Acts of Citizenship

Acts of Citizenship

EDITED BY
ENGIN F. ISIN
& GREG M. NIELSEN

Zed Books
LONDON & NEW YORK

Acts of Citizenship was first published in 2008 by Zed Books Ltd, 7 Cynthia Street, London N1 9JF, UK and Room 400, 175 Fifth Avenue, New York, NY 10010, USA

www.zedbooks.co.uk

Designed and typeset by Long House, Cumbria, UK
Cover designed by Andrew Corbett
Printed and bound by Gutenberg Press Ltd, Malta

Distributed in the USA exclusively by Palgrave Macmillan, 175 Fifth Avenue, New York, NY, 10010, USA

A catalogue record for this book is available from the British Library
Library of Congress Cataloguing in Publication Data is available

ISBN 978 1 84277 951 4 hb
ISBN 978 1 84277 952 1 pb

Contents

❖

Illustrations

Preface

The theoretical concept 'acts of citizenship' was created by Engin Isin and was first developed into a series of encyclopedic entries under his direction at the Citizenship Studies Media Lab (CSML) at York University, Toronto, before being edited for this volume. He also organized two key workshops on the concept at the same university on 15 January 2003 and 25–27 March 2004. Some papers from these workshops have been published elsewhere: Ranu Basu (2007) 'Negotiating Acts of Citizenship in an Era of Neoliberal Reform: The Game of School Closures', *International Journal of Urban and Regional Research*, 31 (1), 109–127; Glen Norcliffe (2006) 'Associations, Modernity and the Insider-Citizens of a Victorian Highwheel Bicycle Club', *Journal of Historical Sociology*, 19 (2), 121–50; Peter Nyers (2006) 'The Accidental Citizen: Acts of Sovereignty and (Un)Making Citizenship', *Economy and Society*, 35 (1), 22–41; and Patricia Wood (2006) 'The "Sarcee War": Fragmented Citizenship and the City', *Space and Polity*, 10 (3), 229–42. The chapters included in this book either draw from or were inspired by a Social Sciences and Humanities Research Council of Canada (SSHRC) workshop organized by Greg Nielsen, Yon Hsu and Engin Isin on 'Mediated Acts of Citizenship: Between City and Nation' held at Concordia University, Montreal, 13–15 October 2005. We would like to thank SSHRC, York University, and Concordia University for helping make these workshops and this book possible. We also thank John Jackson, John Keane, Barbara McLoskey, Marc Raboy, Paul Moore, Brian Walker, Daiva Stasiulis and Agnes Czajka for their participation in the Montreal workshop, as well as graduate students Mircea Mandache and Leah Desjardin for their help. We are grateful to all the contributors to the workshop and the book for their trust in the project. When we began working on the concept 'acts of citizenship' it was much vaguer than it is now; without the persistent and determined efforts of our contributors over the years, it would have remained a gesture rather than a concept. Finally we thank our editorial assistant Ian Morisson for his careful and diligent preparation of the manuscript, and Susannah Trefgarne and the Zed Books staff for their thoughtful help and suggestions.

❖

About the Contributors

Bettina Bergo is Associate Professor of Philosophy at the University of Montreal. She has translated six works, including three by Emmanuel Levinas. Her current research concerns the history of anxiety as a theme in philosophy and psychoanalysis.

Kieran Bonner is Professor of Sociology and Director of the Human Sciences Initiative at St Jerome's University in the University of Waterloo. He is the author of *A Great Place to Raise Kids: Interpretation, Science and the Urban–Rural Debate* and *Power and Parenting: A Hermeneutic of the Human Condition*, as well as articles on Dublin, Montreal and Toronto, phenomenology, hermeneutics, reflexivity, interdisciplinary dialogue and student motivation. He was a co-investigator on the *Culture of Cities: Montreal, Toronto, Berlin, Dublin* SSHRC project and Chair of its Executive Committee (2000–5). He is currently a co-investigator on the interdisciplinary research project *City Life and Well-Being: the Grey Zone of Health and Illness*, funded by the Canadian Institute of Health Research (2006–11).

Irus Braverman is an associate professor in law at the State University of New York at Buffalo. Her research focuses on the relationship between law, geography, and anthropology. Her previous publications include 'The Power of Illegality: House Demolitions and Resistance in East Jerusalem', *Theory and Criticism* 28: 11–42 (Hebrew); 'Powers of Illegality: House Demolitions and Resistance in East Jerusalem,' *Law and Social Inquiry* 32 (2); and 'The Place of Translation in Jerusalem's Criminal Trial Court,' *New Criminal Law Review* 10 (2).

Darryl Burgwin currently lectures in sociology and communication at Wilfrid Laurier University. His research focuses on the communicative imagination and creativity of institutions.

Karine Côté-Boucher is a PhD candidate in sociology at York University, Toronto. Her research concerns articulations of securitization and neoliberalism in North America, as well as their transformative impact on the political-social hierarchies of race, gender and class and the shaping of new subjectivities. 'The Diffuse Border: Intelligence-Sharing, Control and Confinement along Canada's Smart Border' will appear in *Surveillance and Society*, 5 (2/3).

Erkan Ercel is a PhD candidate in the Department of Sociology, York University, Toronto. His research involves investigating remembrance of Ottoman citizenship and of how the empire governed subjects from various ethnic and religious communities. His MA thesis, completed in 2005, was 'Desiring Jews: The Fantasy of Ottoman Tolerance'.

Fred Evans is Professor of Philosophy and Coordinator for the Center of Interpretive and Qualitative Research at Duquesne University. He is the author of *The Multi-Voiced Body: Society, Communication, and the Age of Diversity* (Columbian University Press, forthcoming) and *Psychology and Nihilism: A Genealogical Critique of the Computational Model of Mind* (State University of New York Press, 1993). He is also co-editor of *Chiasms: Merleau-Ponty's Notion of Flesh* (SUNY Press, 2000) and has published numerous articles and book chapters on various continental thinkers in relation to issues concerning psychology, politics and technology.

Yon Hsu is an independent scholar. Her research focuses on international communication and Chinese citizenship.

Engin F. Isin is Chair and Professor of Citizenship in Politics and International Studies (POLIS) at the Faculty of Social Sciences, the Open University, where he is also director of the Centre for Citizenship, Identities, Governance (CCIG). Between 2001 and 2006 he served as Canada Research Chair and Professor in the Division of Social Science at York University, Toronto. He is the author of *Being Political* (2002).

Bora Ali Isyar is a recent graduate of the doctoral programme in sociology at York University, Toronto. His research interests include social theory, nationalism, republican theory and the ontology of responsibility. His article 'The Origins of Turkish Republican Citizenship: The Birth of Race' appears in *Nations and Nationalism*, 11 (3).

Ian Morrison is a PhD candidate in the Department of Sociology, York University, Toronto. His research involves historical investigations of citizenship, secularism and the problematization of religion. 'Rethinking the "Problem" of Religious Pluralism in Canada and the EU' will appear in a forthcoming special issue of the *Journal of European and Russian Affairs* on 'Islam, Secularism and Diversity'.

Greg M. Nielsen is Professor of Sociology and Director of the Center for Broadcasting Studies at Concordia University in Montreal. He is the author of a book on public broadcasting, *Le Canada de Radio-Canada: sociologie critique et dialogisme culturel* (Editions GREF), and of *The Norms of Answerability: Social Theory between Bakhtin and Habermas* (SUNY Press), an application of ideas on transcultural communication to citizenship studies. His current research concerns dialogic critiques of contemporary journalism and press coverage of immigration and poverty.

Peter Nyers is Assistant Professor of the Politics of Citizenship and Intercultural Relations in the Department of Political Science at McMaster University, Canada. His research is on global refugee politics with a focus on the implications for sovereignty, citizenship and human agency. His publications include *Rethinking Refugees: Beyond States of Emergency* (Routledge, 2006) and *Citizenship Between Past and Future* (Routledge 2008, co-editors Engin Isin and Bryan Turner) as well as journal articles in *Citizenship Studies*, *Economy and Society*, *International Political Sociology*, *Millennium: Journal of International Studies* and *Third World Quarterly*.

John Saunders is a Post-Doctoral Fellow at the City Institute, York University, Toronto. His research is on governance and information technologies in the city of Toronto, particularly the spaces and politics produced through the implementation of new technologies.

Brian C. J. Singer is a professor at Glendon College, York University, Toronto, and is associated with the graduate programmes in sociology and social and political thought. He has published one book, translated several books from the French, and written several articles for various journals.

Bryan S. Turner is Professor of Sociology in the Asia Research Institute at National University of Singapore. He is the author of numerous books, among them *Citizenship and Capitalism* (1986) and *Vulnerability and Human Rights* (2006).

Ebru Üstündag is Assistant Professor of Geography at Brock University, St Catherines. Her research focuses on urban, political and feminist geographies. Her previous publications include (with Valerie Preston)

'Feminist Geographies of the "City": Multiple Voices and Multiple Meanings' in *Companion to Feminist Geography* (Blackwell, 2005).

William Walters teaches in the Department of Political Science at Carleton University, Ottawa. His research explores the geopolitical sociology of borders and migration in Europe and North America. His previous publications include *Global Governmentality* (co-edited with Wendy Larner) (Routledge, 2004) and *Governing Europe* (with Jens Henrik Haahr) (Routledge 2005).

Charles Wells is a PhD candidate in the social and political thought programme at York University, Toronto. His research interests include psychoanalytic theory, ethics of responsibility, and the act of suicide bombing.

Melanie White is Assistant Professor in the Department of Sociology and Anthropology at Carleton University, Ottawa. Her current research develops the work of Émile Durkheim and Henri Bergson towards a sociology of creativity. Her previous work on the habits of citizenship has appeared in *Economy and Society*, *Citizenship Studies*, *Journal of Civil Society* and *Canadian Journal of Sociology*.

Introduction

❖❖

Acts of Citizenship

ENGIN F. ISIN
& GREG M. NIELSEN

Ways of being or becoming a citizen have proliferated in our times. The trinity that defined modernity – worker-citizen, warrior-citizen and parent-citizen – has expanded to include ecological-citizen, aboriginal-citizen, market-citizen, consumer-citizen, cosmopolitan-citizen, global-citizen, intimate-citizen, youth-citizen and many more. For some critics this expansion breeds confusion. What exactly is citizenship? Is it legal membership in the state? If so, many new citizens don't have a legal membership to which their citizenship refers. Environments, markets, lifestyles and sexes are not things for which you can hold legal member-ship. Nor are these new forms of citizenship mutually exclusive. One can be an environmental, sexual, cosmopolitan and consumer citizen all at once, but it is only recently, and only for the few states that have agreed, that one can hold dual or multiple state citizenships. This absence of legal status, critics argue, makes these ostensibly new ways of being or becoming citizens flimsy, if not ineffective. Since there are no authorities that can recognize claims for rights when they are made, there can be no authority to assume obligations either. Since citizenship involves the mutual constitution of rights and obligations, these news ways of being or becoming citizens remain passive forms of participation rather than active forms of engagement. For others this proliferation indicates a sort of vitality that is significant. If people invest themselves in claiming rights, we are told, they are producing not only new ways of being subjects with rights but also new ways of becoming subjects with responsibilities, since claiming rights certainly involves 'responsibilizing' selves.

Whether this proliferation is seen as confusing and effective or vital and significant, the object of analysis remains the citizen as individual. It is always the citizen whose acts, conduct and habitus are at stake, whether problematized or valorized. Many fundamental issues of our times implicitly or explicitly revolve around or even hinge on the conduct and habitus of the subject called the citizen. Whether it is 'ecology', 'security', 'immigration', 'cohesion', 'integration' or 'energy', attention immediately turns towards how governing subjects should produce the intended result, which is the citizen as individual.

In this book we introduce the concept 'acts of citizenship' as an alternative way to investigate citizenship. Our claim is that this concept constitutes a significant departure from the way in which the study of citizenship has been approached over the last decade. Often it is stated that what is important about citizenship is not only that it is a legal status but that it involves practices – social, political, cultural and symbolic. In other words, formal citizenship is differentiated from substantive citizenship and the latter is seen as the condition of the possibility of the former. Yet, whether the focus is on status or practice, it remains on the doer rather than the deed. To investigate citizenship in a way that is irreducible to either status or practice, while still valuing this distinction, requires a focus on those acts when, regardless of status and substance, subjects constitute themselves as citizens or, better still, as those to whom the right to have rights is due. But the focus shifts from subjects as such to acts (or deeds) that produce such subjects. The difference, we suggest, is crucial.

We propose to shift focus from the institution of citizenship and the citizen as individual agent to acts of citizenship – that is, collective or individual deeds that rupture social-historical patterns. Acts are not passively given, nor do they emerge from a natural order; as such, they can be opposed to the naïvely formulated definition in which to be a citizen simply means to exercise rights or fulfil obligations, as if these neutral forms of individual choice could be sanctioned outside multiple networks of authority. Whereas citizenship practices like voting, paying taxes or learning languages appear passive and one-sided in mass democracies, acts of citizenship break with repetition of the same and so anticipate rejoinders from imaginary but not fictional adversaries.

Theorizing acts means investigating everyday deeds that are ordinarily called politics. But acts of citizenship are also ethical (as in courageous), cultural (as in religious), sexual (as in pleasurable) and social (as in affiliative) in that they instantiate ways of being that are political. These ways of being constitute the existential conditions of possibility of acts. Most, if not all, of the chapters in this book focus on acts of citizenship through concepts posited by a key theorist or sets of theorists that address these conditions. Several chapters grapple with historical and contemporary issues that are of extreme importance to citizenship studies today.

Our focus on acts of citizenship has been developed over the last five or six years in the Citizenship Studies Media Lab at York University, directed by Engin Isin, and through the Centre for Broadcasting Studies at Concordia University, directed by Greg Nielsen. Through building a network of scholars and supervising a group of advanced doctoral students we have engaged with the question of investigating citizenship without restricting it to already-held status or embedded practice. We gradually came to the understanding that by focusing analysis on acts of citizenship we were moving against the mainstream, but could also build an alternative theoretical model without negating the accomplishments of contemporary citizenship studies. In this book we especially grapple with questions concerning theories that help us understand the moment an act of citizenship occurs and how it shapes itself through a two-sided answerability. Are these moments creative and, if so, how do they gain audibility and visibility? We ask vexing legal and political questions. Do acts of citizenship encompass claims of justice as well as forms of domination? Are acts of citizenship inherently (or always) exclusionary or inclusionary? How are beings thrown into acts that enact us/them as citizens, strangers, outsiders or aliens? If indeed acts of citizenship are fundamental ways of being with others, where might we find the best sites and scales to theorize their special form of answerability?

The inquisitive and creative spirit of our collaboration is retained in this volume, which features two different but complementary genres of writing that include longer in-depth theory and analysis chapters and more condensed encyclopedia-style entries that highlight different dimensions in acts of citizenship through concrete examples. Each group of chapters is followed by several entries that help clarify and extend reflections raised by the chapters. The chapters and entries are grouped under three sections according to themes raised by the above questions: (1) Politics, Ethics and Aesthetics; (2) Citizens, Strangers, Aliens and Outcasts; and (3) Sites and Scales of Answerability. Each section features case entries, which are accounts that focus on a specific event, delineated by a place and a date, and ask questions about the grounds and consequences of these events as acts of citizenship.

Politics, Ethics, Aesthetics

Treating acts of citizenship as 'deeds' rather than as some neutral repetition of practices structured by the expectation of passive reception means that our first step must be to theorize citizenship as simultaneously political, ethical and aesthetic. The chapters in Part I by Engin Isin, Melanie White and Bettina Bergo explore the philosophical backdrop of each of these fields as they apply to acts of citizenship. To perform a 'deed' means politically and aesthetically to anticipate and thus partly shape the possibility of a rejoinder. If aesthetics is about creating or shaping appearance, and the possible is a key element in the definition of politics, then the question of responsibility is always at the heart of ethics. Acts of citizenship create a sense of the possible and of a citizenship that is 'yet to come'. Without necessarily being ethical, such acts implicitly ask questions about a future responsibility towards others. While this question is explicit in deeds that anticipate rejoinders from others, the more difficult relation to theorize is the one between political and aesthetic questions of answerability that shape the deed into larger wholes, which in turn create loopholes for counter-acts to emerge.

In Chapter 1 Isin addresses these folds of politics, ethics and aesthetics by placing the contribution our problematic has made to citizenship studies over the last decade. He quickly identifies the key difference in our approach and situates it within a longer philosophical tradition, focusing discussion on Mikhail Bakhtin and Martin Heidegger as well as others. The chapter explains the methodological consequences of our proposed alternative and shows how acts of citizenship are a political mediation between two sides of answerability that include the requirement to respond to challenges with a creative and unique performance that can claim no alibi, yet also defend a general idea that is immanent rather than transcendent. An 'act' is that moment in which a being comes away from everyday politics and at the same time renews the openness of the subject to the world. This difference between responsibility and answerability is examined as key to explaining the condition that enables subjects to disrupt their everyday.

Drawing from a parallel and complementary line of thinkers that stretches from Henri Bergson to Gilles Deleuze, White strengthens the theoretical argument around aesthetics and politics; she argues that if we conceive acts of citizenship as a break from habitus, they must be defined as creative. For an act of citizenship to be creative it must arise from a breakdown of our capacity to recognize how we should act while simultaneously responding to its crisis with an invention. Creativity, therefore, depends upon encounters or situations that mark the failure of our habits and recognition to act as usual. A genuine encounter forces one to pose the question of how to act, exposing the need to develop new, creative responses to those occasions where we no longer recognize the context of action. When this line of inquiry is situated in relation to the concept of the act of citizenship, it becomes possible to argue that the act can be creative in so far as it emerges, negatively, as a consequence of the breakdown of our capacity to recognize how we should act, and, positively, as the creation of new modes of citizenship able to respond effectively to the situation.

Examining a gap between Levinas's theory of justice and his ethics, Bergo asks if acts of citizenship must encompass normative claims as well as a darker political dimension that repeats a form of abuse within civil society. Levinas's contribution to 'acts of citizenship', she argues 'lies in his phenomenological ethics'. This ethics describes a relational dimension of immediate lived experience (a dimension we obscure when we represent it to ourselves) in which a person is affected by the experience of the suffering of another. What Levinas can teach us about mediating acts that promote citizenship, and the equity we expect from its institutionalization, requires thinking through the mediations that make up civil society – including those that have been damaged.

The shorter, 'encyclopedic' entries in Part I focus on those acts that intrude into law. Charles Wells examines an act when Abraham almost sacrifices Isaac. Although this act does not immediately present itself as an act of citizenship, it nonetheless lends itself to this form of interpretation if one considers that the commandments handed down to the community of believers are structurally equivalent to a set of laws that structure a body of citizenship. Next – through an examination of Antigone, whose act demonstrates the ambivalent nature of acts and which hovers in the interstices between acts of heroism, suicide and faith – Wells recognizes the significance of rupture as the grounds of the act. The death of Socrates makes Bora Ali Isyar recognize the tension between responsibility and answerability. This death becomes essential for understanding those answerable yet irresponsible acts that may not be enacted in the name of the law but come to be considered acts of citizenship. Then – this time in the setting of Australia's Northern Territory – Isyar sees a similar tension in the legal controversy surrounding the case of Bob Dent and the Rights of the Terminally Ill Act (1995), which depicts the legal conflict over death and the productive potential of citizenship with startling clarity. Darryl Burgwin sees a more popular example of the heroic act in the ultimate sacrifice of Pat Tillman as a US soldier-citizen. Here the act of heroism refers, for its greater good, to a body of citizenship.

Abraham and Isaac, Antigone, Socrates, Dent, and Tillman are examples that reveal ambiguities within acts of citizenship. These cases focus on moments when beings, who claim, assert and impose rights and obligations, enact themselves as citizens beyond the law. In Part II we focus more on the history and process in which acts of citizenship differentiate others or outsiders as those who are not citizens or insiders.

Citizens, Strangers, Aliens, Outcasts

We contend that many other avenues of research become apparent once citizenship is examined as an act or deed that produces new subjects. Each of the chapters in Part II explore acts of citizenship as the production of subjects, whether citizens, strangers, aliens or outcasts. Brian Singer's discussion of the origins of citizenship in America begins with the double reminder that citizenship is most directly affiliated with democracy, and that as such it demands a political definition regarding rule and order. He asks the question what political subjects would be without reference to a *polis* that structures their authority. By focusing on the relationship between acts of piety in the religious City and acts of citizenship in the political City, Bryan Turner draws a parallel between political and religious subjects, on the one hand, and politics and religiosity, on the other. Kieran Bonner's chapter follows, exploring Hannah Arendt's work to clarify this same sense of the political in the City, with Dublin as a case study. Peter Nyers' chapter asks what acts of citizenship might mean without the *polis* in a different way. He explores the question of what political subject is produced in the 'No One Is Illegal' movement. The final chapter in this section, by William Walters, draws on recent work on the enactment and performance of citizenship to examine the subterranean movements that materialize the figure of the irregular migrant.

Singer begins his chapter with a review of two founding moments invoked in Alexis de Tocqueville's classic *Democracy in America*. The first is an original, political founding on the East Coast, which can be said to follow the scenario of contract theory. The second founding concerns the West, and takes the form of individual homesteaders. The implications of each are carefully reviewed to identify acts of citizenship and assess their influence on the development of contemporary global civil society. The extension of the genealogy of these founding acts into contemporary cosmopolitan politics provides an opportunity to discuss how in Western thought the *polis* has always been considered as the space of appearance of politics or the site of acts of citizenship. Tocqueville's interpretation of American democracy departs from this model – and helps explain why American democracy remains fragile and volatile as a democracy whose site, by contrast, is not the *polis*.

Following Augustine, Turner argues that the religious is constituted by acts associated with the sacred that are performed within 'the city of God', namely the sphere of such enactments. An old problem is presented here within a somewhat more exact theoretical framework in order to ask how the political city relates to the city of God, or in more concrete terms how acts of piety relate to acts of citizenship. Acts of piety can empower actors in the same way that acts of citizenship do, and so a person becomes a valuable member of the inspirational city by undertaking these acts of piety – especially through taxation, reproduction and, if necessary, military defence of the community. Pietization of everyday life has significant implications for the political city and for relationships between different religious communities within the public sphere. Acts of piety and acts of secular citizenship in effect create two separate cities – the inspirational and the secular. The tensions between the inspirational city and the political city may not constitute a clash of civilizations, but do indicate the intensification of religious identities within the public domain, raising questions about how social interactions between different groups that involve rituals of intimacy can take place without conflict.

Bonner's chapter engages the issue of appearance and uses Arendt's account of *vita activa* to think through a case study of acts of urban citizenship within the city of Dublin. A recent municipal policy initiative is discussed in terms of its intention to increase moments in which citizens might act (participate). Analysis of an unintended outcome of city planning suggests the disappearance of the political as an experienced form of diversity. Arendt's contrasts between direct and representative democracy in the city enable Bonner to develop distinctions between act, activity and action. '[A]n act of citizenship', he argues, 'in its full worldly reality is more than voting for someone else to act and speak on one's behalf. It requires the full experience of acting and speaking' itself.

When acts of citizenship produce strangers, aliens and outcasts, they emerge not as beings already defined but as active and reactive ways of being with others. Along these lines, Nyers raises critical questions about the toxic effects of state control of illegal immigration and refugees in North America. Nyers examines 'how refugee and migrant activists and their allies are presently demanding and, in some places, constructing a world where "no one is illegal". This phrase is at once a radical cosmopolitan chant, the name taken by many pro-migrant groups, and also an emerging political project.' The chapter focuses on the latter dimension and asks: what is the political theory of 'no one is illegal'?

Two themes in the emerging discourse of acts of citizenship are examined by Walters in the section's final chapter. The first comes from Giorgio Agamben's theorization of the 'ban' and its production of 'naked life'. His concept has been widely used to analyse the ways in which contemporary immigration authorities, and the regimes of citizenship which they embody, ensnare 'irregular migrants' in an indeterminate space ('the camp'). For researchers in the second theme, migration is a social movement capable of confounding and destabilizing the distributions and markings of sovereign power. Walters ends by arguing that while the latter take has much potential for analysing questions of migration, we should not overlook those moments when political interventions purposefully and strategically refuse to make strong claims about citizenship.

The 'Acts' section of Part II explores the history of citizenship and the meaning of exclusion and inclusion in ways that aid reflection on the themes and arguments raised by Singer, Turner, Bonner, Nyers and Walters. Another way of thinking about claiming rights and recognition for the excluded is to examine a contemporary case between two separate state authorities. Erkan Ercel provides a creative interpretation of the treaty signed between the Turkish state authorities and the executives of the European Union Council in Brussels in 2005, whereby Turkey is promised full membership provided it meets the accession criteria. Irus Braverman presents an analysis of the activities – seen as creative collective acts – of Machsom-Watch (MW), an organization established by Jewish-Israeli women in response to Israel's oppressive policies in the occupied territories. Karine Côté-Boucher illustrates how Guatemalan refugees living outside the country actively negotiated and shaped conditions for their return in 1993. Ebru Üstündag shows how the struggles of Romani people for recognition take the form of an outcast 'non-territorial nation' – a direct challenge to the history of citizenship as 'minoritization'. Ian Morrison allows Milan Kundera's novel *The Joke* to raise several vital questions about East and West Europe and offers important insights into acts of citizenship with relation to intention and temporality.

Sites and Scales of Answerability

Acts of citizenship are considered as political in so far as these acts constitute constituents (beings with claims). Part III draws attention to examples from New York, Beijing and Hong Kong as Fred Evans, Yon Hsu and Greg Nielsen explore how citizenship can articulate itself simultaneously in the public domain and everyday ethical sites where specific claims or counter-claims are made about rights, responsibilities, identity, recognition and redistribution. The section also explores examples of how cities act as interlocutors in encouraging interaction (sometimes conflictual) across diversity, giving opportunities free from formal, institutional restraints and permitting experimentation with identities and cosmopolitan belonging.

Evans's chapter presents a study of public art as an act of citizenship in New York City. His analysis of Krzysztof Wodiczko's *Homeless Projection* in Union Square takes inventiveness and creativity as acts that debunk oracles of the city. With extensive reference to Bakhtin, the example of public art is used to illustrate both the dialogic hybridity of the city's voices and the role of art in debunking oracles, specifically the real estate industry's 'revitalization' campaign in New York City during the 1980s. In illustrating this struggle around the moment an act of citizenship takes place, or what might better be called 'the audibility of voices', the link between citizenship and the city is theorized as a multi-voiced body in a way that overcomes the limitations of political liberalism's appeal to the universality of abstract right and communitarianism's tendency to rely on exclusionary group identities as a basis for justice.

Hsu invokes Derrida's argument for 'democracy to come' and Bakhtin's ethics and implied politics in an analysis of the 1989 Tiananmen crackdown in Beijing. As the confrontational moments of acts and counter-acts between the young man and the tank en route to the square were broadcast globally, the act itself was mediated into the icon of Chinese defiance against repression and the struggle for democracy. This orientalist reading is placed squarely within the liberal tradition and radically challenged from the alternative approach we are calling acts of citizenship. Beyond the heroic or iconic meaning of the act, the chapter theorizes spontaneous acts by juxtaposing and challenging axiological positions between 'the people' and the liberators of the 'people' at the political level. At the ethical level, the chapter elucidates a deeper concern for answerable acts in the once-occurrent moment.

Nielsen closes this section by responding to the call for answerability sounded in several earlier chapters. He proposes an alternative approach to acts of citizenship that constitute a cosmopolitan ethics and politics. Analysis of an intense verbal conflict between two individuals, recorded live on a Hong Kong bus and broadcast with English language subtitles on the Internet, is presented as an example of a failed act of citizenship in everyday urban culture. The example demonstrates how ordinary acts of citizenship emerge, breaking with assumed civic norms and habits. An alternative approach to citizenship studies focuses on acts that challenge the non-participatory stance assumed when we travel under the assumption that we live together not only across difference but also out of a much-needed indifference. Acts of citizenship with cosmopolitan intent are situated within the irony of a necessary indifference towards otherness in urban culture.

These acts are defined as events that contain several overlapping and interdependent components: they claim rights and impose obligations in emotionally charged tones; pose their claims in enduring and convincing arguments; and look to shift established practices, status and order.

While previous examples of acts defined citizenship through forms of struggle that involve encounters between social groups and state authorities, the acts in this section are about the complexities and eccentricities of acts of citizenship that often cross the boundaries of city, nation and region. Ian Morrison provides an analysis of the act of commemoration and shows how celebrating the 1916 Easter Uprising in contemporary post-national Ireland involves not only legal status but also those practices and rituals through which the commemoration is enacted. John Saunders investigates municipal voting rights for non-citizens by using the example of the case of Cambridge, Massachusetts, which raises the issue of belonging in urban citizenship. Saunders is also interested by a paradoxical form of urban street theatre performance called a 'flash mob'. 'Residents coming together as a group, claiming space and interrupting the everyday order in the city can be seen as a form of resistance to established patterns and practices.' To illustrate unmediated and unspeakable acts of citizenship, Erkan Ercel draws upon an intensely urban scene from a film by the director Spike Lee, *25th Hour* (2002), where we follow the last 24 hours of one Montgomery Brogan (Edward Norton), who has only one day left before he has to hand himself over to the state penitentiary.

Conclusion

Acts of citizenship are understood as deeds that contain several overlapping and interdependent components. They disrupt habitus, create new possibilities, claim rights and impose obligations in emotionally charged tones; pose their claims in enduring and creative expressions; and, most of all, are the actual moments that shift established practices, status and order. Acts of citizenship should be understood in themselves as unique and distinct from citizenship practices in the sense they are also actively answerable events, whereas the latter are institutionally accumulated processes. Like citizenship practices, acts of citizenship step into the participatory out of the non-participatory and are answerable to both general ideals and unique performances. Acts of citizenship are thus politically effective in so far as they help organize public presentations or appearances of often-contradictory statements from actors who claim rights or impose social responsibilities. But at another level such statements or creations are potentially transcultural as they are named in and across the languages of domestic and international flows. Acts of citizenship need each of these overlapping and interconnecting components to sustain their effectiveness; otherwise they might dissolve, collapse, fragment or break down into uncivil or violent acts.

The concept of acts of citizenship thus leads to a rather sharp break with current citizenship studies in that it stetches the field well beyond the dominant liberal trajectory that dwells on a linear, formal and legal language of status, rights, obligation, justice and order. This tradition delineates boundaries between 'us and others' and makes claims about social goods (security, governance, services, community and moral precepts) and identities (cultural, ethnic, religious, class, gendered, local, national and cosmopolitan). In contrast, acts of citizenship may be cultivated by or may transgress practices and formal entitlement, as they emerge from the paradox between universal inclusion in the language of rights and cosmo-politanism, on the one hand, and inevitable exclusion in the language of community and particularity on the other.

Each contribution to this book draws on and in turn supports a well-knit set of arguments within a common problematic (acts of citizenship as ruptures from social-historical patterns), while the chapters and essays on exemplary acts complement one another within each part and as a whole. This does not mean uniformity around a single subject, theoretical idea or historical understanding, but rather the coming together of a common critique and reasoned alternative approach so as to make convincing the claim to originality and the significant expansion of a field of study. By investigating phenomena that range from collective to individual deeds of heroism, and from social and political struggles to representations of acts in art (film, novel, tragedy), we have identified acts, investigated their conditions of possibility (legal versus illegal) and recognized the subjects that they produce (citizens, strangers, aliens, outcasts): these procedures have enabled us to think about citizenship in dynamic, concrete, effective and critical ways. By understanding acts of citizenship in this way, this book seeks to contribute to our unfolding view of their structure of answerability as well as responsibility, calculability and intentionality. By including two genres or writing and different styles of thought while creating an original focus for investigating citizenship, we hope to widen the appeal of the book and also to generate debates over whether 'acts' can become distinct objects of investigation in citizenship studies. Thus we have not aimed to demonstrate that acts of citizenship should and must be investigated so much as to elaborate upon them as an object of analysis. This has both theoretical and political ramifications at a time when investigating citizenship can easily be seen as merely reflecting on matters ranging across multiculturalism, cohesion, integration, civics and belonging. This book shifts the focus away from these fairly limiting categories and recasts what is to be understood by 'active citizenship' by genuinely engaging with the question of what constitutes 'action' in the first place. Thus the book should engage a scholarly interest at least as wide as the interdisciplinary and cross–genre approaches of its contributors.

PART I

❖

Politics, Ethics, Aesthetics

Chapter 1

Theorizing
Acts of Citizenship

ENGIN F. ISIN

Citizenship in Flux: Subjects, Sites, Scales

It is now widely recognized that the social and political struggles over citizenship have acquired a new intensity (Isin and Turner 2002, 2007). What has become apparent more recently is that while citizens everywhere may be contained legally within state boundaries that enact rights and obligations, their own states are not subject to such containment. All states, through multilateral arrangements and international accords, implicate (or fail to implicate) their citizens involuntarily in a web of rights and responsibilities concerning the environment (wildlife, pollution), trade (copyright, protection), security, refugees, crime, minorities, war, children and many other issues. While the enforceability of these accords is a contested matter, every state exists in social, political or economic integration and is implicated in varying degrees of influence and autonomy. These complex webs of rights and responsibilities implicating citizens in various ethical, political and social decisions are important to keep in mind when thinking about citizenship today. What complicates this image further is that many citizens and non-citizens (illegal aliens, immigrants, migrants) of states have become increasingly mobile, carrying these webs of rights and obligations with them and further entangling them with other webs of rights and obligations. The status and habitus (ways of thought and conduct that are internalized over a relatively long period of time) of the subject we call the citizen is made infinitely more complex by its entanglements with these overflowing webs of rights and responsibilities.

15

Much has been debated concerning these matters in the past two decades, especially in the field of citizenship studies. By taking stock of these debates and suggesting that much of the focus has been on the status and habitus of citizenship, this chapter aims to outline a different perspective on the question of how subjects of the new overflowing rights and responsibilities enact themselves as citizens. It aims to constitute acts of citizenship as an object of investigation that is distinct from (but related to) the status and habitus of citizenship. After further defining the new context of global movements and flows, and articulating the need to focus on the concept of the act itself, I draw from several interdisciplinary thinkers who have investigated the concept of the act and outline a set of principles for theorizing acts of citizenship that will indicate the approach to citizenship we are building.

There is no doubt that the new intensity of struggles over citizenship is associated with global movements and flows of capital, labour and people. The movements of capital have created new sites of production and exchange of commodities across various boundaries and stretched limits of regulation. The creation of various zones, regions and territories to enable competitive production and exchange has created new sites of domination, exploitation and resistance. Similarly, global movements of labour across nations and states have generated new sites of struggle for both redistribution and recognition. As well as major movements into European, Anglo-American and Australian labour markets, there have been population movements within major states such as China and India. Meanwhile, within Anglo-American states, the post-war consensus on the welfare state and social citizenship has ended in a morass of vague disavowal, while neo-liberalization of the provision of social services has created new injustices and inequalities (Clarke 2004). This intensification of social relations through movements and flows has generated new affinities, identifications, loyalties, animosities and hostilities across borders.

Thus, whatever names are given to these processes of 'globalization', 'neo-liberalization' and 'post-modernization', and one can certainly question the adequacy of all or any of these names, various processes have combined to produce new, if not paradoxical, subjects of law and action, new subjectivities and identities, new sites of struggle and new scales of identification. Through these new subjects, sites and scales of struggle, citizenship, while typically understood as a legal status of membership in the state, if not the nation-state, became increasingly defined as practices of becoming claim-making subjects in and through various sites and scales (Isin 2008, forthcoming). These debates have illustrated that when combined with various adjectives such as 'intimate citizenship', 'multicultural citizenship', 'sexual citizenship', 'transgendered citizenship', 'consumer citizenship', 'cosmopolitan citizenship', or 'ecological citizenship', new identities could be investigated as the formation of new subjects, sites and scales of claim making (Clarke *et al.* 2007; Isin and Wood 1999; Kymlicka 1995; Kymlicka and Norman 2000; Lister 2002). This is not to say that there has been less emphasis on status but, rather, to suggest that most critical studies on citizenship focus on how status becomes contested by investigating practices through which claims are articulated and subjectivities are formed (Benhabib 2004; Soysal 1994). The effect of this shift to practices has been the production of studies concerning routines, rituals, customs, norms and habits of the everyday through which subjects become citizens. We can suggest that the impact of this body of work has been to include habitus (internalized or embodied ways of thought and conduct) alongside status within studies of citizenship (Bourdieu 1994; Schatzki 1997). This body of research has demonstrated effectively that virtues are cultivated, that citizenship is not inherited but learned, and that cultivating citizenship requires establishing supportive and relatively enduring practices and institutions (Allman and Beaty 2002).

Theorizing Citizenship: Status, Habitus, Acts

To put it another way, critical studies of citizenship over the last two decades have taught us that what is important is not only that citizenship is a legal status but that it also involves practices of making citizens – social, political, cultural and symbolic. Many scholars now differentiate formal citizenship from substantive citizenship and consider the latter to be the condition of possibility of the former. Not only has this been a productive development but it also corresponds and responds to the broad transformations mentioned earlier.

While this body of work has been useful and effective in demonstrating how citizenship involves habitus that is formed over a relatively long period of time, the question of how subjects become claimants under surprising conditions or within a relatively short period of time has remained unexplored. We know virtually nothing about how subjects become claimants when they are least expected or anticipated to do so. Granted, for subjects to become claimants they must have been embodying certain practices. Take, for example, the civil rights or feminist movements. Both developed over a relatively long period of time various resistance practices ranging from folklore, theatre or music to social and political networks. But both movements transformed subjects into claimants of rights over a relatively short period of time through various acts that were symbolically and materially constitutive. Who can forget the Montgomery Bus Boycott in 1955, when those named as 'negroes' claimed they could sit anywhere they wanted on the bus (Burns 1997)? Who can forget the hunger strike staged by British suffragette Marion Wallace Dunlop in Holloway prison in 1909, in protest against being refused the status of political prisoner (Fulford 1976)? These momentous acts required the summoning of courage, bravery, indignation, or righteousness to break with habitus. Without such creative breaks it is impossible to imagine social transformation or to understand how subjects become citizens as claimants of justice, rights and responsibilities. Thus, the difference between habitus and acts is not merely one of temporality but is also a qualitative difference that breaks habitus creatively.

The importance of making this difference cannot be overstated. Under what conditions do subjects act as citizens? How do subjects transform themselves into actors? How do subjects become claimants of rights, entitlements and responsibilities? If acts of citizenship cannot be reduced to status (for those who do not have status also demonstrate that they are capable of acting as claimants, while those who do have status may not be able to act as citizens), how do we name these acts without inferring them from the status of actors already named? Furthermore, acts cannot be reduced to practices because to enact oneself as a citizen involves transforming oneself from a subject into a claimant, which inevitably involves a break from habitus (Farnell 2000). Yet acts are necessary but not sufficient conditions of the social transformation of subjects into citizens. If this is so, how do we investigate acts through which subjects transform themselves into citizens?

It is now vitally important to expand our investigations to enable us to understand the decisions involved in making subjects into citizens. To investigate acts of citizenship in a way that is irreducible to either status or habitus, while still valuing this distinction, requires a focus on those moments when, regardless of status and substance, subjects constitute themselves as citizens – or, better still, as those to whom the right to have rights is due (Arendt 1951; Balibar 2004; Rancière 2004). To investigate acts of citizenship is to draw attention to acts that may not be considered as political and demonstrate that their enactment does indeed instantiate constituents (which may mean being part of a whole as well as being a member of a constituency). The enactment of citizenship is paradoxical because it is dialogical. The moment of the enactment of citizenship, which instantiates constituents, also instantiates other subjects from whom the subject of a claim is differentiated. So an enactment inevitably creates a scene where there are selves and others defined in relation to each other.

These are not fixed identities but fluid subject positions in and out of which subjects move. In other words, being always involves being with others. These subject positions can be analytically identified on a spectrum of intensity ranging from hospitality to hostility: citizens, strangers, outsiders and aliens. Becoming a subject involves being implicated in this spectrum (Isin 2002, 2005). The dialogical principle of citizenship always involves otherness. Several questions thus arise regarding theorizing acts of citizenship. How do subjects such as citizens and others such as strangers, outsiders or aliens break away from these positions? If indeed acts of citizenship are fundamental ways of being with others, how do beings *decide* between solidaristic (generous, magnanimous, beneficent, hospitable, accommodating, understanding, loving), agonistic (competitive, resistant, combative, adverse) and alienating (vengeful, revengeful, malevolent, malicious, hostile, hateful) acts towards others? What actualizes those acts? Could theorizing acts of citizenship provide the means through which to differentiate acts that are worth resisting and those that are worth cultivating? These questions cannot be answered without constituting acts as an object of investigation. Only then can we begin to understand what makes certain acts 'acts of citizenship'. There are acts of violence, hospitality, hostility, indifference, love, friendship and so on, and, while they can be intertwined with acts of citizenship, these different kinds of acts are not reducible to each other. They must remain distinct and distinguishable for our investigations. To investigate these questions, however, requires going beyond the field of citizenship studies. It requires working through some of the crucial issues of social and political thought. What theoretical sources can we draw on from social and political thought for investigating acts? We now turn our attention to that question by using concepts developed by Adolf Reinach, Martin Heidegger and Mikhail Bakhtin, and then taken up by Jacques Lacan, Hannah Arendt, Emmanuel Levinas and Jacques Derrida: all these thinkers, I argue, have investigated the nature of acts implicitly and partially, albeit in different – yet congruent – ways. (The notable exceptions are Reinach and Bakhtin, who argued that acts should be an object of investigation.) Then we shift our focus to address acts of citizenship specifically and discuss how they might be investigated.

Orders, Practices, Acts

How does social and political thought constitute acts as an object of investigation? This is a more complex question than it first appears, for two reasons. First, social and political thought has not given much attention to acts as an object of analysis. Searching scrutiny has been devoted to the concept of 'action' but very little to the concept of 'the act'. We shall articulate a difference between the concepts of 'act' and 'action' later; suffice it for now to say that analysis of the former remains fragmented, varied and mostly contained within the concept of speech acts (Austin 1962; Searle 1969; Smith 1990). Second, it would be fair to suggest that modern social and political thought, at least, has been dominated by a concern with order rather than disruption. This is despite a voluminous literature on revolutions, which really investigates them as different kinds of order – as Žižek (1999) illustrates. Both reasons are provocative, so let us briefly discuss them before we turn our attention to theorizing acts.

If we survey the state of social and political thought today there are a number of concepts that are dominant but the concept of the 'act' is not one of them. We are concerned about 'practices', 'conduct', 'discipline', 'rule', 'governance' and 'action', to describe what agents do and how they behave, but not 'acts'. This state of affairs often values routine over rupture, order over disorder, and habit over deviation. When the second concepts in these pairs come into focus they are often considered as 'distortion' of the first concepts. It appears that to describe, explain or account for those routines by which humans order their social and political relations is more important than their ruptures or breaks. The predominant focus has become the way in which people conduct themselves and routinize certain habits in their bodies, develop certain behaviours, and follow certain rules. It seems that social sciences in general and social and political thought are oriented towards understanding orders and practices and their conditions of possibility. Consider, for example, the enormous influence of the concept of habitus popularized by Pierre Bourdieu (1972; 1980; 1994), or the critical influence Foucault has had with his studies on 'discipline' (1975), 'care of the self' (1984) or 'conduct of conduct' (1988). These concepts are oriented towards how subjects constitute themselves through relatively enduring modes of conduct. There is a sense in which social and political thought is really oriented towards the way in which humans conduct themselves in routinized and ritualized ways. It seems as if social and political thought is fascinated by how bodies, habits and practices, are intertwined to produce conduct. Admittedly, certain issues and controversies emerge from this focus: for example, the problem of the relationship between structure and agency, the problem of the agent, the problem of the universal and the singular, the problem of the individual and society, and problem of continuity versus discontinuity. What is the relationship between structures of action and the patterns of action? How do people conduct themselves? What do disciplines accomplish? Do disciplines produce bodies? If so, how? If it is through routines, how do those routines become practices? How are subjects enabled to act upon the actions of other subjects? Do subjects follow rules? Does following a rule involve routinized habits or is it a rational process? How does governing the actions of others work as conduct of conduct?

These examples are not exhaustive but they are sampled from nearly a century of social and political thought. I am inclined to suggest that social and political thought has been dealing with a cluster of problems that we can define as problems of orders and practices. Theodore Schatzki has given a good account of how orders and practices have become objects of social thought (2002, 2003). It is fair to say that it is this dominant focus on orders and practices that undergirds modern social and political thought. To insist on investigating acts is to call into question this dominant cluster of problems itself.

If indeed orders and practices have become the dominant objects of thought, finding theoretical sources that can help us investigate acts is a major problem. All the same, it is possible to assemble together those concepts that will enable us to investigate acts, or constitute acts as objects of analysis. There are segments of social and political thought that either explicitly or implicitly address the question of acts separately from (but in relation to) other objects such as conduct, practice, routine, habit, and so forth. We have as many fragments as we need to mould from them a certain style of thought. That work still needs to be done and is beyond the scope of this chapter. Meanwhile, we can begin with the core question.

What does an act mean? Strangely, while both as verb and noun 'act' is one of the most provocative and affective words in the English language, it is also not easily neutralized by being absorbed into or flattened as 'action'. As Ware (1973, p. 403) illustrates, at least in the English language, replacement of 'act' by 'action' either is impossible or changes the meaning of everyday phrases. We have expressions such as acts of courage, acts of generosity, acts of terror as well as court actions, social actions, affirmative actions but these will not work by exchanging 'act' with 'action' and vice versa. A brief digression into the Oxford English Dictionary (OED) illustrates this. As a verb, to act primarily assembles meanings such as 'to put in motion', 'move to action, 'impel, actuate, influence and animate', 'to bring into action, bring about, produce, perform, or make', or 'to carry out a project, command or purpose'. To act implies simultaneously being *directed* and *oriented* towards something. But it also implies to perform an action either as genuine (a play) or counterfeit (simulation). To act embodies actions that can produce both genuine and counterfeit effects. Moreover, it can be coupled with phrases to assemble meanings such as to 'act out', which means to represent unconscious impulses, desires, instincts and drives. Being directed or oriented towards does not only or necessarily involve consciousness but also the unconscious. To 'act up' can imply conducting oneself disgracefully or anti-socially. To act can also mean to act or enact a character, or to impersonate or assume a character by mimicking or mocking. To act may also mean 'to perform on the stage of existence' or 'to do things in the widest sense' or 'to conduct oneself' or to serve or stand in for something or somebody. To act on or upon implies regulating conduct according to certain norms or imperatives. Finally, to act, when used in conjunction with things, can mean to produce effects, fulfil functions or exert influence. As a verb, then, what is remarkably missing from the English usage is to begin, create or disrupt. It is defined by rather neutral verbs such as make, move and animate, but there is no sense in which an act actualizes.

As a noun, an act is equally non-interchangeable with action. Most significantly, an act stands for a deed or a performance but not for a thing done. In the same vein, it also stands for any operation of the mind such as desiring and willing. An act can be opposed to intention or possibility and can mean actuality of a condition, state or quality. An act can refer to the process of doing, action or operation ('act of God') as well as a moment of the process ('in the act'). Equally significantly, an act refers to anything transacted by a political body such as a council or deliberative assembly. It is therefore – as a decree passed by a legislative, judicial or other body – the most fundamental declarative political and legal instrument. By extension, it also refers to the instrument itself as a record of this transaction and declaration. As such, its genealogy shares the same origins as the Acts of the Apostles. Finally, and equally interestingly, an act refers to parts or divisions of a drama in which a definite segment of the whole action is performed. By extension, it also evokes communion, collaboration, affiliation and fraternization by 'getting into the act'.

Obviously, both as verb and noun, the word 'act' implies and evokes an impressive range of conduct and outcomes that are related to but irreducible to action. Yet 'action' has long been a concern of modern social and political thought. By contrast, 'acts' has never been a consistent and persistent object of thought. When Stout says, 'Being an agent is being something that acts, something that does actions', it sounds promising (2005, p. 3). But when he continues to say that 'in the philosophy of action we are dealing with two types of entities: agents and actions', acts disappear from analysis. Similarly, Bennett simply assumes that acts can be called actions (1995, p. 29). The fact that acts can refer to deeds as well as to performance, to process as well as to outcomes, and to conduct as well as to enactment already confuses the ground for developing a concept that focuses on the passage between a performance and its outcomes, or between an act and its actualization.

In contemporary social and political thought, Robert Ware (1973) remains, as far as I am aware, the sole figure to have argued for a distinction between acts and actions. Ware argues that while both acts and actions concern doings rather than happenings, acts are different kinds of doings than actions (p. 404). As mentioned above, this distinction can already be found in our common use of the expressions 'act' and 'action', but Ware thinks it has been curiously neglected. By noting that many things can be called acts or actions, the fact they cannot be substituted for each other should be taken to illustrate that these are different entities (p. 403). Ware proposes six necessary conditions for something to be called an act. (I will state these in my own words as Ware's specification of acts and their difference from actions is not always consistent with mine.) First, to specify an act is to indicate a doing. While actions also involve a doing, it is necessary that they involve movement, change, and motion of objects and bodies. 'What is important for actions is that there be action. Actions and motions are rather alike. They both involve action or motion' (p. 408). The kind of doing that acts indicate does not need to involve such objects and bodies. Second, acts are doings of actors. Actions can happen without actors. Thus, acts are either human or humanized (acts of God or acts of nature). There are actions of non-human beings just as there are actions of human beings, but there are acts only of human beings (p. 406). Third, acts happen because of a decision to perform the act. The decision can be intentional or non-intentional but an act will always involve a decision. Fourth, while acts take time and space for doing, they do not have spatio-temporal coordinates: 'acts do not have a place or position in the world and thus cannot be seen [or observed]' (p. 414). Fifth, acts must have completion. They involve accomplishments. 'The accomplishing of some-thing is not an action although it may take action to accomplish some-thing, and doing something will usually involve action' (p. 407). That is to say, acts exist as entities whose absence or presence can, in equal measure, specify an accomplishment. 'Doings that go on for a period of time and that can be continued or broken off might be action or activities [routines or practices], but they are not acts' (p. 413). Sixth, acts build upon acts. Acts involve accomplishments, with moments when they start and end, but they also have continuity within themselves. They accrete over time.

While Ware's is a welcome argument for making a distinction between acts and action, it falls short of articulating this distinction as ontological difference. Thus, he also conflates acts and action by interchanging them several times with contradictory results. How, for example, can acts take time and space but lack spatio-temporal coordinates?

An act is neither a practice nor a conduct nor an action, and yet it implies or perhaps makes all those possible. When theorizing acts we are dealing with three types of entities (and not two, as Stout thought): acts, actions and actors. When I use the term 'theorizing acts' I have in mind an approach that focuses on an assemblage of acts, actions and actors in a historically and geographically concrete situation, creating a scene or state of affairs. Yet, if investigating acts is impossible without focusing on acts *themselves* that exist independently of actors, it is also important to recognize that acts cannot be actualized without actions. In this I follow Reinach (1983). It was he who argued that acts should be distinguished from action and that they should be accorded ontological existence that is prior to both actors and actions. He interpreted the essence of an act as an expression of the need to be heard. He investigated various acts such as willing, promising, commanding, requesting and contemplating, and concluded that for an act to be a social act it must enact (via linguistic or non-linguistic means) a need felt by one party to be heard by another (p. 19). As he put it, '[t]he turning to another subject and the need of being heard is absolutely essential for every social act' (p. 20). This made acts for Reinach inescapably dialogical. It is beyond the scope of this chapter to discuss how Reinach then used his concept of social acts to demonstrate the foundations of law, or to show how his conception can be said to have anticipated speech act theories and can perhaps be used to critique them (Crosby 1990; DuBois 1995; Smith 1990).

The importance of Reinach is that he belonged to a milieu at the turn of the twentieth century that included Franz Brentano, Edmund Husserl, Edith Stein, Max Scheler and Dietrich von Hildebrand. This milieu was both familiar to and influential for Martin Heidegger and Mikhail Bakhtin. It is interesting that despite their familiarity with this milieu Max Weber (1978), Talcott Parsons (1968) and Hannah Arendt (1958) often reduced 'acts' into 'action'. Thus, both Weber and Parsons conflated acts and action, albeit in different ways. Similarly, Habermas (1998), also despite the aforementioned milieu, takes Parsons as his starting point and develops, with the speech act theories of Austin and Searle and Mead's pragmatism, his concept of communicative action as 'reaching understanding'. As Habermas states, the interest in social action is oriented towards what he calls 'the classical question of how social order is possible' (1998, p. 234). Yet, it is possible to argue that in certain moments Weber, Parsons, Arendt and Habermas indeed implicitly indicate that they have an intuitive understanding that there are differences between acts and action. It is possible to find the uses of 'act' to indicate a general class of deeds and 'action' as a concrete behaviour bound by a place and time.

If there is one conclusion that one can draw from the work of the milieu discussed above it is that acts are a class of phenomena that indicate transcendent qualities (this is called ontological) of an action, whereas an action indicates a deed, a performance, something that is done (this is called ontic). To begin theorizing acts there does not need to be an action at all. We can investigate, for example, 'acts of forgiveness' and consider under what conditions certain actors may come into being by becoming implicated in acts that we can identify as 'acts of forgiveness'. Thus, it can be said that acts have a virtual existence that may be actualized under certain conditions. They are actualized, that is, made actual, by action. We can argue, as Derrida does (2001), that for an act of forgiveness to be an act of forgiveness it needs to be unconditional, and that there can be no conditional act of forgiveness. To be able to develop this argument we don't need to make reference to actions that actualize an act of forgiveness. By contrast, investigating actions would always involve the assemblage of action, actors and acts in a concrete scene. Thus, we can say that Greek aristocrats in 594 BCE committed an act of forgiveness when (via Solon) they cancelled all debts owed by peasants. Known as *seisactheia*, this action belongs to a class of acts that we call forgiveness. Thus, actualization of an act of forgiveness involved an action, *seisactheia*, in 594 BCE in Athens by aristocrats in their response to peasants. For the reason that there is a difference between ontological and ontic, and vitual and actual, an act should not be reduced to a deed or an action.

Now that I have asserted an ontological difference between acts and actions, how do we theorize acts? I would suggest that the essence of an act, as distinct from conduct, practice, behaviour and habit, is that an act is a rupture in the given. This is very close to what Ware (1973) had in mind when he considered that acts must be accomplishments. I have already mentioned how much attention is paid to orders or to what Bourdieu (1994) eventually called habitus, relatively enduring dispositions in contemporary social and political thought. But we can suggest this was the case for a long while rather than being a contemporary phenomenon. When we consider other major concepts of social and political thought in the twentieth century such as discipline (Foucault 1975), practice (Bourdieu 1980), society (Giddens 1984), identity (Rajchman 1995), citizenship (Turner 1986), government (Dean 1999), state (Tilly 1992), nation (Anderson 1983), sovereignty (Hinsley 1986), globalization (Hirst and Thompson 1999) and cosmopolitanism (Held 1995) it is almost as if social and political thought is exclusively focused on given orders. Or, rather, it is the givenness of orders that becomes an object of investigation. Accounts are provided of orders either found, diagnosed or anticipated. It seems almost as if social and political thought is fascinated by how an order holds and aims to give an account of it. When we consider the disagreements that were prominent in the 1950s and 1960s over habit versus 'following a rule' as the object of explanation in social sciences, for example, we observe how much concern there was about 'behaviour'. It is instructive to read Winch (1958) again today to realize how much he worried about establishing habit or routine behaviour as the exclusive object of social science. We may as well recall, too, that it was in the twentieth century that social sciences were almost absorbed into what was then called and persists today as 'the behavioural sciences'. While social sciences or social and political thought may concern themselves with ruptures and breaks, as did Foucault (1969), the focus almost always remains the difference between orders. This is ironic because modern social and political thought was born in the age of revolutions and its main concern can be said to have focused on giving an account of change, even revolutionary change. Marx (1848) and Freud (1964) perhaps represent the beginning and end, respectively, of that concern. I do not mean to suggest that there has been no concern with 'disorder'. Rather, acts are contrasted with habitus and other concepts that stand for relatively enduring dispositions of men and women that account for the persistence and stability of an order or the grounds of the emergence of another order.

I have already mentioned some thinkers whose work will be essential for theorizing acts. But I want to sharpen the difference between acts and action before I proceed with outlining some principles of theorizing acts. Lacan illustrates an interesting way to wrestle acts from action. He begins with a distinction between mere behaviour and acts (Lacan 1977, p. 50). He says that all animals engage in mere behaviour but only humans act. He goes on to suggest that 'acting out' and 'passage to the act' are not acts at all. (The passage to the act is a psychoanalytical concept that designates impulsive acts that are often violent and are a response to the intense pressure of anxiety to be resolved.) Lacan discusses both kinds of acts and appears to make a distinction between authentic or proper acts and acting out or passage to the act. Consider acts in terms of their scene of enactment. Acting out presupposes a scene that is already formed, in which the actor performs a script. By contrast, the passage to the act assumes that the actor actually flees or departs the scene (Evans 1996, pp. 136–7). But if an act is neither a mere behaviour nor acting, nor passage to the act, then what is the essence of the act? While some Lacanian commentators argue that what makes an act proper is responsibility, others suggest that indeed the act proper is passage to the act, which is a violent rupture. The issue remains unresolved. Like Lacan, Arendt also defines the act as a fundamental human capacity. Arendt often argues that being political means the capacity to act (Arendt 1969, p. 179). But if to act is no mere behaviour, what is its essence? She ascribes particular importance to the ancient Greek conception of act, which means both *governing* and *beginning* (Arendt 1958, p. 177). To act means to set something in motion, to begin not just something new but oneself as the being that acts to begin itself (p. 177). Since we are beings endowed with the capacity to act (or, as Sartre would say, since 'to be is to act'), and because to act is to realize a rupture in the given, 'to act' always means to enact the unexpected, unpredictable and the unknown (Sartre 1957, p. 613). As Arendt puts it rather evocatively, '[T]he human heart is the only thing in the world that will take upon itself the burden that the divine gift of action, of being a beginning and therefore being able to make a beginning, has placed upon us' (Arendt 2005, p. 322). To act, then, is neither arriving at a scene nor fleeing from it, but actually engaging in its creation. With that creative act the actor also creates herself/himself as the agent responsible for the scene created.

To maintain a distinction between acts and action and acts and habitus requires isolating acts as those entities that create a scene by involving actors who remain at the scene. Acts are ruptures or beginnings but not impulsive and violent reactions to a scene. By theorizing acts, or attempting to constitute acts as an object of analysis, we must focus not only on rupture rather than order, but also on a rupture that enables the actor (that the act creates) to remain at the scene rather than fleeing it. If an act is understood against habitus, practice, conduct, discipline and routine as ordered and ordering qualities of how humans conduct themselves, we can then perhaps understand why the question of acts would remain minor and fragmented within social and political thought and the social sciences.

We can now turn to a close reading of the young Bakhtin's incomplete manuscript, *Toward a Philosophy of the Act*. The reason we focus on this text is twofold. First, being aware of the Husserl circle and especially Max Scheler's work on ethics, the young Bakhtin makes the distinction between acts and action an ontological difference. Since the text is incomplete, some might say incoherent, it is useful for understanding what he finds at stake in making an ontological difference between acts and action. Second, in making this distinction Bakhtin introduces another distinction: between responsibility and answerability. So far we have left the issue of decision in the background but if it is a condition of acts then we need to anchor the decision in relation to something. Bakhtin's distinction is between what he calls two sides of answerability. I will reinterpret the two sides of answerability as responsibility (ontic and action-oriented) and answerability (ontological and acts-oriented). The question reacts to a tradition of understanding acts that reduces them to theoretical categories by orienting these acts towards their calculability, responsibility and intentionality. For this tradition acts enacted by beings such as we ourselves are intelligible only in so far as they are calculable, responsible and intentional. These terms bring about an understanding of the subject of the act as a calculating, responsible and intentional being. Of course, acts have calculable, responsible and intentional moments, but they are not reducible to them. How do we understand and interpret acts beyond calculability, responsibility and intentionality?

Theorizing Ethical Acts: Responsibility and Answerability

Bakhtin's *Toward a Philosophy of the Act* was written in the 1920s but was not published until the 1990s (Bakhtin 1993). By and large cast as an attempt at creating a first philosophy from an ethics, and in the process joining a critique of Kantian and neo-Kantian categorical imperatives, the manuscript produces vital insights on theorizing acts and crystallizes its genuine object of critique, of which Kantianism is only a special case (Nielsen 2002).

Bakhtin critiques three styles of thought that, he says, are inadequate for theorizing acts. He does not designate them clearly. Nor does he name anyone. I shall call these aestheticism, theoreticism and historicism. The two essential distinctions that Bakhtin introduces, again in my own words, are between acts and action and responsibility and answerability. The problem that Bakhtin sets out is the one that we have already emphasized. There is a world in which people perform actions and have their reasons and motives for doing so – or, as Weber would say, they attach subjective meanings to their actions. But can these actions be explained by giving an account of these meanings, motives and reasons? According to Bakhtin aestheticism would account for these actions in so far as they make sense within an order. Aestheticism would turn the focus away from the unique and once-occurrent aspect of these actions. Aestheticism reduces actions to acts. By contrast, theoreticism would account for them by interpreting them as an instance of something abstract. Theoreticism reduces acts into actions. Historicism sees both acts and actions but fails to write the actor into the act and the scene. Historicism lets the actor flee the scene that it creates. To investigate acts, Bakhtin seems to be saying, we need to fashion a style of thought that does not split the acts and actions but sees them as two aspects of events and places the actor at the scene. To put it another way, the beginning point for Bakhtin is that acts and action ought to be kept apart but considered together, along with our act of investigating as part of the scene, if we are to make sense of acts at all. Bakhtin urges us to see how acts create actors that decide to remain at the scene.

The concept that becomes decisive for Bakhtin is answerability to the Other. An act constitutes its unity (acts and action) via what Bakhtin calls a two-sided answerability. The content and occurrence of an act are answerable in different ways. These two sides of answerability are not reducible to each other and they cannot be understood without each other. When these two sides are understood together the split between acts and action can be surmounted in theorizing acts (Bakhtin 1993, p. 3). Bakhtin criticizes aestheticism and theoreticism for attempting to derive the content of an act from its moral law: both reduce the unique occurrence of the act to its interpretation, or, in Bakhtin's words, its special answerability to its general answerability. This, Bakhtin says, happens when the normative content of an act is understood to derive from a categorical imperative. By contrast, theoreticism constitutes the actor as a transcendental or theoretical actor rather than a concrete, historical performance. 'Thus, in so far as we detach a judgment from the unity constituted by the historical act/deed of its actualization and assign it to some theoretical unity there *is* no way of getting out from within its content/sense aspect and into the ought and the actual once-occurrent event of Being' (p. 7). What Bakhtin seems to be getting at is the difficulty of interpreting what actors do when they act: if interpreted with already existing concepts (by assuming calculable, responsible and intentional actors) the act is already folded into an event and thus into an order. Yet, if one resists the temptation of this kind of interpretation, one may have nothing at all to say about the act. This is the paradox of acts.

If it is impossible to investigate an act through abstracting its content from its occurrence, how does one investigate it as a unified act? If we fail to overcome these three styles of thought, we are thrown back into a split between what is and what ought to be (p. 20). Yet Bakhtin recognizes that overcoming aestheticism, theoreticism and historicism is not as easy as it sounds:

> My participative and demanding consciousness can see that the world of modern philosophy, the theoretical and theoreticized world of culture, is in a certain sense actual, that it possesses validity. But what it can also see is that this world is not the once-occurrent world in which I live and in which I answerably

perform my deeds. And these two worlds do not intercommunicate; there is no principle for including and actively involving the valid world of theory and theoreticized culture in the once-occurrent Being-event of life. (p. 20)

But modern ethics – understood as either content ethics, construing the act from universal or categorical norms, or formal ethics, construing an act by deriving its ought from the concrete act itself – cannot bridge these two worlds (pp. 24–5). Neither form of ethics can capture the fact that 'the actually performed act – not from the aspect of its content, but in its performance – somehow knows, somehow possesses the unitary and once-occurrent being of life; it orients itself within that being, and it does so, moreover, in its entirety – both in its content-aspect and in its actual, unique factuality' (p. 28). Thus, the answerable act must be investigated as the 'actualization of a decision – inescapably, irremediably, and irrevocably' (p. 28).

What an act actualizes or performs is a decision that is answerable to the Other. Bakhtin seems to reach the conclusion that once we understand an act as the actualization or performance of a decision in its unity, neither objectivism nor subjectivism, and neither rationalism nor voluntarism, can provide adequate grounds for theorizing acts. For the act itself unites both objective and subjective, both rational and volitional, as constitutive moments of the act. Bakhtin suggests, in fact, that language is historically structured in a way that captures participative thinking and performed acts (p. 31). To investigate an act would articulate not the world produced by the act 'but the world in which that act becomes answerably aware of itself and is actually performed' (p. 31). That moment of becoming aware of itself is the unfolding of the actor to her being in the world – a world that does not contain already given objects and subjects (thus a given scene), but in which those subjects and objects unfold in their relations to each other in that world (thus creating the scene). It is not a world of objects that theorizing acts creates but relations amongst those objects and subjects as they unfold to each other and the investigator.

This is one of the most interesting aspects of Bakhtin's thoughts on acts, as he attempts to write the investigator into the act as an actor. Bakhtin says when investigating an act that 'the mere fact that I have begun speaking about it means that I have already assumed a certain attitude towards it – not an indifferent attitude, but an interested-effective attitude' (p. 32). Bakhtin will designate this aspect of theorizing as 'emotional-volitional intonation'. By this concept Bakhtin attempts to surmount both the subjectivism–objectivism and emotionalism–rationalism dichotomies. An act embodies both individual consciousness and cultural consciousness, but the decisions enacted by an act are beyond the bounds of individual consciousness (p. 35). The concept 'emotional-volitional intonation' designates 'precisely the moment constituted by my self-activity in a lived experience – the experiencing of an experience as *mine*: *I* think – perform a deed by thinking' (p. 36). To investigate an act is to understand that this 'moment constituted by the performance of thoughts, feelings, words, practical deeds is an actively answerable attitude that I myself assume – an emotional-volitional attitude towards a state of affairs in its entirety, in the context of actual unitary and once-occurrent life' (p. 37). An act therefore constitutes that moment when an actor enacts not merely the content of an act, but also its sense. As Bakhtin says 'What we shall find everywhere is a constant unity of answerability, that is, *not* a constancy in content and *not* a constant law of the performed act (all content is only a constituent moment), but a certain actual fact of acknowledgement, an acknowledgment that is once-occurrent and never-repeatable, emotional-volitional and concretely individual' (p. 39). Thus, we can argue, the two sides of answerability correspond roughly to responsibility and answerability. To act or actualize an act, which is a decision, on the one hand produces an actor within the concrete, calculable, immediate conditions of the act that result in responsibilities towards others; on the other hand, the act reveals an actor to herself in her answerability to the Other. The paradox of the act is that responsibility and answerability may well contradict one another. Being immediately responsible towards others may well go against being answerable to the Other. It is this paradox that Derrida explores as two forms of responsibility (Derrida 1991, 1992). Thus, we have two sides of answerability in Bakhtin and two forms of responsibility in Derrida. I suggest using responsibility to specify the calculable (ontic) orientation towards others and answerability to specify the incalculable (ontological) orientation towards the Other.

While it is fruitful to see how the young Bakhtin struggled to make a distinction between acts and action, responsibility and answerability, and content and sense of acts, a question that remains is the essence of answerability to the Other. It is this question, I think, that Heidegger (1927) and Levinas (1978) struggled with and to which Derrida (1992) returned. The question can be rephrased as: who is the Other? As we have seen, as there are several references in the young Bakhtin to Being and beings and Being-as-event it would be simplistic to assume that answerability answers other beings. We have already specified that as responsibility and we do not wish to reduce answerability to responsibility. We have seen above that when Bakhtin emphasizes a difference between two forms of answerability, he is on the verge of developing a difference between responsibility (ethical relations of obligation between given beings in a given scene) and answerability (ethical relations between beings and Being). Answerability is not a commitment or promise that one pledges to another being. If answerability is not towards another being, whom does it answer and who calls?

This is where Heidegger's ontological analysis of conscience is significant. As is well known, in *Being and Time*, after demonstrating how 'beings such as we ourselves are' are constituted by attunement, understanding, fallenness and discourse, Heidegger says that it is conscience that discloses ourselves in our potentiality-as-being. As beings whose existence is a concern for ourselves, we disclose our being to ourselves through our potentialities and possibilities. Heidegger says that his existential analysis of conscience reveals the character of this disclosure as a 'call' (Heidegger 1927, p. 249 SZ 269). It is possible to see the resonance between 'call' and 'answer', between Heidegger and Bakhtin. The call of conscience appears as summoning the being such as we ourselves are into its own unique possibilities. Can we interpret Bakhtinian answerability as an answer to the call of conscience? In order to move in that direction, we need an understanding of conscience that is beyond its everyday meaning of guilt as debt (Nietzsche 1887, pp. 41–5).

That is what Heidegger does in roughly the following way. The call of conscience discloses our being to ourselves. The call of conscience appears precisely because we fall prey to others, or lose ourselves in them. How do we lose ourselves in others? We flee from our own thrownness into the ostensible freedom of others by being responsible towards them. But this also becomes a flight from the uncanniness of our thrown being (Heidegger 1927, p. 255 SZ 276). Conscience reveals itself as the concern over our own thrownness. The caller is our own being concerned about its thrownness. The summoned is also our own being called forth to its potentialities. The call comes from and is directed towards the being that I am. Yet, the call is something that I have neither planned nor willed. It calls (p. 254 SZ 275). The call of conscience directs the being that I myself am out of uncanniness. The call of conscience discloses my potentiality-as-being. Can we not consider this as a possible reading of the distinction between responsibility and answerability in Bakhtin?

To inflect answerability with Heidegger's analysis of conscience, we need to focus briefly on the character of the summons. Heidegger insists on interpreting conscience existentially and ontologically, which means to wrest it from the everyday notion of conscience as guilt or debt. Instead, Heidegger moves towards being guilty about something other than the immediately present. He says '[t]he idea of guilt must not only be removed from the area of calculating and taking care of things, but must also be separated from relationship to an ought and a law such that failing to comply with it one burdens himself with guilt' (p. 261 SZ 283). Thus Heidegger recognizes that the call of conscience is a response to guilt, but he refuses to interpret that guilt in its everyday understanding of debt as owing something, that is responsibility. The everyday understands guilt as the absence of what ought to be and conscience as that which makes guilt present. While the quality of the 'not' is present in the idea of guilty, it is not lack understood as absence. Heidegger articulates guilt ontologically as follows. In our thrownness beings such as we ourselves always lag behind our possibilities. We understand ourselves as these possibilities. We ground ourselves, or our ground of being discloses itself as those possibilities – not only those we can pursue but also those we cannot. The ground discloses itself as the 'not' of being (pp. 262–3 SZ 284–5). This nothingness means being free for our possibilities and yet, at the same time, it is the ground for being guilty. The existential guilt, then, is not about this or that debt that can be calculated, but about the fact that I exist as such. It is this existential guilt that makes us answerable to our being. Beings such as we ourselves are, who concern ourselves with our being (care), will not only concern ourselves with everyday guilt as owing something (responsibility) but will also be guilty in the very ground of our being (answerability). What makes conscience possible is the existential fact that we are guilty in the ground of our being and close ourselves off from our thrownness and flee from uncanniness (p. 264 SZ 286). It is this fleeing that the call of conscience makes us understand. The call of conscience as care gives us an understanding of existential guilt. It is through the call of conscience as care that uncanniness brings us face to face with our nothingness, which belongs to our own potentiality-of-being. If that is the case, Heidegger reflects, then the call, as that which makes us answerable, is tantamount to understanding ourselves in our own potentialities – and hence not fleeing. Moreover, we recognize our own potentiality-of-being as potentiality of becoming guilty. When we constitute ourselves in our answerability we make ourselves ready for the call of conscience as care. This readiness includes our becoming free for the call. By understanding the call we have listened to our own possibility of existence (p. 265 SZ 287). We can suggest with Heidegger that answerability answers the call of conscience as care from the uncanniness of being-in-the-world that summons beings such as we ourselves are to our own potentiality-for-being-guilty (p. 266 SZ 289).

Heidegger illuminates Bakhtin's analysis of the act from the perspective of answerability. The affinities between *Being and Time* and Bakhtin's style of thought in *Toward Philosophy of the Act* are prodigious. After all, both shared a deep interest in Scheler (1916) and Kierkegaard (1983), and aimed to develop an ontological conception of the ethical act by calling Kantian ethics into question. Heidegger grounds Bakhtin's investigation of the answerability of acts by his existential analysis of conscience. The two share an insistence on the irreducibility of the act to its immediate responsibility, calculability and intentionality (acting out) and a refusal to interpret acts as absolute ruptures (passage to the act).

The answerability of an act is irreducible to calculation, responsibility and intentionality. An ethical act precedes and indeed makes possible any action. An act is always oriented towards its objects before calculation, responsibility or intention. These terms (calculation, responsibility, intention) arrive at the scene (action) too late to understand or interpret it. An ethical act also precedes and indeed makes possible any actors. The actor is produced through the scene and is constituted by the act itself. It would be questionable then to assume that the answerability of the act is to another actor. An act acknowledges its answerability to Being. This is where there are significant affinities between Heidegger and Bakhtin. Or, to put it more modestly, Bakhtin's concept of answerability is best elaborated, enlarged and refined with Heidegger, especially with his concept of 'conscience as the call of care'. Again, Heidegger provides guidance in answering the question of who this being that acts actually is (p. 107 SZ 114). He has fundamental reservations about assuming that that being is the 'simple perceiving reflection of the I of acts' (p. 109 SZ 115). The whole point of thinking through being-in-the-world is the conclusion that a mere actor without a social world is impossible. The world in which we exist is a with-world: 'Being-in is being-with others' (p. 112 SZ 119). Being-with is an existential concept and it does not assume objective presence or absence of other beings; even in their objective absence being still has the character of being-with. As being-with we essentially exist as beings concerned with others and the Other. Whether this concern expresses itself as tolerance or intolerance, difference or indifference, it is still being-with. The being that acts, therefore, is already a being-towards-others and has an understanding of others because it is a being whose essence is being-with. Thus being-with-one-another cannot be understood as the presence of several actors together (p. 118 SZ 125).

An ethical act in the way in which we articulated it – as answerability – perhaps prepares the ground for understanding other acts, but cannot explain them. As we are interested in acts of citizenship, the question that presents itself is that of political acts. That citizenship and the political are related concepts does not require elaboration, merely a reminder. But how do we investigate the passage from ethical acts (answerability and responsibility) to political acts? How do ethical acts articulate themselves into political acts? When Heidegger elaborates upon being-with, he insists that 'others' are those from whom one mostly does not distinguish oneself, or that others are always others with their kind (p. 111, 113 SZ 118, 120). I find this both troubling and confusing. Disagreeing with Heidegger, while still remaining within ontological and existential analysis, we can observe that beings are also being-with others other than those beings that they understand as their kind. Beings are always being-with their kind as well as with those whom they constitute another kind of other. This is the question of the political to which Heidegger's thought remains a stranger. To put it another way, the question of the stranger as the essence of the political eludes Heidegger. It is this question of the political as the question of the third party that Levinas and Derrida introduce.

Theorizing Political Acts: Law and Justice

Acts involve others and the Other, but if others are not an undifferentiated mass then what differentiates them? Theorizing political acts raises the question of a third party, as political acts cannot always take place amongst beings of the same kind. A political act will always involve a third party. When a third party is present, the two parties will constitute themselves in their answerability towards being political, which constitutes the essence of the political. The issue of the third party was introduced by Levinas to address the question of justice and politics rather than a question involving relations between enemy and friend or self and the Other (Critchley 1999, pp. 214–15). For Levinas an act proper is enacted when a third party enters into it (Levinas 1978, pp. 157–9). When Levinas says, 'The third party is other than the neighbour, but also another neighbour, and also a neighbour of the other, and not simply his fellow', he is emphasizing that an act always brings into assemblage more than those who are immediately caught in the scene that the act creates (p. 157). A scene of an act therefore always involves a spectrum of others, rather than two others facing each other. With the introduction of a third party, there will be a breach between the other, the third party and the 'I'. The third party is the birth of the question of justice. Being gathered together through space, with a breach but proximity, there will be a question of comparison, coexistence, visibility, difference and all that stands for justice. But here justice itself does not stand on law: 'justice is not legality regulating human masses, from which a technique of social equilibrium is drawn, harmonizing antagonistic forces' (p. 159). Thus, 'It is important to recover all these forms beginning with proximity, in which being, totality,

State, politics, techniques, work are at every moment on the point of having their centre of gravitation in themselves, and weighing on their own account' (p. 159).

For Levinas 'justice remains justice only in a society where there is no distinction between those close and those far off, but in which there also remains the impossibility of passing by the closest. The equality of all is borne by my inequality, the surplus of my duties over my rights' (p. 159). Thus, because justice is 'an incessant correction of the asymmetry of proximity' (p. 158), seeking it will involve answerability. Levinas says that the answerability of an act is what institutes the original locus of justice, 'a terrain common to me and the others where I am counted among them, that is, where subjectivity is a citizen with all the duties and rights measured and measurable which the equilibrated ego involves, or equilibrating itself by the concourse of duties and the concurrence of rights' (p. 160). Justice seeks answerability when one makes a claim upon the other in the presence of another. If the ethical act arises as answerability in the absence of a third party (surplus of obligations over rights), then the political act arises as justice (surplus of rights over obligations) in its presence. The distinction Derrida (2002) insists on between justice as incalculable and law as calculating aspects of order is intimately connected with the difference between responsibility and answerability as regards theorizing acts.

Theorizing political acts must then mean investigating these ways as expressed in the everyday that are ordinarily called politics. In other words, the political is irreducibly different from politics but cannot be investigated and delineated without investigating politics. How to proceed from theorizing politics to the political is complicated, which exemplifies how everyday politics can be mapped onto the acts of the political and interpreted as ways of being political. This way of theorizing acts can be called transcendental empiricism (Deleuze 1994). The upshot is that politics constitutes relatively enduring and routinized ways of being that can only be investigated through the political when it ruptures these ways of being. If these ways of being (habitus) constitute the existential conditions of possibility of politics, acts constitute the conditions of possibility of the political, a rupture of politics.

We can summarize our initial findings as follows: (1) Acts and action are distinct and separate (but related) classes of phenomena. While acts have a virtual existence, action is always actual. (2) Acts rupture or break the given orders, practices and habitus. Creative ruptures and breaks take different forms that are irreducible. They can, for example, take forms of resistance or subservience. What actualizes an act is not determinable in advance. (3) Acts produce actors and actors do not produce acts; actors actualize acts and themselves through action. (4) Actualization of acts provokes both responsibility and answerability. Acts always concern others and the Other. The tension between responsibility and answerability produces acts as ruptures in the given. (5) Answerability and responsibility are distinct and separate (but related) classes of phenomena. While responsibility invokes the given, immediate and calculable, answerability orients acts towards the Other. (6) Ethics and the ethical, politics and the political are distinct and irreducible (but related) aspects of acts that one must investigate separately while keeping them together.

Investigating Acts of Citizenship: Becoming Activist Citizens

If each act is simultaneously both ethical and political (because it is not merely calculable, responsible and intentional), is every act an act of citizenship? If not, when is an act an act of citizenship? The insistence on acts as the object of investigation rather than the status and habitus of subjects already breaks new ground. Citizenship studies often proceeds with a focus on the three ontic aspects of citizenship: extent (rules and norms of exclusion and inclusion), content (rights and responsibilities) and depth (thickness or thinness of belonging). We can suggest that these aspects of citizenship arrive at the scene too late and provide too little for interpreting acts of citizenship. They arrive too late because the actors of extent, content and depth are already produced; for acts produce actors that do not exist before acts. They provide too little because the scene has already been created. If acts produce actors (or actors are produced through acts) then initially we can define acts of citizenship as those acts that produce citizens and their others.

Theorizing acts is part of a larger body of work that proposes a way of investigating genealogies of citizenship as a generalized question of otherness that includes strangers but also outsiders and aliens. It draws upon Heidegger and Levinas on the question of the political (Isin 2002). Briefly, this analysis regards the formation of social groups as a fundamental but dynamic process through which beings such as we ourselves come into being. Through orientations (intentions, motives, purposes), strategies (reasons, manoeuvres, programmes) and technologies (tactics, techniques, methods) as forms of being political, beings enact solidaristic, agonistic and alienating modes of being with each other. These forms and modes constitute ways of being political in the sense that being implicated in them is not necessarily calculable and rational but may also be unintentional or affective. It is in these ways that we become political: that is to say, we enact ourselves as citizens, strangers, outsiders and aliens rather than identities or differences that are already there. For this reason, it is impossible to investigate 'citizenship' – the name that citizens, as distinguished from strangers, outsiders and aliens, have given themselves – without investigating the specific constellation of orientations, strategies and technologies that are available for enacting solidaristic, agonistic or alienating modes of being with each other. The question of acts emerges from this analysis precisely because it raises the question as to what accounts for subjects refusing, resisting or subverting the orientations, strategies and technologies in which they find themselves implicated, and the solidaristic, agonistic and alienating relationships in which they are caught. While we are implicated or caught in these forms and modes, they guide but do not determine our enactments. It is important to investigate these forms and modes of being political, and acts enable us to investigate the transformation of these ways: how do subjects become actors by finding ways into or out of them? If we always find our ways into forms and modes of being political, we also find ways out of them.

How should we approach theorizing acts of citizenship? Are acts of citizenship inherently (or always) exclusive or inclusive, homogenizing or diversifying, positive or negative? Or do these meanings that we attribute to acts only arise after the fact? Following our discussion of acts, we cannot define acts of citizenship as already inherently exclusive or inclusive, homogenizing or diversifying, or positive or negative. These qualities arise after or, more appropriately, through the act. In fact, we as interpreters ascribe these qualities to those acts. That means that acts produce such qualities only as their effects, not causes. Moreover, those acts that are explicitly intended for certain effects (inclusion, diversity, tolerance) may well produce others (exclusion, homogeneity, intolerance). *The first principle of investigating acts of citizenship is to interpret them through their grounds and consequences, which includes subjects becoming activist citizens through scenes created.* Thus, we contrast 'activist citizens' with 'active citizens' who act out already written scripts. While activist citizens engage in writing scripts and creating the scene, active citizens follow scripts and participate in scenes that are already created. While activist citizens are creative, active citizens are not.

Can acts of citizenship be enacted without an explicit motive, purpose or reason? Do those beings that act as citizens, strangers, outsiders or aliens necessarily (or always) attribute reasons to their acts? Acts cannot happen without motives, purposes, or reasons, but those cannot be the only grounds of interpreting acts of citizenship. While acts of citizenship involve decisions, those decisions cannot be reduced to calculability, intentionality and responsibility. But because they are irreducible to those qualities they can be enacted without subjects being able to articulate reasons for becoming activist citizens. Acts of citizenship do not need to originate in the name of anything though we as interpreters will always interpret how acts of citizenship orient themselves towards justice. *The second principle of theorizing acts of citizenship recognizes that acts produce actors that become answerable to justice against injustice.*

Can acts of citizenship happen without being founded in law or responsibility? Do those beings that act as citizens, strangers, outsiders or aliens necessarily (or always) act in the name of the law and responsibility? Are acts of citizenship only legitimate when founded in law and responsibility? Acts of citizenship are not necessarily founded in law or responsibility. In fact, for acts of citizenship to be acts at all they must call the law into question and, sometimes, break it. Similarly, for acts of citizenship to be acts at all they must call established forms of responsibilization into question and, sometimes, be irresponsible. Those activist citizens that acts produce are not *a priori* beings recognized in law, but by enacting themselves through acts they affect the law that recognizes them. *The third principle of theorizing acts is to recognize that acts of citizenship do not need to be founded in law or enacted in the name of the law.*

Acts constitute actors who claim and assert rights and obligations, enact themselves as activist citizens and, in the process, differentiate others as those who are not (strangers, outsiders, aliens). Acts of citizenship are those acts through which citizens, strangers, outsiders and aliens emerge not as beings already defined but as beings acting and reacting with others. We have considered acts of citizenship as political in so far as these acts constitute constituents (beings with claims). But they are also ethical (as when answerable and responsible), cultural (as in the carnivalesque), sexual (as when pleasurable) and social (as in acts of affiliation, solidarity or hostility): in these ways they actualize or perform ways of becoming political. We define acts of citizenship as those acts that transform forms (orientations, strategies, technologies) and modes (citizens, strangers, outsiders, aliens) of being political by bringing into being new actors as activist citizens (claimants of rights and responsibilities) through creating new sites and scales of struggle.

Acknowledgements

I would like to thank the following graduate and postgraduate students who participated in the Citizenship Studies Media Lab (CSML) seminars between 2002 and 2006 as CSML Fellows: Irus Braverman, Darryl Burgwin, Gül Caliskan, Agnes Czajka, Karine Côté-Boucher, Dana Dawson, Erkan Ercel, Gil Gaspar, Bora Isyar, Matt Jackson, Alex Lefebvre, Gabriel Levine, Graham Longford, Ian Morrison, Kim Rygiel, John Saunders, Ebru Üstündag, Charles Wells and Melanie White. Each and all have contributed significantly to the birth and development of the concept 'acts of citizenship'. I am grateful to Greg Nielsen for providing insightful and useful comments on an earlier draft. I am also grateful to Kieran Bonner, John Clarke, Fred Evans, William Walters and Melanie White for their critical comments on the last draft of the chapter.

References

Allman, D. D. and M. D. Beaty (eds) (2002) *Cultivating Citizens: Soulcraft and Citizenship in Contemporary America*, Lexington Books, Lanham.

Anderson, B. R. (1983) *Imagined Communities: Reflections on the Origin and Spread of Nationalism*, Verso, London.

Arendt, H. (1951) *The Origins of Totalitarianism*, Harcourt Brace Jovanovich, New York.

— (1958) *The Human Condition*, Chicago, University of Chicago Press, Chicago, IL.

— (1969) 'On Violence' in *Crises of the Republic: Lying in Politics; Civil Disobedience; on Violence; Thoughts on Politics and Revolution*, Harcourt Brace Jovanovich, New York.

— (2005) 'Understanding and Politics' in *Essays in Understanding, 1930–1954: Formation, Exile, and Totalitarianism*, Schocken Books, New York.

Austin, J. L. (1962) *How to Do Things with Words*, Clarendon Press, Oxford.

Bakhtin, M. (1993) *Toward a Philosophy of the Act*, University of Texas Press, Austin, TX.

Balibar, E. (2004) *We, the People of Europe? Reflections on Transnational Citizenship*, Princeton University Press, Princeton, NJ.

Benhabib, S. (2004) *The Rights of Others: Aliens, Residents and Citizens*, Cambridge University Press, Cambridge.

Bennett, J. F. (1995) *The Act Itself*, Clarendon Press, Oxford.

Bourdieu, P. (1972) *Outline of a Theory of Practice*, Cambridge University Press, Cambridge.

—— (1980) *The Logic of Practice*, Stanford University Press, Stanford.

—— (1994) *Practical Reason: On the Theory of Action*, Stanford University Press, Stanford.

Burns, S. (1997) *Daybreak of Freedom: The Montgomery Bus Boycott*, University of North Carolina Press, Chapel Hill.

Clarke, J. (2004) *Changing Welfare, Changing States: New Directions in Social Policy*, Sage, London.

Clarke, J., J. E. Newman, N. Smith, E. Vidler and L. Westmarland (2007) *Creating Citizen-Consumers: Changing Publics and Changing Public Services*, Sage, London.

Critchley, S. (1999) *The Ethics of Deconstruction: Derrida and Levinas* (2nd edn), Edinburgh University Press, Edinburgh.

Crosby, J. F. (1990) 'Speech Act Theory and Phenomenology' in A. Burkhardt (ed.), *Speech Acts, Meanings and Intentions: Critical Approaches to the Philosophy of John R. Searle*, W. de Gruyter, Berlin.

Dean, M. (1999) *Governmentality: Power and Rule in Modern Society*, Sage, London.

Deleuze, G. (1994) *Difference and Repetition* (trans. P. Patton), Columbia University Press, New York.

Derrida, J. (1991) *Given Time: I. Counterfeit Money* (trans. P. Kamuf), University of Chicago

Press, Chicago, IL.

—— (1992) *The Gift of Death* (trans. D. Wills), University of Chicago Press, Chicago, IL.

—— (2001) *On Cosmopolitanism and Forgiveness* (trans. M. Dooley and M. Hughes), Routledge, London.

—— (2002) 'Force of Law: The "Mystical Foundation of Authority"' in *Acts of Religion*, Routledge, New York.

DuBois, J. M. (1995) *Judgement and Sachverhalt: An Introduction to Adolf Reinach's Phenomenological Realism*, Kluwer Academic Publishers, Dordecht.

Evans, D. (1996) *An Introductory Dictionary of Lacanian Psychoanalysis*, Routledge, London.

Farnell, B. (2000) 'Getting out of the Habitus: An Alternative Model of Dynamically Embodied Social Action', *The Journal of the Royal Anthropological Institute,* 6 (3), 397–418.

Foucault, M. (1969) *The Archaeology of Knowledge and the Discourse on Language* (trans. A. M. S. Smith), Pantheon, New York.

—— (1975) *Discipline and Punish: The Birth of the Prison* (trans. A. Sheridan), Vintage Books, New York.

-—— (1984) *The Care of Self*, Pantheon, New York.

—— (1988) 'Technologies of the Self' in L. H. Martin, H. Gutman and P. H. Hutton (eds), *Technologies of the Self: A Seminar with Michel Foucault*, University of Massachusetts Press, Amherst.

Freud, S. (1964) *Civilization and Its Discontents*, Vintage and Hogarth Press and the Institute of Psychoanalysis, London.

Fulford, R. (1976) *Votes for Women: The Story of a Struggle*, White Lion Publishers, London.

Giddens, A. (1984) The Constitution of Society: Outline of the Theory of Structuration, University of California Press, Berkeley.

Habermas, J. (1998) 'Actions, Speech Acts, Linguistically Mediated Interactions, and the Lifeworld' in M. Cooke (ed.), *On the Pragmatics of Communication*, MIT Press, Cambridge, Mass.

Heidegger, M. (1927) *Being and Time* (trans. J. Stambaugh), State University of New York Press, Albany.

Held, D. (1995) *Democracy and the Global Order: From the Modern State to Cosmopolitan Governance*, Stanford University Press, Stanford.

Hinsley, F. H. (1986) *Sovereignty*, Cambridge University Press, Cambridge.

Hirst, P. Q. and G. Thompson (1999) *Globalization in Question: The International Economy and the Possibilities of Governance* (2nd edn), Polity Press, Cambridge.

Isin, E. F. (2002) *Being Political: Genealogies of Citizenship*, University of Minnesota Press, Minneapolis.

—— (2005) 'Engaging, Being, Political', *Political Geography,* 24, 373–87.

—— (forthcoming 2008) 'Citizenship in Flux: Sites, Scales and Acts' in P. Pansapa, G. Thomas and M. J. Smith (eds), *Making a Difference! Civic Engagement and Citizenship in a Global Society*, Zed Books, London.

Isin, E. F. and B. S. Turner (2002) *Handbook of Citizenship Studies*, Sage, London.

Isin, E. F. and B. S. Turner (2007) 'Investigating Citizenship: An Agenda for Citizenship Studies', *Citizenship Studies,* 11 (1), 5–17.

Isin, E. F. and P. K. Wood (1999) *Citizenship and Identity*, Sage, London.

Kierkegaard, S. (1983) *Fear and Trembling; Repetition*, Princeton University Press, Princeton.

Kymlicka, W. (1995) *Multicultural Citizenship*, Oxford University Press, Oxford.

Kymlicka, W. and W. Norman (eds) (2000) *Citizenship in Diverse Societies*, Oxford University Press, Oxford.

Lacan, J. (1977) *The Four Fundamental Concepts of Psychoanalysis* (trans. A. Sheridan), Hogarth Press: Institute of Psychoanalysis, London.

Levinas, E. (1978) *Otherwise than Being or Beyond Essence* (trans. A. Lingis), Kluwer, Dordrecht.

Lister, R. (2002) *Citizenship: Feminist Perspectives* (2nd edn), Palgrave Macmillan, Basingstoke.

Marx, K. and F. Engels (1848) *The Communist Manifesto*, Penguin, London.

Nielsen, G. M. (2002) *The Norms of Answerability: Social Theory between Bakhtin and Habermas*, State University of New York Press, Albany.

Nietzsche, F. (1887) *On the Genealogy of Morals* (trans. W. Kaufmann), Viking, New York.

Parsons, T. (1968) 'The Theory of Action' in *The Structure of Social Action* (Vol. 1), Free Press, New York.

Rajchman, J. (ed.) (1995) *The Identity in Question*, Routledge, New York.

Rancière, J. (2004) 'Who Is the Subject of the Rights of Man?', *The South Atlantic Quarterly*, 103 (2/3), 297–310.

Reinach, A. (1983) 'The Apriori Foundations of Civil Law', *Aletheia*, 3, 1–142.

Sartre, J.-P. (1957) *Being and Nothingness: An Essay on Phenomenological Ontology* (trans. H. E. Barnes), Methuen, London.

Schatzki, T. R. (1997) 'Practices and Actions: A Wittgensteinian Critique of Bourdieu and Giddens', *Philosophy of the Social Sciences*, 27 (3), 283–308.

—— (2002) *The Site of the Social: A Philosophical Account of the Constitution of Social Life and Change*, Pennsylvania State University Press, University Park, PA.

—— (2003) 'A New Societist Social Ontology', *Philosophy of the Social Sciences*, 33 (2), 174–202.

Scheler, M. (1916) 'The Being of the Person' in D. Moran (ed.), *The Phenomenology Reader*, Routledge, London.

Searle, J. R. (1969) *Speech Acts: An Essay in the Philosophy of Language*, Cambridge University Press, Cambridge.

Smith, B. (1990) 'Towards a History of Speech Act Theory' in A. Burkhardt (ed.), *Speech Acts, Meaning, and Intentions: Critical Approaches to the Philosophy of John R. Searle*, W. de Gruyter, Berlin.

Soysal, Y. (1994) *Limits of Citizenship: Migrants and Postnational Membership in Europe*, University of Chicago Press, Chicago, IL.

Stout, R. (2005) *Action*, McGill-Queen's University Press, Montreal and Kingston.

Tilly, C. (1992) *Coercion, Capital, and European States, AD 990–1992*, Blackwell, Cambridge, MA.

Turner, B. S. (1986) *Citizenship and Capitalism: The Debate over Reformism*, Unwin, London.

Ware, R. (1973) 'Acts and Action', *The Journal of Philosophy*, 70 (13), 403–18.

Weber, M. (1978) *Economy and Society: An Outline of Interpretive Sociology* (trans. G. Roth and C. Wittich), University of California Press, Berkeley.

Winch, P. G. (1958) *The Idea of a Social Science and Its Relation to Philosophy*, Routledge, London.

Žižek, S. (1999) *The Ticklish Subject: The Absent Centre of Political Ontology*, Verso, London.

Chapter 2

❖

Can an Act of Citizenship
Be Creative?

MELANIE WHITE

The promise of 'the act of citizenship' to generate new ways of thinking about those ways of acting politically that are not easily captured by conventional socio-legal understandings of citizenship is substantial. Defined by Engin Isin as those moments when individuals, beings and groups claim, assert, and impose rights through which they define themselves as active and reactive ways of being with others, the concept of the act of citizenship seeks to address the myriad ways that human beings organize, remake and resist their ethical-political relations with others (2008). The concept attempts to foreground the transformative possibilities of political becoming in the constitutive formation of new and innovative ways of acting politically. As such, the 'act of citizenship' seeks to emphasize moments of aleatory possibility by highlighting the emergent, the new and, ultimately, the creative in becoming political.

This heuristic potential has motivated me to interrogate one aspect of the concept – its claim to creativity – by posing the question: can an act of citizenship be creative? This question is prompted by a possible tension between those citizenship 'practices' that engender reasonably durable, resilient and predictable ethical-political relations with others and those citizenship 'acts' that disrupt them through transformative action. The question of whether the exercise of citizenship is capable of generating creative acts engenders a theoretical problem for a traditional conception of citizenship that depends on organized, disciplined and habitual practices to demonstrate one's citizenly competence. In short, to what extent do the habitual practice and the creative activity of citizens stand in opposition to one another? Do habits hinder or support creative practice?

The question of whether acts of citizenship can be creative is investigated here by way of a very specific sense of 'creativity' found in the work of Henri Bergson (2001, 1991, 1974a, 1974b), and subsequently developed by Gilles Deleuze (1988, 2004a, 2004b). For Bergson, as for Deleuze, creativity expresses itself as *duration*. Duration is the flow and movement of time that resists and exceeds its division into seconds, minutes and hours. It is a conception of time that is necessarily distinct from space and is defined as that which differs from itself in so far as the passage of time marks a perpetual process of change in and for the being that lives and endures. Thinking about creativity as duration is potentially useful for theorizing the creative capacity of the act of citizenship for at least two reasons. First, it is a conception of creativity that requires no external criteria in evaluating innovation and change. Creativity is an expression of duration, as that which changes from itself. This understanding allows us to sidestep moribund debates over the necessary form and substance of what 'counts' as creative – for creativity is a becoming, one that is by its very nature transformative. Next, creativity does not organize an individual's specific talents and capacities into a specific state of being; rather creativity is expressed in terms of an aspiration to change. Creativity is neither evaluated as a product nor as an end result; rather it is best expressed as a tendency to change, as an expression of movement through time.

The understanding of creativity discussed here is not to be confused with the kind celebrated by popular psychologists who seek to bring fulfilment to those struggling with the spiritual and emotional complexities of late-modern life (Csikszentmihalyi 1996). Such popular conceptions of creativity tend to organize human capacities so as to render them calculable such that they may achieve specific goals like economic success, emotional fulfilment and spiritual balance. This is a conception of creativity that inevitably organizes human beings into calculable, predictable subjects through different technologies of government (Osborne 2003, pp. 508–10). For Bergson, such popular attempts to define creativity would run counter to the whole spirit of creativity as duration, for genuine creative movement is necessarily unpredictable, incalculable and altogether unknowable in advance. As Bergson argues, '[T]ime is what hinders everything from being given at once. It retards, or rather it is retardation. It must, therefore, be elaboration. Would it not then be a vehicle of creation and choice?' (1974, p. 93).

The purpose of this chapter is to consider whether acts of citizenship can be creative in this Bergsonian sense. This task involves reading Bergson as a social theorist, a task which poses some difficulty given that Bergson is not typically interpreted as such. This is curious given that Bergson's last significant publication, *The Two Sources of Morality and Religion* (1977) is easily his most sociological work and contains many useful insights on the nature of social obligation and creativity that should be of interest to both social theorists and citizenship scholars alike. Certainly many contemporary philosophers have taken an interest in Bergson; this interest, however, is often at the expense of *The Two Sources*, arguably his most important work from the standpoint of social and political theory (Alliez 2004; Ansell-Pearson 2002; Kolakowski 1985; Mullarkey 2000). Thus, this chapter proposes to think with Bergson on the problem of citizenship and creativity by focusing almost exclusively on *The Two Sources,* especially its first chapter, in order to take advantage of its insights for the problem of citizenship and its creative potential.

Essentially, my argument boils down to the claim that in order to be truly creative, the citizen must overcome the force of habit by provoking a genuine encounter that poses the problem of how to act. This may seem like truism, but it complicates a major sociological strain *à la* Durkheim (1961) and, possibly, Foucault (1977), that highlights habits as necessary and useful limits placed on the self by society that enable subjects to learn to exercise their 'freedom'. Bergson argues, conversely, that in the spirit of genuine creativity, habits cannot be creative because they are oriented to calculable outcomes of action. Indeed, the problem with habits is that they give us the illusion that our conduct is predictable and calculable; the effect is to stifle unforeseen and unknowable aspects of untapped creative potential. This is not to suggest that habits are insignificant or unimportant, for they are crucial for social cohesion and the preservation of society, and a necessary foundation for citizenship. But what Bergson allows us to see is how forceful and compelling habits are in conditioning and organizing durable, institutionalized action, and that in order to overcome the pull of habit, we must open ourselves up to the experience of a genuine encounter, one that forces us to temporarily abandon our habitual ties and inclinations by opening us up to unpredictable and incalculable experiences. It is in this context that it becomes possible to argue that if the act of citizenship is to be creative, it must have the aspiration towards a genuine encounter at its heart. It must affirm the unforeseeable and contingent, and consequently aspire to transcend the limits imposed by habits (even if momentarily) in order to disrupt the static and sedimented dimensions of human action. This is the nature of the creative act of citizenship.

Bergson's Method of Intuition

It is an irony of sorts that Bergson's work has been so neglected in philosophy and social theory, given his substantial intellectual presence in the early twentieth century. It has been thanks to Deleuze's careful and inspired treatment of Bergson that we have a contemporary point of departure in assessing Bergson's thought. One of Deleuze's significant contributions to understanding Bergson is that he systematizes Bergson's remarks on intuition as a philosophical method (Deleuze 1988, p. 13). Intuition is usually thought of as a feeling or as a form of immediate knowledge, but for Bergson, intuition is a method that helps us to resolve the tendency of the intellect to eliminate duration from our philosophical concepts. Bergson argues that our intelligence is unable to capture duration because the language we use to express ourselves uses representations that cannot express the movement and flow of duration. The intellect prevents us from seeing duration in things and, in so doing, reflects a 'habitual, normal, commonplace act of our understanding' (1974b, p. 31). Bergson argues that duration always exceeds our attempt to represent it, and as a consequence, we typically fail to grasp the duration of an object when we create concepts because they stress the object's resilience and durability. Our concepts tend to combine the static and dynamic without sufficient attention to the ways that these tendencies differ in kind. Thus, we fail to see the composite concept as composite because 'the state of the composite does not consist only in uniting elements that differ in kind, but in uniting them in conditions such that these constituent differences in kind cannot be grasped in it' (Deleuze 1988, p. 34). Accordingly, our experience is such that we are unable to see the movement and change in ostensibly static, immobile objects.

Bergson's method of intuition resolves this problem in so far as it attempts to capture the dynamic qualities of the object it seeks to represent: '[I]ntuition starts from movement, posits it, or rather perceives it as reality itself, and sees in immobility only an abstract moment, a snapshot taken by our mind, of a mobility' (1974b, p. 34). Intuition proceeds by the division of pure tendencies that differ in kind; it divides the false composite into pure tendencies – one static, the other dynamic – that are irreducible to one another. The static tendency exhibits a propensity towards immobility whereas the dynamic tendency is oriented towards movement and change (Deleuze 1988, p. 31; 2004a, p. 26; 2004b, pp. 39–40). Bergson argues that by dividing a composite into its constitutive tendencies, a new concept is formed that 'will now be cut to the exact measure of the object' because it reveals its tendency to change and evolve over time (Bergson 1974b, p. 29).

The Habits of Citizenship

Bergson's method of intuition becomes immediately apparent in *The Two Sources of Morality and Religion* ([1932]1977) in that 'society' appears as a suspect composite subject to division into static and dynamic tendencies that he terms 'pressure' and 'aspiration'. Pressure expresses the tendency of a society to preserve itself through obligation and habit; it is associated with a society's tendency to close in on itself and is, henceforth, associated with what Bergson terms the 'closed society'. Aspiration reflects the dynamic movement and evolution of society; it is a creative tendency that expresses itself as a transformative emotion that 'stirs the soul'. Aspiration is associated with a society's tendency to open itself up to change, and is, consequently, associated with the 'open society'. We must take care to remember that the open and closed society are expressions of pure tendencies and, as such, can never be found in actually existing social life. We always experience society in its composite form; its pure tendencies to pressure and aspiration are obscured by the failure of our intellect.

With this in mind, I want to suggest it might be possible to think of citizenship as a composite concept, much like society, that is comprised of a pure tendency towards stasis and a pure tendency towards movement and change. For citizenship, like society, consists of a range of collective beliefs and habitual practices necessary for the continued stability and relative permanence of the conduct it seeks to represent. At the same time, there is a dynamic dimension to the category – as the attempt to theorize acts of citizenship would attest – that exceeds habitual obligatory practice through a creative appeal to change.

Let us now move to Bergson's depiction of the closed society in *The Two Sources* as a way of thinking about static understanding of citizenship, one that is necessary for the sustained organization and coordination of goods and resources in society. The closed society reflects this orientation to self-preservation by means of three principal themes – obligation, habit and pressure – that work concertedly to stabilize the social. Bergson begins with the question of obligation, for he notes that it is customary that we obey (at least most of the time), but the compelling question is 'why'? (1977, pp. 9–10). The obligation to obey is not based on the particular quality of the relationship one has with others, but rather has to do with the authority invested within social roles such as 'parent', 'teacher' or 'citizen'. Each of these social roles expresses a pressure, understood as a pure tendency, that acts on each and every one of us such that 'vaguely perceived or felt, there emanates an impersonal imperative from society' (1977, p. 10). These obligations reinforce one another such that they form a society of 'total obligation', so that each time we obey, we reaffirm the general principle of obligation in society: '[c]onceive obligation as weighing on the will like a habit, each obligation dragging behind it the accumulated mass of the others, and utilizing thus for the pressure it is exerting the weight of the whole: here you have the totality of obligation for a simple, elementary, moral conscience' (1977, p. 25).

It is possible, therefore, to deduce two important characteristics of obligation. First, obligation relates human beings to one another inter–subjectively such that obligation itself does not inhere in any specific relation, but is a necessary feature of all social relations. Obligation, in other words, is fundamentally impersonal. Second, obligation is 'extra-rational' in so far as it is founded upon a tautological dictum: 'you must because you must' (1977, p. 23). We might use reason to dispute a particular obligation, but we abide by the very principle of obligation for the successful functioning of the social. Obligation coordinates the social satisfaction of our needs, and while we may retroactively apply a rationality to introduce legitimacy to our acts, the principle of obligation is primarily what organizes our needs as beings that are free, but necessarily dependent on social organization to live and to prosper.

So, while Bergson does not speak directly to the problem of citizenship and the kinds of obligations it inspires, we might infer a general impression from his discussion of the way obligation and habit underlies the 'closed' society about citizenship and its practices. In this view, citizenship constitutes a web of obligatory social beliefs and practices that derives its strength from the impersonal force of pressure or authority in society. Bergson argues that the strength of relations of obligation is attributable to the extent to which society effectively 'interpolates intermediaries between itself and us: we have a family; we follow a trade or a profession; we belong to our parish, to our district, to our country' (1977, p. 18). If citizenship constitutes one of these intermediaries, we find society organized as a series of concentric circles with the individual at the centre and society at the periphery. Thus, citizenship represents an 'impersonal' set of obligations to action that structures relationships between individual citizens, and those between citizen and society. Thus, citizenship coordinates the satisfaction of our needs, such as food, shelter, and social and political well-being. This is an understanding of citizenship that is relatively homogeneous, and is defined as an expression of the citizen's location in a system of obligation.

Returning now to the problem of obligation, we see that it clearly derives its strength from habits, those coordinated sets of regular and repeatable activities that reflect the social organization of pressure in a society. They are governed by social pressures that both organize the internalization of the system of obligation in a society and relate individual habits to the larger whole. Habits mediate individual expectations and social necessity – indeed, one might say that they simultaneously individualize and totalize. Habits allow one to anticipate solutions to the problem of how to act before the need to act is realized; indeed for Bergson they assume an almost automatic response to the problem of responding to one's needs. To this end, Bergson argues that the nearly automatic quality of habitual action bears a marked resemblance to the instincts of non-human social animals. The 'instincts' of hymenopterans such as bees or ants, for instance, represent automatic behavioural codes that are performed by individual members of the society. But where social insects of this sort cannot modify or alter their conduct by will, given that their action is based on a biological coding that we call instinct, human beings, in contrast, have the capacity to alter their conduct even in spite of the strength of social pressure (1977, p. 27). Because the force of habit is so strong, Bergson points out that it is fair to say that habit functions for human societies as instinct does for non-human societies. In other words, habit subtends the totality of obligation and gives it a powerful strength such that it operates as if it were instinct.

What characterizes human conduct, therefore, is the 'habit of habits', such that although each of our habits is contingent and locally organized, the tendency towards cultivating habits is nearer to instinct than one normally assumes. This habit of building habits bears some resemblance to the way the habit of speech expresses a 'virtual instinct' (1977, p. 28). But it is important to stress that Bergson does not imply that habits are reducible to natural or biological forces, for habits are clearly socially and culturally constructed – rather it is the 'habit of contracting these habits' that is irreducible – for the 'habit of habits' is the very basis of human societies and a necessary condition of their existence. It is in this specific sense that Bergson argues that any social morality has a natural or biological basis (1977, p. 101). Accordingly, the habit of acquiring habits is a relative constant in human societies and operates much as instinct does for insects and animals: habits 'have a force comparable to that of instinct in respect to both intensity and regularity' (1977, pp. 26–7). Habits reinforce the existing structure of obligation, given that human beings typically do not use their intelligence to modify their conduct. We might say, in other words, that human beings have fallen into the habit of complying with the social pressure of obligation. Indeed, if obligation depended on reason, we would be able to challenge, argue and debate the validity of the rules at hand. But the reality is that we tend blindly to accept our social obligations without dispute, and consequently obey with habitude.

Now this is instructive for thinking about the concept of the act of citizenship, specifically in terms of those static forms of citizenship that are grounded by habit. If we accept that citizenship is typically embedded within a system of obligation as a means of coordinating and organizing our social and political needs through the language of rights and entitlements, then we find that habits play an important role in structuring our obligations to each other and to society. These obligations, however, tend to be oriented towards self-preservation, a concern that is necessarily and essentially conservative. Obligation organizes our intelligence in such a way that we feel a habitual tie that can be expressed as affection towards our families, community and nation. This affection is channelled into a duty that we feel towards these groups when they are threatened – we defend our family honour or our national interest in an effort to preserve them. Bergson characterizes this instinct to defend ourselves as an instinct for war, given that our affection and duty often take the form of hostility and violence if that which we love is threatened: '[w]ho can help seeing that social cohesion is largely due to the necessity for a community to protect itself against others, and that it is primarily as against all others that we love those with whom we live?' (1977, p. 33). In other words, obligation implies a sense of cohesion and solidarity that is ultimately embedded in relations of inclusion and exclusion.

In sum, we might say that when citizenship is taken to be organized solely by habits, our ability to conceive of the creativity of citizenship is inhibited in the following ways: first, habits impair the capacity for human intelligence to challenge, debate and critique our repetitive activity; and, second, such a commitment to habits engenders a logical error in so far as it presumes that it is possible to calculate and predict future action on the basis of past action. Moreover, as we have seen above, habits engender relations of inclusion and exclusion that reinforce ties to duty that do not allow us to appreciate the tendency towards creative movement, one that citizenship can and must express by virtue of its location in time. Habits, in sum, express the tendency of pressure to congeal, and to fix action into specific states, or snapshots of activity.

Creativity and the Act of Citizenship

We return once again to the motivating question of this chapter: can an act of citizenship be creative? Let me present Bergson's image of creativity before turning to assess the implications for thinking about how this might apply to thinking about the concept of the act of citizenship. In order for the human mind to 'open' itself up to the new and creative, Bergson sketches those human tendencies that must be activated in order to disrupt the tendency towards closure. Indeed, as we have seen, the pressure of habits is so strong that it stifles creativity. Recognizing this, Bergson argues that it is through the expression of emotion – understood not as a surface agitation, but as a wellspring of emotional upheaval – that the shackles of habit can be disrupted. Characterized as an expression of a pure tendency, emotion stimulates human intelligence by thwarting the pressure of habit and by 'opening' one up to the new. Emotion is accordingly defined by Bergson as 'affective stirring of the soul' that does not simply register as a superficial emotion, but rather as 'upheaval of the depths' (1977, p. 43). This is a truly creative emotion, one that has the effect of fundamentally displacing that which was previously arrested and of driving it forward. It is not pressure that animates emotion, therefore, but rather an aspiration – one which 'vivifies, or rather vitalizes, the intellectual elements with which it is destined to unite' (1977, p. 46).

Such stirrings of the soul are usually the product of a creative emotion that is organized by an aspiration towards openness, an openness towards movement and change that provokes us to dispense with habitual modes of thinking and to embrace profoundly new insights and ideas. The source of this 'opening' is not found in the repetitive activity of habits, but in the general disposition towards a non-predictive, incalculable creative impulse that is accessed by opening oneself to emotional experiences that rattle the very depths of one's being: '[t]he soul within which this demand dwells may indeed have felt it fully only once in its lifetime, but it is always there, a unique emotion, an impulse, an impetus received from the very depths of things. To obey it completely new words would have to be coined, new ideas would have to be created' (1977, pp. 253–4). This aspiration towards openness is not to be understood as a logical extension of the closed society; rather, it represents a profound and fundamental break, for it is only through rupture of this kind that the truly new can emerge. It is an altogether different tendency from pressure. Without the kind of aspiration that characterizes an emotional upheaval of this sort, one is unable to overcome the force of habit found in the totality of obligation. This kind of creative emotion is a stimulus towards action that incites 'the intelligence to undertake ventures and the will to persevere with them' (1977, p. 43). Put simply: creative emotion motivates the new, and, in so doing, becomes the new. It is the 'source of the great creations of art, of science and of civilization in general' (1977, p. 43).

The appeal of thinking about acts of citizenship from this perspective is that it forces us to consider those 'openings' where citizens break or destabilize the bonds of habitual activity, and, in so doing, unleash a creative energy. Now, this creative expression is necessarily sporadic and temporary, but the effect is to breathe new life into previously static, and potentially stagnant, modes of thought and life. In this context, creative acts of citizenship might be understood as those 'stirrings of the soul' that disrupt habitual activity. Now this experience of the 'new' will eventually become habituated over time, but, for Bergson, this process reflects the opening and closing of all objects of our experience.

For Bergson, the aspiration towards openness finds its ultimate expression in mysticism, understood here as a sustained aspiration to stir the soul (1977, p. 96). The mystic serves as a figure who has a gift of sight, one who can see – if only haltingly – a way of moving beyond our sedimented habits. The mystic serves as a vehicle of change, but one that is also necessarily rooted in the habitual practices of everyday life; these, we must be clear, are inescapable because they are constitutive of social life. Through the mystic's ability to perceive an openness where previously others perceived stasis, we find a 'return to movement', one that 'emanates from an emotion – infectious like all emotions – akin to the creative act' (1977, p. 53). It is necessarily a solitary endeavour, for one's relationship with the divine, with creativity and the energy of life is for Bergson an individual effort. As such, the mystic exemplifies the attitude or tendency towards openness by making a leap of faith; it is through the example of the mystic that we are able to access this kind of creative energy, for the mystic suggests the means for us to 'open' ourselves. The mystic helps us to 'see' that we must leap without explicit direction, without knowing where we will end up; in other words, we must embrace the impossibility of knowing the future by simply leaping, and, in so doing, we accept the movement, that is our movement, of life that is duration. Bergson argues that the example of the mystic offers one way to disrupt the tendency towards habit, prediction and calculability that is so characteristic of the closed society (1977, pp. 44–5).

Bergson is not suggesting that we all need to become mystics to be creative, but rather that the mystic infuses an aspiration to creativity in each of us. Mysticism represents an encounter where one opens oneself to the unknown and does not calculate possibilities in advance – one simply leaps. Now mysticism is not the only expression of an encounter, but it is the one Bergson emphasizes in *The Two Sources*. It is this language of the encounter and the leap that becomes useful for thinking about the creative potential of the act of citizenship. It is important to note that Bergson does not discuss the concept of the encounter in *The Two Sources;* it is developed earlier in his analysis of the ontological presuppositions of duration in *Matter and Memory* (1991). In this context, an encounter can be defined as the meeting or confrontation between people and things; such a confrontation disrupts habitual activity in so far as there is not an immediate automatic or 'instinctual' response to the need to act (Bergson 1991, p. 45). Rather, the encounter poses the problem of how to act – it is the site of a genetic convergence between a thing (or things) and a body that perceives. The encounter necessarily comes from without, from the outside, and is thoroughly unanticipated.

What is significant about the encounter is that it is an accident of sorts that forces one to pose the question of how to act: that is, to ask the question of why one might act one way and not another. Gilles Deleuze suggests, in his reading of Bergson, that encounters prompt the question of 'should I act' along with 'to what extent am I capable of acting' and 'how should I act?' (1986, pp. 61–3). They are at once the site of a problem posed and a solution rendered. Questions of how to act are entertained and enacted by all agents that pass through duration; they redirect energies, and in so doing disrupt habitual activities by prompting the question. The encounter represents an indeterminate zone where outcomes are unknowable and where things could have been otherwise (Bergson 1991, p. 64; see also Deleuze 2004b, p. 51). In other words, in the encounter one exercises a degree of choice over whether to act one way and not the other – and it is in this context, I want to suggest, that a creative act is born. We might therefore understand the exposition of the different acts of citizenship collected in this volume as different expressions of an encounter, of a moment of non-recognition, and accordingly of the movement, continual and necessary, between the closed and the open.

This discussion makes it possible to argue that the creative act of citizenship is one that affirms the unpredictable and contingent by provoking encounters that disrupt one's habitual tendencies. This is of course easier said than done, particularly given the power of social authority and pressure contained within the totality of obligation, one that is of course necessary for endurance and stability over time. Bergson argues that creativity (in its pure tendency) is found in the aspiration to openness, that is in the leap of 'faith' that allows us to explore forms of expression whose outcomes are not always already calculated in advance. Thus, the creative act of citizenship is one where the answer to the question of action is not already assumed; it means that one must pose the question, and, in response, one must leap with uncertainty.

While Bergson presents the closed and the open as pure tendencies, it is important to stress that we never experience them as such. In actually existing society, and consequently for actually existing citizenship, one never finds the open and closed in any degree of purity. Moreover, the tendencies towards pressure and aspiration are both evident to a greater or lesser degree: pressure ensures a commitment to cohesion and self-preservation, and aspiration engenders an openness to dynamic innovation. Thus, when one is faced by an encounter that engenders aspiration, we have an expression of creative possibility. This aspiration continues until such time as it is checked by the tendency towards pressure. Consequently, the tendency towards aspiration is never sustained for very long: as one opens oneself up to take the leap, the pressures of society, and of citizenship, seek to conserve themselves and close in on themselves. To this end, a society and its citizens are, therefore, constantly in motion: 'between the closed soul and the open soul there is a soul in the process of opening' (1977, p. 63). If the open and the closed represent pure tendencies, we must be reminded that there is only one soul, one citizen, one society that is opening and closing on itself.

Conclusion

We have here the beginnings of what a 'creative' act of citizenship might look like, at least assuming that one accepts the individual ethos of creativity on which Bergson's argument depends. At a conceptual level, this account mediates the rootedness (habits and belonging) and rupture (creativity and potentiality) of social life in accounting for social transformation. The creative act of citizenship is one that transgresses the confines of habitual practices and, consequently, reorganizes and reconstitutes those very habits in the process. What appears to us as an 'act' of citizenship, therefore, is simply an expression of the continuous passing of duration, the indivisible process of leaping from habits of citizenship to acts of citizenship, thereby territorializing and reterritorializing the terrain of citizenship in the process (Deleuze and Guattari 1987). Thus, if our aim is to identify a specific, tangible, 'creative' act of citizenship as such, it seems to me that we can only identify it in retrospect. Why? To be truly creative in Bergson's sense, something cannot be constituted as an 'act' from its genesis in an encounter. For to call an act creative, from the outset establishes boundaries that limit the full range of creative movement. One cannot claim to be performing a creative act of citizenship beforehand, for this suggests that a genuine encounter has not occurred. Here, the problem of how to act has not been posed, for we know the answer already – it is an act, and it is a creative act of citizenship. Rather, it is only after the fact, only after the encounter has been resolved, when we have solved the problem of how to act, that we can come to claim the 'act' as a 'creative act' as such. The point is that creativity in Bergson's sense implies a movement beyond the habitual and its necessary return. Accordingly, if we return to the question that motivated this chapter, we might say 'yes', but we must be wary because an act of citizenship can only be constituted as a creative act retrospectively when we wish to attribute special significance to a moment of political becoming. Otherwise we stand to undermine the truly creative.

Acknowledgments

Special thanks to Alex Lefebvre for comments on an earlier version of this chapter.

References

Alliez, E. (2004) *The Signature of the World: What is Deleuze and Guattari's Philosophy?* (trans. E. R. Albert and A. Toscano), Continuum, New York.

Ansell-Pearson, K. (2002) *Philosophy and the Adventure of the Virtual: Bergson and the Time of Life*, Routledge, London.

Bergson, H. ([1911] 1974a) *Creative Evolution* (trans. A. Mitchell), Modern Library, New York.

— ([1941] 1974b) *The Creative Mind: An Introduction to Metaphysics* (trans. M. Andison), Citadel Press, New York.

— ([1932] 1977) *The Two Sources of Morality and Religion* (trans. R. A. Audra and C. Brereton), University of Notre Dame Press, Notre Dame, IN.

— ([1908] 1991) *Matter and Memory* (trans. N. M. Paul and W. S. Palmer), Zone Books, New York.

— ([1889] 2001) *Time and Free Will: An Essay on the Immediate Data of Consciousness* (trans. F. L. Pogson), Dover, New York.

Csikszentmihalyi, M. (1996) *Creativity: Flow and the Psychology of Discovery and Invention*, Harper Collins, New York.

Deleuze, G. ([1983] 1986) *Cinema 1: The Movement-Image* (trans. H. Tomlinson and B. Habberjam), University of Minnesota Press, Minneapolis, MN.

— ([1966] 1988) *Bergsonism* (trans. H. Tomlinson and B. Habberjam), MIT Press, Cambridge, MA.

— (2004a) 'Bergson, 1859–1941' in *Desert Islands and Other Texts, 1953–1974*, Semiotext(e), New York.

— (2004b) 'Bergson's Conception of Difference' in *Desert Islands and Other Texts, 1953–1974*, Semiotext(e), New York.

Deleuze, G. and F. Guattari ([1980] 1987) *A Thousand Plateaus: Capitalism and Schizophrenia* (trans. B. Massumi), University of Minnesota Press, Minneapolis, MN.

Durkheim, E. ([1925] 1961) *Moral Education: A Study in the Theory and Application of the Sociology of Education* (trans. E. K. Wilson and H. Schnurer), Free Press, New York.

Foucault, M. ([1972] 1977) *Discipline and Punish: The Birth of the Prison* (trans. A. Sheridan), Random House, New York.

Isin, E. F. (2008) 'Theorizing Acts of Citizenship', Chapter 1, this volume.

Kolakowski, L. (1985) *Bergson*, Oxford University Press, Oxford.

Mullarkey, J. (2000) *Bergson and Philosophy*, University of Notre Dame Press, Notre Dame, IN.

Osborne, T. (2003) 'Against "Creativity": A Philistine Rant', *Economy and Society*, 32 (4), 507–25.

Chapter 3

❖❖

What Levinas Can and Cannot
Teach Us About Mediating Acts
of Citizenship

BETTINA BERGO

Does Levinas's phenomenological ethics teach us anything about mediating acts of citizenship?[1] Formally speaking, Levinas's is an inquiry into the conditions of possibility of our interest in the good, shared life, good actions, and social responsibility. However, his philosophy is unfolded with a surreptitious difference − the kind of difference that Kant called transcendental and which the young Heidegger made into his ontological difference. From the moment philosophy proceeds on two tracks, a transcendental and an anthropological one, we confront difficulties. The most notable difficulty lies in the desire to make action or knowledge flow from conditions of possibility that are impossible to describe exhaustively, like Kant's famous transcendental schematism. Given that, Levinas's ethics cannot tell us what we ought to do, or even what we could hope to do. So there has been a longstanding debate: is Levinas's in any way a practical ethics, or is it an interpretive phenomenology concerned with the openness of our bodily existence to relations with others? I want to stage this debate in what follows, starting with Jacques Derrida's 'The Word of Welcome' (in Derrida 1997), moving through the observations of a left-leaning political theorist from Argentina (Benasayag, in Benasayag and Scavino 1997), and finishing with the Hegelian Gillian Rose's proposed critique of 'post-modern' thought (Rose 1992).

Derrida characterized Levinas's first great work, *Totality and Infinity* (1961), as a treatise on hospitality (Derrida 1997, pp. 39–210). He deemed it that in his 1997 homage to Levinas. At that time, some three hundred undocumented African refugees had been holed up in the Église Saint-

Bernard, in Paris's 18th Arrondissement, for five months, carrying on a hunger strike that collapsed with their forcible round-up and deportation. A 'treatise on hospitality' suggests that from Levinas's transcendental descriptions, acts of hospitality could arise, *de facto* hospitality towards the other person and even the stranger. Derrida clearly understood that Levinas's thought, even if elaborated at a transcendental level, was meaningless unless it told us something about our concrete social existence.

Herein lies the enormous difficulty of working with Levinas in considering acts of citizenship, not to mention the ways in which they can be mediated. Part of this difficulty is due to the tension that Levinas himself creates when he defines existence, or 'Being', as violence – and politics as the science of distributing and regulating violence. The irony of this, of course, is that Levinas, having studied with Husserl and Heidegger in the 1920s, seems to carry with him a conception of Being that comes out of the thinking of 'occasionalism', resoluteness, and the Weimar Republic's fixation on life and death questions. We find that thinking in Heidegger, with his resolute anticipation, his decision, his *Volk*; but we also find it in Carl Schmitt, for whom the political was the science of determining who is an enemy and acting on that determination. Life and death, action as decision, friend versus enemy: however we define Being – as revelation, as *Dasein* [there-Being], or as the context of the political decision – the Weimar environment of political thought was imbued with the urgency and contrastiveness (life and death) that we find embraced by Levinas himself in 1961. Anything but innocence, Being is Heraclitean, rapacious, some would say social Darwinist, though they forget that Herbert Spencer had a cosmology of progress for his *telos*, not just a sociology of progress. Levinas's conception of Being means that ethical acts, punctual acts demanding justice, can only be interruptions of an ongoing state of affairs that is always on the verge of showing the violent underpinnings of its structures. He calls these acts 'transcendence'; he calls this the 'good beyond Being', because Being in itself is paradoxical. Unredeemable, Being is always violence and predation; but, always already redeemed, Being carries strange 'traces' in it of responsibility and generosity. One may object to this logic; indeed, it seems to change somewhat in his 1970s writings. But I believe this is a logic that has two basic sources: first, the confirmation that the Shoah brings to thinkers like Schmitt in regard to politics and political life; second, Levinas's lifelong opposition to Heidegger's conception of Being as the open space in which we emerge, summoned, in *Dasein*'s structure of resoluteness, to have a conscience (Heidegger 1962, p. §59). For Levinas, the neutral atmosphere that Heidegger called 'Being' could only oppress us or recede in the wake of our concern with other people. But Being could never become the source of a call of conscience, much less of revelation, as Heidegger had argued. Levinas therefore returned Being to a Schmittean logic of danger, friends and enemies, and the 'occasion' of the political decision. However, Schmitt taught us something very valuable, which was not lost on Levinas. He taught that theological concepts ultimately give rise to political ones. That will be precious for what we argue shortly.

Support for Derrida's hospitality claim comes from the Argentinean theorist Miguel Benasayag, who revisits Jean-Paul Sartre's existentialist sketch about people gathered at a bus stop (Benasayag and Scavino 1997). As you may remember, Sartre's vignette showed all the struggle and abjection implicit in his conception of the gaze of the other. Benasayag suggests a different scenario for the bus stop.

> Let us imagine a bus stop where individuals await, with anxiety, a bus that does not come. For each of them it is clear that the objective is to get into the bus. Nevertheless, during this time, things come to pass [*il se passe des choses*] at this stop. An elderly woman feels ill and must be helped; a baby needs milk and someone must go and look for some; a few people are carrying snacks in their pockets which they begin to share. And perhaps even someone, the funniest of them, will launch into a brief monologue designed to distract the others. Who knows whether a great passion will arise between two persons there; for this is about life, therefore solidarity, community, sharing and love. Nevertheless, if we ask each one of these persons what they are actually doing, they will respond that they are waiting for the bus. Moreover, there will probably be someone there who attempts to put a bit of order back into this bus queue. (Benasayag and Scavino 1997, pp. 23–4)

We should note here what some might call multiple 'Levinasian moments'. These are moments in which spontaneous responsibility can be seen. Are they really Levinasian moments? Is not Levinas the philosopher of infinite responsibility? Only at the formal level. He certainly says that traces of an unlimited responsibility can be found in disinterested social gestures. But traces are evanescent things, so the matter is not wholly decidable. However, if we say that these bus stop moments are not Levinasian moments, then Levinas's phenomenology slides into rhapsody and formalism.

Derrida's recapitulation and Benasayag's revision of Sartre were designed to set up a tension at the heart of Levinas's work: Levinas is describing a structure of our sensibility, said to be predisposed to an ethical openness prior to intentional reflection on our part. Once we reflect on the vulnerability of our flesh, the instant, in which responsibility comes to pass, closes up as if it had been a gap, lost to conscious representation. Therefore, no transcendental exposition,[2] no effective statement of the source of responsibility, is possible with certainty. On the other hand, how would we ever deduce a transcendental level if not through its own tracing by way of the multiple layers of daily existence in a life world? This difficulty has played itself out in philosophy at least since Solomon Maïmon wrote to Kant and showed him that his categories had no direct application to everyday life. It would seem that this amounts to an insuperable tension in philosophies that claim to deduce the conditions of possibility of our rational and emotional life; this 'disconnect' lies at the heart of Levinas's work as well. Nevertheless, Derrida reminds us that no justice, no political formation, is ever founded on cynical calculation alone, and Benasayag's vignette suggests an empirical exit door. This door is, as Deleuze and Guattari have characterized it: 'expression'. 'The possible world is not real, or is not yet real, and yet, it exists nonetheless; it is something expressed which exists only in its expression, in the face or in an equivalent of the face' (Deleuze and Guattari 1991, p. 22). So the question for us is: if expression and welcome are mediations, can mediations of this degree of fragility take on a life other than sporadic political protests or non-institutionalizable pockets of resistance? It seems to me that that represents the central question of this part of the present work: 'Politics, Ethics and Aesthetics'.

Thesis 1: The Impossible Passage from the Face-to-Face to the Third Party

The late political philosopher, Gillian Rose, was critical of post-modern thought, especially of post-modern political thought. It was as though, for her, writing at the beginning of the 1990s, post-modern political thought was paving the way back to theology whence so many political concepts had already come. Post-modern politics ran the risk of losing secularity itself, because it evacuated secular mediations in favour of disorganized resistance or an aporetic approach to political dialectics. At the heart of post-modernity's separation of pure – if finite – reason and human praxis, there is a decisive absence of categories able to mediate acts of sociality, legality or politics. Rose writes:

> These 'moves', which characterize post-modern thinking, would mend the diremption of law and ethics by turning the struggle between universality, particularity, and singularity into a general sociology of control. Yet the security of this new spectatorship is undermined by the tension of freedom and unfreedom which it cannot acknowledge, for it has disqualified the actuality of

any oppositions that might initiate process and pain – any risk of *coming* to know. Instead the tension between the contraries of subjective freedom and objective unfreedom [within post-modern thought] appears as an unconceptualized aporia … as a singularity without its contraries of universal and particular. (Rose 1992, p. xiv)[3]

Rose's critique of a 'sociology of control' refers to the heritage of the struggle between Hegel's political dialectic and the emergent social sciences, like those of Max Weber and Émile Durkheim, which paved the way to structural-functionalism. Certainly, Michel Foucault understood sociologies of control (he struggled, within a post-structuralist perspective, to show their internal fissures). And, if we believe Jürgen Habermas's charge that Foucault's thought is fundamentally conservative, then Foucault unwittingly participated, himself, in the logic Rose criticized, offering us ultimately a narrow aesthetics of self-creation. The problem has been noted of Levinas's ethics as well: responsibility comes to pass in a split second; it cannot be institutionalized; we can use Levinas's description of it as a model, but that changes nothing about the pre-intentional quality of our encounters with the face as pure expression of need. Perhaps this explains why, for Gilles Deleuze, we are passing from an age of myth into an age of religion: rationality was mythic in its omnipotence, while religion responds to the suffering of the particular to the detriment of a critical analysis of socio-economic structures. In effect, Levinas's 1960s work gives us the ethical moment as an encounter between a self and a face that calls, that is pure expression, and that opens into conversation. Conversation, hospitality, even teaching are core aspects of Levinas's conception of responsibility in the 1960s. But these things certainly have a private quality to them.

When faced with the question of how responsibility actually enters into political history, Levinas answers in two ways: first, the passage is always already there; it arises as a question about justice. Second, Levinas proposes an alternative history, even a 'prophetic history', that is designed to open onto humanity rather than aiming at particular citizens or Western cosmopolitans. Levinas's alternative history is the history of the family and the community. In Levinas's logic, 'I' experience being chosen by my father; and 'I' serve my brothers. For Levinas, this is the concrete experience of responsibility within a micro-society that is as relevant to all of us as standard political history is. Levinas therefore opposes Hegel's state with a conception of the family – better, with the community based on the family. Certainly, we do not want to resurrect a political dialectic in which each human assembly is subsumed by an overarching *telos* which is the state (and its military). Recall that the last avatar – on the political Right – of Hegel's political logic was precisely Carl Schmitt's, with his *coup d'état* against the Weimar Constitution, designed paradoxically to save the German constitution *qua* Idea from the reality of its parliamentary disarray. For Schmitt, the liberal state *must* self-destruct because it assigns equipollence to human institutions other than the state itself, and thereby drains the state of energies vital to its political survival.

Nevertheless, we also do not want Levinas's micro-community or family to structure all our mediations for citizenship and political life. If that does not amount to a kind of tribalism, it certainly entails a re-specification of law to make room for instances like religious tribunals. But a strange connection seems to persist, if not to insist, between the small-is-beautiful communities and the successful perpetuation of socialism.

As the sociologists Robert Putnam and Seymour Martin Lipset have noted, socialism appears to work best as long as socio-economic identification runs parallel to ethnic or national identification, creating a sense of the 'good for *us*', not just the good for everyone and no one (Putnam 2004; Lipset and Marks 2000). Is this not the core of our contemporary dilemma: even if slowed down by regressive forces of imperialism, the economic and political thrust is today towards globalization, with all the problems of 'governance' that that entails? Globalization dissolves family or tribally based institutions or renders them redundant. In the midst of this centrifugal expansion, predictably, spontaneous resistance takes place. In the best of cases, these pockets of resistance are indifferent to the more 'elemental' forms of identification, like the ethnic or the religious. But these are often short-lived. In the worst of cases, resistance relies for its energy on idealized identifications whose condition of possibility is inward-looking, with all the attendant exclusions that introspection entails. For that reason, Levinas's 1961 mediation, the family, which runs between the face-to-face and political actuality, seems implausible, even contrived, under present circumstances – as contrived, in fact, as Hegel's 'Russian doll' conception of imbricating social institutions, all of which are trumped by the state. The problem only grows worse in the 1970s writings when Levinas conceives of the interruption by the Other as a structuring split essential to the birth of our subjectivity itself. How do you get from an immanent division, rooted in the vulnerability of our flesh, to a conception of viable mediations in political and juridical life? Like Jean-François Lyotard in *The Differend*, Levinas argues for the importance of bearing witness (Lyotard 1983, pp. 163–72, 184–6).[4] But bearing witness is one step away from returning to a logic whose religious dimension is unavoidable. As Lacan said in his 1974 talk *Triomphe de la Religion*, we should expect to see a lot more religion in the years to come (Lacan 2004). And, in effect, the religious revival of the past two decades offers mediations that address communities in their particularity. These appear to be rooted in the specificity of individuals' suffering and hope; in what Isin and Nielsen here call the 'enactment, performance and negotiation of citizenship', whether legal-formal or creative-substantive. Not only is religion's appeal strong for that reason, but the promise of reward for acts of witness or martyrdom often combines this-worldly rewards with recompense in a world to come.

I believe that the most tragic case in which Levinas's divorce from political mediations shows up in is his response, in 1982, to the massacre of Palestinians by Christian Phalangists in the refugee camps of Sabra and Shatila. In a radio interview with Alain Finkielkraut, Levinas compares 'utopian' conceptions of love and peace with the actuality of political history. His spontaneous remarks here belie a political scepticism that is rare in his philosophical works. Levinas argues that when we recognize the contrast between utopian political movements, intrinsically weak things, and the violent reality of Western history, then we must admit that *de facto* politics generally eludes ethical responsibility and no nation is better in this than another. Levinas says:

> When you compare world history, where there are so many mystical thoughts and movements ... doctrines of peace and love, with the true political course of this history made up of wars, violence, conquests and *the oppression of men by their fellows*, then you have less cause to worry about Israel's soul and political history. Ethics will never, in any lasting way, be the good conscience of corrupt politics. (Levinas 1982–3, pp. 1–8)[5]

What does this mean if not that institutionalized law and politics tends to destroy utopianism and messianicity, and that everybody, within or without Israel, is thereby corrupted? This is not the only time Levinas found himself before the conundrum of everyday Israeli politics and his philosophical insistence that ethical responsibility survives in political life as a trace. The terrible thing is not Levinas's conundrum – anyone can be caught up in reactions to a history of exclusion and destruction; anyone can be swayed by the power, even the necessity, of ethnic identification, and strike up against the universality of utopias that exist as regulative ideals – the problem is that this tension seems to have no resolution in Levinas's philosophy. That is what Rose pinpointed in her sweeping invective against post-modern thought. Already some twenty years before the conversation with Finkielkraut, in one of his most fascinating essays, the 'Messianic Texts',[6] Levinas asked a question and then answered it, using an inadmissible strategy (Levinas 1963). He writes:

> To conclude, I sincerely wonder if, since Emancipation, we [i.e., Jews] are still capable of messianism … [F]or a long time … Judaism felt it lived in an arbitrary world, in which no reason commanded political evolution … even in the Talmud, the historical confusions and anachronisms committed by the Rabbis are not the result of ignorance, but attest to a refusal to take [political] events seriously … [that is, those] events unfold[ing] in an informal cycle of violence and crime. (Levinas 1997, pp. 59–96)

If messianism means that something higher than politics, like ethical responsibility, inhabits the world-view of pre-Emancipation Jews, then, with Jewish political enfranchisement comes an incapacity for messianism – perhaps even in the form of hope. But that would suggest also a surprising incapacity for anything like the practice of Levinas's transcendental ethics within everyday situations.

Its ambiguities notwithstanding, messianism and its decline are not limited to the Jewish community. Moreover, whatever its punctual intensity, messianism often dissipates with *de facto* political participation. In that way, the difficulty becomes only worse. Enfranchisement, participation, belonging – all understood as the cultivation of just political acts and the creation of emancipatory civic practices, citizenship in form and substance – all diminish the urge towards messianism such as is found in Levinas's Talmudic lessons on justice. Does that mean that the now-predictable political gestures of tokenism destroy the very energy source of resistance groups and communities, not to mention their principal means of self-demarcation? Is this an admission of the unavoidability of political cynicism? This is a problem not easy to adjudicate, because enfranchisement has produced very different results according to the communities brought into the 'fold'. Levinas's question is really: where does the conviction stop that holds that once you are in the game, you too shall learn the strategies of those longtime players who themselves once pursued an extra-political vision? Thus, Levinas closes his 'Messianic Texts' by saying to the assembly of *intellectuels juifs de langue française* that the messianic sensibility, which is inseparable from some knowledge of chosenness as responsibility, 'would be irremediably lost … if the solution of the state of Israel did not represent an attempt to *reunite* the irreversible acceptance of universal [Hegelian] history with the necessarily particularist messianism' (Levinas 1997, p. 96, emphasis added).

It is no longer possible to speak of the reunification of universal history and messianism. And I hope that Levinas is less a naïve Zionist here than a philosopher struggling with the aporia of his entire project, when it is seen through a political, and ethnic, lens. His is not the only messianic aporia: think of Theodor Adorno's exhortation that we venture, within a post-Auschwitz Marxism, to conceive history from the perspective of 'redemption'. Is *this* not another instance of the ethical-political impasse? How do we conceive history in such a perspective? History neither is redeemed nor promises redemption, so this must be an imaginative exercise. Perhaps we see it again in Walter Benjamin's 'Theses on History',[7] when he speaks of a 'weak messianic force', which each generation receives from the past and on which that past has a claim (Benjamin 1980, pp. 691–704). Whether it is understood as a 'principle of hope' or serves to motivate ideology, messianism is the ethical moment that gives the lie to political calculation, even as it falls off the scale of justice. Is it because we cannot bear the ugliness of pragmatic politics that we recoil before arguments like Alan Dershowitz's insistence that, since condemnation of torture will not make torture go away, we must find other ways of bringing torture under international law? How can resolving the aporia between ethics and politics be the task of messianism, when messianism conceives politics either as a religious or an aestheticized struggle? Is messianism, broadly conceived, the *only* way to motivate mediations between citizenship and the state? Is it the only alternative to pragmatic complacency (when Americans admit that 'we' fly suspects to Syria and Romania so as not to torture them on native soil, then we must ask: who has this *we* become that makes this admission)?

Thesis 2: Whose Metaphysics, Whose Hospitality?

If Gillian Rose is right, then post-modern thought is destined either to slide towards a religious impetus for its 'energy source', or to become irrelevant to pragmatic political discussions. What is incontestable is that something must stabilize those social and civic practices that resist the homogenization of the market or the neutralization of the (either late capitalist or phantasmatic) 'global community'. As Hegel already recognized in his depiction of the sad fate of Christianity, institutional stabilization engenders ideological hypocrisy and that institutional survival logic according to which the group ultimately aims solely at self-perpetuation and legitimation – institutional juggernaut logic. In 'The Word of Welcome' (1997), Derrida insisted that Kant's political philosophy of a legislated hospitality – such as we find it in Kant's essay 'Toward Perpetual Peace'

(1795) – was based on a metaphysics different from that of Levinas (Derrida 1997, p. 15). Kant's was a Heraclitean metaphysics. He recognized that life, as becoming, was change and conflict. By consequence, political justice had to avoid both the Hobbesian Leviathan and pacifist dreams. As Derrida puts it:

> [T]he law and the cosmopolitics of hospitality that [Kant] proposes as an answer to that terrible alternative [between Hobbes and utopia], amounted to a set of rules and contracts, an interstate conditionality that limits the very hospitality that it [is supposed to] guarantee, and this, against a Natural Law background reinterpreted on a Christian horizon. For Kant, the right to safe harbor is strictly bounded by such rules. (Derrida 1997, p. 175)

In short, the formal assurance of the welcome of the stranger, not to mention her protection, requires legal determinations about who has a *right* to the status of stranger apt to being protected. Derrida will argue that this approach is a circle, probably vicious, but that this stance appeared to the mature Kant as the only hard-nosed realistic politics of peace: between safe haven and the cemetery (Derrida 1997, p. 174).

It would seem that, on Derrida's reading, the decisive contribution of Levinas's *Totality and Infinity* is found in the direct enactment of hospitality as response – which is always a response addressed *to* something not determinable by the self. As Derrida puts it:

> This preposition *to-* [*à-*], is placed before the infinite [*à-Dieu*], which places itself within the preposition *to-*. The *to-* is not open only to the infinite … *that is to say to-God autrement dit*, it turns in his direction and it addresses itself *firstly to respond to-, firstly to respond for*, it addresses it '*ad*' to the infinite that calls to it and addresses itself to it; [this *to-*] opens infinity, by virtue of its scope, to the reference-to, the relation-to [the other person]. (1997, p. 179)

While Rose would argue that Derrida's explanation of the infinite, provoking an opening-towards, is either anthropological particularism or some dalliance in phenomenological 'theology', Derrida bypasses this alternative completely. Derrida argues that the relation-to is the excess to which all theories of jurisprudence lay claim or which they presuppose. He writes:

> No doubt there cannot be a peace worthy of its name in the space of that '*tyranny*' or of that '*anonymous universality*' [called the state]. But, as we just sensed, the topology of [Kant's] politics seems quite twisted [retorse] in its multiple folds. For Levinas recognizes that that which is '*identified outside the State*' (peace, hospitality, paternity, infinite fecundity, etc.) has a framework *within* the State; it '*is identified outside the State even though the State holds a framework for it*'. (1997, p. 172)

This means that the *source* of hard-nosed legalist hospitality and safe haven is not sublatable within the structure – the state – that is nevertheless entrusted with its macro-management. If the micro-practices of responsibility were only assured their reality by the state, then two things would be clear: first, humans' highest vocation would undeniably be active service to the state (in the army, for instance), and any contestation of this would look absurd; second, there would be no gainsaying Adorno's pessimistic observation, 'You cannot be good in a bad state.' Now, both these claims are persuasive. But when the state promises the good or worthy life within its bounds, no matter how secular its promise, the state is appealing to something beyond itself, to a promise, however underdetermined that promise may be. This allows Derrida to say:

> There is therefore a topological destiny to [Levinas's] structural complication of the political. An enclave of transcendence, as we said earlier. The boundary between ethics and politics loses, in this enclave or complication, and loses forever, the indivisible simplicity of a limit. Whatever Levinas may say about this, the determinability of this limit has never been pure, and it never will be. (1997, pp. 172–3)

By creating a 'complication', or a beyond to which the logic of the state calls, Levinas produces a philosophy from which a politics can arise that is different from Kant's policing and formalism. Versions of this politics have been called alternately a 'principle of hope' (Ernst Bloch), the 'perspective of redemption' on history (Theodor Adorno), or a 'weak messianic force' (Walter Benjamin). And if we look to the ideologues of the counter-revolution, then we find Carl Schmitt insisting, more formally perhaps, that political categories *all* stem originally from theological concepts and therefore, from something like religious life beyond the state. With the return of the messianic theme in Derrida, we recognize its importance as politics' own life energy. But has that gotten us past the instability that messianism invariably brings to politics? Is Schmitt's definition of the political not like a fanatical translation of Aristotle's ethics, in which the essential ethical role of the friend turns into the essential distinction of political friends versus political enemies in the name of the sovereignty and purity of politics? However that may be, what Derrida is trying to do is more modest. He credits Levinas simply with a non-confessional acknowledgment of an excess within the state, an excess that points precisely beyond the state. It would certainly seem that if we recognize the logic of the state as pure immanence or encompassing subsidiary institutions, then individual acts of hospitality, like hiding and protecting persecuted persons, would seem an uncanny narcissism. So something must open up the logic of the state. It is only the boundary *between* the ethical and the political that Derrida is contesting. And it is just this contestation that he credits to Levinas. This contestation is possible because Levinas interrupts the metaphysical totalization that underlies the project of political totalization envisioned by Kant – even if it is never wholly realized. *Totality and Infinity* is a refusal of totalizing metaphysics. That does not mean that metaphysics has an outside or a beyond to it. Metaphysics is interrupted by what philosophical thought cannot wholly frame. And *Totality and Infinity* contains the seeds of an enactment of political resistance, that which turns into messianic witnessing in *Otherwise than Being*. So, political action in Levinas amounts to questioning a neat boundary between ethics and politics. In 1961, Levinas argues that the Third Party looks at me through the eyes of the Other. In 1974, he exhorts: 'Why does the other concern me ... Am I my brother's keeper? These questions have meaning only if one *already supposed* that the ego is concerned only with itself. But ... the self is through and through a hostage, older than the ego' (Levinas 1974, p. 117). I hope the alternative is not between modesty and extremism. The crux of the question is the spirit of messianism itself.

Some have taken Levinas's work as a phenomenology of traumatized affectivity. But do we have to endure the dehumanization of war or illegal detention camps (Bagram, Guantanamo) simply to recognize intersubjective responsibility? Others have taken Levinas's work as proposing a regulative ideal, in the form of a call. The ironist might ask what practical postulates are needed in order to take up this call as ethical-political action. That is, what must we *believe* if we are to accept Levinas's metaphysics as interruptible by an 'otherwise', and his ethics as expressing our pre-conscious intersubjective connections? The answer to these questions (other humans, God, both, neither) determines what we can do with Levinas's philosophy. It is compelling to entertain Derrida's claim that the boundary between the ethical and the political is not an impassable barrier. But that does not wholly solve the mediation question. Messianism motivates the creation of mediations, at a host of levels; but when messianism becomes a practical mediation itself, it supplants other mediations – often secular ones at that.

Derrida's tribute to Levinas shows how the latter's thought has a weight equal to the neo-Hegelian critiques of Levinas, like Gillian Rose's invective against post-modernism. But Derrida's tribute cannot abrogate Rose's doubts about post-modern 'broken middles' – those middles that want to mediate between ethics and politics. Messianic thought is all the rage today, pobably because we have reached such a state of political discouragement that we recur to Lacan's resources of religion to give us the strength to continue to protest or try to create something between Scylla and Charybdis: American hegemony and globalization.

Messianism has two basic aspects to it. This is true, outside of considerations of messianic *time*, of that kind of intense present moment of anticipation which so many readers of Saint-Paul picked up on in the 1920s (among them Schmitt, Heidegger and Benjamin), and which we are again debating today. If we ignore, for a moment, the distressing insistence by some that messianism must shape itself into a political party, then messianism's two aspects are simply a promise of hope and the insistence that an excess inheres at the heart of intersubjectivity. But this excess would have all the unpredictability of Benasayag's bus queue. Now, whether we theologize this excess or hold it in its indeterminacy as a call, Kant's pessimism is still right on one point: messianic energy motivates best within structures that provide political and juridical stabilization. However, as the impetus to creating those structures, messianism itself must be protected from an excess of desire. Never in Levinas can responsibility solve the problems traditionally called 'good versus evil' or 'state versus society'. If nothing else, our desire that Levinas provide us paths towards an irenic politics bespeaks the enduring interest in messianism which, in turn, demonstrates the endurance of Levinasian responsibility in some kind of memory ... and perhaps *phantasy*. It would seem that the lesson of New Orleans – already long since vanished from our television screens – is that mediations are possible within functional states, whereas with the demise of equitable state structures and institutions, fragmented civil and economic mediations turn into messianic calls for justice. These calls sometimes give rise to movements and resistance, but not always. In the latter case, the messianic impetus moves between ethical hope and the extremism of desperation. Of course, extremism itself poses the question of how to stop institutions from moving towards absolutism when established mediations, like courts and parliaments, collude in this movement or lack the resolve to stop it.

Levinas's contribution was to see that responsibility and justice come not from me or my inborn moral sentiments, but from interruptions by the Other, or better, from the relation between the other and me. That is a different metaphysical beginning than Kant's. Derrida is right about that. It comes out of Hermann Cohen and Franz Rosenzweig even as it recalls Carl Schmitt's insight that political categories arise out of religious ones. But Levinas's conception of Being or existence remains frightening, at least in the Preface to *Totality and Infinity*. Levinas bears out Carl Schmitt when he urges that politics is linked to concrete existence, much the way the art of winning a war is linked to the violence intrinsic to natural (and social) beings. With ethics thus opposed to Being, even the metaphysics of the 'complication' that Derrida perceived in Levinas cannot supplant Kant's 'Heraclitean metaphysics'. If Levinas's correlational responsibility goes some way towards explaining why Frankfurt School thinkers like Habermas exert an attraction on theorists of democratic politics, we cannot also say that Levinas's thought, by itself, is enough to do what the Frankfurt School was attempting to do – establish the conditions for critical but egalitarian speech situations. Can it be the case that failing to elaborate mediations – whether creative aesthetic ones or more humdrum traditional ones – leaves us vulnerable to the extremist face of messianic hope? It seems that the answer is clear.

Notes

1 Heartfelt thanks to Gabriel Malenfant, Département de Philosophie, Université de Montréal, for his comments, suggestions and unflagging assistance.
2 By 'transcendental exposition', I mean a presentation of a complex of lived experiences in which distinctions between what is subjective and what is objective, what is inner and what outer, are temporarily put out of consideration. The purpose of transcendental description, as Edmund Husserl intended it, is to reveal the life of consciousness in its immediacy, that is, before we reflect on the experience, classify it, and categorize it.
3 Rose targets Levinas and his two-term politics, which starts in responsibility to a singular other and opens, enigmatically according to her, into social existence. But social existence is a hybrid, carrying the violence of 'being' together with the peaceableness of the face-to-face encounter. Rose also targets Derrida in this critique – all of this from an Adornian-Hegelian perspective.
4 In the English translation, see pp. 107–18, 126–28.
5 In the English translation, see pp. 289–97; cited by Rose 1992, p. 248.
6 For the English, see Levinas 1997, pp. 59–96.
7 In the English, see Benjamin 1969, pp. 253–64.

References

Benasayag, M. and D. Scavino (1997) *Pour un nouvelle radicalité: puissance et pouvoir en politique*, Éditions la découverte, Paris.
Benjamin, W. (1969) 'Theses on the Philosophy of History' in *Illuminations: Essays and Reflections* (ed. H. Arendt), Schocken Books, New York.
— (1980) 'Über den Begriff der Geschichte', *Gesammelte Schriften*, Vol. I.2, Suhrkamp Verlag, Frankfurt am Main.
Deleuze, G. and F. Guattari (1991) *Qu'est-ce que la philosophie?* Éditions de Minuit, Paris.
— (1994) *What is Philosophy?* (trans. H. Tomlinson and G. Burchell), Columbia University Press, New York.
Derrida, J. (1997) *Adieu à Emmanuel Levinas*, Galilée, Paris.
— (1999) *Adieu to Emmanuel Levinas* (trans. P.-A. Brault and M. Naas), Stanford University Press, Stanford.

Heidegger, M. (1927) *Sein und Zeit*, Max Niemeyer Verlag, Tübingen.

— (1962) *Being and Time* (trans. J. Macquarrie and E. Robinson), Harper and Row, New York.

Lacan, J. (2004) *Triomphe de la religion précédé de Discours aux Catholiques*, Éditions du Seuil, Paris.

Levinas, E. (1961) *Totalité et Infini: Essai sur l'extériorité*, Martinus Nijhoff, The Hague.

— (1963–76) 'Textes Messianiques', *Difficile Liberté. Essais sur le Judaïsme*, Albin Michel, Paris.

— (1982–3) 'Éthique et Politique', *Les Nouveaux Cahiers*, 18, Paris.

— (1989) 'Ethics and politics' in S. Hand (ed.), *The Levinas Reader*, Blackwell, Oxford.

— (1997) 'Messianic Texts', *Difficult Freedom. Essays on Judaism* (trans. S. Hand), Johns Hopkins University Press, Baltimore.

— (1998) *Totality and Infinity: An Essay on Exteriority* (trans. A. Lingis), Duquesne University Press, Pittsburgh.

Lipset, S. M. and G. Marks (2000) *It Didn't Happen Here: Why Socialism Failed in the United States*, W. W. Norton, New York.

Lyotard, J.-F. (1983) *Le différend*, Éditions de Minuit, Paris.

— (1988) *The Differend: Phrases in Dispute* (trans. G. van den Abbeele), University of Minnesota Press, Minneapolis, MN.

Putnam, R. (2004) 'Who Bonds, Who Bridges: Finds from the Social Capital Benchmark Survey', paper at American Political Science Association, Annual Meeting, Chicago, IL, September.

Rose, G. (1992) *The Broken Middle: Out of Our Ancient Society*, Blackwell, Oxford.

ACTS I

❖

Heroic Intrusions
and the Body of Law

Act 1

Abraham's Sacrifice

CHARLES WELLS

Acts of citizenship can be seen as political when they move against religious or legal codes. Such acts rupture the habitus of citizenship and create moral paradoxes that ripple across the power structures that govern ethical and legal communities. While remaining answerable towards the Other, such acts uproot the taken-for-granted ethical or legal subject. The greatest classical example of this is seen in the 22nd chapter of the Book of Genesis when God tests Abraham by commanding him to sacrifice his younger son, Isaac, as a burnt offering. While interpretations of this story have generally been limited to the domains of theology and moral philosophy, it can also be thought of as an act of citizenship – perhaps the original act from which all others issue.

Telling Isaac that God himself will provide a lamb for the sacrifice, Abraham leads his son to the top of a mountain in the land of Moriah, builds an altar, and prepares for the bloody deed. Having bound Isaac, and drawn his knife, Abraham is stopped at the last moment by the angel of the Lord, who explains that he has passed a test by showing his fear of God. Looking around him, Abraham finds a ram caught in a thicket and sacrifices this in place of Isaac on the altar. Finally, the angel, returning a second time from heaven, announces that Abraham's reward will be that his progeny will multiply, and possess the gate of their enemies.

This story, at the heart of the Jewish, Christian and Islamic religions, has been the object of both an endless stream of theological and philosophical inter-pretations and a stubborn silence. In God's command that Abraham sacrifice his son lies an unbearable contradiction. If he carries out this command, Abraham will be disobeying the universal ethical laws that God has laid down. However, if he refuses to carry out the command, Abraham will be disobeying God's explicit order. Even if this is not understood as a strict deadlock, in the sense that Abraham is rewarded for his readiness to disobey the universal ethical law in favour of an explicit order from God, this does little to ease the anxieties that the story of Abraham and Isaac provokes. The story remains at least a terrifying precedent for sinning in the name of God, if not evidence for the notion that obedience to God is, precisely, to sin.

Through the work that has been undertaken on citizenship in the last decade, citizenship has come to be associated with the existence of a body of citizens founded on universally comprehensible and applicable codes and laws. In prescribing the characteristics of the citizen, these laws serve to determine the external limit of the body of citizenship. That is, the laws erect a set of rights and obligations that apply to all citizens, and those who transgress the laws may well face becoming non-citizens or outsiders as punishment.

When imagined in the terms of citizenship presented above, the dilemma of Abraham and Isaac is irresolvable. Clearly, there is a body of citizenship constituted by God's commandments. But it remains incomprehensible how God, as the principle that underwrites the laws of the body of citizenship, could nonetheless command the transgression of His own laws. Here, obedience is equivalent to disobedience in a strict paradox. Even the angel's appearance to stay Abraham's hand does not alleviate this tension, as what remains determinative is Abraham's willingness to do the killing. If his will is sufficient to prove his faith, it is surely sufficient to convict him of sin.

There is, however, another approach to citizenship that suggests a way out of this deadlock. This approach focuses on the notion of the act of citizenship: an act that disrupts and undermines the stability of the laws that determine the limits of the body of citizenship. This act is a transgression, but one that simultaneously refuses the punishment prescribed by the law. Here, the non-citizen or outsider lays claim to the (ontological) principles that underwrite the (ontic) written laws of the body of citizenship, and turns them back on those same written laws. The non-citizen demands recognition as a citizen without, at the same time, giving up the characteristics that have determined his or her non-citizen status – that is to say, the non-citizen demands precisely what is impossible under the existing written laws. Thus, the act of citizenship appears as a demand that the existing written laws be cleared away to make room for something new.

When imagined in the terms of this approach to citizenship, the deadlock of Abraham and Isaac loosens somewhat. If, through an act of citizenship, a non-citizen can lay claim to the principle that underwrites the written laws, and use that principle as a justification for transgression, then God's command to Abraham may be read in this same way. As that which grounds the (written) ethical laws, God may nonetheless approve an act that clears away those laws to make room for something new. This interpretation is still tentative, however, and it gives rise

'The Sacrifice of Isaac', Rembrandt van Rijn (© State Hermitage Museum, St Petersburg)

to pressing questions. Why has God chosen this moment to demand an act of citizenship, and why must that act be Abraham's sacrifice of his own son?

The answer to these questions emerges from what has gone unsaid in the above explanation of this new approach to citizenship. Although this approach is associated with an act of citizenship that demands the clearing away of the old laws, it is nonetheless simultaneously associated with a demand for something new, implicit in which is a recognition of the need for laws as such. This approach to citizenship does not condone a state of permanent lawlessness, especially in so far as it sees laws as representative of a larger field of human interaction: convention, language, exchange and culture. Without law, there would be no society, ethical or otherwise. Nonetheless, every set of laws necessarily constitutes an outside of non-citizenship. As a result, there will necessarily always arise a moment in which the punishment suffered by the outsider becomes unbearable. A call may then emerge for an act that will temporarily clear the ground for something new.

But when is this moment? When does the punishment suffered by the outsider become unbearable? This is the fundamentally unanswerable question at the heart of this approach to citizenship. Because this moment demands the transgression of universal, ethical laws – because these laws are seen, in this moment, to have failed – the criteria for determining when the moment has come cannot be based on any universal, ethical law. The act of citizenship is strictly inexplicable and incomprehensible because the sole basis for explaining and for comprehending anything is the field of convention and language, which is precisely the field that this act seeks to disrupt. There is no way to describe the moment that demands an act, other than as a call.

God's command to Abraham can thus be seen as representative of the call that demands an act of citizenship. According to this interpretation, the laws that govern the body of citizenship of which Abraham is a citizen (which prohibit murder and human sacrifice) must have become oppressive, prescribing a level of injustice and unethical treatment for non-citizens (perhaps specifically for murderers or those who practise human sacrifice) that are intolerable to Abraham. As readers of the story, however, we are not privy to the specific situation of injustice, precisely because the characteristics of the situation itself cannot justify such an act. The only way this kind of justification would be possible is through the application of a universal rule, which is precisely what the act of citizenship disrupts. Instead, the story refocuses our attention from the situation onto Abraham himself, who, in his singularity, experiences that situation as a call. This call is inexplicable in universal terms. It becomes a command from God that neither has nor needs any other justification.

Act 2

❖

Antigone's Offering

CHARLES WELLS

A claim to be a citizen belongs to the first level of abstraction in an act of citizenship. This plea is most often heard in the formal language of status. Status in turn gains access to the substantive language of rights and obligations as the second level of the same abstraction. The first level is the moment in which outsiders and insiders appear in the barest conceptual opposition. The second level appears through another discourse but also embodies the same binary opposition. The question arises as to what happens if each side becomes the other at a third cosmopolitical level? Can the insider and outsider distinction be retained in the same binary? A founding text in the Western tradition that best reveals these complex levels in acts of citizenship is the tragic story of *Antigone*. This act can be interpreted as an act of citizenship on all four levels of abstraction: as an attempt to assert the status of her brother, the traitor Polynices, as a citizen of Thebes; as an attempt to assert Polynices's status as a citizen of a different body, the family; as an attempt to assert Polynices's status as a citizen of a transcendent or cosmopolitan body; or as an attempt to radically defy the concept of citizenship itself.

The tragedy *Antigone* was written by Sophocles in 442 BC. Chronologically last in the trilogy of Theban Plays after *Oedipus the King* and *Oedipus at Colonus*, *Antigone* was nonetheless written first. It has had a major impact on the history of modernity, and continues to exert a powerful force of fascination on the modern imagination. The tragedy begins after Antigone's two brothers, Eteocles and Polynices, have killed each other over the rulership of Thebes, their home city. Antigone's uncle, Creon, has risen to the throne to fill the void of power, and as Eteocles defended the city from within, he is treated as a hero. Polynices, who enlisted foreign aid and assaulted Thebes from without, is treated as a traitor and

'Antigone confronted with the dead Polynices', Nikiforos Lytras
(© National Gallery – Alexandros Soutzos Museum, Athens)

condemned by Creon to lie unburied on the field of battle. In the course of the play, Antigone contravenes Creon's law and tries to bury Polynices. When she is apprehended in the process of carrying out this resolution, she is brought before Creon, where she compounds her crime by refusing either to deny or repent for her act. Instead, she reaffirms it, wilfully accepting any attendant punishment. Consequently, Creon sentences her to be sealed alive in a tomb. Speaking her last words from the threshold, Antigone laments the life she will never lead and, once the tomb is sealed, hangs herself.

How can Antigone's act be interpreted as an act of citizenship? As a *polis*, Thebes clearly constitutes itself as a body of citizenship. When Polynices departs from this body, and returns aggressively from without, he is identified as an enemy and a traitor, and Creon responds by stripping him of his rights (rites) of citizenship. If Antigone's act is to be interpreted as an act of citizenship in relation to this scenario, it appears as one of the four possibilities discussed below.

First, she may be attempting to reassert Polynices's status as a citizen of Thebes. This possibility appears to be the least likely. When Creon asks Antigone to affirm that Polynices was a 'traitor [who died] attacking his country', she does not hesitate in her agreement. Indeed, from her response, one can see that she takes it for granted. 'Even so,' she says, 'we have a duty to the dead.' Although one might be tempted to argue that death, in some way, returns Polynices to his rightful status as a citizen of Thebes, this does not seem to be Antigone's intention. When Creon asserts that our duty to the dead is 'not to give equal honour to good and bad', Antigone's response is: 'Who knows? In the country of the dead, that may be the law.' It seems clear that the right to burial, which Antigone attempts to grant Polynices, is not based on his status as a citizen of Thebes.

The second possibility, that Antigone may stand for another body of citizenship that exists over and against that of the *polis*, is more tenable. Typically, this other body has been interpreted as the family, whose laws occasionally (if not continuously and essentially) contest those of the *polis*. In this interpretation, Antigone enacts her duty to Polynices as a member of his family. This interpretation often coincides with a gender analysis of Antigone's role as a woman challenging the patriarchal authority of the polis. Creon's pronouncement, 'We'll have no woman's law here, while I live', certainly offers a great deal of support for this position. However, Antigone's insistence that she 'would not have done the forbidden thing for any husband or for any son' disturbs this reading, suggesting that it is not simply Polynices's status as a member of her family that calls on her to act, but rather something particular about his status a brother.

The third possibility is that Antigone's act is an assertion of Polynices's status as a citizen of a transcendent body. This body, which transcends both the family and the *polis*, is referred to in the Greek tradition as cosmos and is typically represented as humanity as a whole. This may be thought in parallel with the country of the dead to which Antigone refers in her conversation with Creon. This body is organized around a set of laws whose relation to the particular laws and customs of a given *polis* or family is transcendent. Here, Polynices's death appears as a boundary beyond which the laws and interests of the *polis* do not extend. This suggests a kind of moral citizenship. As a citizen of the transcendental body, Polynices is guaranteed the right to burial by a fundamental moral law that structures human exchange, and the good of Thebes ceases to be a consideration. What disturbs this interpretation is the necessarily arbitrary character of any specific content attributed to the law structuring the transcendental body. Typically, the law of the transcendental body is associated with structures such as the incest taboo, which are already thrown into flux by Antigone's status as the offspring of an incestuous union. Even leaving this aside, however, the rite of burial must be acknowledged as a culturally specific act, whether the corpse is present or absent when acknowledging the dead.

Finally, it is possible that Antigone's act is one that is purely disruptive, challenging the notion of citizenship in its entirety. It may be that Antigone is motivated by an absolute refusal of the category of citizen in so far as it is a term of exclusion. From this perspective, Antigone's act usurps and deconstructs the stable forms of citizenship by deliberately applying rights reserved for citizens to a non-citizen par excellence. Here, Antigone does not assert Polynices's status as a citizen within any body, but rather throws everyone else's citizenship into question.

Act 3

❖

The Death of Socrates

BORA ALI ISYAR

A key dimension within acts of citizenship is hidden in its immediacy. As a noun an act is an event. The realism of the event, though, also contains a sense of another possible or potential event. In the presence of the act there is also an act yet to come. To get at this difference between the sense of the real and the sense of the possible in acts of citizenship it is helpful to think through the example of Socrates's discussion of death and philosophy. As an act of citizenship his discussion focuses on its meaning at the time as well as its meaning to come. In his death he has allowed a bad law to continue to govern citizens but he has also created a philosophy to come. His act both maligns the law and creates a rupture in the history of citizenship that gives credibility to philosophy, as a way of being a citizen that was, and perhaps still is, yet to come.

In 399 BC Socrates was summoned to defend himself against charges of impiety in front of an Athenian jury consisting of 501 fellow male citizens. For Socrates, being summoned to King Archon's court was a moment of simultaneously fulfilling a duty and claiming the rights of Athenian citizenship. It is a duty in that Socrates must both appear before the court in order to defend himself and abide by the decision of the jury. However, his appearance before the court also provides him with the opportunity to develop a 'reasonable discourse' concerning the nature of philosophy and the valuable life of a citizen. Thus the death of Socrates becomes a moment of the performance of citizenship not only through his acceptance of the jury's decision, hence a duty, but also through practising philosophy, hence a right.

For years, accusations were aimed at Socrates relating to his way of practising philosophy. For Socrates, these allegations were particularly dangerous as they took the form of rumours and gossip. The danger in such allegations is that they do not allow the opportunity to defend oneself. Thus, at the beginning of the *Apology*, it becomes clear that for Socrates a courtroom defence is not only his duty as a citizen, but also a space in which he can argue for himself with fellow citizens. That is why, before defending himself against Meletus, Socrates begins his apologia by defending himself against the anonymous accusations.

The anonymous accusations are as follows: Socrates is a wise man who, by argument and by philosophizing, turns the weaker argument to the stronger argument, thereby corrupting his listeners, especially the youth of Athens. In order to disprove the possibility of this argument, Socrates outlines what it means to practise philosophy. For Socrates, it turns out, philosophy is not one of the many practices that make up life, but is a way of life itself. It is a way of life in which the primary goal is to search for truth.

A wise philosopher, however, not only searches for and establishes truth; he also questions already established truths by way of 'reasonable arguments'. Consequently, for Socrates, the search for truth is a mission that can only be accomplished by the soul. The body, with its immediate needs to be satisfied, is always a barrier to the way of life of a true philosopher. A true philosopher, in his everlasting search for truth, must escape from the body as much as possible in order to be guided by what the soul demands: the truth. This definition informs Socrates's political claim to citizenship. To fully realize this claim we must return to Socrates's last words and their double interpretation in Western philosophy.

According to *Phaedo*, Socrates's final statement was as follows: 'Crito, we owe a cock to Asclepius; make this offering to him and do not forget.' Two aspects of this statements are essential for a discussion of the death of Socrates: 'we' and 'do not forget'.

Before Socrates swallows the poison, he engages in a final discussion concerning death and philosophy with the twelve other people in his cell. Throughout the discussion, Socrates argues that death is not something to be feared. This judgement is based on two factors. First, no one can know what kind of a thing death is. Therefore, fearing death means claiming to know something that one cannot know and, consequently, is against the philosophical life. Second, if death means the complete separation of body from soul, and the complete ruin of the body, then death is the essential goal of anyone who wishes to become a philosopher.

According to the dominant reading of the last words of Socrates, which Nietzsche considerably influenced, Socrates wants to sacrifice a cock to Asclepius, the god of healing, because he is healed from life, the worst of all diseases. However, this reading does not sufficiently address the issue of the use of 'we' by Socrates. What if Socrates uses the word 'we', as Foucault has suggested, to refer to the friendship between Socrates and the people in his cell?

As he and his friends were very close, Socrates may have argued that any harm and healing would be lived in the plural sense. Common to both these readings is that Socrates despises life and, therefore, death is a healing.

Throughout *Phaedo*, Socrates and his friends discuss the good life, which prioritizes the soul, and, therefore, the search for truth over other ways of life. In the end, they reach the understanding that a life led in the philosophical way is supreme. In other words, they discard any other form of life. However, what is also always extant in the dialogues is the suspicion the listeners have about the validity of the arguments of Socrates In the end Socrates realizes that there is no suspicion left in his friends and that they have understood that they need to lead a life that is based on searching for the truth through the care of the soul. Thus, they are healed. That is why Socrates says 'we' have to sacrifice a cock for the god of healing.

This is also better understood when the second part of the statement, 'do not forget' is carefully examined. Socrates uses the Greek word *αμελησητε*, which means both 'do not forget' and 'do not be careless'. If we adopt the second meaning, Socrates makes a final warning to his friends to care for their souls for the rest of their lives in order to follow a philosophical way of life.

Where does this argument lead us? Socrates, as will be remembered, was found guilty of corrupting the youth through his practice of philosophy, which was a way of life for him. By referring to two opposing interpretations, we can see the multiple ways in which Socrates challenges the Athenian court decision against philosophy. As a living being, a citizen, Socrates, by accepting the death penalty, is deprived of the right to philosophize. He performs his duty by drinking the poison. Yet he also becomes a living soul through death. He completely rids himself of bodily barriers and becomes the true philosopher. In other words, at the moment of being deprived of his right to be a philosopher and to life, he gains the right to become the good philosopher. However, if 'we' refers to the friends who will live after Socrates, then, at the moment of death and by arguing the possible benefits of death he continues teaching his friends and leading them to a life for which he was sentenced to death. In other words, the court's decision to punish him with death for his philosophy leads to the enrichment of that philosophy, which is meaning yet to come.

Act 4

Euthanasia

BORA ALI ISYAR

Contemporary claims to the right of euthanasia provide an interesting case for thinking about the two-sided problem of answerability in acts of citizenship. On one side there is a claim for the right to die. On the other side, the claim is contingent on the condition of unbearable pain, loss of dignity and no hope of survival. As the claim is performed it creates a unique political space where the contingency of the claim tells us about the right of citizens to make decisions about their lives. Yet when the attempt is made to make the claim universal it loses its contingency and falls back into its outlaw status, continuing to disturb the habitus and its legal institutions.

Take for example the case of Bob Dent, who ended his life on Sunday 22 September 1996 in the Australian city of Darwin under the Northern Territory's short-lived Rights of the Terminally Ill Act of 1995. Dent's death was the first case of legal euthanasia. Intense debates on the right to die by numerous parties including legal theorists and practitioners, religious and medical institutions, and citizens who demanded the right to euthanasia followed his death. The act was terminated two years later but the debates, now incorporating experiences in the Netherlands and Oregon, USA, continue with the same, if not greater intensity. By simply asserting his right to his own life, including his death, Dent's act must be seen as an act of citizenship.

The Northern Territory Legislative Assembly passed the Rights of the Terminally Ill Act on 25 March 1995. Four people died under the provisions of the act: Bob Dent on 22 September 1996, Janet Mills on 2 January 1997 and two anonymous persons on 20 January and 1 March 1997. As Bob Dent was the first person to request to perform his right to die, his death was preceded and followed by extensive academic and media debates.

In general, supporters of euthanasia in Australia have made two interrelated arguments. The first concerns autonomy. Supporters of euthanasia claim that every individual has the right to decide on the way to live his or her life and that this decision must include the moment of the end of life. Two different definitions of the 'final exit', as it came to be called, were offered. One offered by the vast majority of the supporters of euthanasia argued that anyone experiencing pain or disability had the right to choose the time and circumstances of death. A second group favoured extending the right to choose one's own death to wider contexts. Neither group, however, supported an unconditional right to die.

The second argument in favour of euthanasia concerned the question of fairness. This position stated that the denial of the right to die was a cruel act, as it would continue the suffering of those who wished to die. Again, the right to die was made conditional upon the level of pain, an ostensibly measurable quantity. In other words, for supporters of euthanasia, life was still superior to death in the sense that it had to be preserved until the hope of a 'life with dignity' disappeared. Bob Dent's death was supported because, as both doctors and Dent himself argued, his life had turned into an unbearable existence. This condition led him to lose his dignity and he had no hope of survival.

Suicide, once seen as a rival to the sovereign who was the sole power over death, became an object of sociological and psychological analysis as early as the nineteenth century. At this time suicide was not a crime because it challenged the sovereign power's right over death, but because it was considered an act that is not 'rightfully' – in the legal sense of the word – exercised: 'You do not have the right to die!' What is crucial is that the duty to live is suspended at particular moments. Traditionally it is not only allowed but also expected that citizens have the duty to die for the nation. Being-one as a nation, as a condition for the allowance of one's autonomy over one's death, probably constitutes the most effective discrepancy in the exercise of power over life. It is effective in the nationalist discourse, where the ostensibly most precious element of a being – life – is suspended for nation and society, the supreme being-together of beings in 'modern times'. The question that needs to be asked is this: does Bob Dent's death constitute a somewhat different issue, which accommodates the possibility of disturbing power over life without referring to some higher form of being, nation? In other words, does the act of euthanasia accommodate the possibility of challenging the power over life without defending the society?

Despite the immanence of that possibility, in Bob Dent's case the practice of euthanasia, the suspension of life, was constructed to be in defence of what is more valuable than either Bob Dent, death itself or the life of one individual: society and a particular conduct of life in no way separate from the two poles mentioned earlier. This is not to say that the claiming of the right to die did not challenge the power over life. On the contrary, the debates it produced challenged the dominant discourse of life to a large extent. However, we must be very careful not to ignore the elements that constitute this discourse of life.

Bob Dent was allowed to die because his life was no longer dignified. Bob Dent and his body came to be what the undesired life would be, if it were allowed to exist – a body that cannot take care of itself, one that is weak and that cannot be for the society. The effect of the death served to perpetuate the distinction between good life and bad life in the discourse of life. A body that could not be disciplined, a body that could not be effective, could be allowed to disappear. The political arguments that followed, however, did not address these issues.

It was at the moment of the emergence of calls, although few in number, for the universalization of the right to die, an argument claiming the right to end good life, that the Australian government banned the practice of euthanasia. At that moment, the distinction between good life and bad life lost ground; life became one again, sacred and in need of defence.

Act 5

Pat Tillman:
Soldier-Citizen-Hero?

DARRYL BURGWIN

The manufacturing of simulated images in cultural industries and their often-hidden national and global interests complicate contemporary struggles over the naming of acts of citizenship. To read acts of citizenship through media critically means juxtaposing the struggles around their naming and then negating each claim to have fully defined the meaning of the act. Once each image is linked to its specific ownership claim – whether local, national, or transnational – it becomes possible to demonstrate the unfolding of acts of citizenship in a mediated public logic.

A good example of this is seen in the story of the soldier-citizen-hero, Pat Tillman. Galvanized by the 11 September 2001 attack on the World Trade Centre in New York City, he gave up a multi-million-dollar contract with the National Football League's Arizona Cardinals to fight 'terror' in the Middle East. In June 2003, Tillman and his brother signed up with the elite Army Rangers and subsequently were sent to Afghanistan. Tillman refused to discuss publicly his reasons for giving up his successful pursuit of the American Dream in order, instead and presumably, to protect that dream. On 22 April 2004, as a member of 'A' Company, 2nd Battalion, 75th Ranger Regiment, Tillman died in an ambush near the village of Khost in eastern Afghanistan. Upon his death, Americans looking to put a human and heroic face on America's occupation of Iraq embraced his story of patriotic self-abnegation.

Three Acts of Citizenship

Act 1: Tillman's personal decision to fight terrorism in the name of his country – what he later expressed as a desire, 'to support my brothers' – can be considered an act of citizenship. By all accounts, Tillman was deeply affected by the 9/11 attacks as a shattering indication that America's situation in the world had changed to the degree that he could not continue to live as he had previously. It is also clear that he wished to follow this call not as a media-packaged hero but as a rank-and-file soldier. This contributed to a reticence on Tillman's part when he was asked to speak about his decision. He refused all interviews and opportunities to explain his actions up until his death. At this level, Tillman's act can legitimately be seen as a responsible act of citizenship tied to identification with the American nation, forged anew in the heat of 9/11.

Act 2: It was only after Tillman was killed on the battlefield that his unselfish act was subjected to the American promotional machine and to political interests. The media picked up the story and ran with the 'true American hero' angle. The audience was presented with parallel images of two warriors: the football player and the army ranger. The square-jawed intensity of the white, football Safety – the last line of defence on the field – translated into the point man against foreign terror. In this representation, Tillman's heroic selflessness is transferred to the nation-state and consequently, America itself becomes heroic. Here Tillman stands in for the USA and the USA stands for Tillman. Tillman's deification confounded the popular stereotype of Americans as wealth-obsessed, self-involved figures mindlessly pursuing fame and lacking any moral purpose. Thus, a second act of citizenship occurs when the American state recuperates Tillman's personally responsible act, reinterpreting it as a jingoistic story deployed to justify the actions of that state. Tillman's private support of a public good is thus converted into nationalistic publicity, something that Tillman went out of his way to avoid when he was alive. In this way, Tillman is depicted as the responsible individual fighting for his country in its time of need, and the ideal American citizen untainted by the messiness inherent in modern imperial encounters. This representation was especially important for national unity given the failure to find 'weapons of mass destruction' in Iraq, which contributed to weak support for the American actions both at home and elsewhere. Other questions also remained as to whether the purpose of the occupation was to fight terror or to maintain US access to Middle East Oil resources; was its purpose to promote democracy or was it a business enterprise, a search for new resources and new markets? Tillman's image helped to obscure these issues at least for a time.

Act 3: As the second act of state recuperates the selfless first act, a third act emerges: the establishment of a discourse of 'us' and 'them'. Tillman's familiar face stands in for the American people ('us') and the Islamic enemy becomes completely other to that image ('them') – strange, inhuman, anonymous. The second act of representation sets the limits of the discourse involving both the celebration of Tillman's selflessness and patriotism and the reaction against the external Islamic enemy, as well as the expulsion of internal dissent – those

Americans who oppose the Iraqi occupation. One example of this latter move were the attacks on University of Massachusetts graduate student, Rene Gonzalez, who in a student newspaper brashly called Tillman an idiot for giving up so much for so little. The vehemence of the abuse that Gonzalez received demonstrated the effectiveness of the second act in establishing the symbolic divide between Americans and those against America. But it does not stop there. The pictures that emerged from Abu Ghraib indicate that the third act is an example that demonstrates not all acts of citizenship can be seen as even a qualified good. The naked and hooded Iraqi soldiers, stacked like inert lumber or lifeless cattle – just so much standing reserve – offers a striking contrast to the personalization of the American soldier accomplished through the living mediations of the dead Tillman.

Tillman has been portrayed as a noble warrior citizen who wilfully sacrificed himself to stop any further crimes being committed against his people. The similarity of his story to that of the 'terrorists' who sacrificed themselves for Islam is rarely commented upon. To an observer not caught in the immediate fray it is obvious that the mediated Tillman is positioned as an American martyr. That word is never used, of course, since it is reserved by the discourse for the irrational acts of the religious fundamentalist. The national fundamentalist, however, as long as he is American, is accepted as having good and noble reasons, justified by grief and mourning. With Tillman's sacrifice, it is as if Americans can look at themselves and say, 'See, we are pure of heart and true of cause too. We are not just power- and money-obsessed hedonists who only care about ourselves.'

The revelation that Tillman was killed by friendly fire has served to undermine much of the power of the second and third acts by re-immersing Tillman's story within the inherent ambiguity of the modern imperial encounter. This serves to cloud, once again, the clear distinction between 'us and them'. While the second, state-driven, act attempted to cleanse the American presence in the Middle East of failure and moral doubt, and in the process made the enemy anonymous and other, the revelation of the messiness of Tillman's death establishes once again the difficulty of cleansing any war of its ambiguous elements. Thus, one must think twice before accepting, in any unqualified manner, the heroism of the first act, as, in the context of this ambiguity, nationalism is more readily understood as an alibi that obviates responsibility to those who are positioned outside of the nation. Tillman's responsibility to his nation leads to a devastating irresponsibility to those not defined in those terms; hence the link between citizenship and war. Traditionally, going to war for your country has been the penultimate cost of citizenship – the ultimate being death while fighting. Tillman's act should, at the very least, bring this linkage into question.

PART II

❖

Citizens, Strangers,
Aliens, Outcasts

Chapter 4

❖❖

Citizenship Without Acts?
With Tocqueville in America

BRIAN C. J. SINGER

The following is an essay in chiaroscuro. Citizenship is not usually under-stood in terms of acts. This essay seeks to examine the usual understanding of citizenship, but in contrast to that understanding, it begins with a problematic of 'disenactment'. In this manner, the idea of acts of citizen-ship will, it is hoped, stand in bolder relief by the added shading.

Citizenship is generally associated with democracy (monarchies have subjects, not citizens), and as such is deemed a political matter. The political entails relations of rule – rule by, of, or with others.[1] Democracy, of course, is rule by the *demos*, that is, by everyone; but modern democracy, at least, is also rule by no-one: that is, relations of rule appear suspended over large areas of collective life, and many individuals would claim, or would like to claim, that they are their own boss. Such is the two-sided character of modern democracy: it opens up, in a way that is historically unprecedented, the question of relations of rule and, therefore, of justice; simultaneously, it seeks to avoid that question. This two-sided character reappears relative to citizenship: the latter may be deemed political, but most of us, most of the time, are citizens without having to engage in political acts, actions or performances. Citizenship appears a function of the *jus solis* or *jus sanguinis*, the consequence of a status rather than an act, and therefore as pre-political (Singer 1996).

We can, indeed we must, say that citizenship is constituted by a political act or, better, is instituted through a discontinuous series of acts. However, once instituted, citizenship is provided with a second origin, one that over-lays particular historical acts with the appearance of a general ontological condition. This essay seeks to examine citizenship in view of the appearance of this latter non-political condition. What does citizenship look like when separated from all relations of rule? How does citizenship appear when without a *polis*? The question may surprise; it seems contrary to a very long tradition of political thought. And yet the question receives a response in a well-known if somewhat neglected classic, Alexis de Tocqueville's *Democracy in America*. In effect, Tocqueville gives a name to this ontological foundation that modern democracy gives itself: he refers to it in terms of the 'social'. It is the conceit of this essay that it is worth examining Tocqueville's analysis of modern democracy's social foundation and its implications for an understanding of the ambivalent character of contemporary citizenship. Before proceeding, however, two warnings are in order. First, this is not an exercise in Tocqueville scholarship. Rather, it is a thought piece that treats Tocqueville as an intellectual *agent provocateur* – despite and because of his distance from the present as a nineteenth-century author, from his own times as a displaced aristocrat, and from the United States as a Frenchman. Second, like Tocqueville's original work, this essay treats the United States as both exceptional and exemplary. We are and are not, for better and worse, Americans.

The Political and the Social

Tocqueville begins with a conventionally political analysis, but as his examination of American political institutions proceeds through the first volume, the question of democracy is posed in increasingly social terms.[2] By the time of the second volume, published some five years after the first, the examination of the social characteristics of American democracy moves to the fore, the first three of its four books being about American manners, feelings and thoughts. The fourth and last book, which concerns 'the influence of democratic opinions and sentiments on political society', presents the relation between the social and political as fundamentally uncertain: on the basis of a democratic society there can arise either 'democratic republicanism' or 'democratic despotism'. If today it may appear difficult to decide whether, on the basis of Tocqueville's criteria, we live in a despotic or republican democracy, he clearly held the two to be very different. A democracy can take on different, even opposite traits at the political level; the consistency, nay, the substance of democracy must be sought at a social level.

The question is what is this social character at the base of American democracy? It would be incorrect to identify this substance with American manners, feelings and thoughts, say, in the manner of Montesquieu's *moeurs* (1989). American *moeurs* are more the effects or symptoms than the substance of the democratic social state. Moreover, all political regimes in Montesquieu's view are underwritten by *moeurs*, with different *moeurs* underlying different regimes. In Tocqueville, by contrast, only in democratic regimes can one speak of properly social *moeurs*, seemingly abstracted from political relations of rule. It would be even less correct to identify the social substance with the transformation of the *oikos* into the economy in the manner of Hannah Arendt (1958). In her understanding 'the rise of the social' implies the extension to all of society of the characteristics associated with labour, and originally confined to the domestic household. In her view neither the *oikos* nor the social are considered spheres of action proper, because they are both deemed to be unfree (subject to natural necessity) and unequal (subject to either patriarchal or bureaucratic domination). By contrast, the 'social' in Tocqueville, as demanded by its link with democracy, is associated with liberty and equality, if not an explicitly political liberty or equality. Finally, it would not be entirely correct to speak of democracy's social character as synonymous with civil society, though the former certainly renders the latter possible. Tocqueville's social is not to be identified with a sphere of activity, let alone a set of institutions; for the democratic social substance appears to exist, to borrow Heideggerian terms, not at an ontic but an ontological level of collective existence, being rooted in a claim about the being of being human. To be sure, to the extent that such a claim lays the basis for the contrast between the social and the political, one can read into Tocqueville's argument the more common oppositions between civil society and the state, capitalism and democracy, the bourgeois and the citizen, where the former terms are deemed the more 'real', and sometimes seen as underpinning, sometimes as undermining, the latter terms. However, by placing the social on the side of democracy, the opposition is made much more complex, because it can no longer function as a direct opposition in, say, the manner of Marx. In effect, if the democratic social is at the root of civil society, then the bourgeois cannot simply be denounced as anti-social, nor can civil society simply be condemned as unequal, atomistic or materialistic. It is as though the bourgeois was only a bourgeois because he believed himself a citizen without, thereby, ceasing to threaten to undermine what is most valuable about citizenship, the capacity for political activity. Americans, after all, are far more likely to claim that they live in a democratic as opposed to a capitalist society, and they will claim possession of democratic citizenship even if they do not engage in that most minimal of political acts, voting. Tocqueville's argument allows us to understand why such claims are to be deemed neither unpatriotic nor idiotic (in the Greek sense). The social and political remain in opposition, but as an opposition within democratic citizenship. By situating the social as the substance of modern democracy, Tocqueville introduces an irresolvable tension into its very heart. But what does he mean when he speaks of the social? And how exactly does the social foundation of democracy differ from its more typical political foundation? The response to this question becomes evident when one realizes that there are two founding moments in *Democracy in America*.

The first concerns the original colonists who landed on the east (particularly north-east) coast. They came as religious communities and, on their arrival, established towns on the basis of a charter that established the basic laws – clearly an act of *political* foundation that corresponds to the typically contractualist terms Tocqueville otherwise eschews.[3] The first founding, then, establishes an essentially political community, which becomes the basis of what he terms 'township democracy'. The second, *western* founding involves neither towns nor contracts, but solitary families plunging into the wilderness, and living miles from their closest neighbours (1992, p. 56; 1961, I, pp. 43–4). One is tempted to say that the second founding is the contract in reverse: one quits the community and its laws and returns to the state of nature. Yet the homesteader, whatever his taste for the garden, is no *homo naturalis*. Tocqueville insists these settlers are, more or less, like all other Americans as regards their sense of identity, education, speech, passions, manners and possessions (if one thinks of 'the Bible, an axe and a file of newspapers' as the cultural staples of Americans of that time) (1992, p. 352; 1961, I, p. 356). Socially they are as American as any other; it is just that they do not live in concrete, political communities. We have here two paradoxes: first, that of a democracy without a *polis*, a paradox made possible only because democracy is defined socially, not politically. The second is that of a social that does not seem to require actual social relations.

The figure of the solitary settler now appears banal, but Tocqueville found it most surprising, even unprecedented.[4] Settlement usually follows empire, and is accompanied by government; here government follows settlement. Frontier culture is generally different from that of the metropole, often because it is hybrid, mixing with 'native' societies; but here there is almost no 'commerce' – commercial, civilizational or sexual – with the native populations. The differences between the American east and west are, to repeat, considered more political than cultural. Usually settlement occurs in and around towns. If individuals set off on their own, they are seen as leaving society and entering the 'desert' in order to become hermits, often in order to come closer to God. The American settler does not quit American society, and is not deemed to be particularly asocial. On the contrary, he may well see himself as bearing a privileged relation to what it means to be American.[5]

What is at stake here is, of course, not strictly empirical. One cannot simply say that because there are no towns, there is no township democracy. That would imply that as the populations expand, towns will form, and the democratic politics of the east will be reproduced in the west. Tocqueville, however, is adamant: a new form of democracy is developing. This form follows settlement across the West, and when it reaches the Pacific, will reverse itself and move in the opposite direction, overwhelming the earlier, 'Atlantic' forms. The settler, in effect, becomes a metaphor for a new, soon-to-be-dominant type of *homo democraticus*. In order to understand this personage, one must consider more closely Tocqueville's characterization of township democracy.

He portrays the latter in strokes reminiscent of the eighteenth century's portrayal of the ancient republics. Both are small in size, frugal in character, and marked by an emphasis on virtue. And in both politics is highly participatory, with positions filled by a mix of representation and lottery.[6] And yet, even as township democracy replicates many of the traits of Greek *polis*, and does so far more democratically (equality having far greater purchase in the United States),[7] the townships do not constitute a sort of democratic baseline, but are contrasted with another, more basic and, in Tocqueville's view, more extreme form. For township democracy is analysed as tempering more strictly democratic tendencies, and that because it is 'enacted', and enacted in always specific conditions of diversity. Thus township democracy is presented as inculcating a sense of place, and a public spirit tied to place. It educates citizens about institutional and legal procedures, develops their capacity to negotiate compromises and to recognize superior qualities in their neighbours. With its particularistic emphasis on local conditions, it focuses individual ambition; and with its continuous commerce between neighbours, it limits individual egoism. If democracy is not so tempered, it tends, by contrast, towards the general, the homogeneous and the abstract. If not domesticated by township politics, democracy encourages an excessive extension of individualism, characterized by an impatience with political process, an indifference to public spirit, and hostility to broadened horizons and talent. The result is 'democracy arrived at is most extreme', which can be observed precisely in the west (1992, p. 56; 1961, I, p. 43).

In truth, such a wild, undomesticated democracy – a *démocratie sauvage*, to coin a term – is tied less to a particular space than to a movement across space, and not just across space. Democracy here becomes synonymous with mobility: geographical mobility, social mobility, and the mobility of fortunes. The American is in constant movement; he is often tempted to abandon even the settled habits of the work ethic in order to pursue the main chance, becoming a gambler, literally and figuratively.[8] Democracy 'at its most extreme' appears too restless, too unsettled and too unsettling, to be contained within political institutions bound by *polis* walls. Note that, in the second volume, where Tocqueville confronts the social characteristics of American democracy head on, there is almost no discussion of township democracy.

Equality, Association and Dissociation

The problem, when asking what Tocqueville means by the social, is that one immediately runs up against our second paradox: a social state can exist without actual social relations. Tocqueville himself is sometimes ambiguous. At one point he writes: 'The new States of the West are already inhabited; but society has no existence among them' (1992, p. 56; 1961, I, p. 44) And one of the better commentators on Tocqueville glosses: 'The radical severing of the social links that democracy introduces, opens us to the image of democracy as a "dis-society"' (Manent 1996, p. 12). No political community, no society. We have here an image of atomization, understood as the dissolution of the social bond, here attributed to democracy (others will attribute it to capitalism). Nonetheless, I would submit that, no matter how isolated and, therefore, uncontrolled the individual,[9] society remains intact. Remember our solitary settler: though not empirically in society, he is still an American with all the requisite characteristics. It is as if one can be of society without being in society; or as if the social, once separated from the political, was compatible with the dissolution of concrete ties. Most authors, particularly those influenced by contract theory, would view such a condition as inherently nonsensical. The social, the social bond, is equated with association, itself understood as the very basis of society (and, simultaneously, polity) – particularly in democracies. Tocqueville, by contrast, does not see association as the underlying, defining moment of democracy. True, he has much to say about associations (always in the plural), but precisely, in the second volume, as a means by which to tame the excesses of the underlying *démocratie sauvage*.[10] In this sense, 'association' is logically posterior to the social state that defines democracy. In a word, the social suggests a state of 'sociation' compatible with both association and dissociation.[11] Better, it allows for associations, including political associations, but supposes dissociation. After all, in order to associate one first has to be dissociated. And how can one be mobile if one cannot dissociate from settled conditions? Ancient and township democracies suppose, by contrast, stable populations in continuous face-to-face relations, not the continuous comings and goings of dissociated individuals. Tocqueville, in effect, is suggesting a new 'deterritorialized' democracy adapted to 'deserts' (and large urban conurbations). But if the social is to be defined in terms of a sociation that enables citizens to be both associated and dissociated, one still wonders how such sociation is possible.

In order to respond to this question, it might be useful to open up a parenthesis. The reader may realize that I am forcing Tocqueville to speak to the now rather tired debate between liberals and communitarians. It is as though he were claiming that the disencumbered individuals of the liberals exist, but not because this is their 'natural' state, or because reason dictates that they bracket their concrete attachments under a 'veil of ignorance'. Individuals are disencumbered because they are members of a very specific community, the community of Americans, considered as, in many respects, the exemplary modern democratic community. That such a community may appear as a 'community without community' is due to the character of the bond that binds Americans together. It is a social, as opposed to a political, bond where, as suggested by the solitary settler, the imaginary relation need not be doubled by a concrete, enacted relation. An imaginary relation, it is fundamentally abstract: one can be an American citizen without an act of citizenship; one can even be a citizen without having actual relations with other citizens. Of course, one cannot live within entirely imaginary relations indefinitely (no more than one can live entirely without such relations). Nonetheless, even as the democratic social temporarily suspends political relations of rule, the abstraction of the social momentarily suspends the hold of concrete, communal ties. Tocqueville is disturbed by the very real political consequences that can result from the abstraction of sociation, and seeks all sorts of devices, most famously a rich associational life, to counter its effects. And as an advocate of associational life, Tocqueville has become the darling of those who would trumpet the many benefits of 'social capital'. But one must not forget that, for Tocqueville, the voluntarism of associational life supposes the dissociation of earlier, more embedded relations.

What lies behind the imaginary social relation? What gives it its energy and force? For Tocqueville, the American democrat is impelled not so much by the individual pursuit of rational self-interest (as liberals claim), or the virtuous pursuit of the public interest (as communitarians would claim); he is motivated less by interest than by passion and, more specifically, the passion for equality (Blackell 2004). This passion is deemed democracy's 'generative principle' and is at the basis of its essentially social character. Because democracy is defined in the horizontal terms of equality, it is no longer primarily defined politically in the 'vertical' terms of the rule of the many. For the opposite of democracy is not monarchy (considered as compatible with democracy's 'levelling' tendencies) but aristocracy, understood not as the rule of the few, but as a form of society populated by, in Louis Dumont's words, *homo hierarchicus*.[12] Now what distinguishes an egalitarian from a hierarchical society is not really the degree of its inequalities, at least not inequalities in wealth or life chances. Tocqueville admits that that there is a considerable economic inequality in the United States and that such inequality will probably increase.[13] Equality is viewed less as an economic fact (or any kind of fact)[14] than as, to employ Castoriadis's term (1987), an 'imaginary social signification'. Democracy, simply put, claims that people are fundamentally equal; aristocracy claims they are not. Both claims are imaginary in Castoriadis's sense; both make fundamental assertions about the being of being human (though the democratic claim can be considered the more abstract as it renders all humans equivalent). Neither claim is factually demonstrable; instead, each produces its own facts. Political institutions will have to be very different when all are deemed equal, as all particular relations of rule cannot but appear contingent. And as all such relations cannot but appear contingent, there arises a need to establish relations that do not appear as relations of rule. Accompanying the emergence of specifically social relations, Tocqueville suggests, is a mutation in the individual's sense of self.

In an aristocratic society, the self is immediately faced with other selves who are different, and different because of relations of rule. Indeed, one's sense of self requires one's subordination to a higher principle and to the person who incarnates that principle, for one's 'identification' with that person raises one above oneself, and situates oneself in relation to the ultimate principle from which the order, coherence and sense of the world proceed.[15] Thus in aristocracy social relations, being immediately imbricated in relations of rule, are inextricably political, even as their imaginary dimension is immediately imbricated in the reality of the relations of rule. In modern democracy, by contrast, relations of rule can be (momentarily) bracketed, such that one's sense of self appears to depend on oneself alone, and not on one's relation with one's superiors or inferiors. This point can be clarified by extending the comparison to ancient democracies. The ancient citizen saw himself as always implicated in relations of rule, whether in the private sphere as ruler of the *oikos*; or in the public sphere as ruler and ruled in turn. This is why his citizenship was unthinkable without his active participation in public matters. In modern democracy one sees oneself as neither ruler nor ruled; one believes that 'no-one is the boss of me' – and where better to prove that one is one's own boss, if not the frontier? To hold that everyone is equal by definition is to imply that they can establish amongst themselves – outside the realms of kinship, religion, law and politics[16] – social relations independent of all relations of rule. This momentary suspension of all vertical, political relations explains the emergence of a seemingly autonomous civil society. And when strictly political relations do appear, it explains why they appear as secondary, indirect and specular. In short, it helps explain why this is representative, as opposed to direct, democracy.

In aristocratic societies, as one's sense of self depends on one's superiors or inferiors, others necessarily appear different from the self. In modern democracy, by contrast, one sees others as essentially similar, as one's *semblable* (to use Tocqueville's term). But isn't one's sense of self then, dependent on one's *semblables,* rather than being independent of all others? At one level, Tocqueville replies, one believes that one is not so dependent: one sees oneself as submitting to oneself alone; one may even believe that others, being similar to oneself, are largely redundant. At another, deeper level, however, one still requires *semblables* if one is to be of society. But one requires less an actual *semblable* than the figure of a *semblable,* an imaginary *semblable.* The argument, in a sense, anticipates George Herbert Mead's concept of the 'generalized other', the abstract sum of all one's significant particular others which, once internalized, is capable, by virtue of its generality, of being detached from all actual others.[17] One's sense of self, in short, does not depend on the direct, continuous presence of a particular other, but supposes the indirect, imaginary presence of one's equals in their abstract generality. Once one has internalized the 'general other', one does not require the actual presence of particular others. Our American can live in the wilderness, and still be fully socialized. In his isolation, he is not just aware of the existence of similar others; he sees these similar others as forming the set of American citizens of which he is a part, precisely because it is made up of people like him.

Consider again the character of the social in its relation to the political. At the level of the social, the self does not rule anyone, and cannot countenance being ruled by anyone; the self believes herself to be equal to everyone else, such equality being not the consequence of a political accord, but a supposition or, better, a presupposition borne by passion and principle, and rooted in an imaginary relation between *semblables.* As a consequence, the social appears as the locus of multiple, uncontrolled, horizontal movements disconnected from the stability of relations of rule. In view of their differences, one cannot but think that the relation between the social and the political will be tenuous. I said earlier that, for

Tocqueville, the character of democratic politics, given its separation from its social base, is fundamentally indeterminate. This is not quite true. Tocqueville holds that the greater the numbers of associations, both civil and political, the greater the likelihood of democratic republicanism, and the fewer the numbers, the greater the chances of democratic despotism. Still, the suggestion is that the social, as a place of sociation, proves an unstable basis for political life. On the other hand, in its separation from the political, the social is relatively insulated from political shifts. One might be surprised at Tocqueville's relative lack of interest in American party struggles, and this despite the fact that many of his interlocutors – and notably, those closest to him in terms of their social background – were quite distressed at the rise of Andrew Jackson, claiming that he was jeopardizing the republic's very existence. Instead he insisted that American society was fundamentally stable, despite the sound and fury of American politics (1992, p. 463; 1961, I, pp. 502–3).

Such stability is only possible because the bond that ties Americans together does not appear to depend on a political act. The fact of citizenship, as well as the existence of relations between citizens, is always already supposed, having been instituted at an imaginary social level. Thus there is, arguably, no need to posit an act of contract at the origin of American citizenship[18]; and there is even less of a need to continuously renew the act of association in order to maintain the citizen body. The separation of the social from the political implies a separation between the world of concrete collective action and that which is its basis, the abstract immanence of sociation. The latter, to repeat, appears to provide the ballast that ensures that the ship of state does not tip too violently. The social, in effect, serves to temper political conflict by reducing its stakes. This would not be the case, however, if it appeared to dictate the content of political action, which is to say that the social is not some submerged principle of order that political action seeks to render visible. In this regard, the immanence of the social cannot be compared with the transcendence of power during the *ancien regime*; during the latter, political speech and action took on an overtly ritualistic character in order to convey the presence of the deity, the source of the order and intelligibility of the world. Nor can the immanence of the social be translated into the terms of enlightenment reason; if such were the case, political action would have to present itself as the direct realization of political speech, itself the transparent expression of a timeless, fully coherent rationality. The social may appear to anchor the political, but it does not and cannot determine the latter's content; understood as sociation, it is simply too abstract, too inchoate, too undecideable to suggest an underlying, positive order.

The social, in this regard, is not without relevance for thinking about 'acts of citizenship', as defined in the introduction to this book. Without the buffering of the social, every act of citizenship would have to refer to the fundamental lines constitutive of the order, coherence and identity of the collectivity as a whole, which is to say that every such act would have to appear not just responsible, but almost impossibly so. Without the social, all acts of citizenship would, in order to move beyond the existing, instituted order, have to present themselves as instituting a fundamental rupture with what preceded it. But backed by the social, acts of citizenship need not be acts of foundation, and can take on an explicitly tentative, responsive character.

At the same time, however, the social also presents difficulties for acts of citizenship. One such difficulty has already been discussed: in its purer, less domesticated form, the social threatens to make political action appear redundant, with potentially noxious consequences for political rule. There is another, related, and more theoretical difficulty already noted *ab ovo*. As the social appears a state of being that precedes political acting, democratic common sense tells us that social subjects produce political activity. The idea of 'acts of citizenship' seeks to contest such a commonplace by claiming that instituting political acts, if not instituted political actions, produce subjects.[19] Such contrasting claims would not really be significant if the subject in the common sense version were without a subject 'position' that influenced the content of his acts. But if the social appears without definite content, the same cannot be said of the subjects of the social. As citizens, these subjects position themselves as *semblables*, which makes it very difficult for them to engage in acts of citizenship as defined here. For *semblables* cannot really be answerable to others in their otherness.

Self and Other

One might think that, with self and other situated as *semblables*, their difference would disappear, and with their difference, all tensions between the two terms. However, rather than disappearing, differences takes on different, more problematic forms. Three types of difference can be discussed: differences between *semblables* (here between Americans); differences where self and other are clearly dissimilar (here between Americans and their racial others, denied full citizenship); and differences where self and other are neither clearly similar nor dissimilar (when it is not certain what it is to be an American). Tocqueville has much to say about the first type of difference, a long chapter on the second type, and nothing concerning the third.

When Tocqueville speaks of the relation between self and other as a relation between *semblables*, he cannot eliminate all signs of difference. Once one realizes that the abstraction that constitutes their relations is actually composed of two abstractions, difference reappears on both sides of the equation, with both self and other marked as particular. In effect, there is an abstraction of the self relative to particular others, and an abstraction of the other relative to the particulars of the self. In certain respects, the two abstractions appear contrary to each other; in others, they appear complementary. Tocqueville considers both abstractions, and considers both to be potentially problematic. I will examine first the abstraction of the self relative to particular others, as it underwrites much of the previous analysis.

With this abstraction one's sense of self is abstracted from the particulars of one's circumstances. That is to say, one's sense of self-identity is not directly defined through these circumstances; it appears as if insulated from its environment, including the personal dependencies and interdependencies associated with that environment. This is the abstraction at the root of individual mobility. One can only be mobile because one's core sense of self remains relatively impervious to changes in one's situation. And when one is in little danger of losing the bearings of the self by moving, one has potentially much to gain. Our solitary settler does not move to escape persecution, nor to preserve a way of life, nor out of curiosity about 'exotic' others. He is moved more by of a spirit of adventure, or the desire to be his own boss. Above all, he seeks, in a change of circumstances, a change in fortune – a change that will provide an occasion to test and, thereby, reveal the self and its potential (1992, pp. 325–30; 1961, I, pp. 348–52). To be all that one can be is the promise of individual autonomy, the abstraction of the self being the premise of the individual's representation of this autonomy. The problem is that when one's sense of self is not immediately dependent on one's proximate others, one will probably not be close to them, however much one might resemble them. It may even be that the more similar they are, the more distant one is from them. This may be why Americans can compete with each other so ferociously without breaking the bonds that join them (at one point Tocqueville speaks of Americans as 'the most avaricious nation on the globe') (1992, p. 384; 1961, I, p. 412). Or why Americans, though they find everyday conversation 'simple and easy', 'neither seek nor avoid intercourse' (1992, pp. 681–4; 1961, II, pp. 201–3) They seem to lack strong attachments because, ultimately, they are indifferent to each other.

The second abstraction, the abstraction of the other relative to the particulars of the self, is perhaps the better known. It supposes that the image of the general other remains external, even as it is internalized. Briefly, Tocqueville argues that, while the democratic individual is unwilling to suffer the influence or authority of any particular person or group, he may, by himself, be uncertain of his place, opinions and orientations; and, in the face of the many, he may feel weak, isolated and impotent. In order to overcome this sense of uncertainty and powerlessness, he will identify with, and submit to, the authority of an imaginary general other (as opposed to the actuality of a particular other) (1992, pp. 283–4, 521–3; 1961, I, pp. 299–300, II, pp. 11–13). As this general other presents itself as an extension of the self, identification with said other appears to multiply the power of the self exponentially. At the same time, however, this abstract other, in its immensity and externality, also appears other than the self, threatening it with a new form of tyranny, one that confuses repression without with repression within. Modern democracy may release individual activity from direct subordination to institutionalized relations of rule; but it also reintroduces a new, strictly social form of domination beneath the properly political form. This social form of domination proves to be all the more effective for being largely imaginary. For it is able, in the absence of an institutionalized "reality principle", to enslave the soul without having to enslave the body (1992, p. 293; 1961, I, p. 311).

For Tocqueville, there can be no orderly relations with others without relations of rule, the latter being implicated not just in the institution of a societal order, but in the constitution of a sense of self. Thus it is not entirely surprising that, when concrete, political relations of rule appear momentarily suspended, they would be doubled with imaginary social relations of rule. Prior to Tocqueville, the more republican wing of the Enlightenment tried to conceive of political relations without the rule of particular persons in terms of either 'the rule of law' or the 'rule of the people'. Tocqueville rejects both solutions, if for different reasons. The law can be only a supplement to political rule, and is deemed to be aristocratic, almost by definition (because of its institutional formalism, specialized corporate bodies and esoteric forms of knowledge). While the 'people', the purported national sovereign, can never institutionalize its rule directly, precisely because it forms less a real than an imaginary entity, incapable of engaging in the particulars of political action without undermining its abstract unity. If rule by the people, one and indivisible, is to be more than momentary, it must be extra-political, even anti-political. In the first volume domination by the people takes the form of the 'tyranny of the majority', understood as the momentary eruption of mob rule.[20] By the second volume, the principal danger no longer lies with revolutionary crowds rushing the public stage, and overwhelming all institutional/ juridical safeguards. Instead it lies with the more durable, passive, know-nothing majorities who, in their desire to pursue their private affairs unhindered, call for increased security and public order. Rather than a source of disruptive political acts, the 'people' now appear as a source of depoliticization resulting from the fear of disruption occasioned by poten-tial conflicts (1992, p. 812; 1961, II, p. 352). As such, the people become the alibi for a new authoritarianism whereby the state, in the name of public tranquillity, extends its iron, if paternalist, grip over an increasingly passive and dependent population. Beware of political leaders who speak in the name of the people; they would use the desire to be left free to pursue one's interests in the social domain to pursue authoritarian projects in the political domain. The appeal to a rich associational life must be understood as an attempt to prevent the potential hiatus between the social and political by the introduction of concrete, institutional mediations. As an education in, and expression of, the manifold, particularistic character of collective life, associations would loosen the hold of the imaginary general other while giving flesh to the promise of democratic participation.

Tocqueville's discussion of the rule of the general other is not without its weaknesses, from both the perspective of his time and our own. There is, to begin with, the failure to consider that the division between the particular individual self and the abstract general other gives rise not just to excessive conformity, but also to resistance to such conformity. One can imagine different versions of such resistance: for example, a 'Protestant' version (where the general other within, in the form of individual con-science, is seen as more 'universal' than the general other without presented by public *doxa*), or a Romantic version (where the concrete universal associated with the spontaneity and creativity of the "deep self" is deemed superior to a shallow, artificial 'social self'). However expressed, the point remains: the division between self and other resulting from their '*semblance*' is as much the grounds for the rejection of social domination as its source. Thus the division that establishes the figure of the general other also ensures that its ascendancy remains incomplete. Failing to see this, Tocqueville makes claims that appear at best premature, and by the 1850s simply false – notably the claims that Americans are, as a result of conformist pressures, incapable of original thinking, great literature and other national achievements (1992, p. 294; 1961, I, p. 312).[21]

From the perspective of the present there is another problem, one that can serve to introduce the next section. It is no surprise that, when Tocqueville speaks of the people, he has in mind the nation-state, and a relatively homogeneous one at that. If democracy constructs citizens as *semblables*, the implication is that those who are not citizens are clearly not similar. There can be no totalized, even reified image of Americans as a body of *semblables* without the specification of borders, whether in terms of geography, politics, language, race or other markers. Yet the idea of democratic equality troubles the distinction between self and other, similarity and difference. In effect, equality erases certain differences, notably the stable, hierarchical differences between self and other of the *ancien regime*, while reintroducing others, including those consequent to the division between the abstraction of the self and the abstraction of the other. What I want to argue now is that, under the sign of the *semblable*, the very character of difference is potentially destabilized. It is not a matter of some differences being more salient and, therefore, more resistant than others. The problem is that it is not clear what is to count as a difference. With democratic equality, the distinction between the similar and the different can lose its clarity, such that the signs of difference become more arbitrary and volatile. This is particularly true today, when the self-evidence of the nation-state has begun to fade, whether because of increasing internal diversity or the increased weight of external influences. In such a context acts of citizenship take on a changed significance. They are less likely to be foundational acts constitutive of communities of *semblables*. Nor are they likely to be acts that confirm the citizens' *semblance* in the face of their evident differences. Acts of citizenship must be, above all else, acts between citizens and non-citizens (or not-yet-full-citizens), that is, acts in view of those who, while deeming themselves different, seek to establish the lineaments of a common space in order to put their similarity and difference to the test.

Similarity and Difference

This is not the situation of Tocqueville's nineteenth-century American. He knows who his fellow-citizen is, that person being someone much like himself. And he knows that those with whom he does not share citizenship are not like him. Most of these live in other countries and belong to other polities, notably those not dedicated to the idea of natural liberty. In this regard, Tocqueville describes how Americans become fast friends abroad when they would have ignored each other at home (1992, pp. 681–4; 1961, II, pp. 201–3).[22] There are also those who live in the United States, but whose *dissemblance* marks them out as less than full citizens. Here the discussion of the 'three races' in the last chapter of the first volume is essential. This chapter, it has been said, does not really belong to the tome, as its subject matter appears contrary to the principles at the heart of the idea of democracy.[23] Yet a careful reading suggests that the condition of the 'inferior' races in the United States cannot be fully understood if one fails to consider the country's democratic character. Thus, while slavery certainly suggests the inequalities of an aristocratic society, when slavery does exist in a democracy, all similarities must be denied the slaves who, by a mark of nature, are relegated to the rank of sub-humans. This makes American slavery much worse than ancient slavery; for the latter could accept the existence of skilled, educated or even intellectually superior slaves, and could permit, even encourage, manumission (1992, pp. 395–6; 1961, I, pp. 424–5). Moreover, racism, in Tocqueville's view, will not disappear with the end of slavery. Although no longer written into law, racial prejudice will remain, becoming all the more intractable as it settles into the thickets of social *moeurs*. One might say that racism is contrary to the principles of democratic equality, but where it exists, it is overdetermined by democracy.

In certain respects, Tocqueville's discussion of America's treatment of its native population is even more ambiguous. Here, arguably, democratic principles are never systematically violated. Indeed, Tocqueville suggests that if there is inequality, much of the blame lies on the other side.[24] For he views Amerindian males as primitive aristocrats not unlike the ancient Franks, who, with their love of war and disdain for field work, resist the white man's ways out of a sense of pride. As for the attitude of Americans to the Amerindians, once the latter no longer pose a direct physical threat, that attitude is marked by, above all, indifference. The abstraction of the self insulates the American settler from life-changing involvement with the native population; there is little cultural hybridization, even fewer 'go native'.[25] Tocqueville speaks of genocide, but it is less the result of violence or disease than neglect and greed. An egalitarian society cannot, without denying its principles, incorporate a subject population through its explicit subordination, which would imply its exploitation but also, potentially, its protection. Thus the American government, rather than seeking a subordinate niche within society, moves the population to reserves where they can largely be ignored. Meanwhile, the local settler population resents even the most minimal resources being reserved for these others, preferring, often in opposition to the government, to engage in individual competition with the Amerindian population, though the latter are hardly in a position to compete on equal terms. This is all the more the case as the minimal solidarity between the two populations, necessary to keep such competition within the limits of the law, is lacking. In effect, assimilation proves imperative yet impossible, resulting in marginalization and degradation, with Amerindians stigmatized less for their communal difference than their individual failings. They are, it would seem, *semblables manqués*, and the indifference that attends this population appears an extension of a more general indifference at the heart of the modern democratic imaginary.

There is something paradigmatic about this description, which one is tempted to extend far beyond this particular case. Any such extrapolation, however, supposes that Tocqueville be moved forward, beyond the nineteenth century, and beyond the America of the 'three races'. One imagines a world where the presence of ascribed differences appears less salient than the absence of assumed similarities, where difference becomes the marker of an individual rather than a collective fate, though still often associated with marginalization, disassociation and invisibility (if not domination, subordination and exploitation). One imagines an acceleration of mobilities such that the distinctions between the similar and different, self and other, are destabilized and volatilized, causing durable, particularistic identities to give way to a moveable juxtaposition of hyphens subject to both instrumentalization and sentimentalization. One conceives of a world where the language of the nation-state has lost much of its purchase, such that political borders appear increasingly arbitrary, though sub-political frontiers proliferate. One posits a world where most people, contrary to Karl Schmitt, appear as neither friends nor enemies, but as objects of well-intentioned indifference. Such a world may well not exist. Still it has a name – the network society – and, with its name, a semblance of reality. The network society is often presented as an extension of democracy, though its relation to politics and political institutions is ambiguous. It is as if one could picture democracy emancipated from the fetters of its institutionalization within a *polis*, thereby allowing the individual's course of activity to expand to the entire world, if not beyond. As these themes find echoes in Tocqueville's characterization of democracy in America, it may be worth examining, however briefly, the implications of the network society by drawing on the theoretical resources he provides.

The very idea of networks is suggestive of something central to modern democracy; the practice of voluntary association. But networks are not associations. [26] An association implies the establishment of a group for some purpose and, in view of the realization of that purpose, the establishment of a certain institutional consistency as given by the creation of member-ships, rules, positions and similar features. Networks have neither goals nor the institutional coherence required for their realization – which is not to say that individuals do not have goals when connecting to networks. One could say that networks adopt the principle of voluntary association, but from the perspective of the individual alone; or, alternatively, that networks sought to supersede associations by becoming better adapted to the exigencies of dissociation demanded by increased individual mobility. The contrast can be rendered even starker if one compares networks with the 'association' constitutive of the democratic polity (which, admittedly, is not really an association except in the minds of contractualists). The modern democratic polity supposes one has a common relation with all those within a delimited territory, that is, with all one's 'neighbours', most of whom one does not, and cannot, know personally. Networks, by contrast, do not require neighbours, even as one generally knows, if only minimally, those with whom one networks. In this respect, networks may appear more concrete, though they suppose and extend the abstractions of self and other linked to the rise of the social. Networks may also appear, this time with greater credibility, more voluntary. After all, in a democratic polity, one does not choose with whom one associates; one chooses the rules under which one associates. In networks one chooses one's associates, and one can choose to dissociate with them, even as the rules become far more elastic. This, to be sure, is a way of saying that networks do not require a notion of public space, however much they may promote continuous, unrestricted free speech. Network speech is neither strictly private nor strictly public, but inhabits a sort of in-between zone where it is possible to ensure that what is most audible is what one most wants to hear. This last point suggests that networks still involve *semblables*. One networks with those whose interests are similar or, at least, comple-mentary to one's own; and to the extent that networks appear indefinitely expandable, one assumes, somewhat narcissistically, that there exist indefinite numbers of people like oneself with whom one can network. Nonetheless, the *semblable* of the network is not the *semblable* of the democratic polity. The latter refers to some notion of the 'people' under-stood as a bounded whole that exceeds its individual parts. With networks the image of the people dissolves, the *semblable* of the network suggesting not a circumscribed political space, but an indefinite, deterritorialized seriality of persons with whom one may choose to connect or disconnect. As a consequence, the generalized other is less likely to appear as a single, unified abstraction, and so loses the sharp edges of its externality. As such, the division between self and similar other loses much of its conflictuality; there is no longer the same pressure to conform or, alternatively, to resist conforming. The network does not face the self as an external projection before which it feels powerless; instead the network appears as a field for the indefinite expansion of the self's initiatives. If the self does feel powerless, it is not because it is crushed by the network's presence, but because it feels disconnected without that presence. In this sense, networks appear as the very metaphor of a new mobility, at once geographical and social, real and virtual, in a world that appear ever more compressed and unsettled. No wonder that the network society is proclaimed an enlargement of democracy, but an enlargement that occurs, precisely, outside the framework of a *polis*. It is, in effect, a new figure of a *démocratie sauvage*, one that seamlessly combines association with dissociation, and one better suited to post-modern conurbations than to Tocqueville's 'deserts'.

Still, the question of the other in her difference remains. One may be similar to those with whom one networks, but one is not certain how similar: probably not enough to identify with them, particularly if one belongs to multiple networks that overlap at only a few nodal points. The other may be one's *semblable*, but the terms of semblance appear much weakened. And what about all those others with whom one does not network, or no longer networks? Are they similar or different? And how is one to know? When there are no durable, *a priori* solidarities, boundaries dissolve, leaving the markers that distinguish the similar from the different more uncertain and mobile. Most people, most of the time, one suspects, will project a weak sense of semblance onto these unknown, indefinite others. In this manner, those outside the network can slip comfortably beneath the radar screens of concern, enabling benign neglect to appear as a form of tolerance. If, however, for one reason or another they cannot be ignored, if, for example, they should appear to represent a threat, weak semblances are liable to mutate into glaring differences. The problem is that, without concrete interactions, the representation of these differences cannot be subjected to reality testing, and may instead become the object of considerable imaginary elaboration. This is all the more likely where the networks, as is their wont, seek only to confirm their own voices; where there are no clear markers for the identification of difference; and where there is no common space for negotiating differends. The threat represented by difference will be presented, one expects, as a threat to democracy, understood less as a threat to a determinate set of political institutions than to 'our values' or 'way of life'. Where the threat appears as an unexpected shock and what is threatened as highly nebulous, the characterization of the difference will prove highly elastic, easily becoming an uncontainable, totalized figure of alterity. One can even envisage an infernal cycle between self and other where indifference based on an imagined sameness alternates with an imaginary threat based on irredeemable difference. And where this latter threat cannot but appear, in the absence of political mechanisms for parleying with difference, as sheer, inexplicable violence.[27]

Cautionary Notes for an Ambiguous Conclusion

Before one begins to panic, it might be prudent to take a few steps back, and recover something of the equivocation of Tocqueville's original text. This essay has argued that the status or habitus of citizenship supposes the rise of the social. But the social itself cannot be identified with an order, or discrete set of practices or institutions; it appears instead as an onto-logical rather than an ontic category. In this regard, the social's difference with Bourdieu's habitus must be underlined: it does not mediate between position (structure) and position-taking (agency), but precedes both position and position-taking, status and practice. The social certainly entails a disposition, a democratic as opposed to a hierarchical disposition, with all that that implies. As a democratically oriented ontological disposition, the social need not, in principle, be any more exclusive of the dynamics of citizenship as an act, than of the statics of citizenship as a status. Compared to the hierarchical disposition towards stable positionalities, the mobile restlessness of the social can encompass a penchant for, as well as an aversion to, the act. One might even wish to claim that the ontological character of the social prepares the way for the ontological character of the act that the introductory essay of this volume seeks to establish.

In its link to democracy, the social remains, despite appearances, tied to the political understood in its broadest sense. As the introduction of individual self-rule, the social doubles the rule of everyone with the rule of nobody. In consequence, the relation of the social to the political proves quite complex. The social anchors the political in a way that permits a new opening and, at the same time, a new closure of the political. This essay has focused on the closure, i.e. the capacity of modern democracies to seemingly ignore the verticality of relations of rule. Acts of citizenship, by contrast, speak to the opening; for such acts must, by definition, move beyond the social to become explicitly political. Even more significantly as regards this opening, acts of citizenship do not just focus on relations of rule, they question such relations in the name of a common justice. Nonetheless, they also suppose the social; for the apparent ontological solidity of the latter ensures that divisive and disruptive political acts do not appear to threaten the bonds that hold society together. Because of the presence of the social, acts of citizenship need not refer to fundamental, foundational acts, and so can appear tentative, incomplete and, therefore, answerable. In this manner, these acts are able to break with existing practices without implying a revolutionary *tabula rasa*. This is not to say that such acts involve politics as usual. Acts of citizenship demand an opening to the difference of others, whereas normal politics supposes that the protagonists are sufficiently similar that a common belonging is a given. The question that must be posed then, concerns the democratic individual's capacity to welcome difference.

The word that perhaps best describes the relation between democratic selves, as described in this chapter, is indifference. This word, I would suggest, can be used in two, different senses. In the first, more common sense, indifference would refer to the closure of the political, for it blunts the summons of the call of conscience that is at the heart of acts of citizenship. In the second sense, indifference would be neither opened nor closed to such acts, for it would lie between semblance and difference, poised to move in either or both directions.[28] If we are to imagine another democracy, one that is both radical and domesticated, we must become sensitive to the undecidability of this opposition. And here the democratic self is not without resources. Because abstracted from its contextual particulars, its sense of self need not feel threatened when faced with different others (as would be the case in an 'aristocratic society' when these others cannot be fitted into the existing hierarchical framework). And when the sense of self feels relatively secure, it will not feel constrained to deny or demonize differences, particularly those that have yet to be codified within an existing world of sense. In other words, the abstraction of the self can prove favourable to the acceptance of others in their difference, particularly when that self is willing to suspend any final claim as to the significance of that difference. And this may be all the more likely to occur if the self feels its own difference relative to its purported *semblables*, and struggles to come to terms with the sense of this difference. In this case, the difference of the self can resonate with the difference of the other in a way that encourages the simultaneous exploration of the significance of both differences. This, of course, will not occur without an actual encounter with the other as an equal. There must be a genuine engagement of self and other if they are to become answerable to each other across their differences. Such an engagement would produce a commonality in difference, a shared, dialogic space where the differences of self and of other would be summoned, relativized and reconfigured. One might call this an association of *dissemblables*.

This idea of an association of *dissemblables*, as it cuts across the social into the political, can help clarify what might be meant by 'acts of citizenship'. By speaking of an association of *dissemblables*, one would not only oppose the tendencies of normal politics to ignore difference; on those occasions when difference cannot be ignored, one would counter its characterization as an absolute difference, that is, as a difference so radical that all communication necessarily appears barred (a characterization that is often the projection of one's own closure onto the other). With an association of *dissemblables,* all differences would be deemed relative, and their significance would be revealed only in the course of the interaction, and then only tentatively. Differences would be returned, in effect, to a world of concrete engagements, where their imaginary elaboration could be controlled, their ethical potential explored, and their implications communicated. Through their differences, self and other would be made answerable to, and ultimately responsible for, each other.

As an association with those excluded from the normal circuits constitutive of the status of citizenship, acts of citizenship cross and contest borders. Where borders are weakened and differences proliferate, such acts will prove both more likely and more necessary. At the same time, such acts, even as they cross borders, cannot but institute the durable relations that constitute a delimited public space – which is to say that acts of citizenship bear the risks of instituting new borders, however porous. One should not confuse acts of citizenship with the complacent tolerance of an abstract cosmopolitanism. An act always involves specific others and specific contexts, which is to say that decisions have to be made as regards which set of strangers, aliens or outcasts to associate with, and according to what criteria. Acts of citizenship are born of choices (including, first of all, the choice to choose); but these are not arbitrary choices, as they entail the establishment of a horizon of justice. And since justice implies the institution of a common terrain, one such criterion must concern the other's proximity, as it results from a shared geography and history, however difficult or contested. Justice, however, extends beyond the proximate other, even as the other may be made proximate by the choice to associate. Moreover, the movement need not be in only one direction. Acts of citizenship still have to bear the burdens of modern democracy. The others with whom one wishes to associate still have the right to preserve not just their difference, but also their distance, whether through the terms of their representations or, more simply, through an act, always possible, of dissociation.

Notes

1 Relations of rule should be based on justice; unjust rules, however, are still political. This is not to say that the is and the ought are divided, but that their conjoining can only be made from within particular relations of rule.

2 This was very much noted at the time. 'But the word [democracy] is going to take on … a new meaning. It is going to designate a modern, egalitarian society, and no longer the political regime associated with the Greeks or Roman republics, or with the idea of the direct intervention of the people in public affairs. The semantic turning point

is consecrated when, in 1835, Tocqueville publishes the first of part of *Democracy in America*' (Rosanvallon 2000, p. 117) (my translation).

3   Tocqueville gives an example of the preamble to such a contract:

> Do by these presents solemnly and mutually, in the presence of God and one another, covenant and combine ourselves together into a civil body politick, for our better ordering and preservation, and furtherance of the ends aforesaid: and by virtue hereof do enact, constitute and frame such just and equal laws, ordinances, acts, constitutions, and officers, from time to time, as shall be thought most meet and convenient for the general good of the Colony: unto which we promise all due submission and obedience... (1992, p. 38; 1961, 1, p. 22)

All page references to *Democracy in America* are first to the Pléiade edition of the *Oeuvres* (1992) and then to the English translation in two volumes (1961).

4   His first reaction to the frontier can be found in the essay 'Quinze jours dans le désert', posthumously published by Gustave de Beaumont (who accompanied Tocqueville on his American adventures) in 1861, and republished in English as a 'Fortnight in the Wilderness'. In the latter Tocqueville writes:

> I had observed that in Europe, the more or less isolated a province or a town, its wealth or poverty, its smallness or its extent, exerted an immense influence upon the ideas, manners, the entire civilization if its inhabitants and often made the difference of several centuries between various parts of the same area. I had imagined that it would be like that in the New World, even more so, and that a country only partially populated in America ought to present all of the conditions of existence and ought to offer an image of society in all its ages... Nothing is true in this picture. Of all the countries in the world America is the least appropriate to furnish the spectacle I was seeking. In America, even more than in Europe, there is only one society. (Tocqueville 1962, pp. 346–7)

5   The United States may be unique in not associating democracy with cities. Certainly there is a long tradition that expresses the American ambivalence to cities, if not to small towns. (White and White 1964) Nonetheless, even if it is true that Americans have a preference for living in relatively homogeneous suburbs, with maximal distance between themselves and their neighbours, one must not exaggerate the American prejudice against cities. Modern cities are neither ancient city-states nor medieval communes, and the critique of the 'moral corruption' of large urban conglomerations is hardly unique to the United States.

6   In the townships 'selectmen' are rotated by lot (1992, p. 68; 1961, 1, p. 57). It should be noted that, for Tocqueville, the townships are the 'base' of the original American democracy, the federal and, even, state levels being something of a later, superstructural add-on.

7   For reasons that will become evident, Tocqueville considers the ancient democracies, as well as England, to be essentially aristocratic.

8   Such continuous restlessness may even drive Americans insane (1992, p. 651; 1961, II, pp. 164–5).

9   'The inhabitants exercise no sort of control over their fellow-citizens, for they are scarcely acquainted with each other' (1992, p. 357; 1961, 1, p. 382).

10 In this regard, associations, both political and civil, must be seen, in part, as the second volume's replacement for the township democracies of the first volume.

11 To carry forward the parallel with Heidegger in the claim that the social is an ontological and not an ontic category, one could say that it entails both association and dissociation in the way that Being supposes both presence and absence, revealing and concealing.

12 Louis Dumont acknowledges Tocqueville and his significance for comprehending 'the egalitarian ideology of modern men' (Dumont 1980, p. xlviii).

13 When faced with the first signs of the industrial revolution, he asks whether the industrial capitalists will constitute a new aristocracy, and answers with a qualified 'no' – despite his claim that the wealth, economic power and general callousness of the industrialist far exceeds that of the *ancien* aristocrat (1992, pp. 671–3; 1961, II, pp. 190–4).

14 Tocqueville does speak of equality as a fact, a 'providential fact', by which he means the movement to equality is historically ineluctable. Sometimes he seems to contrast equality as a fact to freedom as an idea, by which he implies that freedom has no history: it has appeared in the past and can appear in the present, but its appearance remains fundamentally contingent. This argument has little bearing on the one being made here: the providential fact being that the idea of equality is spreading, not that life conditions are becoming increasingly similar. Note that the distinction between equality and freedom, as a difference between fact and idea, cannot be sustained within the text. See 'From Equality to Freedom. Fragments of an Interpretation of *Democracy in America*' (Lefort 1988, pp.183–209).

15 'Identification' is in quotes because the servant does not 'identify' with his master in the sense that he sees himself as the master. Nonetheless, he cannot see himself independent of the master, even as the master sees the servant as an extension of himself. (1992, pp. 690–9; 1961, II, pp. 211–21)

16 These four realms, for Tocqueville, necessarily entail relations of subordination. He thus calls on family, religion and law to counter the tendencies of '*la démocratie sauvage*'. Consequently, he tends not to see (and would, no doubt have deplored) the egalitarian tendencies at work in these spheres.

17 Mead, of course, understood the generalized other as necessarily present in all societies; whereas here the suggestion is that it is unique to democratic societies. In aristocratic societies the identification of the self passes through an identification with a particular (read: superior) other, which implies, to repeat, not simply an internalization of the other within the self, but an externalization of the self within the other (who views the inferior other as a sort of personal appendage) (Mead 1934).

18 For Tocqueville, Americans have always been democratic, even before they reached America.

19 In hierarchical societies, one only acquires a subject position – or a subject position worth having – through an act of consecration. The act, as it were, precedes the status, but only because status proceeds from a higher being. Acts of citizenship, by contrast, would give precedence to the act in its immanence.

20 In the context of the United States, mob rule appears less as a revolutionary act that disrupts a settled institutional order, than the defence of an existing order that cannot openly admit its very real inequalities (almost all the examples involve the defence of the colour line). In other words, the tyranny of the majority emerges in the disjunction between the 'people' defined strictly according to universalist, democratic principles, and the 'people' understood in more particularist terms as *semblables*.

21   In truth, in the first part of the second volume, while still commenting on the difficulty of independent thinking in America, he does allow for the independent growth of literature and the arts, and even the emergence of 'speculative genius'. The cause is the increasing leisure that comes with growing prosperity; no consideration is given to the presence of a general other that was supposed to prevent such developments.

22   The contrast is with Englishmen who cannot drop the claims of class and, when faced with fellow nationals abroad, must affirm the distance that class implies.

23   Sheldon Wolin claims that the book is not called *American Democracy* but *Democracy in America* because the ideal of democracy in America must be separated from America's reality. In his view, this last chapter is a concession to reality and, therefore, forms a sort of postscript (Wolin 2001, p. 266).

24   'The lot of the Negro is placed on the extreme limit of servitude, while that of the Indian lies on the uttermost verge of liberty; and slavery does not produce more fatal effects upon the first, than independence upon the second' (1992, p. 370; 1961, I, pp. 396–7).

25   Historically what were called 'mountain men', who did intermarry with the native population, tended to be *canadiens*. Those who were taken hostage by Amerindian war parties and then integrated into the communal life of their captors were considered 'worse than dead' (1992, p. 383; 1961, I, p. 411).

26   In truth, Tocqueville comes close to discussing networks when he discusses 'private circles' (and *not* associations): 'in democracies [men] are divided by a number of small and almost invisible threads, which are constantly broken or moved from place to place' (1992, p. 731; 1961, II, p. 258).

27   'The struggle against terrorism will perhaps be the founding myth of our depoliticized postmodernity!' (Freitag 2002, p. 188)

28   For Tocqueville, the movement is clearly towards semblance, in part because he equates semblance with equality, a debatable claim. But also in part because he is examining the United States, with its relative absence of class differences, itself the consequence of the relative absence of the hierarchical residues that fuel both revolutionary and counter-revolutionary forces (Gauchet 2005).

References

Arendt, H. (1958) *The Human Condition*, University of Chicago Press, Chicago, IL.

Blackell, M. (2004) 'Symptoms of Democracy: Ambivalence and Its Limits in Modern Liberal Conceptions of the Political', unpublished PhD thesis, York University, Canada.

Castoriadis, C. (1987) *The Imaginary Institution of Society*, MIT Press, Cambridge, MA.

Dumont, L. (1980) *Homo Hierarchicus*, Chicago University Press, Chicago, IL.

Freitag, M. (2002) 'The Dissolution of Society within the "Social"', *European Journal of Social Theory*, 5 (2) (May).

Gauchet, M. (2005) 'Tocqueville, l'Amérique et nous. Sur la genèse des sociétés démocratiques' in *La condition politique*, Gallimard, Paris.

Lefort, C. (1988) *Democracy and Political Theory*, Polity Press, Cambridge.

Manent, P. (1996) *Tocqueville and the Nature of Democracy*, Rowman and Littlefield, Lanham, Maryland, MD.

Mead, G. H. (1934) *Mind, Self and Society*, University of Chicago Press, Chicago, IL.

Montesquieu, Baron C. de (1989) *The Spirit of the Laws*, Cambridge University Press, Cambridge.

Rosanvallon, P. (2000) *La démocratie inachevée. Histoire de la souveraineté du peuple en France*, Gallimard, Paris.

Singer, B. C. J. (1996) 'Cultural versus Contractual Nations: Rethinking their Opposition', *History and Theory*, 35 (3).

Tocqueville, A. de (1961) *Democracy in America*, 2 vols, Schocken, New York.

—— (1962) *Journey to America*, Yale University Press, New Haven, CT.

—— (1992) *Oeuvres*, Vol. 2, Gallimard, Paris.

White, M. and L. White (1964) *The Intellectual versus the City*, Mentor Books, New York.

Wolin, S. (2001) *Tocqueville between Two Worlds: The Making of a Political and Theoretical Life*, Princeton University Press, Princeton, NJ.

Chapter 5

❖

Acts of Piety:
The Political and the Religious,
or a Tale of Two Cities

BRYAN S. TURNER

The analysis of 'the political' in recent years has been significantly influenced by the re-evaluation of the political philosophy of Carl Schmitt who in *The Concept of the Political* (1996) placed sovereignty at the core of any inquiry into the nature of politics. The idea of the political as the power to declare a state of emergency is contrasted with politics, namely the humdrum activities of political parties, elections and lobby groups. We can see this Schmittian influence in the work of Giorgio Agamben, for example, who in *Homo Sacer* (1998) explored the relationship between sovereignty as the power to declare an emergency and the distinction, derived from Aristotle, between *zoe* or natural life and *bios* or the form of life. When Aristotle said that man is a political animal, he invoked this idea of the *polis* as a form of life in which men could rise above mere nature and construct a city in which sovereign power could be institutionalized. We might also note that this discussion of the political recognizes that politics involves actions – creating cities, forming contracts or debating in the public arena. Politics consists, we might say, in the acts of citizens, especially in terms of creating and participating in the public sphere.

If the definition of the political is in itself a controversial issue, then the definition of the religious is equally contentious. The contribution of Émile Durkheim to this debate is still highly influential. In *The Elementary Forms of Religious Life* in 1912, Durkheim (2001) attempted to avoid the idea that religion consisted primarily in holding to certain beliefs about the world – for example that there is an all powerful God who controls the universe – and sought instead to direct attention to rituals and the emotions that are generated by and attached to ritual activity. Religion consists in ritual activities with respect to sacred objects and the consequence of these ritual acts is the creation of community. Of course, these ritual acts give expression to a conceptual distinction between sacred and profane, but religion as such is best understood in terms of religious actions rather than religious beliefs. These rituals represent beliefs through collective actions and at the same time create collective emotions that contribute to the social glue of communities (Barbalet 1998). Religion consists, we might say, in the acts of people, especially in terms of their participation within the religious sphere. The intensity of these religious experiences has perhaps been diminished in the secular environment of a consumer society in which religious participation becomes part of the choices that individuals make to construct a life style in what Philip Rieff (2006) has called the 'deathworks' of the third world of modern consumerism, but secularization is neither uniform nor universal. Alongside secularization, there are also, as I shall attempt to show, powerful movements of pietization that seek to counter-act the secular.

It is obvious from these introductory comments that I am drawing a close parallel between the idea that the political consists in acts relating to sovereignty and that the religious consists in acts towards the divine. In addition 'politics' in the everyday world finds its parallel in pious acts regarding the everyday practices of religion relating to food, sex and domestic arrangements. These acts take place within given spheres of action and thus for the political actor there is the sphere of 'the city'. One might assume that the sphere of action for the religious is within the Church, the mosque, the *sangha* of Buddhism, or whatever institution functions as the meeting place for religious actors. To make more precise the parallel between the political and the religious, on the one hand, and politics and religiosity, on the other, we might borrow a term from Augustine and argue that the religious is constituted by acts relevant to the sacred that are performed within 'the city of God', namely, that sphere where religious acts are enacted.

This formulation allows us to present an old problem within a some-what more exact theoretical framework in order to ask how the political city relates to the city of God or, in more concrete terms, how acts of piety relate to acts of citizenship. Augustine in this sense provides the classical location for the distinction between acts of piety and acts of politics, since it was Augustine who struggled to make sense of the emerging relationship between the Church and the imperial power of Rome (Atkins and Dodaro 2001). The ambiguities of the relationships between ecclesiastical power and state power remain an unresolved problem of modernity. One para-mount issue in modern politics is that there is a crisis of liberal secularism because the separation of Church and state that was institutionalized by the Treaty of Westphalia in 1648 as the international foundation of the system of nation-states appears to be finally unravelling, and hence the relationship between acts of piety and acts of citizenship is becoming increasingly problematic. In particular the civil space that is present in the Islamic community or *umma* in the context of the global diaspora of Muslims no longer comfortably maps onto the secular space of Western liberal democracy. The liberal solution of private religion may have been compatible with certain Protestant sects but not with many other religions (Spinner-Halev 2005). The city of God appears to be increasingly out of joint with the political city, and this lack of fit encourages us to re-examine and question many of the assumptions that have underpinned the liberal view of the civil sphere as a secular domain (Mufti 2007).

My discussion of acts of piety is partly inspired by Luc Boltanski and Laurent Thevenot's *On Justification* (2006), in which they explore various discourses or 'polities' as they call them by which the worth of a person is measured, and partly by Jeffrey Alexander's *The Civil Sphere* (2006), in which he examines the role of social movements in constituting democratic spaces. *On Justification* considers the many ways in which the worth of a person and hence the different values that might attach to different persons can be justified by moral argument. The most obvious example is an economic model (from the classics of political economy) in which a person's worth is measured in monetary terms. Differences in income might be justified by reference to the contributions people make to society and the length of time they have invested in training (Davis and Moore 1945). But they also recognize an 'inspired polity' in which a person is measured by their religious worth or, to use the language of Christianity, by 'grace'. I propose that we can in principle measure a person's inspirational worth in terms of 'acts of piety', where piety creates a hierarchy of values or grace. Modern religious revivalism in the Abrahamic religions (Judaism, Christianity and Islam) has spelled out a new piety for lay people to counteract unorthodox ways of traditional life and the secular life styles of consumerism in global capitalism. Acts of piety thereby often represent a challenge to the secular world, but also the traditional world of taken-for-granted religiosity. This argument applies to many forms of religious revivalism in modernity (Berger 1999), but in this chapter I shall concentrate primarily on the issue of piety in the Islamic public space.

In order to understand piety as such I employ the anthropological notions of body, practice and disposition that have been so carefully developed in the work of Pierre Bourdieu. Thus a range of concepts relating to the 'logic of practice', habitus and hexis can be redeployed to consider that practical nature of piety (Bourdieu 1990). Acts of piety typically involve bodily practices related to diet, comportment, deportment, bodily discipline and clothing. The worth of a person in the inspirational city is measured by the value of their acts of piety that are expressions of a particular religious habitus.

Finally, individual acts of piety have to be seen and understood within a wider social context and within a deeper historical framework. For example, the modernization of the everyday world (or habitus) in Islam is articulated through acts of piety that create post-traditional life styles – religious or pious life styles that are in competition with tradition, with the secular habitus of other Muslims and with other religious traditions such as Christianity, Buddhism and Hinduism. Acts of piety provide a sense of empowerment as individuals come to take on practices that may cut them off from their traditional environment. As a pious Muslim I may demand a change in office hours in a secular corporation to undertake my daily prayers. There is also what one might call a tendency towards the inflation of religious acts as the pious demonstrate their superior worth within the religious field. The inspirational polity shares important features, in Boltanski and Thevenot's model, with the polity of fame in which reputational value is paramount. This competitive struggle over the price of piety provides an insight into the pietization of women in modern Islam and furthermore helps us to understand why there is a mounting conflict between two cities – the secular and the inspirational. Finally, this competitive struggle over the worth or price of piety brings out an important contradiction in piety, because there is a well-established religious tradition that says that true piety is always hidden. The truly pious do not flaunt their piety just as the genuinely rich do not need to exhibit their wealth – but if piety is hidden from view, how can we measure the worth of the pious?

The Body and Religion

'Piety' is from the Latin *pietas*, or reverence and obedience to God, but it is also associated with pity, as in God showing pity to mankind. It refers, in short, to habitual acts of reverence and obedience, and hence it is the habits or habitus of the pious. In sociological terms, the concept of habitus in the sociology of Bourdieu means the everyday practices that embody a set of dispositions which in turn determine taste, in this case a taste for particular religious beliefs, practices and objects. Bourdieu's book on *Distinction* (1984) was in fact about 'the distinction of taste'. In Bourdieu's notion of social capital, taste is determined by social stratification, producing a hierarchy of preferences (for leisure, for aesthetic objects, consumer goods and life style). A criticism of Bourdieu's understanding of habitus may be appropriate here, because Bourdieu implicitly treats dispositions as relatively stable sets of preferences. The word 'habit' is derived from 'habitus' and hence suggests that our dispositions and tastes are merely routine, whereas an act of piety may involve a radical change of habits. For Bourdieu, the individual is inculcated into a relatively stable habitus and as a result it is not self-evident that Bourdieu's sociology has in fact transcended the dichotomy between structure and agency. In this chapter my argument is that acts of piety do not simply reproduce habits, but rather challenge existing arrangements both secular and religious. For example, the spread of Qur'an reading groups and recitation competitions are not simply institutionalizing a set of traditional assumptions but creating new forms of religious practice that challenge many existing assumptions (Gade 2004). Similarly, when young Muslim women adopt the veil they are not conforming to traditional practice, since their mothers and grandmothers were typically not veiled. In this respect we need to be aware that acts of piety in empowering people characteristically involve some challenge to the existing order or 'city'. In particular, acts of piety are a deliberate challenge to the secular city.

Bourdieu's work is ultimately derived from Aristotle, who was concerned to understand how virtues can be produced in individuals as a result of education, including the training of the body. Hence in Greek culture excellence in the gymnasium was seen to be a foundation for the character of the citizen. The Greek word for 'virtue' in the *Nichomachean Ethics* is *arête* or excellence, in which moral virtue is excellence of character. The habitus of the individual involves what Bourdieu following Aristotle calls a hexis in which bodily dispositions embody values and virtues. This type of argument has been applied recently to Islam, for instance in Saba Mahmood's *Politics of Piety* (2005). Although this discussion might appear to be focused on Western notions of piety and excellence, Mahmood's discussion of Muslim piety shows clearly the interchange between classical Arabic philosophy and Greek culture in which Aristotle is shared mutually by Arab and Greek civilizations – as in the commentaries of Averroes on Aristotle.

Although I have so far couched this debate within exclusively Western terms, we could easily present a parallel set of arguments from the works of Confucius and Mencius. For example, Mencius says:

> That which a gentleman follows as his nature, that is to say benevolence, rightness, the rites and wisdom, is rooted in his heart, and manifests itself in his face, giving it a sleek appearance. It also shows in his back and extends to his limbs, rendering their message intelligible without words. (Lau 2004, Book 7, Part A, paragraph 21)

Mencius belongs to a tradition in which the self is the outcome of a process of self-development and hence it is a tradition which recognized the mutability of character. Both speech and bodily decorum are indicative of an underlying character and hence a set of virtues. Within a cultivated and disciplined self, character is expressed unintentionally through a virtuous disposition. Hence for Mencius a noble character is expressed through the clarity and brightness of their pupils; an obscure look in the pupil conveys the idea of obscurity of character and weakness of virtue (Heng 2002).

The study of pious acts is thus an important aspect of the sociology of religion, because the spread or revival of religion in any social group or society requires some degree of pietization, involving the reform of practices in the everyday world that give otherwise secular activities (eating, sleeping, dressing and so forth) a religious significance. Body and embodiment play an important role in religious belief and practice, and pietization is aimed at excellence or virtue in the practice of religion. Women, in educating and disciplining their children, are critically involved in the intergenerational reproduction of these dispositions. The study of female piety in modern reformist movements is a crucial stage in understanding the modernization of the everyday world by the intensification of religious practice.

Apart from his occasional comments on Islam in the study of Algeria, Bourdieu did not undertake a sociological study of religion as such. His perspective is widely viewed as a valuable approach to theory and research on the body (Shilling 2007). Bourdieu's emphasis on practice and habitus also lends itself conveniently to an appreciation of religion as a social practice. We can define habitus as the ensemble of attitudes, dispositions, and expectations that individuals share as members of a particular social environment, for which he employs the term 'field'. In Bourdieu's terms, taste is not individual, random or unstable, but organized in terms of social positions, practices and institutions. The habitus is an 'acquired system of generative dispositions' (Bourdieu 1977, p. 95) within which individuals think that their preferences are obvious, natural and taken-for-granted. In the everyday world, individuals are not typically reflexive about their dispositions, because

> [w]hen habitus encounters a social world of which it is the product, it is like a 'fish in water': it does not feel the weight of the water and it takes the world about itself for granted… It is because this world has produced me, because it has produced the categories of thought that I apply to it, that it appears to me as self-evident. (Bourdieu and Wacquant 1992, pp. 127–8)

For Bourdieu, tastes and dispositions are clearly related to our embodiment, and things that we forcefully dislike cause us disgust. The seventeenth-century notion of disgust as an offence to our sensibilities connects this feeling of repugnance with actual nausea.

Habitus and embodiment are obviously interconnected, because 'the way people treat their bodies reveals the deepest dispositions of the habitus' (Bourdieu 1984, p. 190). Our bodies express the habitus of the field in which they are located: in his famous study of the French status systems, Bourdieu showed that social differences in preferences for sports were related to different social classes, and that these social classes express different 'preferences' for body weight, shape and disposition. Whereas weightlifting and the cultivation of powerful bodies are part of the working-class habitus, badminton and tennis are more closely associated with the dispositions of the educated middle and upper classes. In *Distinction* (p. 190) there are important connections between social class, preferences for food and body shape, because '[t]aste in food also depends on the idea each class has of the body and of the effects of food on the body, that is, on its strength, health and beauty; and on the categories it uses to evaluate these effects, some of which may be important for one class and ignored by another, and which the different classes may rank in different ways'. Because different bodies (strong and squat, lithe and athletic, or voluptuous and sexual) have different aesthetic values in their social fields, we can distinguish between the physical and symbolic capital of bodies. Bourdieu identified social capital (the social relations in which people invest), cultural capital (educational qualifications) and symbolic capital (honour and prestige), but the human body is also part of the capital to which human beings ascribe values.

The physical and symbolic capital of the body necessarily stand in a contradictory relationship. Sporting and dancing careers can be understood in terms of these contradictory pressures, where retired celebrities can retain their symbolic capital by becoming stars in related or adjacent fields, for example on TV or in films. Bourdieu's work has been particularly useful in the study of sporting bodies: can we deploy his work with equal success to think of the religious body as one where pious practices or investments have produced graceful outcomes? The habitus of elite religiosity generates dispositions or tastes towards the body that establish norms of propriety, gracefulness and spirituality that can be thought to embody charisma as a manifestation of orthodoxy or authenticity within the field of competing definitions, legacies and causes. These graceful enactments are the work of lengthy training, education and practice, and hence can be contrasted with the practical religiosity of the populace who do not fully understand and therefore cannot artfully practice religious acts. The mass are impious because their *doxa* is, for one thing, contaminated by syncretism.

Justification and the City

To understand acts of piety and acts of citizenship it is important to understand the changes that have transformed modern capitalism. One place to start our examination of these transformations is with a major analysis of modern society: *The New Spirit of Capitalism* by Luc Boltanski and Eve Chiapello (2006). In order to grasp the point of their study, one has to take note of the special vocabulary that has been invented by Boltanski and his colleagues over several decades. This new vocabulary expresses the view that critical social science – especially critical theory inspired by Marxism – has been in decline since the social effervescence of May 1968. Boltanski, Thévenot, Chiapello and others want to reinvent a post-Marxist critical theory in which a sociological critique of society engages with the great variety of public debates that also challenge social institutions, and as a result demand some justification of power. This approach means that sociologists need to take seriously what social actors themselves have to say about society and their place in it, and also to pay attention to how their agency is manifest in social change. For example Boltanski and Chiapello are particularly interested in the role of indignation in social movements. They argue that 'indignation emerges in historically situated forms, while doubtless being rooted in anthropologies that possess very general validity. Forms of indignation may be regarded as emotional expressions of a meta-ethical anchorage, and concern infringements that are believed, at least implicitly, to affect people's possibilities of realizing their humanity' (p. 491).

Boltanski and Chiapello want a sociology of action and justification in which agency is given its full recognition and in which actors are seen to be knowledgeable and capable of bringing about change through protest, action and debate. Their emphasis on agency and justice leads them to describe public order in terms of confrontations between different orders of value. Their analysis of the public sphere attempts to steer a course between conceptualizing society as an endless arena of violence, power struggles and confrontation (Nietzsche, Marx, Foucault and Bourdieu) and a contractual and consensual vision of social order (Rawls, Habermas and the communitarians). Boltanski and Chiapello wish to avoid the idea that justification is merely an ideological superstructure, since, for them, justification also exerts constraints on industrial capitalism that limit the impact of alienation and exploitation. Boltanksi, Thévenot and Chiapello share with Durkheim, Parsons and Habermas a recognition of the importance of social norms in both constraining and justifying social action, but they do not assume that actual capitalist societies are built on a stable value consensus. On the contrary, the public sphere is seen as one of endless debate between different orders of value. They are specifically concerned with disagreements over values and thus develop the idea of six logics of justification that they call 'cities' or political communities, namely the inspirational city, the domestic city, the reputational city, the civic city, the commercial city and the industrial city (pp. 23–4). To this list they add their own interpretation of the modern political community, namely the network city.

Each city has been the topic of classical political and social theories: thus, for example, Rousseau was the philosopher of the civic city and Saint-Simon of the nineteenth-century industrial city. Each city needs to find a balance between the principle of a common humanity and the existence of pluralistic values and interests. This superior principle creates a hierarchy of values involving an order of greatness or *grandeur*. The order of greatness in the inspirational city was sanctity; in the industrial city it was inventiveness and expertise. Disputes between values result in the creation of tests to settle disputes. These tests often fail, because there is no agreement on a common principle and people in the network city can always appeal to other earlier cities – such as sanctity as a principle of conflict resolution. However, while disagreements are not easily resolved, they also open up the possibility of critique.

The New Spirit of Capitalism can be criticized on empirical grounds for what it does not say about modern capitalism. However, these empirical gaps in the book's account of French society may only serve to reinforce the vitality of its theoretical framework. For example, as class membership and identification have declined, so religio-ethnic identity has become far more salient in the public domain. Public contestations over identity, ethnicity, citizenship, race and religion, Islamism and *laicite* spilt onto the streets of Paris suburbs in a dramatic fashion in 2006, and yet there are no references to ethnicity or religion in their study of French society. Why is ethnicity not part of their analysis of the exclusionary regimes of advanced capitalism? In part this is because they do not have enough to say about globalization and hence do not consider the presence of diasporic communities within the network city. The European Union has become heavily dependent on global labour migration and hence Europe is confronted by the problem of how to manage multicultural civil societies. Despite their concern with exclusion and justification, they say relatively little about the ethnic composition of the labour force in modern societies. The justification of exclusion on the basis of ethnicity and indignation against racism ought to be an important part of their analysis.

In modern Europe, multiculturalism has become a polite way of describing 'the management of religious diversity' and 'coping with religious differences' in fact means simply 'the management of Muslims'. France of course could be said to have been at the coalface of the problem, given the state's problematic response to the 'headscarf affair'. Critical sociology and Marxism were in retrospect notorious for their neglect of religion, which was seen as either an ideology of pre-capitalist societies or a superstition that would, in the face of scientific knowledge, wither away. Although Boltanski and Chiapello want to distance themselves from Marxist materialism and Max Weber's relativism, it is interesting that they also fail to engage with the issue of religion in modernity. They want to draw a parallel between Weber's spirit of capitalism and their new spirit of capitalism, but the difference is that Weber took religion very seriously, albeit from the standpoint of Kantian post-Christian ethics.

The problem for secular states with religious fundamentalism (in Judaism, Christianity and Islam) is that it wants to draw its values from the inspirational cities of Jerusalem and Mecca rather than Athens and Rome, from the holy city rather than from network society, and hence it is difficult to resolve value disputes in modern society by a test that could be mutually acceptable (Orr 1995). Therefore, civil society remains unstable. The debate is especially acute in France given the legacy of republican secularism and the cultural dominance of the Catholic Church against the alternative voices of reformist Islam which owe more to Sayyid Qutb and Ayatollah Ruhollah Khomeini than to Saint Simon, Rousseau and Condorcet. Although a conceptual analysis of capitalism does not require any empirical reference to Islam, any discussion of regimes of justification in modern Europe can hardly avoid it. Can any study of indignation and justice avoid the social movements that have coalesced around women, domesticity and the labour market, or around ethnicity, exclusion and housing, or around religion, dignity and national values? France has been virtually the European social laboratory for such contestations of value.

It is interesting to compare *The New Spirit of Capitalism* with another major work on the civil sphere: Jeffrey C. Alexander's *The Civil Sphere* (2006). Alexander shares with Boltanski and Chiapello the view that civil society is a secular city, and as a consequence these critical studies of modern society have little to say about the challenge of Islam to Western liberal views of the public sphere – and yet reformist Islam is a significant challenge to liberal theories of multiculturalism and secularism. I am not here referring to something that we call 'fundamentalism' or worse still 'political Islam'. My reference is to the broad movement of Islamic reform and development involving, for instance, the Islamization of law in Malaysia, recognition of Islam in Turkish public life, the growth of Qur'an reading groups in Indonesia and Bangladesh, and the peaceful demand to wear headscarves in French schools: this movement calls for a recognition of Islam as itself a public sphere, but a sphere that is not necessarily compatible with secularism. In this situation, acts of piety – such as adopting the veil – is a disruptive act that questions the underlying assumptions of republican secularism. The veil explicitly recognizes the prior exclusion of the migrant and the underclass from mainstream French society.

Rituals of Intimacy in South-east Asia

Although Islam is now connected, at least in the Western press, with the idea of political Islam and violent opposition to the West, these journalistic ideas overlook or ignore the fact that Islam has been undergoing a peaceful *jihad* of renewal that is better known as *da'wah* or Islamic outreach (Lukens–Bull 2005). These peaceful movements typically involve some degree of pietization in which the ordinary lives of Muslims are increasingly brought within a framework of devotion and pious practice. Renewal and the methodical development of correct practice involves the development of religious virtue or habitus. In *Politics of Piety* Mahmood has employed concepts from Bourdieu to explore the growth and implications of the Muslim habitus for pious women in modern Egypt. Her ethnographic study provides an excellent framework for thinking in more global terms about Islamic renewal.

In Egypt, of course, Muslims practise within a predominantly Islamic culture in which other groups such as the Copts are small minorities. However, norms of renewal are invoked more sharply when Muslims find themselves in a minority and hence under much greater pressure for secularization and assimilation. These group norms of conformity are more likely to be invoked when a community is a minority, or where the majority feels it is under threat by a minority – one, for example, that is economically dominant. These everyday norms that are important for defining religious differences, sustaining group identities and maintaining the continuity of the group may be called 'rituals of intimacy'. Erving Goffman in *The Presentation of Self in Everyday Life* (1959) documented the daily practices that are necessary to present the self in interaction with others. These everyday rituals are part of the drama of representing the religious self in contexts that may be ambiguous, contradictory or dangerous. These rituals are guides to good action. Can I serve alcohol to strangers and maintain my identity as a 'good woman'? How can I be pious?

These rituals or codes of conduct provide a series of answers to questions about how to behave towards strangers who are not co-religionists, and how to maintain religious purity in societies that are secular.

Norms regulating correct everyday behaviour have of course been present in all traditional religious systems. In traditional Muslim cultures, there are well-established customary guides to correct action. These behavioural guides were often fashioned in traditional societies along social class lines, and what applied to court administrators would not apply to peasants (Hodgson 1974). What then is new in the contemporary situation? One can argue that Islamic norms were originally constructed for the guidance of behaviour in societies which were wholly or predominantly Muslim. With the growth of the world-wide Muslim diaspora, there is a new need to define correct behaviour and to expunge 'foreign elements', whether these are Western or indigenous folk components. For example, Al-Kaysi's *Morals and Manners in Islam* (1986) warns of the need to Islamize customary behaviour and ensure that children are raised according to correct norms. The second issue is that with fundamentalism there is, as it were, an inflationary pressure to increase the scope and depth of these norms. As Muslim *imams* compete for lay followers, there is a tendency to increase the strictness of norms that are seen to be required by Shari'a. One interesting example is that while *halal* food such as the prohibition of pork is well known, in an inflationary religious setting these norms also come to include the idea of *halal* water. The pornography bill before the Indonesian Parliament will inflate the range of activities and circumstances that can be defined as pornographic from kissing in the street to revealing 'sensual' body parts. A third factor is that the growth of the Internet has greatly increased this sense of the global *umma*, and the importance of strict adherence to norms (Mandeville 2001). Finally, there are a series of contingent circumstances that have enhanced the perceived need to defend Islamic practice. In particular 9/11, the notion of a clash of civilizations and the war on terror have all conspired to enhance the norms of group identity.

Rituals of intimacy define the religious habitus. These daily practices include preferences for food and dress, the selection of intimate friends, and the organization of courtship and marriage. How do women in different social classes manage the everyday life of immediate intimate contacts? How do they sustain separate and pure religious practices? Where do they get advice about proper conduct? Are these rituals changing over time to become more exclusive? The notion of habitus is thus useful in defining the religious dispositions of individuals and how their taste for a range of religious services and commodities (such as *halal* food) is shaped.

However, this modern usage often obscures the fact that the notion of habitus is actually derived from the tradition of so-called 'virtue ethics' in the philosophical tradition of Aristotle. In this tradition, habitus contributes to the shaping of ethical practices that in turn create particular types of character. The religious habitus is designed to create a particular character, namely the good Muslim or the good Christian.

The rituals of intimacy are by definition in fact rituals of exclusion. If a ritual or norm defines a person as my co-religionist or peer, it automatically defines some other person or group as neither peer nor co-believer. Intimacy is an inclusive mechanism as well as an exclusionary practice that creates a circle of intimates and outsiders. The stronger the code of intimacy, the more intense the web of exclusion. These rituals of intimacy that are a component of acts of piety are partly a creation of modern times (through religious inflation), where religious identities are becoming more critical and challenging. At the same time these rituals quarantine the everyday world, making future inter-group conflicts more likely, and reducing the conditions of general social reciprocity.

Conclusion: the Global *Umma* and the Crisis of Secularism

The struggle to purify religion in an age of globalization and of increasing cultural hybridity is being fought out around the idea of piety, and piety is typically manifest not in correct beliefs but in correct albeit disruptive and reflective practice, and in turn pious practice involves a special government of the body (or a diet). The overt aim of pious practice is of course to produce a particular type of mentality or person or technology of the self, but the covert aim of piety or its unintended consequences are to define and demarcate social groups within a society or within a field of diverse religious traditions and legacies. Piety and purity, I argue, are connected closely with cultural struggles against traditionalists (who are associated with synthesis and syncretism) by modernizing social groups who embrace piety as a strategy to purify the social body by purifying the physical body. We can therefore talk about movements of pietization as an alternative to the idea of fundamentalism and fundamentalization. Because piety redefines identities, pietization has or can have important implications for politics.

I have suggested that while the liberal model separates religion and politics, we can no longer isolate or separate piety and acts of citizenship. This question becomes especially problematic in the case of Islam, which increasingly defines its own social and political space. Acts of piety in the context of religious renewal increasingly articulate a separate inspirational city and as a result a secular network society sits alongside and in tension with the city of God. We can argue that historically secular citizenship has been constructed around three principal activities: work, public service (such as military duty) and reproduction (or parenting) (Turner 2001). The citizenship entitlements of liberal capitalism are a set of what we may call contributory rights: that is, claims against society are based on contributions to the community through work, public service and reproduction. Let us take work as the principal example. By entering the labour market, I not only contribute to the economy but, in paying taxes to the state, I acquire entitlements in later life to a pension and health benefits. The most obvious characteristic of modern citizenship is the act of paying taxes, and the absence of tax evasion and economic corruption can be taken as measures of a successful state. If I pay my taxes in a context of trust and transparency, then citizenship exists. These activities are essential aspects of acts of citizenship. This model of citizenship presupposes that some degree of consensus already exists, but in many societies – those that are now highly diverse in religious terms or in which the civil sphere is highly disputed – it is no longer clear that paying our taxes is unproblematic. Should I pay my taxes to the mosque, the brotherhood or the state? When the secular city and the inspirational city no longer enjoy a symmetrical relationship, then acts of piety and citizenship may diverge.

We can argue, therefore, that within Islam there are a parallel set of acts that constitute a religious community. Just as acts of citizenship are necessary to construct a commonwealth, so acts of piety are necessary to create a community. The worth of a citizen within the civil city is measured by his or her contributions to the community through activity in three arenas or 'pillars' such as work, war and reproduction. These are very obvious in the case of Islam where the worth of an individual is measured formally in terms of the Five Pillars of orthodoxy, namely the *Hajj* (pilgrimage), *Salat* (the prayer ritual), *Sawm* (fasting during Ramadan), *Shahada* (the profession of faith) and *Zakat* (almsgiving). We can perceive a certain parallel here in which *zakat* is a tax, and hence a Muslim who pays his or her taxes is an active member of the *umma*, which is a global political community. Some Muslim communities such as the Ibadis add a sixth pillar, namely the *jihad*. Although *jihad* basically means to undertake a personal struggle against evil in one's own life, it has of course become defined by the Muslim Brotherhood (*al-Ikhwan al-Musulimun*) as a military struggle against the West. Hence there is a parallel between the idea that the ultimate act of citizenship is to lay down your life for the sake of the communal good and the idea that an act of piety might involve a violent struggle against an enemy. Attempts by reformist Islam to imbed the religious law or *Shari'a* in the public domain as a universal system of law move the *umma* closer to statehood. For women, acts of piety also involve child bearing and child rearing, and thus the worth of a woman is measured by her reproductive contribution to the community.

Acts of piety can empower actors in the same way that acts of citizenship do. A person becomes a valuable member of the inspirational city by undertaking these acts of piety especially through taxation, reproduction and if necessary military defence of the community. I have therefore attempted to show how the pietization of everyday life has significant implications for the political city and for relationships between different religious communities within the public sphere. The greater the piety of the social group, the greater its social distance from other groups. The more intense the piety, the greater the potential through rituals of intimacy for tensions in the everyday world in terms of interactions with outsiders. The greater the piety of a social group, the more likely the trend towards homogamy in marriage. The most significant illustration of this problem is the controversial ruling about apostasy in recent cases in countries such as Malaysia: this ruling prevents a person exiting a religious group. Acts of piety and acts of secular citizenship in effect create two separate cities – the inspirational and the secular city. The tensions between the inspirational city and the political city may not constitute a clash of civilizations, but do point to the intensification of religious identities within the public domain, and raise questions about how social interactions between different social groups involving rituals of intimacy can take place without conflict.

References

Agamben, G. (1998) *Homo Sacer: Sovereign Power and Bare Life*, Stanford University Press, Stanford.

Alexander, J. C. (2006) *The Civil Sphere*, Oxford University Press, Oxford.

Al-Kaysi, M. I. (1986) *Morals and Manners in Islam: A Guide to Islamic Adab*, The Islamic Foundation, Leicester.

Atkins, E. M. and R. J. Dodaro (eds) (2001) *Augustine Political Writings,* Cambridge University Press, Cambridge.

Barbalet, J. M. (1998) *Emotion, Social Theory and Social Structure: A Macrosociological Approach*, Cambridge University Press, Cambridge.

Berger, P. L. (ed.) (1999) *The Desecularization of the World*, William B. Eerdmans Publishing Co, Michigan.

Boltanski, L. and E. Chiapello (2006) *The New Spirit of Capitalism*, Verso, London and New York.

Boltanski, L. and L. Thévenot (2006) *On Justification: Economies of Worth*, (trans. C. Porter), Princeton University Press, Princeton.

Bourdieu, P. (1977) *Outline of a Theory of Practice*, Cambridge University Press, Cambridge.

—— (1984) *Distinction: A Critique of the Judgement of Taste*, Routledge and Kegan Paul, London.

—— (1990) *The Logic of Practice*, Polity Press, Cambridge.

Bourdieu, P. and L. Wacquant (1992) *An Invitation to Reflexive Sociology,* Polity Press, Cambridge.

Davis, K. and W. E. Moore (1945) 'Some principles of stratification', *American Sociological Review*, 10 (2), 242–9.

Durkheim, É. (2001) *The Elementary Forms of Religious Life*, Oxford University Press, Oxford.

Gade, A. (2004) *Perfection Makes Practice: Learning, Emotion and the Recited Qur'an in Indonesia*, University of Hawaii Press, Honolulu.

Goffman, E. (1959) *The Presentation of Self in Everyday Life*, Doubleday Anchor, Garden City, NY.

Heng, J. (2002) 'Understanding Words and Knowing Men' in A. K. L. Chan (ed.) *Mencius. Contexts and Interpretations*, University of Hawaii Press, Honolulu.

Hodgson, M. G. S. (1974) *The Venture of Islam: Conscience and History in World Civilization*, 3 vols, University of Chicago Press, Chicago, IL.

Lau, D. C. (ed.) (2004) *Mencius*, Penguin, London.

Lukens-Bull, R. (2005) *A Peaceful Jihad: Negotiating Identity and Modernity in Muslim Java*, Palgrave Macmillan, New York.

Mahmood, S. (2005) *Politics of Piety: The Islamic Revival and the Feminist Subject*, Princeton University Press, Princeton and Oxford.

Mufti, A. R. (2007) *Enlightenment in the Colony: The Jewish Question and the Crisis of Postcolonial Culture*, Princeton University Press, Princeton and Oxford.

Orr, S. (1995) *Jerusalem and Athens: Reason and Revelation in the Works of Leo Strauss*, Rowman and Littlefield, Lanham, MA.

Rieff, P. (2006) *My Life among the Deathworks*, University of Virginia Press, Charlottesville and London.

Schmitt, C. (1996) *The Concept of the Political*, University of Chicago Press, Chicago, IL and London.

Shilling. C. (ed.) (2007) *Embodying Sociology: Retrospect, Progress and Prospects*, Blackwell, Oxford.

Spinner-Halev, J. (2005) 'Hinduism, Christianity, and Liberal Religious Tolerance', *Political Theory*, 33 (1), 28–57.

Turner, B. S. (2001) 'The erosion of citizenship', *British Journal of Sociology*, 52 (2), 189–210.

Chapter 6

❖

Arendt's Citizenship
and Citizen Participation
in Disappearing Dublin[1]

KIERAN BONNER

Citizen Participation and Dublin – A City of Possibilities

> The *polis*, properly speaking, is not the city-state in its physical location; it is the organization of people as it arises out of acting and speaking together, and its true space lies between people living together for this purpose, no matter where they happen to be… It is the space of appearance in the widest sense of the word, namely, the space where I appear to others as others appear to me, where men exist not merely like other living or inanimate things but make their appearance explicitly… Whatever lacks this appearance comes and passes away like a dream, intimately and exclusively our own but without reality. (Arendt 1958, pp. 198–9)

As a European city in a country that is an enthusiastic member of the European Union, Dublin has developed a vision document, *Dublin – A City of Possibilities* (*DACP*) that sets out what the city is to look like in 2012. It is a document of the Dublin City Development Board (DCDB), established in 2000 by the government (local and municipal government in Ireland falls under national government legislation) 'to address coordination at a local level, improve participation of local communities in local decision-making and tackle social exclusion' (DCDB 2002, p. 11). The DCDB is 'a unique city partnership where different agencies and organizations involved in the development of Dublin City come together to facilitate the identification of shared values and key priorities facing the city' (p. 12). Its 27 members are drawn from local government, statutory agencies, local development and social partners (e.g., community agencies, a trade union, the chamber of commerce.)

In 2002 DCDB unveiled *DCAP*. Divided into 15 strategic themes, this vision document is to serve as the integrated 'economic, social and cultural strategy' for the City of Dublin, covering the period from 2002 to 2012. The first theme, 'A City of Neighbourhoods', is central and is therefore referred to as the 'heart theme'. The next four are called 'enabling themes' 'because they represent key cross-cutting principles that underpin the entire strategy… Finally there are ten outcome themes which will directly impact upon the way people live, how people live and where people live' (p. 13).

'A Democratic and Participative City' is one of the four enabling themes of the document, and its aim is to increase citizen participation, accountability and democratic participation. As with the whole document, the need for this enabling theme emerged as a consequence of the issues brought to light during consultation about the document, issues that are endemic to all modern contemporary democracies, such as 'falling levels of participation in local organizations and projects', 'low election turnouts, general apathy about politics', 'feelings of isolation from local government and elected representatives', 'absence of policy networks in the City to facilitate a participative democracy', and 'the growing appetite in the community to participate in a more meaningful and constructive way in the workings of local and central government' (p. 55). In other words, the city of Dublin, which up to 30 years ago was the capital of a country that had a nationalist, Catholic and rural ethos (the capital, thus, of a more traditional society [Bonner 2004]) is now trying to respond to issues that pervade almost all modern representative democracies.

In the light of the issue being addressed in this book, the DCDB would seem to be engaged in an act of citizenship. As expressed in the Introduction and in Isin's Chapter 1, acts of citizenship involve those constitutive and disruptive moments when rights are claimed, responsibilities asserted and obligations imposed. 'Acts rupture or break given orders, practices and habitus' (Chapter 1, p. 36). In the case of the DCDB, we have an initiative that is disruptive with regard to current patterns of citizen participation and that seeks to be constitutive in so far as its aim is to change low citizen participation fundamentally by creating the possibility of a new set of practices. Clearly, Dublin City Council, through its agency the DCDB, has assumed the responsibility of redressing the deficit in citizen participation. As described in the various chapters in this book, to focus on acts of citizenship is to focus on activity over passivity, on doing over receiving, and on process over product, all of which this initiative aims to effect. The initiative also recognizes that 'acts of citizenship are not necessarily founded in law or responsibility' (p. 39), though it does seem to provide a name or alibi for the act. Though this initiative provides a name and alibi – the importance of citizen participation – it could reasonably be interpreted as desiring to create an environment where the participation on the part of citizens 'produce[s] actors' rather than the production of subjects by the formal entitlement of citizenship (the rights and obligations built into law). If an enactment of citizenship 'inevitably produces a situation where there are selves and others defined in relation to each other' and '[t]hese are not fixed identities but fluid subject positions in and out of which subjects move.' (pp. 18–19), then this initiative could reasonably be defined as an act of citizenship. As an initiative of the DCDB, it aims to create a situation where 'acts [citizen participation] produce subjects' rather than actors producing acts' (p. 2).

'How are beings thrown into [this] act that enact(s) them as citizens, strangers, outsiders and aliens' (p. 39)? Is the non-participating citizen, as constituted by this discourse, a stranger or, by virtue of the alienation of citizens from the political system, an alien? Does the focus on local participation as against the narrow view of mere ballot participation mean that those formally considered outsiders and aliens would now, in so far as they participate in community concerns, constitute themselves as citizens? Is this DCDB initiative both an attempt to create an environment that encourages acts of citizenship and an act of citizenship in its own right? In what way is this initiative similar to or different from examples provided in this book – Antigone, Socrates, the 1916 commemoration ceremonies, and so on? In what way are these examples acts of citizenship? In what way can the investigation of this initiative reveal ambiguities within the concept of acts of citizenship? More specifically, in what way do these examples help articulate what an act of citizenship means in a way that prevents this suggestive term from suffering the fate of many new ideas, where 'the blurring of boundaries is celebrated as the all-purpose cure for the deformations of the modern age' (Villa 1996, p. xii)?

Hannah Arendt, Democracy and Citizen Participation

In order to help work through these issues, and as one way of specifying an act of citizenship, I will engage the work of Hannah Arendt, particularly her notion of action, politics and participation. As we can see from her description of the *polis*, the life of the citizen is one of participation. The *polis* 'is the organization of people as it arises out of acting and speaking together … the space of appearance … where I appear to others as others appear to me'. Citizen participation, for Arendt, creates a *polis*, a public realm, and it emerges when people live together for the purpose of speaking and acting with each other. That is, the *polis*, in contrast to the city state, is not a mere structure or institution that can exist independently of the acting and speaking people; rather, the latter is constitutive of the former. In a direct democracy like ancient Athens – a democracy that excluded women, foreigners and slaves – the citizen participated in this political space and sought through words and deeds to persuade his peers in action. Through this participation, the clear-sighted ability to include in one's thinking the perception of others validated one's political position and brought about a shared sense of reality (Arendt 1958, p. 57). Without this space of appearance, life and life's activity becomes that which 'comes and passes away like a dream, intimately and exclusively our own but without reality' (Arendt 1958, pp. 22–78; 1968, pp. 227–64; Villa 1996, pp. 3–41; Canovan 1992, pp. 129–49). Explicitly appearing to others in a context where others take up the opportunity to appear (through words and deeds) is how Arendt would understand an act of citizenship. While the act of exercising one's citizenship by marking a ballot paper in the privacy of a voting booth is often taken as the contemporary example of people exercising their responsibilities and rights as citizens in a representative democracy, it cannot be an act of citizenship in the fullest sense of the term if we use Arendt as our guide.

The form of democracy in Ireland, as well as almost all modern democratic countries, is representative democracy. Yet representative democracy, parliamentary or otherwise, does not require that citizens appear through their own words and deeds. In representative democracy, the citizen delegates action and speech to the elected representative. 'The most the citizen can hope for is to be "represented", whereby it is obvious that the only thing which can be represented and delegated is interest, or the welfare of the constituents, but neither their actions nor their opinions' (Arendt 1963, p. 268). Yet, it is precisely the appearance through words and deeds that defines an act of citizenship in Arendt's terms. 'Only the political life, the life of action and speech, is free; only the political life is human. To be human is to be a citizen' (Villa 1996, p. 28) and to be a citizen requires that one appear through one's words and deeds.

In representative democracy, as Canovan (1992, p. 232) describes it, 'if the individual is given a vote in a secret ballot, he is liable to … use his vote as a means of defending his private interests, something to be bartered to politicians in return for election promises'. She goes on to say that 'representative government therefore seemed to [Arendt] a standing invitation to corruption'. It has led to mass parties, spin management, media manipulation, government by polling (a more effective way of assessing the wants and desires of the electorate on a more ongoing basis than term elections) and elections that are more often like a promise competition than a debate about political issues. Representative government has shown itself to be reasonably effective in protecting the civil rights of all citizens and, given the horrors of the twentieth century, this is no small achievement. Yet this accomplishment, by itself, does not lead to the rise of a *polis*, public realm, or *res publica*. The enjoyment of civil rights as a private person, however crucial, 'is not the same thing as being the citizen of a republic and enjoying political freedom' (Canovan 1992, p. 233). As Arendt herself says (1963, p. 218), 'political freedom means the right to be a participator in government, or it means nothing'.

For Arendt, then, an act of citizenship in its full worldly reality is more than voting for someone else to act and speak on one's behalf. It requires the full experience of acting and speaking; it is this criterion that Arendt would use to assess whether acts were either social or political and so acts of citizenship. Of course, to understand this distinction we need to explore more fully the distinctions involved in acting and activity *per se* in order to distinguish the uniqueness of citizen acts. Arendt's critique of representative democracy as inimical to the development of full citizenship needs to be understood against the background of her analysis of human activity in general.

In relation to the discussion of the nature of acts of citizenship in this book, the attempt to make Dublin a more 'democratic and participative city' at the very least implicitly acknowledges the limitations of representative democracy and the idea of citizenship it both originates from and encourages. In many ways it seems to speak to the concerns that Arendt raised about governance in modern society. For example, the document states that 'Participation in decision making has been traditionally limited to the ballot paper. Increasingly, however, the concept of participation is being broadened' (DCDB 2002, p. 55). It goes on to suggest that 'the strengthening of participation in the governance of a city relies on the strengthening of direct citizen and community involvement in decision-making channels' (p. 56). These assertions seem clearly to echo Arendt's version of citizenship and political freedom regarding the relation between 'political freedom' and 'the right to be a participator in government'. The intention to move participation beyond the limitations of the ballot paper, and the interest in nurturing and responding to 'the growing appetite in the community to participate in a more meaningful and constructive way in the workings of local and central government' (p. 55) address the desire to encourage acts of citizenship and a sense of real political freedom.

Here also we seem to have some recognition of the limitations of representative democracy and an attempt to do something about these limitations, an attempt that would seem, on the surface, to be an application of Arendt's principles. The vision document says that citizen participation will be brought about through the development of various forums at the city, area and neighbourhood level. These forums aim to 'increase transparency in the process through which non-elected representatives are invited to participate in strategic policy formulation within Dublin City Council' (p. 58) and as such aim to be more than merely consultative.

The DCDB initiative seeks to repair a commonplace problem in all modern democracies – the alienation of the citizens from the political system of democracy, under a system of modern liberalism that views politics as 'the chambermaid of private interests' (Barber, as cited in Villa, 1996, p. 4). Arendt

> challenges our most deeply rooted liberal preconceptions about the *nature* of politics. Following Aristotle, Arendt passionately asserts that the essence of politics is *action*. Laws and institutions, which to the liberal mind are the stuff of politics, for Arendt supply the framework for action. The activities of debate, deliberation, and participation in decision making come to occupy centre stage. Moreover, since politics *is* action, we need to recast our notion of citizenship in a participatory mode: not to be active in the political affairs of one's community is to cease to be a genuine, full member of that community. (p. 4)

Arendt's sentiments cohere with the idea that 'acts of citizenship do not need to be founded in law or enacted in the name of the law' (Isin, this volume, p. 39).

This is one way of interpreting the meaning of the idea of the space of appearances. Using this method, the DCDB initiative seeks to provide an environment where acts of citizenship are not only open to all but encouraged in all. In so far as it promotes participation rather than representation, and through participation seeks to develop 'a pyramidal structure of representatives sent on from the lower levels to the higher councils' (Canovan 1992, p. 236), a process that Arendt thought could form a practical alternative to the party method of representation, the initiative embedded in the *DACP* moves in an Arendtian direction.

Acts of citizenship are not delegated in the way voters delegate their participatory rights to those they elect. An act of citizenship means nothing if it does not show itself and its meaning through the very act of its being accomplished. As described in this book, Antigone's act to bury Polynices, Socrates's act to show up in response to the summons of the Athenian court, and the decision by the Irish Taoiseach (Prime Minister) to commemorate the 1916 Easter Rising are all acts that show themselves through their enactment. In this sense, as is articulated both in the Introduction and Chapter One, acts of citizenship need to be understood as escaping the means–end paradigm of rational thinking or the instrumental plea of having been elsewhere.

The DCDB initiative may be caught in a tension here, given its position as part of the master plan called the vision document. It finds its being within the discourse of planning and specifically within this plan. As part of the plan it ultimately gets its legitimation and meaning as a programme embedded in Dublin's 'Economic, Social and Cultural Strategy'. That is to say, this particular 'enabling theme' is part of the overarching design of 'building a meaningful strategy based on shared values' (DCDB 2002, p. 4). A consequence of this tension is that the initiative to increase citizen participation may be undermined by what critical theorists like Habermas and Bernstein see as the 'threat posed by the universalization of technical rationality'. That is, 'as ever-larger areas of social existence are subjected to the dictates of instrumental reason and to the prerogatives of rational administration, the space left for the exercise of citizenship gradually disappears' (Villa 1996, p. 5; Habermas 1973; Bernstein 1983, pp. 171–232). This initiative therefore lies uneasily between a production paradigm, where the initiative is part of an overall strategy for Dublin, and a praxis paradigm, where citizenship participation is understood to be an end in itself (Bonner 1998, pp. 47–57). As we will see, this tension may end up undermining in practice what is intended by the initiative.

Action and the Human Condition

In order both to be able to assess the *DACP* vision and to provide a way of specifying further what an act of citizenship means in this case, we first need a stronger sense of what Arendt means by action. This concept pervades all her writings from *The Origins of Totalitarianism* to the *Life of the Mind* but it finds its clearest phenomenological articulation in *The Human Condition*. Many contemporary theorists, while acknowledging the originality of her contributions, find this particular work to be limited and even flawed. Some see it as validating an ethnically cleansed, patriarchal *polis* that is out of synch with the strengths and virtues of modern citizenship (Habermas 1983; Bernstein 1986). As Villa puts it, 'even the most sympathetic of her commentators accuse her of succumbing to the longing for Greece that has been the occupational hazard of German philosophy since Kant' (Villa 1996, p. 3). Yet he concedes that 'descriptive conceptualizations of labour, work and action in *The Human Condition* leave no room for confusion or conflation: each activity emerges in sharp contrast to the other two' (p. 18).

The Human Condition, it is argued (Parekh 1981, pp. 68–9), is best read as oriented to doing a phenomenological description of human activities in a way to help distinguish political activity from other kinds of activity. And yet, 'Arendt's phenomenology is enclosed within theoretical commitment arising out of her reflections on totalitarianism and modernity as well as on the limitations of the Western tradition of philosophy' (Canovan 1992, p. 102).[2] Arendt's experience of the horrors of the twentieth century – Nazism and Stalinism in particular – led her to re-engage and question the very nature of so-called Western civilization and the political structures that grew out of it, which not only failed to protect Europe from this barbarism but, in the case of Stalinism, was complicit in its development. Her preoccupation with the concept of action follows directly from her meditations on totalitarianism, Marxism and the Western philosophical tradition, all of which seemed to her to have denied or ignored the most politically relevant characteristic of human beings – their plurality. Totalitarianism represents for her a deliberate attempt to erase all traces of plurality and spontaneity from human beings, while Marxism, she thought, saw mankind as a herd of animals with no individuality or initiative. Within the philosophical tradition forged by solitary thinkers since Plato, Man was an abstract subject that existed only in the singular (Canovan 1992, p. 130).

As we are all shaped by this Western civilization, coming to terms with her analysis involves a radical and reflexive questioning of the horizon of understanding that shapes our thinking. If Arendt is correct, this reflexive engagement is necessary if we are to avoid the barbarism that drew on the very features of Western civilization we often celebrate – our problem-solving and organizational abilities, our modern rationality, our belief in the benefits of human mastery. That is, a strong embrace of reflexivity is essential if we are to grasp the nature of Arendt's distinctions, as they challenge the very horizon of understanding (Gadamer 1975) we use to navigate our way through the concerns of our world, including a concern with acts of citizenship.

The original title of *The Human Condition* was 'The *Vita Activa*'. Arendt acknowledges that the Western tradition of political philosophy conceptualized the *vita activa*, and did so in a narrowing and hierarchical fashion. That is, the active life, which in ancient Greece found its highest expression in the *bios politikos* or political life, was formulated from the standpoint of the *bios theoretikos* or life of contemplation, and as inferior to that standpoint (1958, pp. 7–21). Marx sought to reverse this hierarchy in his 'Theses on Feurbach', but Arendt argues that, in turning the tradition on its head, he still remained trapped within the conceptual framework of the very tradition of political philosophy he saw himself as rejecting (1968, pp. 17–40). 'While Arendt believes that Marx and Nietzsche, in their rebellion against the Socratic-Christian valuation, succeeded in reversing the traditional hierarchy of the contemplative and active life, the very success of this reversal did nothing to remedy the original blurring of the inner articulations of the *vita activa*' (Villa 1996, p. 17). (It is in this sense that we could say that political theory, as instanced by the canon of Western political philosophy, arrives too late to help with the understanding of acts of citizenship.) Thus, we have Arendt's sense of the need for a more radical destructuring or deconstruction of that tradition – a method that she, like Derrida, would have learned from Heidegger (Villa 1996, p. 9; Gadamer 1989, pp. 102–13) – in order to recover the full multidimensional reality of human activity.

Arendt develops her understanding of the active life in explicit defiance of the Western philosophical tradition because, she says, 'My contention is simply that the enormous weight of contemplation in the traditional hierarchy has blurred the distinctions and articulations within the *vita activa* itself and that, appearances notwithstanding, this condition has not been changed essentially by the modern break with the tradition and the eventual reversal of the hierarchical order in Marx and Nietzsche' (1958, p. 17). Through her 'respectful but radical debate with Marx' (Kristeva 2001, p. 162) and the relation of this work to Stalinism, she came to the recognition that political action was formulated in terms of 'making' or fabrication. This orientation goes back to Plato, who conceptualized statecraft in terms of the craftsman (Arendt 1968, pp. 104–15; Gadamer 1975, pp. 278–89; Plato, *The Republic*). This ideal is politically problematic because it makes violence intrinsic to the political process. Just as one has to cut a tree down to make a table, so one must destroy a society to bring about a revolution (Arendt 1963, pp. 62–6). This orientation is also politically problematic because it sustains the illusory goal of mastery and control. Again, as we will see, it is this understanding of politics, which takes for granted the *poeisis* (production) perspective, that may well be where the well-intentioned DCDB citizenship initiative flounders.

For Arendt, political action is not about control but about stories that have the power to reconcile us to human limits, and such stories emerge in a *polis* made up of freely participating citizens (1958, pp. 175–247). Thus, to engage fully the issues surrounding mediating acts of citizenship and the modern city, one has to be aware reflexively of the standpoint or perspective that goes into thinking the political.

Citizenship, Freedom and the Public World

Against the weight of the tradition of political philosophy, and in order to articulate a conceptually clear alternative to our modern situation, Arendt, with the aid of Aristotle (Villa 1996), returned to the experiences of the ancient Greeks in order to recover the inspiration behind their interest in establishing a public realm dedicated to developing the human capacity for speech and action. While the ancient Greeks were surrounded by tribal organizations, by monarchies, and by tyrannical empires, and themselves had experienced all of these forms of political organization, they went on to create the world's first democracy, the *polis*, the Greek word for city and the root word of politics. Now, as already stated, the *polis* does not refer to the Greek city-state, literally speaking. It is not an empirical designation but an eidetic one and realms like the *polis* continue to appear when the desire for freedom expresses itself in revolutionary action. 'The American Revolution, the Paris Commune, the original *soviets* of 1905 and 1917, the *Räte* (workers councils) of the German Revolution of 1918, the Hungarian revolt: all are cases in which the overthrow of tyranny led to the founding of a space for freedom and the (tragically brief) flowering of action and speech' (Villa 1996, p. 29).

In ancient Greece, the *polis* was established in contrast to the household, and it was only in the *polis* that one developed one's capacity for speaking and acting well (Arendt 1958, pp. 28–38). This public realm was established as one where freedom and excellence could flourish, as these qualities are displayed in and through action. By virtue of both speech and action, human individuality and uniqueness could appear in the full light of the public realm. Dealing with, and responding to, the unexpected is the *sine qua non* of action. It was the public realm that made it possible for humans to discover, develop and exemplify the reality of the potential: that what is unique about humans is that 'the unexpected can be expected from us'. The experience of genuine plurality makes possible the appearance of individual uniqueness. If acts of citizenship 'rupture or break the given orders, practices and habitus' (Isin this volume, p. 36), then this is due to the potential for action as distinct to the potential for work or labour that is built into the human condition.

Because 'labour assures not only individual survival, but the life of the species', it was undertaken for reasons of necessity.

> The distinctive trait of the household sphere was that in it men lived together because they were driven by their wants and needs... That individual mainte-nance should be the task of the man and species survival the task of the woman was obvious, and both of these natural functions, the labour of man to provide nourishment and the labour of woman in giving birth, were subject to the same urgency of life. Natural community in the household therefore was born of necessity, and necessity ruled over all activities. The realm of the *polis*, on the contrary, was the sphere of freedom, and if there was a relationship between these two spheres it was a matter of course that the mastering of the necessities

of life in the household was the condition for freedom of the *polis*. (Arendt 1958, pp. 30–1)

Thus, the point of the Greek example is not to valorize a sexist, racist and slave-based society but rather to illustrate 'that the difference between public and private corresponds to the difference between freedom and necessity' (Villa 1996, p. 19).

The *polis,* in privileging both action and speech, was the realm of persuasion. Just as Homer's heroes had to be persuaded to join in the Trojan adventure (Arendt 1958, pp. 186–7), so, too, in the *polis*, one could not be forced but only persuaded to participate.

> The good life, as Aristotle called the life of the citizen, therefore, was not merely better, more carefree or nobler than ordinary life, but of an altogether different quality. It was 'good' to the extent that by having mastered the necessities of sheer life, by being freed from labour and work, and by over-coming the innate urge for all living creatures for their own survival, it was no longer bound to the biological life process. (Arendt 1958, pp. 36–7)

Thus the life of the citizen is not different in degree but 'of an altogether different quality'. This life shows its identity through its freedom from being mastered by the urgencies of life; it is only in this way that acts are political and citizen-like. For Arendt, then, an act of citizenship is a display of political freedom.

If mastering the necessities of life was the condition of entry into the *polis*, this did not mean that wealth was the crucial entrance requirement. In Athens, there were comfortably well-off slaves and there were poor citizens. What was essential was not wealth but valuing one's freedom. 'A poor man', Arendt says (1958, p. 30), 'preferred the insecurity of a daily changing labour market to regular assured work, which, because it restricted his freedom to do as he pleased everyday, was already felt to be servitude, and even harsh painful labour was preferred to the easy life of many household slaves.' Citizen action shows itself in a commitment to political freedom, a commitment that can and most often does involve significant sacrifice (Canovan 1992, pp. 224–32).

This notion of citizenship is a radical alternative in consumer society where the association between wealth and freedom is assumed. (The lottery in Canada used to advertise winning by saying, 'Imagine the Freedom'.) Arendt describes the life of citizenship that, by virtue of the value put on political freedom, is willing to suffer the economic harshness of an insecure daily labour market. Thus, through her analysis, she formulates a kind of political action that seems irrational and unproductive to our ears. In Bakhtinian terms, 'the world of modern philosophy, the theoretical and theoreticized world of culture' (as cited in Isin this volume, Chapter 1, p. 29) is not the lived world of a public realm. Yet, though modernity privileges an economic conception of freedom, this notion of political freedom is not completely alien to us – at least as intelligible action that enables us to understand twentieth-century icons like Gandhi, Martin Luther King, or Mandela. 'The political way of life, when contrasted to that lived in the household or the "barbaric" life outside the state, was characterized by the fact that here "speech and only speech made sense"' for 'the central concern of all citizens was to talk to each other' (Villa 1996, p. 32).

In this view then, acts of citizenship display freedom in their enactment, they appear through the speech and actions of individuals, and that appearance attains a worldly reality in a public realm where equal and plural individuals also appear (through words and deeds). Equality and diversity are the essential elements of a public realm where acts of citizenship can appear. 'Domination, liberation, administration, representation– determined by force of necessity and destructive of plurality, they are all pre-political in character. Mistaken for the stuff of politics they become anti-political, denaturing the public realm by subjecting it to the life process' (Villa 1996, p. 31). As Kateb (2000, pp. 133–4) says, 'There must be diversity of opinion if politics is to go on. Socioeconomic matters seem to be amenable to conclusively right answers; or contrastingly, to the mere expression of preponderant will. Neither feature is authentically political.'

Diversity is required for the art of political thinking to be developed; true citizen participation, in Arendt's terms, is not about compromise regarding different private interests, whether collective or individual. Such compromise happens regularly in business dealings but these are business acts, not political acts. Neither is politics about assessing the general will in Rousseau's sense. 'The difference between [Arendt's] position and Rousseau's can in fact be summed up by saying that according to the former, citizens are held together not by a common will but by a common *world*, by sharing a common set of worldly institutions' (Canovan 1992, p. 226).

In this sense, the 'Proclamation of the Republic' by the leaders of the 1916 Easter Rising (which, as Morrison states in his 'Acts of Commemoration' entry in this book, is being commemorated as a courageous act of citizenship to found the Irish Republic) is grounded in Rousseau's orientation to the general will (in this case of the Irish people) rather than a set of institutions to make central debate and deliberation. As Morrison states, 'in this transcendental vision of republicanism [embodied in the Proclamation], a being emerges that is meant to be enacted in an identical fashion in all members of the republic', thus undermining the pluralism essential for politics. For Arendt, however, the issue would not be the problem of 'continually marginalizing all other identities that individuals or groups politically construct' (Morrison) but rather the nationalist vision with its deep sense of a unitary people that misinterprets the nature of politics and political action. Political action involves deliberation and debate amongst equals where no one is forced to accept the opinion of the other because 'political debate is end-constitutive; its goal does not stand apart from the process ... but is performed in the course of the "perform-ance" itself' (Villa 1996, p. 32), thus requiring a common set of worldly institutions. It is this concern with the public realm that, for Arendt, defines an act of citizenship.

Labouring, Work and Citizenship Acts:
The Significance of Reflexivity

One way of further specifying this notion of citizenship is to develop ideas about other kinds of acts or activities that at some fundamental level are not political and cannot reasonably be said to be citizenship acts. According to Arendt, there are three fundamental activities of the human condition: labour, work and action. 'Labour is the activity which corresponds to the biological processes of the human body, whose spontaneous growth, metabolism and eventual decay are bound to the vital necessities produced and fed into the life process by labour' (1958, p. 7). That is, the activity of labour is concerned with individual and species survival. 'Work provides an "artificial" world of things, distinctly different from all natural surroundings' (p. 7). This activity builds a 'world' which becomes a home for humans; this is more than a mere environment to survive in: rather, it is made of objects intended to outlast our individual earthly existence and so connect us to past and future generations. Work fills the world with 'meaningful' artefacts – from heirlooms, to houses, to works of art, and ultimately to texts of stories of great deeds and great words (like Homer's *Iliad*). The latter artefacts (stories) depend on and connect with action. Action, the third dimension of human activity, is 'the only activity that goes on between [humans] without the intermediary of things [of the world] or [the] matter [of survival]' (p. 7). By action, Arendt means individual initiative, the beginning of something new. 'As a general category of human activity, action is closely related to speech, and Arendt often talks about speech and action in the same breath, as phenomena that arise from human plurality and disclose the uniqueness of each individual' (Canovan 1992, p. 131). Through the capacity for speech and action, humans can begin something new and unpredictable, which, in turn, provides a space for the revelation of human uniqueness (Arendt 1958, pp. 175–88; Canovan 1992, pp. 99–154; Kateb 2000, pp. 130–48). Thus, from Arendt's perspective, we have three kinds of acts: acts of labouring, acts of production, and acts of speaking and doing. From Arendt's very strict but clear elucidation, it is only the latter acts that are truly political and earn the name acts of citizenship. It is only the latter that truly give rise to the *polis*.

What makes the public realm different from the social realm, or the private realm, or the realm of the state? We can answer this question by resolving the question of what the *polis* makes possible. The public realm, Arendt says (1958, p. 57), makes available to the participants a sense of worldly reality. This sense of reality 'relies on the simultaneous presence of innumerable perspectives and aspects... Only where things can be seen by many in a variety of aspects without changing their identity,' she goes on to say, 'can worldly reality truly and reliably appear.' Where the act of labouring provides a sense of solidarity and community through the shared struggle for survival, and the act of production provides a sense of mastery and control over nature, acts of speaking and action provide humans with a sense of worldly reality. 'Only where things can be seen by many in a variety of aspects without changing their identity, so that those who are gathered around them know that they see sameness in utter diversity, can worldly reality truly and reliably appear... The end of the common world has come when it is seen only under one aspect and is permitted to present itself in only one perspective' (p. 57). Thus, there is a strong and necessary relation between experiencing plurality and developing the art of recognizing worldly reality. This necessary relation may denote that acts of citizenship, while they provide crystallizations of the capacity of human spontaneity, freedom (Antigone) and resistance (Socrates), by themselves are not enough (at least according to Arendt) if they do not have a public realm. And perhaps the very focus on acts of citizenship, its relevance and significance in these times, is a reflection of our worldlessness; that is, the focus may be a reflection that *we lack a shared world*. If '*commonality* ... dissolves or is shattered, it is no longer possible to view the same thing from a variety of perspectives' (Villa 1996, p. 34, italics in original). This concern will be taken up later in this chapter.

Labour, work and action are 'all are intimately connected with the most general condition of human existence, birth and death': labour with the survival of the individual and the species; 'work and its product ... bestow a measure of permanence', which survives the death of individuals and connects us to generations past and future; and 'action in so far as it engages in founding and preserving political bodies, creates the conditions for remembrance, that is, for history' (Arendt 1958, p. 9). Here is one way of understanding the various entries in this book that interpret acts of citizenship and as such re-engage our remembrance of the human ability to act without an alibi, without an instrumental plea of having been elsewhere – though again the issue as to whether an act can be an act of citizenship if it is not oriented to founding or preserving a public realm remains to be addressed.

Applying the reflexive or radical interpretive perspective (Bonner 1997, 2001) to what Arendt says about the multidimensional nature of worldly reality, we can see that her description of human acts is pluralist, itself reflecting the significance of plurality. She is looking at one phenomenon – human activity – and sees three fundamental activities, none of which are conceptually reducible to the other. Her approach is multi-perspectival, and, for Arendt, this multidimensional perspective is not just another theoretical orientation but one crucial both to the preservation and practice of freedom and to the art needed to recognize reality in all its full multidimensionality. It is an art that the theorist must develop in order to approximate the multidimensional nature of reality, and it is an art for the active citizen who seeks to develop conclusions and *doxai* (opinions) valid for the political sphere.

Political thinking (unlike philosophical thinking) involves 'considering a given issue from different viewpoints, by making present to my mind the standpoints of those who are absent … being and thinking my own identity where I am not' (Arendt 1968, p. 241). Understanding reality is both a theoretical concern, in so far as it is intrinsic to the understanding of the nature of political activity, but it is also a concern of *praxis* in so far as it is intrinsic to strong political action. Arendt's method of analysis coheres with the content of her argument, displaying not 'an indifferent attitude' but a version that Bakhtin calls 'an interested effective attitude' (Bakhtin, as cited in Isin this volume, Chapter 1, p. 30). Arendt both calls for and (through her texts) exemplifies the thinking of the citizen who acts – in the words that inspired the title of Elisabeth Young-Bruehl's biography (1982) for love of the world: 'For this world of ours, because it existed before us and is meant to outlast our lives in it, simply cannot afford to give primary concern to individual lives and the interests connected with them' (Arendt 1968, p. 156).

The underlying ethical element in Arendt's description is that a fully rich relation to our own human potential for action involves all three activities in a way that places each activity in proportion with the other two. We need labour to survive, we need to make things so the earth can become a human home, and we need to act and speak with each other in order to found public realms for the sake of appearance. The problem with the modern age is its emphasis on – nay, through consumerism, its celebration of – the activity of labouring. The urgency of the biological life process, which drives the labouring activity, has taken over the free space the other activities require and has put in its place an image of the good life as the life of consumption.[3] In Arendt's terms, not only is the potential to develop a rich relation to human activity stifled, but our individual and collective ability to recognize reality and question the ethical implications of our actions is seriously impaired.

Arendt identifies two modern developments in particular that enervate the collective sense of worldly reality: the development of reductionism in the social sciences and the development of ideology in politics. As she showed in many of her works, but most especially in the *Origins of Totalitarianism*, this surrender to illusion had profound political consequences in the twentieth century. Though our contemporary consumer society differs in significant ways from the totalitarianism of Nazism and Stalinism, both kinds of social organization become real in part because worldlessness, or the absence of commonality, becomes more pervasive in mass society. While totalitarianism enervates the art of reality recognition through the pervasive acceptance of the logic of ideology (Arendt 1951; Canovan 1992, pp. 86–94), consumerism does it by pandering to our fantasies and desires and exploiting our anxieties and fears.

It is now more apparent why Arendt develops a critique of representative democracy. Consumer society distorts and exacerbates the dangers inherent in a system of contemporary representative democracy because citizens, who are only citizens because they vote and not because they participate in the public realm, are in danger of choosing a public representative based on fantastic promises or anxious private fears. The utopian fantasy pervades contemporary consumer society, as can be seen in the pervasiveness of media and advertisements. The political environment further panders to the human fantasy of wanting it all, having it all, doing it all. The apathy and cynicism about politics and politicians, endemic in all modern democracies, is a reflection of these unfulfilled fantasies, itself an instance of the demise, not of the shared fate on this planet, but of the sense of reality that can emerge from the sense of a shared world, when we engage in acts of citizenship to found or preserve a public realm.

Our very socialization into modernity makes thinking through the multidimensional reality of the *vita activa* difficult. Implicit in Arendt's argument (but only implicit, as she eschewed methodological concerns), is that any theorizing about citizenship requires the development of skills to see and understand an object from many perspectives, or in my own terms, to be rigorously reflexive about the object we seek to understand (Bonner 2001, 1997, pp. 176–200). We do not theorize in a vacuum or from an illusory position of scopic transcendence, but rather from within a horizon shaped by dominant and embedded prejudgements. To quote Nietzsche, our relation between past and future 'is understood in terms of what is strongest in the present, or not at all' (cited in Villa 1996, p. 10). Thus, our concern with acts of citizenship and with the case study of the DCDB initiative has to demonstrate a critical reflection on what is strongest in the present. Arendt's thought exercise on the distinctions between labour, work and action give us a clearer perspective to aid in the struggle for reflexive awareness. An embrace of dialogical reflexivity is therefore crucial to the understanding and critical assessment of these distinctions, and of the reason for them. What would an assessment of the *DACP* look like if we were to apply the same reflexive criteria? What would it tell us about the multidimensional nature of the reality of Dublin? As we shall see, it is precisely this lack of reflexivity with regard to what is strongest in the present (consumerism) that threatens to deconstruct the Dublin City Development Board initiative.

A Reflexive Analysis of the Tension between the Planning Discourse and the Culture of Dublin

How is one to assess the DCDB initiative to bolster citizenship participation? It remains to be seen whether the culture of Dublin will be changed by this initiative or whether an active and participatory citizenry will emerge. Recent evidence suggests that the problem of social exclusion and poverty is in the process of being addressed successfully (Potter 2007). However, as has now been established, social inclusion could mean a greater opportunity for all to participate in citizenship acts or it could mean an opportunity to participate more equally in consumer society. The latter does not necessarily lead to the space of appearance for plurality. One way to assess the DCDB initiative, therefore, is to apply the reflexive orientation already applied to Arendt. In this case, we would apply what we know about action and speech to *DACP*, as a speech act itself. As political speech is end-constitutive, one can assess the speech or language of the document itself. The discourse of *DACP* can be taken as an exemplary case study because it is an outcome of the kind of participation that the citizen participation initiative seeks to establish.

The vision of *DACP* emerged out of what it calls 'stakeholder participation'. 'The first step involved the establishment of a City Community

Forum, comprising of community and voluntary organizations in the city. The forum provides for a coordinated and recognized structure for two-way consultation with this sector and the mechanism for participation on a level platform with state agencies and other organizations and bodies' (DCDB 2002, p. 18). This consultation took place over three phases: Phase 1 involved developing the 'Strategy Working Papers'; Phase 2, the 'Draft Strategy'; and Phase 3, 'Refining the Draft Strategy' (DCDB 2002, p. 18), leading to the final document. This process seems to mirror the process for developing citizen participation.

As described earlier in the chapter, citizen participation is going to be encouraged through forums at various levels ascending from the neighbourhood through the area to the city. This process coheres with Arendt's notion of direct political participation based on a pyramidal structure, where representatives from the lower levels would be sent on to the higher levels, based on their appearance through words and deeds at each level. *DACP* is an outcome of the pyramidal process and so can be seen as an exemplification of what the citizen participation initiative seeks to bring about. In Phase 1, 162,100 participated, 73,548 in Phase 2, and 90 in Phase 3 (DCDB 2002, p. 19). Though it is never explicitly stated, this document itself is presented as one example of what citizen participation looks like – and so as a microcosm of what Dublin might look like when citizens participate around issues of its future.

Yet, even though it is Dublin's plan, the uniqueness of the culture of Dublin is not reflected in it; it looks remarkably similar in orientation and language to the kind of plans that emerge in almost all Western cities – with its heart theme ('Neighbourhoods'), its enabling themes ('A Diverse and Inclusive City', 'A Connected and Informed City', 'An Integrated City', and 'A Democratic and Participative City') and its outcome themes ('A Safer City', 'A Greener City', 'A Moving and Accessible City', 'A Family Friendly City', 'A Healthy and Active City', 'A Cultural and Enjoyable City', 'A City of Homes', 'A Learning City', 'An Enterprising City', and 'A Community Friendly City'). If one were to list only these themes, without identifying the city whose vision they seek to embody, one would be hard pressed to identify the source city. It could very easily be Toronto or Montreal. Here we have a classic example of the way a discourse shapes an object. In this case, the planning discourse shows the priority of the discourse over the object being described. Within that discourse, Dublin can only be seen to be quantitatively different (whether it has more creative workers as a percentage of its population) and not qualitatively or generically different to other cities. In this discourse, it is also difficult to see the uniqueness or identity of the speakers (the Dubliners) who produced it.

The uniqueness of Dublin's voice or identity now looks as if it has been erased. Might this not be an example of the way the common world of Dublin disappears when viewed from a single perspective, despite the desire to establish Dublin as a city that exemplifies citizen participation? How does this erasure happen? Having been involved in a similar process in Alberta, I realized through my participation that the inclusive process is not about encouraging diverse opinions but precisely about generating lofty goals with which it is difficult to disagree. The utopian fantasy celebrated in consumer society pervades such political documents. The *DACP* vision statement itself shows this generic characteristic: 'to facilitate challenge and change, actively involving citizens, business, communities, and statutory agencies in determining and developing a strong, vibrant, successful, inclusive, multicultural and healthy city where all can achieve their full potential' (DCDB 2002, p. 12). The goals or ideals or vision of participation, competitiveness, safety, learning, culture, sustainability, and so on are 'of course' goals. Rather than being issues around which legitimate differences emerge, leading to the possible emergence of the public realm, disagreement now looks regressive, primitive, or unenlightened. Rather than an image of the worldly reality of Dublin, where its identity is revealed in its diversity, we end up with a discourse of utter sameness.

In the light of this document, the process of citizen participation seems directed towards managing the different viewpoints in a way that, however well-intentioned, eliminates rather than fosters the public realm. Precisely because there is no adequate understanding and protection of the nature of the public world, at least as instanced by the document itself, the process is in danger of threatening the very outcome citizen participation should result in: a vibrant and diverse public realm.

The language of the document is the language of a planning discourse, diversity of opinion is washed out through the production of generic goals and aims with which one cannot disagree. Who would argue against the outcomes listed above? There is no real public issue at stake that would bring diverse or even opposing opinions to the table for deliberation. The aim of the process is precisely to produce a controlling will; the *DACP*, through its anesthetized language, represents this process. It functions as though it is a post-modern consumer solution to the problematically essentialist claim embedded in the 1916 Proclamation of the Republic. To that extent, though it says the right things about citizen participation, and though its process includes citizen participation, it does not say or include participation in a way that brings a common world into appearance, or shows the uniqueness of either the speakers or the city.

It is precisely this danger of homogenization that Arendt saw as threatening the health of public citizenship in an era when no distinction is drawn between needs that address the urgencies of life and the need to care for the world that makes individual and species survival secondary.[4] Could this be one reason why the distinctiveness of Dublin or Toronto might be rendered deeply invisible in the discourse of cultural planning? Has action been conflated with making, *praxis* with production? The goal to produce a 'strong, vibrant, successful, inclusive, multicultural and healthy city' – rather than generate a public forum where diversity of opinion about the good of the city can show itself – shows the dominance of the production paradigm. If the aim is to produce a certain kind of city, has the logic of production become the ground of intelligibility of citizen action? If so, increased citizen participation through the creation of one or many public forums is not seen as an end in itself, but rather as a means to produce the 'strong, vibrant, successful, inclusive, multicultural and healthy city'. The problem with conflating practical action with technical action is that now 'things make sense only as means to ends. With this "instrumentalization of the world", Arendt argues, usefulness and utility are established as "the ultimate standards for life and the world of men". *All* things are ultimately degraded into means, thus losing whatever "intrinsic and independent value" they once may have had' (Villa 1996, p. 23). The intrinsic and independent value of Dublin is what is lost here.

It is interesting that the *DACP* shares the same political orientation to the public (that it is an expression of the general will) as the 1916 Proclamation of the Republic, though it does so in opposition to the appeal of the Proclamation. Instead of an appeal 'to the dead generations from which she receives her old tradition of nationhood', in which 'Ireland, through us, summons her children to her flag and strikes for her freedom', the *DACP* offers the post-modern vision of 'challenge and change … in determining and developing a strong, vibrant, successful, inclusive, multi-cultural and healthy city'. And while this change in vision would meet Morrison's concern for inclusion, what seems to be excluded is the identity of Dublin itself. Thus, there is no reference to the meaning of the city within which 'change and challenge' is to happen. It is as if the place has no value and so does not really exist. The *DACP* assumes that in challenge and change there is no common world to preserve, and so, to all intents and purpose, no reality to Dublin.

'The end of the common world has come when it is seen only under one aspect and is permitted to present itself in only one perspective' (Arendt 1958, p. 57). Is it fair to say that, despite the well-intentioned efforts of the initiators of this process and the participants in it, the *DACP* is the end of Dublin as a common world? Is this end brought about as a result of its discursive exclusion of the multidimensional nature of the reality of the common world? This plan as a discourse is the end of Dublin as a common world because it is seen only under one aspect and is permitted to present itself in only one perspective.[5]

This is not to say that Dublin does not have a reality or an identity outside the discourse that embodies the disappearance of its identity. Thus, at an analytic level, it is ironic, as Kevin Dowler (2004, p. 27) said in his comparison of the master plans of Toronto and Dublin, that 'plans, though they may seek to promote difference (through heritage, architecture, innovation, etc.) as a key strategy, undertake to do so in the same manner – and thus paradoxically (or ironically) reproduce sameness in the very act of attempting to do otherwise'. The collapse of the distinction between *poeisis* and *praxis*, between work acts and citizenship acts, helps provide us with a way of understanding how, despite good intentions and significant resources, the disappearance of Dublin's identity could happen.

So participation is a necessary but not sufficient condition for the creation of a full sense of citizenship. For this, something else is needed, perhaps pointing to what is needed for the concept of the act of citizenship. As we can see from the examples described in this book, an act of citizenship does not need a political space for its enactment. Antigone or the anonymous person who stood in the way of the tank in Tiananmen Square were both able to act and thus show their freedom despite their lack of citizenship. Yet, to be fully political – that is, to make forums for debates and deliberations as an end in itself – acts of citizenship need to be more than isolated and lonely examples of heroic sacrifice.

In this light, the inspiration behind this book may well have as its unrecognized ground the need to provide a sense of hope in an era of worldlessness. 'The modern growth of worldlessness, the withering away of everything between us, can also be described as the spread of a desert' (Arendt, 2005, p. 201). Seeking to provide images of acts of political freedom in an era that lacks the commonality required to see them as part of the space of appearance is a hopeful enterprise, a sense of faith that the desert can be reclaimed; heroic acts appear without a public space but their appearance is itself an isolated reminder that acts of citizenship are always a possibility.

Notes

1 This chapter emerges from my research on the *Culture of Cities: Montreal Toronto Berlin Dublin* research project, funded by Canada's Social Science and Humanities Research Council under its Multi-Collaborative Research Initiative programme. I thank SSHRC

for making my research visits possible and Greg Nielsen, Carolyn Dirks, Roisin Bonner and Margaret O' Shea Bonner for their responses, suggestions and editorial corrections. I also acknowledge the influence of the work of the principal investigator of the above project, Alan Blum (and that of his collaborator, Peter McHugh), on all of my work – including this essay.

2   In a sense it is more like the hermeneutics of another student of Heidegger, Gadamer, than a Husserlian phenomenology.

3   In the realm of consumption, human activity refers to the exercise needed to keep the body fit and healthy.

4   That economy and cultural production should, in these plans, be seen as natural bedmates is perhaps not surprising given Arendt's insight that 'the greatest threat to the existence of the finished work arises precisely from the [means–end] mentality which brought it into being' (1968, p. 216). That is, just as the economic focus treats the world as a means to an end (of economic growth), so too does an artistic mentality.

5   This is not to say that there are not interesting issues for analysis made available by the document. Even in a discourse where the object, in this case Dublin's vision of itself, is trapped rather than revealed by the language used, we can tease out concerns and anxieties. For example, in selecting 'A City of Neighbourhoods' as the heart or central theme, this vision of Dublin seems post-modernist in orientation. Harvey (1989, p. 67) describes the architect Leon Krier's critique of the planning of the modern city (as a site of symbolic poverty) and his consequent description of the good city as one where 'the totality of urban functions' are provided within 'compatible and pleasant walking distances'. Recognizing that such an urban form 'cannot grow by extension in width and height' but only 'through multiplication', Krier seeks a city form made up of 'complete and finite urban communities', each constituting an independent urban quarter within a large family of urban quarters, that, in turn, make up 'cities within a city'. The vision document may instance what Fintan O' Toole has called Ireland's transformation from traditional to post-modern culture without ever becoming modern (1996).

References

Arendt, H. (1951) *On the Origins of Totalitarianism*, Harcourt Brace Jovanovich, San Diego, CA, New York and London.

—— (1958) *The Human Condition*, Chicago University Press, Chicago, IL.

—— (1963) *On Revolution*, Penguin Books, Harmondsworth.

—— (1968) *Between Past and Future: Eight Exercises in Political Thought*, Penguin Books, Harmondsworth.

—— (2005) *The Promise of Politics* (ed. J. Kohn), Shocken Books, New York.

Baarber, B. (1984) *Strong Democracy*. University of California Press, Berkeley.

Bernstein, R. (1983) *Beyond Objectivism and Relativism: Science, Hermeneutics and Praxis*, University of Philadelphia Press, Philadelphia, PN.

—— (1986) *Philosophical Profiles*, University of Pennsylvania Press, Philadelphia, PN.

Blum, A. (2003) *The Imaginative Structure of the City*, McGill-Queen's University Press, Montreal.

Bonner, K. (1997) *A Great Place to Raise Kids: Interpretation, Science and the Urban–Rural Debate*, McGill-Queen's Press, Montreal.

—— (1998) *Power and Parenting: A Hermeneutic of the Human Condition*, Macmillan/St. Martin's Press, London/New York.

—— (2001) 'Reflexivity and Interpretive Sociology: The Case of Analysis and the Problem of Nihilism', *Human Studies*, 24 (4), 267–92.

—— (2004) 'Continuity Change and Contradiction in Contemporary Dublin', *Canadian Journal of Irish Studies*, 30 (2).

Canovan, M. (1992) *Hannah Arendt – A Reinterpretation of Her Political Thought*, Cambridge University Press, Cambridge.

DCDB (Dublin City Development Board) (2002) *Dublin: A City of Possibilities: Economic, Social and Cultural Strategy (2002–2012)*, DCDB, Dublin.

Dowler, K. 'Planning the Culture of Cities: Cultural Policy in Dublin and Toronto', *Canadian Journal of Irish Studies* 30 (2).

Gadamer, H. G. (1975) *Truth and Method*, Sheed and Ward, London.

—— (1989) 'Destruktion and Deconstruction' in D. Mischelfelder and R. Palmer (eds), *Dialogue and Deconstruction: The Gadamer–Derrida Encounter*, State University of New York Press, Albany, NY.

Habermas, J. (1973) *Theory and Practice* (trans. J. Viertel), Beacon Press, Boston, MA.

—— (1983) *Philosophical-Political Profiles* (trans. F. Lawrence), MIT Press, Cambridge, MA.

Harvey, D. (1989) *The Condition of PostModernity*. Blackwell, Oxford.

Kateb, G. (2000) 'Political Action: Its Nature and Advantages' in D. Villa (ed.), *The Cambridge Companion to Hannah Arendt*, Cambridge University Press, Cambridge.

Kristeva, J. (2001) *Hannah Arendt* (trans. R. Guberman), Columbia University Press, New York.

O'Toole, F. (1996) *The Ex-Isle of Erin*, New Island Books, Dublin.

Parekh, B. (1981) *Hannah Arendt and the Search for a New Political Philosophy*, Macmillan, London.

Potter, M. (2007) 'The Irish Miracle', *Toronto Star*, 7 April, A1, A18-19.

Villa, D. (1996) *Arendt and Heidegger: The Fate of the Political*, Princeton University Press, Princeton, NJ.

Young-Bruehl, E. (1982) *Hannah Arendt: For Love of the World*, Yale University Press, New Haven, CN.

Chapter 7

❖

No One Is Illegal
Between City and Nation

PETER NYERS

'I'm illegal. So what?'
(T-shirt slogan, 'A Day Without Immigrants', New York City, 1 May 2006)

Acts of Non-Citizenship

This chapter investigates acts of citizenship by politicized groups of non-status migrants and refugees, and assesses the normative and political challenges they pose to established norms about citizenship, belonging and political community. Refugees and other migrants with precarious status are emerging as key protagonists in global struggles concerning freedom of movement, social recognition, worker protections and the right of asylum (McNevin 2006). In Australia, to take a well-known case, widespread resistance has been organized both within and outside a country-wide network of asylum-seeker detention centres. Hunger strikes and demonstrations by detainees have been actively supported by citizen movements outside the barbed wire fences, including a 1,000-person convergence on the Woomera detention centre in 2001 during which these fences were torn down. In Canada, over 1,000 non-status Algerians living in Montreal launched a public campaign that successfully pressured the Canadian and Quebec governments to regularize their status (Nyers 2003). In Egypt, frustrations with the refugee determination system provoked over 3,000 Sudanese 'closed file' refugees to occupy Mustafa Mahmoud Park and hold a three month sit-in outside the offices of the United Nations High Commission for Refugees in Cairo (FMRS 2006). In Europe, migrants have organized several 'Migrant Assemblies' in order to assert their voices and raise their agendas amidst the din of the 'citizen groups' that dominate the voices of the European Social Forum network. Examples of political engagement by refugees and non-status migrants could go on and on, but clearly these acts are becoming increasingly important sites of global/local politics (McNevin 2006).

The vibrancy and scope of refugee and migrants' rights movements was perhaps demonstrated most dramatically in the Spring of 2006, when undocumented migrants organized massive, record-breaking protests in major American cities. The *New York Times* (Editorial, 2006) described the events as the result of a 'miracle of grassroots mobilization that turned a shadow population into a national movement in less than a month'. The public protests culminated in a National Day of Action on 1 May 2006 – a general strike in all but name, variously called 'A Day Without Immigrants', the 'Great American Boycott', and 'the new civil rights movement'. The sheer scope of the protests is largely without precedent in American history. The number of people – citizens and non-citizens, documented and undocumented – that took to the streets broke records for public demonstrations in many cities. Conservative estimates counted 600,000 demonstrators marching in the streets of Los Angeles; 400,000 in Chicago; 50,000 in San Francisco and San Jose; 15,000 in Houston; 30,000 across Florida; and so on. Perhaps even more dramatic were the protests not covered by the major media. Small towns like Porterville (California), Yakima (Washington), El Paso (Texas), and Castroville (California) – towns where citizens rarely, if ever, engage in public protest – were witness to public demonstrations by hundreds of undocumented immigrants. While the protests have been criticized for the overuse of American flags and the appeal to American nationalism (Bauder 2006, for example), they nonetheless represent an important moment of claim making and rights taking by non-citizens. In this sense, one of the most remarkable elements of the massive protests associated with A Day Without Immigrants is that tens of thousands of protesters took to the streets *without* any mobilization by established social movement organizations. 'People were caught up in the moment', says one migrant rights activist from New York City.[1]

What insights can be gained about citizenship from these 'moments' when non-citizens with extremely precarious status assert themselves as political by publicly making claims about rights and membership, freedom and equality? In his introduction to this volume, Engin Isin contrasts the relatively enduring institutions and dispositions of habitus with the temporally focused perspective offered by 'acts' of citizenship. He proposes that investigating acts of citizenship involves a 'focus on those moments when, regardless of status and substance, subjects constitute themselves as citizens – or, better still, as those to whom the right to have rights is due'. This chapter will examine acts of citizenship with reference to the growing political movement of non-status migrants in Canada. While smaller in scope than the campaign in the United States, the movement in Canada has been equally significant in raising a number of challenges for how we understand political community and political subjectivity. The chapter will discuss the significance of a number of 'acts' by the action committees of non-status migrants: acts of self-identification as 'non-status'; acts of claim making and rights taking in the form of regularization campaigns at both the state and city levels; acts of protest in street rallies, marches and detention centres. The aim of focusing on this case is to ask some critical questions about acts of citizenship. What are the conditions under which non-status persons can constitute themselves as being political? Does the act of reclaiming the term 'non-status' by the political 'action committees' of non-status migrants qualify as an act of citizenship? Are acts of autonomy and self-representation also acts of citizenship? What kind of acts of citizenship would allow for no one to be illegal? Taken together, do these various 'acts' signal the emergence of a new subjectivity?

To investigate the political movements by non-status migrants means coming to terms with a fundamental disagreement over what counts as political. In Canada, self-organized 'action committees' of non-status migrants and refugees have emerged and asserted themselves as political by organizing against detentions and deportations, as well as pressuring the government to regularize their status. However, the action committees are regularly confronted with the problem that the identity conferred on them is one that historically has been excluded from the political domain. Non-status people not only lack the full range of citizenship rights, but they are also denied the opportunity to express themselves as political beings. Their banishment from the political, moreover, is not merely the result of national and international laws that prohibit (or make it risky for) refugees or non-citizens to act politically. The problem is as much conceptual as it is legal: it turns on the fact that historically citizenship has been the identity through which claims to political being are enacted.

Faced with the myriad ways in which non-status people have been spoken for and silenced, the aim of this chapter is similar to that of Moulier-Boutang's, who has urged us 'to seize the silences, the refusals, and the flight as something active' (2001, p. 227). How exactly to accomplish this ambitious task may always remain elusive. However, surely an important part of the answer must include a consideration of the role that 'voice' plays in the constitution of political subjectivity. To publicly self-identify as 'non-status' is to engage in a political act, or better – an act of political subjectification. What the action committees of non-status refugees and migrants illuminate is that the claim 'I am non-status' is not just a moral plea. It is rather a declaration that is generative of a political subjectivity. In a deeply paradoxical way, to self-identify as a non-status person is to engage in an act of citizenship.

Vocalizing Acts of Citizenship

To act is to put something into motion, to create something new. But the 'problem of beginning', as Said (2004) put it, is always the 'beginning of the problem'. At the origin of Western political thought is the work of Aristotle, the first political scientist, who placed certain vocal acts at the centre of his theory of the political. To be sure, questions about the political seem unavoidably intertwined with questions about voice. Aristotle emphasizes the deeply political dimensions of voice, and provides an account of the political that begins with a partitioning of different kinds of voices. In the opening passages of Aristotle's *Politics*, a crucial distinction is drawn between the voice (*phone*) that can indicate pleasure or pain, and the voice (*logos*) that can articulate the just and unjust. For Aristotle, the former is shared by both animals and humans; the latter is the sole domain of humans. It is this latter form of speech that allows one to say 'I have been wronged', introducing a standard of judgement that allows for the space of the political to emerge (Dolar 2006, pp. 105–6).

Thus politics has emerged as a practice in which the use of voice makes it possible to perform certain acts. Key among these are acts of citizenship. Isin (this volume) argues that acts of citizenship can be authored or anonymous, intended or accidental, individual or collective. In this account of citizenship what counts is not the subject's status (citizen, refugee, non-status migrant) but the act itself. Thinking about citizenship in this way makes one attentive to the enactments of citizenship, how it is performed and negotiated. Traditionally citizenship has been investigated in terms of rights and responsibilities, their substantive content or depth, and the extent to which they are (and are not) distributed across society. This approach, Isin complains, is unsuitable for interpreting acts of citizenship. 'They arrive too late', he says, 'because the actors of extent, content and depth are already produced' (Isin, this volume). For Isin, acts produce actors/subjects: 'acts produce actors that do not exist before acts'. Acts of citizenship, therefore, produce citizens and their others: strangers, outsiders, aliens. Investigating 'acts of citizenship' demands a rethinking of many of the assumptions, dispositions, biases, and fascinations of modern social and political thought: the privileging of order over change, action over acts, the enduring over the momentary, certainty over contingency, planned over accidental, and so on.

Isin's account of citizenship is part of a growing movement within citizenship studies that criticizes the exclusions rendered by the acceptance of formal citizenship as a precondition for political voice. It is becoming increasingly common to hear arguments that criteria for inclusion should rely less on formal membership than on the principle that 'all affected' people should be included in the *demos*. It follows that the right to vote in elections should be granted to resident non-citizens (Beckman 2006). To be able to vote in democratic elections is an important achievement for non-citizens, as it recognizes their autonomy, personhood and capacity to assert themselves as political beings. However, acts of voting should not be taken as the end point for acts of citizenship. What other possibilities exist for the enactment of political voice? As Dolar (2006, p. 202) points out, etymologically 'to vote' draws on the Latin words for 'wish' and 'pledge' and bears no relation to the word *vox*, voice. The relationship of voice to the political involves a much more complicated set of issues than simply the right to vote. What is at stake is the model by which the political community constitutes its subjects, audiences and spaces.

This raises an important aspect of political community that is often unappreciated and undertheorized – that the political community is also an aesthetic community. Constituting the world is always an aesthetic activity, in that it involves a framing of the given, of what can be perceived and seen, heard and heeded. There is what Jacques Rancière calls the 'partition of the sensible' that orders and polices what is visible, what can be said, who can speak. This partitioning is practised in a highly uneven fashion, and so it is important to emphasize that this is a *politics* of aesthetics. Non-status migrants are disqualified from sharing the stage with citizens as (political) actors. The equation between citizenship and the political creates an aesthetic order where non-status migrants are variously seen as a threat, a risk, or a victim. They are rarely perceived as agents, actors, participants or subjects capable of making claims and demanding rights.

Rancière's project is to enact a redistribution of the perceptible, of what can be said and seen. He bases this project on the idea of radical equality. For him, the political involves a miscount of equality. Politics occurs during those moments when those who 'do not count', who have 'no part' in the recognized social order, make a claim to be counted. These claims appear as an interruption of the established speaking order which elevates citizenship to holding a near monopoly of speech acts. In contrast to the optimism for rational and inclusive dialogue that democratic theorists look for in (global) civil society, Rancière's emphasis on interruption and disagreement as foundational political moments is worth reflecting upon and has important resonances with the dissonant speech acts of non-status migrant politics (Rancière 1999; Nyers 2006; McNevin 2006; Panagia 2006, pp. 119–24). Rancière rejects Kantian aesthetics in favour of the Burkean sublime, albeit with a significant change in emphasis. Whereas Burke saw much danger in all the commotion and furor of the sublime, 'Rancière treats the sublime as the sine qua non of political action, precisely because of its divisive nature' (Panagia 2006, p. 88). From this perspective, one does not have to be a formal citizen in order to be heard and seen in a political sense. Those who are denied the status of citizen can break into the 'consensual' system, interrupt this order, and assert themselves as a visible and speaking being. As Rancière (2006, p. 5) says, 'Politics means precisely this, that you speak at a time and in a place you're not expected to speak.'

The task of politics therefore becomes something other than representing the unrepresented. Something much more ambitious, difficult, and radical is at work here. The task becomes theorizing the political in relation to the unrepresentable. As Panagia (2006, p. 122) argues, non-status people 'are unrecognizable, yet they demand acknowledgement. Lacking a proper name, they are unrepresentable, yet they demand equality' (Panagia 2006, p. 122).

Border Lives

Who is a non-status migrant? This is a surprisingly complex question. The simple definition provided by advocacy groups working for the rights of non-status people is that 'non-status migrants are people who do not have the legal status that would allow them to live permanently in Canada' (Khandor et al. 2004). However, people can become 'non-status' for many reasons. For example, their refugee claim and/or appeal may have been rejected; they may not have official identity documents; their sponsorship relationship may have broken down; their student visa, visitor's visa, or work permit may have expired; there may be a moratorium on deportations to their country of origin. Some scholars have begun using terms such as 'uncertain status', 'precarious status', and 'gradations of status' to emphasize that one's legal position in the country – and hence one's relationship to rights, entitlements, access to services, obligations, responsibilities, and so on – cannot always be talked about in strict either/ or terms. Instead, people often move in and out of status, and between different degrees of legal status. To speak of non-status in a legal sense is to consider a number of grey areas (Goldring et al. 2007). The point, however, is that all these areas are political, and they need to be examined critically.

Technical definitions aside, in Canada, as elsewhere, many words are used to describe people without full legal immigration status. Non-status migrants are rarely portrayed in a positive or affirmative light as fully formed subjects who are capable of autonomy, self-representation and claim making. Critics who are opposed to this type of migration typically employ a pejorative discourse in order to define non-status people in terms of criminality ('illegals'), poor moral character ('queue jumpers'), or as a dangerous threat ('terrorists'). Others try to employ more neutral or humanitarian language, but here too the connotations are less than positive. In fact, it is extremely difficult to think of words to describe non-status people other than in terms of absence or lack: lack of documents ('undocumented'), lack of established travel arrangements ('irregular migrant'), lack of visibility ('clandestine workers'), lack of social status ('shadow population'), lack of security ('precarious status'), lack of humanity ('alien'). Academic writers similarly have been unable to use anything but the language of abjection and exclusion when speaking of non-status lives. Balibar (2000) describes them as the 'excluded among the excluded'; Panagia (2006) calls them *anomic:* literally, 'lacking a name'; Coutin (2000) says they occupy a 'space of non-existence'; De Genova (2002) describes the 'space of forced invisibility, exclusion, subjugation, and repression' that non-status people must negotiate in order to survive (cf. Nyers 2003).

The theme of lack is similarly echoed in interviews with non-status migrants living in Toronto and Montreal.[2] One non-status person describes the situation facing members of the Latin American community in Toronto: 'There are many people who live like ghosts.' People living this precarious life regularly describe the limited life opportunities afforded to them because of their lack of formal status:

'I am a lawyer, but if you don't have status then you are nobody.'

'A lot of employers are delighted to hear that you have no papers, because they can overwork you and exploit you.'

'It really drains you that you have to work 12-hour shifts for very little money. I used to be young. Now I feel so old.'

Non-status migrants live in constant fear of detention, deportation and surveillance by the authorities. An activist in the Toronto Philippine community tries to be honest about the ultimate absence or lack involved in advocacy work for non-status people: 'We're getting our people ready for deportation.'

The experience of lack is produced in large part by the way non-status people experience borders. For non-status people the borderline is not just at physical entry points at ports, airports, and land crossings. Clearly, border politics are no longer limited (if they ever were) to the thin lines that separate domestic from foreign, here from there, us from them, the normal from the exceptional (Walker 2006, p. 57). The border is a much thicker, more complicated site of practices; it is not 'primarily a place, but a process' (Aas 2005, p. 198), one that gets enacted wherever and whenever non-status people try to access social services provided by public officials. The border is therefore widespread and seemingly ubiquitous. For non-status people the border has literally become a 'place where one resides' (Balibar 2002, p. 83). It merges places such as health care clinics, social housing cooperatives, schools, food banks, welfare offices and police stations within a ubiquitous elsewhere. For people without status, every-day activities (working, driving, and going to school) are at risk of being transformed into criminal and illicit acts with dire consequences (De Genova 2002, p. 427). Minor transgressions such as jaywalking across a city street can land the non-status migrant in immigration detention. Activists that do support work within the Toronto Immigrant Holding Centre report that many women are incarcerated there as a result of trying to access social services. There are many documented cases in Toronto of non-status women who end up in detention (often with their Canadian-born children) after they telephoned '911' and asked for emergency services. Women making a claim for police protection from domestic violence and abusive partners are placed in detention and eventually deported once their lack of formal status is discovered (Padgham 2006). Here, we can see the highly discretionary – as opposed to law-based – aspect of immigration law (Pratt 2005, pp. 53–72), as city police make it a practice (although they are not directed to do so) to pass on details about immigration status to the deportation arm of the Canadian state, the Canadian Border Services Agency. What begins as a rights claim for protection from domestic abuse ends up with the complainant being detained and deported.

Similar concerns about bordering practices have been directed to school officials, social housing buildings and health clinics. By trying to access basic social services, non-status migrants end up triggering a deportation apparatus that implicates individuals and agencies well beyond those who directly work for Immigration Canada or the Canada Border Services Agency. For example, as a social worker who intervenes on behalf of a child experiencing abuse one may consider oneself to be acting in the best of interests of the child. However, children aid societies are mandated to report abuse to the police. If the parents are without legal status then the police will inform immigration officials, and a deportation order is usually issued. What began as an act of compassion and protection ends up as deprivation of citizenship, as the child (who may well have been born in

Canada and therefore be a citizen) is sent to the country of origin of his or her parents. Intentionally of not, social workers, school administrators, housing workers and other providers of the benefits of social citizenship become functionaries of the deportation apparatus.

Acts of bordering are also acts of citizenship in that they are part of the process by which citizens are distinguished from others: visitors, strangers, outsiders, non-status people and the rest. Like acts of citizenship, acts of bordering can be either deliberate or unintentional. Sometimes a mere visual cue to a memory of border experience is enough to enact the border once again.

> I work at an agency where there is a very large Citizenship and Immigration Canada billboard right beside the main reception area. I find that sign to be one of the biggest barriers to providing services for non-status people. For people just walking in, *even if they know that we offer services to non-status people*, they see that billboard from Citizenship and Immigration Canada and just walk away. They remember the billboard as the same one they saw at the passport office and the Immigration Review Board: the places where they were rejected in the first place! This is a huge barrier to people thinking that they would be safe and treated any different from the institutions that had previously rejected them, making them non-status.

Or as a client support worker at a multicultural healthcare centre that provides services to non-status people complains: 'My referrals are embarrassing. I refer people to more barriers. They report back to me consistently: "I went to that agency you referred me to and the minute they asked me for my documents, I just walked out the door."'

Autonomous Acts of Self-Representation

While non-status people may experience the border as highly ubiquitous, it should be emphasized that this fact does not necessarily overcode the entirety of their lives. Despite the restrictions there still seems to be room for acts of citizenship. Many non-status people speak about life in a way that is not only about fear of authorities: 'Many people live with fear. In one occasion the police got us. And in spite of that we go out. We do not live with fear.' Soumya Boussouf from the Action Committee of Non-Status Algerians also emphasizes the multiple possibilities for living as a non-status person: '[E]ven though you are a non-status person you do not even realize it. You are working; you have friends; you go out; you try to have a life despite all the barriers, despite everything – which is just normal, just human' (Lowry and Nyers 2003, p. 67).

In this context, the emergence of self-organized and autonomous action committees of non-status migrants is quite remarkable, not least for how they disrupt our expectations about what kind of action is possible by non-status migrants. In Canada, diverse communities of non-status migrants are organizing public campaigns with the aim of reframing the terms of their relationship to the political community. As one activist from the Toronto group No One Is Illegal explains:

> One of the interesting trends is that so many different community groups are coming together to support themselves and each other. Like the Philippinos, the Bangladeshis, the Iranians, the Palestinians, the Algerians ... we're really seeing a new trend of self-organized committees coming out of different communities. People in these communities are trying to figure out strategies for lobbying, mobilization, and public actions. This is something unique and we are seeing more and more of it.

The number of these self-organized and autonomous 'action committees' of non-status migrants has indeed grown dramatically in Canada, especially since the aftermath of the 9/11 attacks. A partial list of the action committees includes: the Solidarity Across Borders coalition, the Coalition against the Deportation of Palestinian Refugees, Action Committee of Pakistani Refugees, the Action Committee of Non-Status Algerians, the Human Rights Action Committee, Refugees Against Racial Profiling, and many others. The allies of these action committees are also numerous and diverse, but a growing number of them explicitly define themselves as allies in solidarity with, and not leaders of, this movement, and actively support the work of the non-status action committees. Again, a partial list of these groups include the Ontario Coalition Against Poverty, Justice for Migrant Workers, the STATUS Coalition, the Vancouver Association of Chinese Canadians and the autonomous No One Is Illegal groups in Toronto, Montreal, Vancouver, and other Canadian cities.

The emergence of non-status political action committees demonstrates that, like citizenship, migration can be understood as a strategy of becoming political. In a similar vein, Mitropoulos (2006, p. 8) describes migration as 'a strategy ... undertaken in and against the cramped spaces of the global political economies of work, gender and desire, among other things, but a strategy for all that'. Thinking about migration as a kind of strategy grants a certain autonomy to a phenomenon that is usually understood in relationship to various structural 'push' and 'pull' factors. What is sometimes called 'autonomous migration' is an extra-legal form of self-directed migration undertaken by individuals and communities as a survival strategy when states and other institutions no longer provide the conditions for an adequate quality of life (Rodriguez 1996). This perspective sees migration as a complex social force that constitutes a social and political challenge to global controls on freedom of movement, albeit in ways that are only partially intentional and self-conscious (Mezzadra 2004).

The idea of the 'autonomy of migration' is easily confused with other concepts or processes. For example, autonomy here is not meant to imply a form of migration that is somehow independent of economic or other pressures and forces. Nor is it meant to imply that the migrant, in making the choice to move, is somehow the embodiment of a Kantian self-identical subject, making claims to cosmopolitan rights of hospitality. Instead, as Mitropoulos (2006, p. 10) explains, the autonomy of migration means 'that one does *not* concern oneself with the reasons why an other wishes to move across borders, simply put: it insists that the other is autonomous from oneself, particularly where one's *self* is most liable to assume the pose of deciding on such matters for an other, either because one's own belonging is not in question *or* as a means to prove that it should not be'. The political acts of non-status migrants can therefore destabilize comfortable assumptions regarding political community that equate belonging with citizenship status. Perhaps the most radical consequence of this politics is the recasting of the terms, subjects and spaces of the political itself. As Mitropoulos (2006, p. 10) argues: 'the concept of the autonomy of migration is an insistence that politics does not need to be the property of the state and those who – however implicitly and by dint of a claim to belong to it, as the subject that is *proper to it* (its property) – can claim to reserve for themselves the thought and action that is deemed to be properly political'.

One of the key means by which non-status people in Canada have asserted their autonomy as political actors is by reclaiming the discourse that defines their existence. This is an accomplishment that should not be underemphasized as there has been a significant change in the language and terminology used to describe them. There has been an important, albeit partial and contested, change in Canadian public discourse over the past decade from common references to 'illegal immigrants' to a more regular use of the term 'non-status'. The charge of illegality is meant to undermine the moral character of certain types of migrants to Canada. The term 'illegal' implies a breaking of the legal order, a violation of rule-following norms of behaviour, and an intention to commit a wrong. By contrast the term non-status signifies a set of meanings with a wider range of political possibilities.

As we saw above, non-status people may actually have a variety of statuses within the governmental order. The point of the term is not to designate a strict legal status, an either/or situation whereby one is either legal or not. Such logic is clearly out-of-step with the complex way in which states and migrants negotiate residency, the right to work or study, refugee status and other means through which people come to work, study and live in Canada. The point is that the 'non-status' are without any standing, rank, or position in a political order that privileges citizenship. The non-status migrant is of no consequence; they are 'needed but unwelcome' (Appadurai 2006, p. 44). The self-designation of 'non-status', especially when it is articulated in public through words, images, or voice, is an articulation of a wrong. The demand of 'status for all' is really a demand for 'equality for all'. Equality here means equal access to the rights of social citizenship: healthcare, social welfare and the rest. But it is also a demand for recognition and respect of the dignity of non-status people as human beings. To self-identify as non-status is to articulate a grievance to a community in which one has no legal or moral standing. In this way, the use of the term 'non-status' can signal the emergence of a new political subjectivity.

Acts of Regularization: Between City and Nation

The key means by which the action committees have made claims to equality is through the demand for regularization. As a result of several years of cross-national networking between migrant rights groups and the action committees of non-status people, a series of common demands have emerged. These demands include an end to deportations; an end to the detention of migrants, immigrants, and refugees; and the abolition of 'security certificates' (a measure in Canadian immigration law that allows non-citizens deemed to be a threat to 'national security' to be held in detention indefinitely, without charge, and under secret evidence). The main demand, however, is that the Canadian government should intro-duce a programme to regularize the status of *all* non-status migrants. These are ambitious, even audacious demands – and the political ground is tricky: historically the Canadian state has proved quite adept at excluding large numbers of non-status immigrants in its regularization programmes.

While regularization programmes are usually pitched as humanitarian acts of a compassionate government, the political reality is much more complex. Governments, for example, often introduce regularization pro-grammes when they are planning major changes to Canadian immigration law. Regularization programmes allow people who were still in the clutches of the old system to be dealt with before new – usually more restrictive and exclusionary – immigration procedures are introduced. In this way, regularization programmes can go hand in hand with the imposi-tion of tighter border regimes, more restrictive immigration controls, and harsher punishments on non-status immigrants. Moreover, the selection criteria used in regularization programmes are part of the complex set of practices that work to produce and stabilize notions of citizenship and belonging. As a method of categorization, these criteria (such as criminality, medical inadmissibility, economic wealth, length of residency, level of 'integration', family connections or country of origin) separate those 'worthy' of legal status, permanent residency, and eventual formal citizenship from those deemed undesirable, unworthy of status, and potentially dangerous to the national body politic. As a result, people with criminal records (however minor) and serious medical conditions (even if the illness originated in Canada) are likely be excluded from regularization. In the end, the criteria are implicated in a nationalist production of fear, and reinforce a racialized discourse that constructs the immigrant as dangerous and diseased – to be screened, tested, monitored and contained.

The problems associated with making a claim on the state to regularize status are well known to the action committees and their allies. Increasingly, the demand for regularization is being directed at the level of the city as a way to sidestep many of the exclusions enabled by state-level policies. This strategy has found its inspiration in developments in the United States, where many municipalities have developed 'local citizenship' policies for non-status migrants. These include issuing driver licences, providing in-state tuition rates for public colleges and universities, and even non-citizen voting in local elections (Varsanyi 2006). Another source of inspiration has been the International Parliament of Writers' 'cities of refuge' network, which offers hospitality and refuge to persecuted writers. The action committees of non-status migrants and their allies have begun to construct such a politics within Canadian cities, albeit with an important difference in how to approach sanctuary. The international cities of refugee network inspired by the IPW aims to advance freedom of expression and international solidarity by providing hospitality to persecuted writers. The aims of the city-based non-status campaigns are more ambitious. Instead of sanctuary being enjoyed by a single individual, hospitality would be shown to the tens of thousands of non-status people living in major Canadian cities. The struggle here is to envision emerging forms of international solidarity that advocate not only global freedom of movement and the right to cross borders, but also the right to stay where one already lives.

The action committees of non-status migrants have been active in campaigns to create sanctuary cities. The common tactic is to lobby municipalities to adopt some version of a 'Don't Ask, Don't Tell' (DADT) policy with regard to immigration status. These policies prohibit municipal employees from asking about an individual's immigration status ('don't ask'), and also stop them from sharing this information with immigration or other government authorities ('don't tell'). Such a policy would ensure that municipal funds, resources and workers would not be used to enforce federal or provincial immigration laws. A DADT municipal policy could ensure that city services are available to all city residents on the basis of residency and need, and without discrimination on the basis of immigration status. Since many non-status persons have difficulty obtaining official documents, the criteria of residency could act as a border. A more radical approach to realizing a sanctuary city would be to guarantee these services on the basis of one's presence within the city alone, and without the need to prove one's residency. Membership would be treated as a matter of social fact rather than legal status.

In the United States, over fifty municipalities have adopted some kind of DADT policy. In Canada, a DADT campaign was launched in Toronto in March 2004, with over forty community organizations as active participants. Groups in Vancouver and Montreal are considering similar campaigns. In a short period of time the Toronto DADT campaign has built momentum and received serious attention from the media, city councillors and the community at large. By 2007, both the police and the public school system in Toronto had formally endorsed a DADT policy. A DADT campaign advocates the provision of city services on the basis of residency, not immigration status. If successful, it will constitute a *de facto* regularization programme. This is a canny recognition of the exclusions that are always built into state-level regularization programmes. Those who were excluded from such a programme would continue to be able to access health, education, police and other city services without the fear of having their lack of status exposed and reported to immigration officials and border police.

To the extent that the city becomes a site of immigration policy making – a prerogative reserved for the state – this may be a form of 'municipal foreign policy' (Hobbs 1994) that poses a serious challenge to the state as the site of a transformative politics. Is there the possibility that, as Derrida (2001, p. 4) hoped with regard to the 'cities of refuge' network, DADT cities will 'reorient the politics of the state', 'transform and reform the modalities of membership', and participate in the construction of 'solidarities yet to be invented'?

Mediating Acts of Citizenship

To the extent that the demand for regularization of status is focused on recognition by state and other governmental authorities, is it really all that radical? Is this a politics that envisions formal state citizenship as its end goal? To be sure, the connections between status and the state are deep, right down to the level of language. Etymologies reveal that the words 'status' and 'state' share the same Latin root: *stare* – meaning 'to stand'. The association of 'standing' with immobility, stasis, and lack of change implies a *status quo*, a conservatism regarding the standards of normality. Status, moreover, implies an implicit ranking or standing within society and so assumes a hierarchy of belonging. At the same time, however, a more disruptive reading of the root 'to stand' is also possible. To stand also means to be seen, to become public, to be among the counted, to demonstrate one's existence and presence. Hence, standing requires a certain quotient of courage.

Investigating the moments when non-status people 'act' as political allows us to move beyond the conservative elements of campaigns for status and focus on their potential for novel forms of political subjectification. The transformative dimension of acts of (non-)citizenship can be seen in the many public demonstrations and protests marches organized by the action committees and their allies. The presence of non-status people at a protest rally, for example, will have a mediating effect on the acts available to those citizens also present at the protest. It is quite normal for the rallies and marches organized for non-status rights to define themselves as 'child friendly'. As a result, activists with experience of, and perhaps even a preference for, direct action tactics have had to modify their own performances of citizenship. As Burman (2006, p. 288) notes with regards to anti-deportation actions in Montreal: 'Bold anti-poverty activists – whom I have seen in other contexts antagonize the police – here consent to organizers' insistence that because of the precarious legal status of many of the demonstrators, participants must agree on a peaceful behavioural protocol.' Out of similar concerns, speechmakers at rallies have had to slow down their speeches in order to ensure that all protesters understand their political points. The act of citizens and non-status people raising their voices together in a public space to declare that 'No One Is Illegal' or 'Status for All' or 'So so so! Solidarité! Avec, avec, avec les Refugiés!' can also have the effect of opening new possibilities for collective political engagement.

> The 'nous' in 'donnez-nous nos papiers', when uttered by citizens and non-citizens alike, changes the usual channels of nation-state-based community building and thus challenges the preexisting conduits of circulation ... and makes visible the city as a node of differential temporalities and asymmetric orientations to the nation. (Burman 2006, p. 290)

A flyer handed out during a Status for All march in Montreal in May 2007 underscored this point: 'We march to refute the division between "citizen" and "non-citizen", between "good" and "bad" immigrants, between "guest" and "permanent" workers, between those who deserve rights, and others who don't.'

Must the acting subject be present in order for an act of citizenship to have occurred? The answer would seem to be no. During 16–25 June 2005 hundreds of members of the coalition Solidarity across Borders and their allies walked over 200 km from Montreal to the Parliament in Ottawa to demand the regularization of all non-status persons in Canada. A flyer handed out during the march, titled *Why We Are Marching*, declared that protesting non-status migrants 'refuse to be invisible and silenced'. The flyer explained that the marchers were on their way to Ottawa in order to rectify a wrong that had been committed against them: 'We are marching because there is no such thing as an "illegal" human being, only unjust laws and illegitimate governments.' The flyer also invoked the names of dozens of community members who had 'been removed, detained, forced under-ground or forced into sanctuary'. Key among these names was Shamim Akhtar, a Pakistani refugee claimant and active member of Solidarity Across Borders and the Action Committee of Pakistani Refugees.

The March to Ottawa was an idea proposed by Akhtar in the summer of 2003. The Akhtar family was one of the most active families within the Action Committee, and worked to fight the deportation of hundreds of Pakistani non-status refugees from Montreal. Their asylum claim was rejected by the Canadian state, and the Akhtar family was deported in the summer of 2004. Akhtar, an activist within Solidarity across Borders, proposed the idea of a March to Ottawa in the summer of 2003. Her removal from Canada notwithstanding, her agency left an impression that could not be erased by her deportation. As Burman (2006, p. 281) explains: 'When people are removed, their absence leaves an imprint; the intimates they have left behind restructure their everyday lives around that imprint.' Burman argues that when the 'imprint' of absence is transposed into a presence within the city, all sorts of possibilities emerge for 'radical differ-ence and hybridization' to emerge.

The act of marching is deeply political. Etymologies of the verb 'march' suggest a connection to the Frankish word for 'to mark out, delimit' and so it is related to words such as borderland, boundary and frontier. Surprisingly, one of the meanings of the verb march is 'to have status'. To march, therefore, not only implies a progressive and forward-moving action; it is also related to the limits of the political, where insiders and outsiders, citizens and non-citizens are drawn. The non-status march is therefore a limit act of citizenship.

But is the emphasis on voice and audibility an overemphasis? Does it not retain and reproduce a certain liberal paradigm about citizenship which emphasizes audibility as opposed to visibility? Is it too much of a burden to have to be able to speak in public in order to be recognized as political? Is it not a problematic position to assume that everyone will know what it means to make a claim that can be recognized as such? In December 2003, No One Is Illegal established the Arts in Detention group for women and children being held in the Toronto Immigrant Holding Centre. The purpose of the art group is to 'bring the messages of those incarcerated within its walls to the outside world in order to undermine nationalist assumptions of Canada as a multicultural, immigrant-welcoming nature'. The group also has as its aim to create 'a space to open up discussion on the issues faced by non-status immigrants in Canada'.[3] Detention centres are designed to separate non-status people not only from the world on the outside, but from people within the facility as well. The art group was a special initiative that allowed detainees to actually engage, dialogue and interact with one another. As Farrah Miranda points out: 'The art group is the only thing at the detention centre that pulls all these women from different places to the same table, looking at each other, facing each other. It's really human' (Padgham 2006, p. 181).

While life in detention makes the expression of political voice in any public way very difficult, the Arts in Detention group enabled expression through visual means. The artwork produced by the detainees was displayed to the broader public in May 2005, when the art produced by the women and children in detention was displayed as part of Toronto's annual Mayworks Arts Festival. This has given women detainees the opportunity to constitute themselves as cultural subjects. And since the artwork has been shown in galleries and reproduced in magazines and books, they are also becoming interlocutors in the debate about their condition. Much of their contribution to this debate is raising fundamental political questions about freedom, autonomy and equality. Arts in Detention member Sima Zeheri explains: 'A lot of their work is quite political, whether it's images of their homes and children or families, or explicit political messages and phrases. Often their art talks about wanting to stay in Canada, wanting to be free, stating that they are not criminals and that they shouldn't be in detention' (Padgham 2006, p. 180). The art group had a restorative power Zeheri had not expected:

> I thought it would be a lot grimmer, and it is, but there is more, too. There were days when I was working as a volunteer with an NGO that provides basic services at the detention centre and I would see forty people and thirty of them would be in tears. But in the art group, you also see people supporting each other, you see how they survive and keep up their sense of humour and joy of life and optimism. There is almost a forgiveness of everything that was

happening to them. I feel awed and humbled by the people inside, their courage and their perseverance. (Padgham 2006, p. 181)

Conclusions

What does investigating the political acts of non-status migrants reveal about acts of citizenship? The focus on acts allows one to think about citizenship in terms other than debates over legal status, the distribution of rights, or identity politics (Joppke 2007). Investigating acts of citizenship not only allows for these dimensions to be addressed and discussed, it also insists that the focus be on those moments – those acts – when, regardless of status, subjects constitute themselves as citizens, as those to whom the right to have rights is due. From the perspective of acts, when a group of non-status migrants make a demand for regularization, or protest against an upcoming deportation, or come out in public and shout 'Status for All' and 'No One Is Illegal', we can hear these declarations as more than moral pleas for better, more humanitarian treatment. Rather, they can be heard as declarations that are generative of a political subjectivity. The process of subjectification in this context allows non-status groups to extract themselves from the hegemonic categories by which political identity is normally understood. It is quite a wonderful paradox to say that publicly self-identifying as a non-status migrant is to engage in an act of citizenship.

In his theorization of acts of citizenship, Isin (this volume) suggests that three principles emerge when investigating citizenship. What can we learn about acts of citizenship from our discussion of the political activism of non-status migrants? The first is that acts of citizenship are not inherently exclusionary or inclusive, but can be interpreted as such through their consequences and effects. What are the effects of the acts of non-citizenship that have been discussed in this chapter? The key effect is that we are witnessing an interruption and transformation of the political. The lives of non-status people do not fit neatly into the frameworks of inclusion or exclusion, welcomed or rejected, dangerousness or vicitimage. Non-status migrants may be subjected to all of these discourses and practices, but they are also emerging as something more, something else, something other. They are not merely the citizen's Other, but also other claims-making and rights-taking political beings.

The second principle of studying acts of citizenship is that because acts produce subjects, finding an explicit motive or rationale for action is not a paramount concern. Subjects can enact themselves as political without articulating directly their reasons for acting as citizens. This dimension of acts of citizenship was demonstrated in several ways. Organizing street protests where both citizens and non-status people are active participants has the effect of tempering the speech acts of citizens. The Arts in Detention group allows for non-status detainees to express themselves politically without uttering a word. The 'Don't Ask, Don't Tell' approach to sanctuary cities does not require any intentionality or even an admission of being non-status. Isin's second principle would seem to be confirmed by these examples.

There are, of course, some complex challenges involved in these acts. There is the issue that whereas citizens can speak with an assured voice and assume an audience within civil society, communities of non-status migrants can make no such assumptions. As a result they have had to invent the strategy of interruption: they have had to organize their community, mobilize voices, stretch the norms of acceptable behaviour, and, at times, even break the law. There are also some serious limitations and dangers involved in the key demand for regularization. In addition to the problematic criteria, discriminations, and borderings involved in state-initiated regularization programmes, the sanctuary city approach has limits as well.[4] In the first place, there is the concern that sanctuary cities of this kind operate on the basis of a secret. There is a definite sense of freedom of movement to be gained by the knowledge that interaction with municipal authorities will not inadvertently trip a borderline. However, the whole policy of DADT rests on the assumption of anonymity. Does this not reproduce the logic of silence, subterfuge and secrecy that already determines much of the daily existence of non-status people? Nor does the demand for regularization address how the border is a temporal as much as a spatial experience. Time is a key factor in the logic of border management and control. Like all border experiences, the temporal dimension is experienced differently depending on one's class, status, race, gender, country of origin, and so on. For some, the border can involve delays, increased wait times, incarceration and detention. For others, it can mean expedited movement and speedy processing for being a 'trusted' traveller (Bhandar 2004). Border time still affects people past their crossing into legal status. The point is that border times still affect racialized immigrant communities even when they are regularized: second- and third-generation immigrants still get regarded as 'immigrants', citizens who are somehow foreign to the nation.

Finally, Isin asks us to consider the possibility that acts of citizenship can happen without being founded in law or responsibility. The politics of non-status migrants seems to take a paradoxical stance on this question. On the one hand, the most immediate concern is to pressure governments, both local and national, to regularize the legal status of all non-status migrants.

While contesting territory within the zone of illegality, the movement nonetheless grounds its key demands within the law. On the other hand, these are clearly acts that call the law into question, and even break it. To become recognized as responsible it would seem that acts of irresponsibility must be undertaken. Street protests need to be organized; the offices of bureaucrats with authority to stop a deportation need to be occupied; claims must be made by those without the authority to speak; rights must be taken by those who have no right to have rights. In these ways and many others, politicized groups of non-status migrants are enacting themselves as citizens even when the law does not recognize them as such.

Notes

1   This point was made by Rafael Samanez from the group Esperanza del Barrio at the public forum 'Status for All! Reflections on Immigrant Justice Movements in Canada and the United States', Citizenship Studies Media Lab, York University, Toronto, Canada, 29 March 2007.

2   Unless otherwise noted, quotations for this chapter are drawn from extensive focus group discussions and individual qualitative interviews with non-status immigrants, refugee and migrant rights activists, community agency workers, lawyers and academics. These interviews were conducted in June–August 2004 and June–August 2005 in Toronto and Montreal. The non-status immigrants interviewed for this study represent a diverse group, and included members from the Algerian, Argentinean, Bangladeshi, Brazilian, Caribbean, Colombian, Iranian, Palestinian and Philippine non-status communities in Toronto and Montreal.

3   Information on the Arts in Detention group is available on the No One Is Illegal – Toronto website: <http://toronto.nooneisillegal.org>.

4   For example, a DADT policy does not address the exploitation that non-status people face in areas such as employment. In fact, unscrupulous employers who exploit the labour of non-status people through overwork, dangerous conditions and low pay may actually benefit from such a policy. After all, the physical and mental health of their workforce is likely to improve if non-status people are able to access basic healthcare from the city.

References

Aas, K. (2005) '"Getting ahead of the Game": Border Technologies and the Changing Spaces of Governance' in M. Salter and E. Zureik (eds), *Global Surveillance and Policing: Borders, Security, Identity*, Willam Publishing, Devon.

Appadurai, A. (2006) *Fear of Small Numbers: An Essay on the Geography of Anger*, Duke University Press, Durham.

Balibar, E. (2000) 'What We Owe to the *Sans-papiers*' in L. Guenther and C. Heesters (eds), *Social Insecurity: Alphabet City No. 7*, Anansi, Toronto.

Balibar, E. (2002) *Politics and the Other Scene*, Verso, London.

Bauder, H. (2006) 'And the Flag Waved On: Immigrants Protest, Geographers Meet in Chicago', *Environment and Planning A*, 38 (6), 1001–4.

Beckman, L. (2006) 'Citizenship and Voting Rights: Should Resident Aliens Vote?', *Citizenship Studies*, 10 (2), 153–65.

Bhandar, D. (2004) 'Renormalizing Citizenship and Life in Fortress North America', *Citizenship Studies*, 8 (3), 261–78.

Burman, J. (2006) 'Absence, "Removal", and Everyday Life in the Diasporic City: Anti-detention/Antideportation Activism in Montreal', *Space and Culture*, 9 (3), 279–93.

Coutin, S. B. (2000) *Legalizing Moves: Salvadoran Immigrants' Struggle for US Residency*, University of Michigan Press, Ann Arbor, MI.

De Genova, N. P. (2002) 'Migrant "Illegality" and Deportability in Everyday Life', *Annual Review of Anthropology*, 31, 419–47.

Derrida, J. (2001), *On Cosmopolitanism and Forgiveness*, Routledge, New York.

Dolar, M. (2006) *A Voice and Nothing More*, MIT Press, Cambridge, MA.

Editorial (2006) 'The Sleeping Giant', *The New York Times*, 29 April 2006, A10.

FMRS (Forced Migration and Refugee Studies) Program (2006) 'A Tragedy of Failures and False Expectations: Report on the Events Surrounding the Three-month Sit-in and Forced Removal of Sudanese Refugees in Cairo, September–December 2005', American University in Cairo, Cairo, 65 pp. (June).

Goldring, L. C. Berinstein, J. Bernhard (2007), 'Institutionalizing Precarious Immigration Status in Canada', CERIS Work Paper No. 61, Toronto: Centre for Excellence for Research on Immigration and Settlement.

Hobbs, H. (1994) *City Hall Goes Abroad: The Foreign Policy of Local Politics*, Sage, Thousand Oaks, CA.

Joppke, C. (2007) 'Transformation of Citizenship: Status, Rights, Identity', *Citizenship Studies*, 11 (1), 37–48.

Khandor, E., J. McDonald, P. Nyers and C. Wright (2004) 'The Regularization of Non-Status Immigrants in Canada, 1960–2004: Past Policies, Current Perspectives, Active Campaigns', unpublished report prepared for the STATUS Campaign, Toronto.

Lowry, M. and P. Nyers (2003) 'Roundtable Report. "No One Is Illegal": The Fight for Refugee and Migrant Rights in Canada', *Refuge: Canada's Periodical on Refugees*, 21 (3), 66–72.

McNevin, A. (2006) 'Political Belonging in a Neoliberal Era: The Struggle of the Sans-Papiers', *Citizenship Studies*, 10 (2), 135–51.

Mezzadra, S. (2004) 'The Right to Escape', *Ephemera* 4 (3), 267–75.

Mitropoulos, A. (2006) 'Autonomy, Recognition, Movement', *The Commoner*, 11, 5–14.

Moulier-Boutang, Y. and S. Grelet (2001), 'The Art of Flight: An Interview with Yann Moulier-Boutang', *Rethinking Marxism*, 13 (3/4), 227–35.

Nyers, P. (2003) 'Abject Cosmopolitanism: The Politics of Protection in the Anti-Deportation Movement', *Third World Quarterly*, 24 (6), 1069–93.

—— (2006) 'Taking Rights, Mediating Wrongs: Disagreements over the Political Agency of Non-Status Refugees' in J. Huysmans, A. Dobson and R. Prokhovnik (eds), *The Politics of Protection: Sites of Insecurity and Political Agency*, Routledge, London.

Padgham, O. (2006) 'Arts in Detention: Creating Connections with Immigrant Women Detainees' in D. Barndt (ed.), *Wild Fire: Art as Activism*, Sumach Press, Toronto.

Panagia, D. (2006) *The Poetics of Political Thinking*, Duke University Press, Durham, NC.

Pratt, A. (2005) *Securing Borders: Detention and Deportation in Canada*, University of British Columbia Press, Vancouver.

Rancière, J. (1999) *Dis-agreement: Politics and Philosophy*, University of Minnesota Press, Minneapolis, MN.

—— (2006), 'Our Police Order: What Can Be Said, Seen, and Done', *Le Monde Diplomatique* (Oslo), 8 August 2006.

Rodriguez, N. (1996) 'The Battle for the Border: Notes on Autonomous Migration, Transnational Communities, and the State', *Social Justice*, 23 (3), 21–37.

Said, E. (2004) *Beginnings: Intention and Method*, Columbia University Press, New York.

Varsanyi, M. W. (2006) 'Interrogating "Urban Citizenship" *vis-à-vis* Undocumented Migration', *Citizenship Studies*, 10 (2), 229–49.

Walker, R. B. J. (2006) 'The Double Outside of the Modern International', *Ephemera*, 6 (1), 56–69.

Chapter 8

❖

Acts of Demonstration:
Mapping the Territory
of (Non-)Citizenship

WILLIAM WALTERS

Sangatte, 1999–2002

Sangatte is a remote and by most accounts unremarkable village near the busy port of Calais in northern France. But from 1999 until 2002, and arguably until this day, 'Sangatte' functioned as a signifier for a set of complexities and tensions related to issues of asylum, borders, migrants and citizenship in contemporary Europe. In 1999 the French government requisitioned a vast hangar of 25,000 square metres. Previously the hangar had stored drilling equipment used by the Eurotunnel company to build the undersea link between France and the UK. Placed under the humanitarian auspices of the Red Cross, the hangar was turned into a makeshift refugee reception centre, or, as many observers were to call it, a 'refugee camp'. The aim was to accommodate the increasing numbers of migrants who were drawn to nearby Calais in attempting to cross the Channel to England. Until it was closed by the French government on 5 November 2002, as many as 76,000 people passed through Sangatte. In some ways the changing population of the centre offered a microcosm of shifting 'humanitarian crises' in the wider world. Initially the centre was populated mainly by people fleeing conflicts in the Balkans. That population gave way to refugees escaping Afghanistan. By the time the centre was closed the largest group was predominantly young male Iraqi Kurds (Coureau 2003).

A host of political issues and interests converged on the space of Sangatte. For transportation companies Sangatte was primarily a problem of business. The railway company Eurostar took legal action against the French Government in a bid to close the centre because of the financial burden which security against unauthorized migrants was placing upon its commercial operations. It also initiated legal action in the English courts, where it challenged the UK Government's proposal to fine companies for every 'illegal immigrant' arriving on their trains (*Daily Telegraph* 2001). Journalists and TV cameras also converged in great numbers on Sangatte. In British news reporting Sangatte was associated closely with the migrants' repeated attempts to board moving trains and 'break in' to the tunnel and the UK itself. On at least one occasion TV coverage showed migrants apparently 'storming' the tunnel entrance in a bid to 'walk under the waves to Britain' (*Observer* 2001). For significant sections of British public opinion events at Sangatte stood for a French government bent on offloading its unwanted population upon the United Kingdom, while for others it testified to the 'over-generous' terms of the UK's asylum provisions, terms which made their country an 'Eldorado' for asylum seekers. In the French press Sangatte came to symbolize among other things 'the plight of the refugees, their hellish journeys to the west, their nightmare dealings with the ... people smugglers' (*Guardian* 2001). Never missing an opportunity to play upon Anglo/ French comparisons and rivalries, many commentators in both countries found in the controversy at Sangatte one more occasion to manufacture national identity.

But Sangatte also became a temporary social observatory concerning new forms of migration, not least the risky transit purveyed by *les passeurs*, the 'people smugglers' (Coureau 2003). As a result of a series of intrepid, undercover sorties by journalists, a more nuanced and contradictory portrait of the centre emerged. The public learnt almost at first hand of the dire conditions at Sangatte; the tactics and the resolve with which the migrants sought to 'breach' the fortified entrance to the tunnel; and the extent to which the smugglers now structured life in the centre and its environs. Sangatte also offered sociologists and ethnographers a laboratory where for three years it was possible to observe at relatively close quarters the new kinds of migration that were so troubling European publics. Consequently a sociological and ethnographic knowledge of Sangatte has also emerged (Coureau 2003; Laacher 2002; Schwenken 2003).

I have started with Sangatte because it is an event that condenses two themes that will be central to the first part of this chapter: *homo sacer* and autonomous migration. These are both themes that have become highly topical, and in some ways controversial, within recent social theories of migration and citizenship. The first theme comes to us from Giorgio Agamben's theorization of the 'ban' and its production of 'naked life' (Agamben 1998, 2000). It has been widely adopted within critical migration and refugee studies, sociology, and international relations theory to map the ways in which contemporary programmes of immigration control, and the regimes of citizenship which underpin them, ensnare 'irregular migrants' in an indeterminate space ('the camp') that is neither fully inside nor outside the social and legal order (Diken 2004; Diken and Lautsen 2002; Edkins 2000; Perera 2002; Prem Kumar and Grundy-Warr 2004).

The second theme is in some respects the polar opposite of *homo sacer*. If the latter designates a space and an identity where the migrant appears suspended between an inside and an outside, positioned as a vulnerable, 'bare' existence, the theme of autonomous migration offers a quite different and in certain respects more optimistic view of unauthorized forms of migration – one that signals their transformative potential (Hardt and Negri 2000; Mezzadra 2004; Mezzadra and Neilson 2003; Rodriguez 1996). In the figure and the elusive movement of the irregular migrant, many theorists of autonomous migration have detected a deterritorializing force that is unravelling statist regimes of citizenship and, in some cases, prefiguring new spaces of affinity and community. For researchers in this second vein, migration is a potentially creative social movement capable of confounding and destabilizing the distributions and markings of sovereign power.

Scholarly interest in both themes has advanced rapidly in recent years. Yet it is a somewhat curious fact that, at least as far as studies of migration and citizenship are concerned, to date there has been relatively little dialogue between these positions (but see Mezzadra and Neilson 2003). Perhaps this is because they are quite different in tone and in the political conclusions towards which they tend. Whatever the reasons, the first aim of this chapter is to call for greater interchange between these two trajectories. I am particularly interested in a set of questions that theories of autonomous migration might raise for *homo sacer*. To what extent is the frequently bleak and occasionally apocalyptic vision that Agamben and his followers offer us challenged by the perspective of autonomous migration? How is the argument that the irregular migrant has become *homo sacer* modified once we recognize more fully the strategic and agonistic character of contemporary border crossings – that mobility is, in other words, a site of struggle in its own right? Is 'the camp' an adequate 'diagram' (Deleuze 1998, pp. 34–44) for expressing these struggles, or does it actually obscure new acts and spaces of citizenship?

In the final two sections of the chapter I turn to recent work developing the theme of acts of citizenship. Calling as it does for an analytical focus on the various ways in which citizenship is enacted, performed and contingently assembled, I argue that this discursive theme moves us beyond Agamben's preoccupation with mechanisms of capture. For it helps us to understand better the occasions when those captured outside a given socio-political order have managed to invent or appropriate forms of political subjectivity for themselves, and sometimes to interrupt that order. Further research in this vein will surely serve as a critical provocation to the gloomy image of the camp. But it should also function as a caution to those who, like Hardt and Negri (2000), would found a theory of global citizenship on the evidence of autonomous migration.

While recognizing the merits of an analytical focus on the act, I caution against a generalized application of the notion of acts of citizenship. The key argument towards which the chapter builds is that political analysis should not overlook those moments when political interventions refuse to make strong claims in the name of citizenship. I shall argue that by ignoring the case of those acts which intentionally or unintentionally, strategically or habitually leave relatively open the question of the identity of the protagonists whom they engage, we blind ourselves to the political possibilities that inhere in certain moments of struggle. I develop this point by returning to the scene of Sangatte. More specifically I examine a recent project by the collective An Architektur. This group has produced a series of maps of the migration and security processes that occurred at Sangatte. Reading this political intervention as an act of demonstration rather than an act of citizenship, I argue that An Architektur abstains from making strong claims about the political identity of the migrants at Sangatte. Instead, its activities serve to demonstrate Sangatte as a sort of new frontier, one for which our current forms of knowledge are patently inadequate. All mapping is necessarily selective and partial. But in this case mapping can be interpreted as an act appealing to a public forum that is yet to come, and invoking the possibility of a public discourse in which the identities of its subjects are not predetermined.

Unauthorized Migration and *Homo Sacer*

Few theorists have won as much attention from critical scholars in recent years as Giorgio Agamben. In a series of controversial and highly original studies he has set out a unique perspective on the relationship between sovereign power, biopolitics, law and subjectivity under modern conditions (Agamben 1998; Agamben 2000). Agamben presents a narrative in which contemporary politics tends ever more to become subsumed within biopolitics, and the figure of the citizen approximates a naked, exposed form of life, stripped of rights and vulnerable to the 'decisionistic' operations of sovereign authorities. At the centre of this narrative is the figure of *homo sacer*, which Agamben adapts from Roman history. This was the being who was banned – placed outside both sacred and political domains in such a way that, if he was killed, such a death was capable of counting as neither murder nor sacrifice. *Homo sacer* is thus a form of 'naked life 'which, according to Agamben, was once the 'hidden foundation of sovereignty' but today has become 'the dominant form of life everywhere' (2000, p. 6). Naked life materializes in all manner of circumstances: it is a consequence of the tendency towards the biotechnical management and enhancement of human life, just as it can arise in situations where populations find themselves deported, expelled and stateless, stripped of the rights of citizenship and dependent upon regimes of humanitarian assistance for their existence. It was in the dreadful figure of Auschwitz that naked life achieved perhaps its most vivid expression. But today, Agamben insists, 'we are all virtually *homines sacri'* (1998, p. 115).

Agamben's work has proved particularly influential in critical migration studies, especially amongst those seeking to make sense of new configurations of citizenship and non-citizenship. His concept of the space that he calls 'the camp' has offered critical theorists a paradigm of the complex and ambiguous location – at once social, legal and spatial – that refugees and other forms of unwanted and/or unauthorized migrants occupy today. The camp names a space that is formally outside the juridical and political order, but, because it *captures* its subjects outside, is never a condition of pure externality (2000, p. 40):

> The camp is the space that opens up when the state of exception starts to become the rule. In it, the state of exception, which was essentially a temporal suspension of the state of law, acquires a permanent spatial arrangement that, as such, remains constantly outside the normal state of law. (2000, p. 39; emphasis in original)

It is not difficult to understand why Agamben has been taken up so positively in migration and citizenship studies. His work speaks powerfully to current political circumstances, not least the alarming elevation of 'terrorism' to the point where it now operates as a 'meta-issue' within global politics, capable of re-legitimating torture and other serious viola-tions of human rights.[2] Many would no doubt see the indefinite detention of 'enemy combatants' within the extraterritorial space of Guantanamo as further confirmation of Agamben's hypothesis that the camp is capable of materializing in the most unexpected ways and places. However, Agamben also offers something important to studies of migration and citizenship. For some time, critical scholars have decried what they have seen as the persistent 'exclusion' from institutions and rights of citizenship of certain classes of migrant in Western countries. As perhaps the pre-eminent theorist of the interstitial, Agamben offers an important qualifier here. He draws our attention to the ambiguous, grey zone between the inside and the outside, the social condition of being neither fully excluded nor fully recognized (2000, p. 40). This conceptualization of an in-between space, a 'zone of indistinction', is perhaps one of his most significant accomplishments.

While there can be no doubting the importance of Agamben's work for the analysis of contemporary migration politics, his thinking also raises problems. Too often scholars in the English-speaking world have seized upon Agamben's work in an enthusiastic but insufficiently critical manner. This lack of caution is rather strange given the sometimes hubristic and vaguely apocalyptic nature of his enterprise. In view of the controversial nature of Agamben's claims, I want to suggest that a more cautious engagement with his work is in order. To this end, I want to make two points.

The first point is somewhat tangential to the purposes of this chapter, but worth noting briefly. It concerns the generalization of the idea of the camp. Agamben argues that today the camp materializes in all sorts of situations, whenever there is a 'materialization of the state of exception' and a 'consequent creation of a space for naked life' (2000, p. 41). He insists that the camp can be detected in all manner of sites, ranging from the gated communities of affluence to the *banlieues*, the 'no-go' areas, and the 'inner city' where the poor and workless are gathered. Given the fact that Agamben derives the concept of the camp from Auschwitz, there is clearly a risk that this move 'seriously banalize[s] the Nazi genocide' (Mezzadra and Neilson 2003, paragraph 17). With this point in mind, Mezzadra is surely correct to emphasize a distinction between what he calls the *lager* and concentration camps. The *lager* finds its origins in projects of colonialism in such places as South Africa and Cuba. As 'an administrative space in which men and women who have not committed any crime are denied their right to mobility', he suggests that the *lager* is a more appropriate concept than the extermination camp for thinking about the contemporary practice of detaining refugees and migrants.

But I think that this kind of distinction can in fact be taken further. Rather than identifying ever more expressions of the camp, we might get a better sense of the variable relations of citizenship and non-citizenship by considering a plurality of what Isin and Rygiel (2007, p. 185) call 'abject spaces', embodying 'different strategies' of abjection but also provoking different acts of resistance. Isin and Rygiel suggest that zones (for example, those of 'free' enterprise and export-processing) and frontiers exemplify abject spaces that are not reducible to the camp. We could certainly add to such a list the diagrams of the township, the ghetto and the plantation. The point is not that such a list is exhaustive but that it helps us avoid the kind of mistake that was made by those readers of Foucault who managed to find the sinister presence of the panopticon lurking in all manner of institutional and political settings. If the camp is not to become the new 'panopticon', then it is necessary to attend to the variability of abject space.

My second point of criticism is more central to the overall theme of this chapter. It concerns the fact that Agamben's perspective seems to offer little space for registering the political and social agency of its subjects. In Agamben's account, and even more so in much of the research that has explored his themes in the context of migration studies, refugees and migrants are depicted as *cast* into spaces at the limit of the law, *contained* outside the system of legal protection, *trapped* in zones of indistinction. As one recent study has put it: 'refugees in detention in Australia, Thailand, and Malaysia [can be understood as] *hominis sacri*, bare lives consigned to zones of exemption where the sovereign law ceases to function' (Prem Kumar and Grundy-Warr 2004, p. 38). In these kinds of accounts, they are subjects to whom all manner of things are done, often in arbitrary and violent ways, but rarely agents in their own right.

As a consequence of this depiction we might note that despite all the insights this perspective offers concerning the complex mechanisms of sovereign power, it carries with it a certain irony since it reproduces the view of migrants as passive, almost helpless beings. For all its critical thrust, Agamben's line of thinking seems to lead us away from a dynamic, agonistic account of power relations, and instead fosters a rather one-sided and flattened conception of migrant subjects. Things are always done to them, not by them. Only occasionally are they granted the capacity to act, and then in desperate ways. For the most part it is a narrative in which authority is just that and sovereign power has the last laugh. It is with this criticism in mind that I turn now to a line of research that certainly has placed migrant struggles at its centre.

The Autonomy of Migration

In contrast to the sombre tone of Agamben's reflections, the debate concerning the autonomy of migration has fostered a somewhat more optimistic view of the trajectory of migration politics, and the possibilities of a transformative citizenship more generally.[3] It is important to note that the autonomy of migration is not a singular political theory any more than it is a coherent political movement. It would perhaps be better to regard it as an emergent ethos operating within thought spaces that bridge academic and activist milieus. It is especially evident in debates in Italy, France, Australia and the United States (in the latter case in relation to Latina/o migration) where it has found resonance in the concrete political struggles of migrants.

Research in this vein often starts with a particular observation: the apparent failure of even the most restrictive and concerted state strategies of migration control and border policing to achieve their stated aim, namely the determination of who should enter the country, who should form bonds of community, and on what terms.[4] 'Autonomy of migration is not supposed to mean sovereignty of migrants, but rather that migrants are not simply objects of state control – that migrants defy controls and resist racist discrimination' (Kanak Attak n.d.).

As an ongoing, mass phenomenon, undocumented migration is taken to testify to the presence of a certain autonomy inherent in the act of migration, an autonomy that, in turn, defies the sovereign power of the state. As a politics, the autonomy of migration finds its support in a number of positions including contemporary anarchisms, radical and anti-racist cosmopolitanisms, and post-soviet communisms. Its most immediate tactical demands include the more or less unconditional regularization of undocumented migrants and the extension of their rights. However, its more principled and overarching objective is the struggle for a generalized right of free movement, but also a right to stay. As Schwenken (2003) notes, the latter is sometimes accorded more emphasis since it is assumed that migrants take the right of free movement anyway.

One of the most widely read and influential articulations of the autonomy of migration is to be found in Hardt and Negri's bestselling *Empire* (2000). Expressed as acts of exodus, desertion and flight, autonomous movement in this perspective is a force that works to confound and undermine contemporary systems of political and economic control. In certain respects the power of autonomous movement has been the hidden secret of the history of class struggle. Far from being merely a reaction to the determinations of capitalist production, migration is a causative and constitutive force. Certainly, capitalism incites and exploits the mobility of its subjects, but their mobility always and ultimately exceeds it. For this reason, autonomous movement is the foremost expression of the collective, potential subject they call the multitude.

> Autonomous movement is what defines the place proper to the multitude. Increasingly less will passports or legal documents be able to regulate our movements across borders. A new geography is established by the multitude as the productive flows of bodies define new rivers and ports. The cities of the earth will become at once great deposits of cooperating humanity and locomotives for circulation, temporary residences and networks of the mass distribution of living humanity. (Hardt and Negri 2000, pp. 396–7)

Hardt and Negri push the theme of autonomous movement in a particular direction. Drawing on a particular interpretation of Deleuze and Guattari's 'nomadology' which emphasizes the deterritorializing power of migration, in their hands autonomous migration becomes nothing less than the principal motive force in the passage through Empire to a new global-ized citizenship. For it is through the innumerable, heteroclite pathways that migrants forge that 'the multitude gains the power to affirm its autonomy, travelling and expressing itself through an apparatus of wide-spread, transversal territorial reappropriation' (Hardt and Negri 2000, p. 398). For Hardt and Negri, the concept of autonomous migration does much of the work that class struggle once did within Marxian theories of social transformation, and not without the latter's eschatological tendencies. Following Walzer, Bull has noted that long before the rise of socialism and its revolutionary ideology, it was the myth of Exodus which provided social actors with an image of radical change. A striking feature of *Empire* is that one sees how 'revolutionary ideology is being translated back into the language of Exodus' (Bull 2004, p. 219).

But not all readings of autonomous migration burden it with quite the same degree of historical purpose or political expectation. In my view the kind of research that is in certain respects more valuable are those inquiries which, in contrast to Hardt and Negri's grandiose scheme, register a more modest and, perhaps, minor understanding of autonomous migration. Here I have in mind a range of sociological, ethnographic and anthropological studies. While their authors do not always explicitly identify their work with the idea of autonomous migration, their findings are certainly consis-tent with its main emphases. For they patiently document many of the ways in which unauthorized migrants and stateless persons actively negotiate the world of borders, work, social relationships, bureaucratic entanglements, refugee hearings and much else. Through their various disclosures – showing that the women whom official reports and media narratives represent as victims of 'trafficking' are in fact far from being helpless pawns but actually agents who make strategic calculations even in the most difficult circumstances (Andrijasevic 2003); examining the particular tactics which migrants employ to achieve a status of residence in a particular city like Rotterdam (Engbersen 2001); or revealing how it could be that even the apparent 'invisibility' of certain migrants is not straightforward but in many cases a status that has to be artfully maintained and reproduced as a survival strategy (Coutin 2003) – studies such as these demonstrate the extent to which irregular migration is an intensely strategic, negotiated phenomenon possessing an irreducibly subjective dimension.

This detailed appreciation of the autonomy and subjectivity of migration has developed largely in isolation from debates about *homo sacer* and the camp. In concluding this section we might ask whether a greater recognition of these manifold expressions of agency would challenge the gloomy view of the camp – whether understood as an archipelago of actual spaces of detention and removal, or as a metaphor for the contemporary political condition. Would it unsettle the image of the camp as a regime that captures its subjects within systems of biopolitical management? If even the stateless and the undocumented reveal themselves to be capable of negotiating and shaping their own circumstances, if only in limited and difficult ways, does this suggest it is too soon to declare that we are all 'virtually *homines sacri*' (Agamben 1998, p. 115)?

Perhaps not. Followers of Agamben would probably point out that while the kinds of struggle mentioned above do indeed go on, it is only rarely that they challenge the fundamental 'logic' of sovereign power. Particular migrants may well succeed in gaining residence or even formal citizenship status; their social pressure may indeed underpin the granting of immigration 'amnesties' which regularize 'hidden' sections of the population; but the basic logic of the camp, the distinctions it draws between politically qualified and bare life, remain firmly in place. Hence, Edkins and Pin-Fat insist that it is only particular kinds of resistance that can unsettle sovereign power (Edkins and Pin-Fat 2004). They highlight two tactics. The first involves the refusal to make distinctions, to draw lines and to differentiate the deserving and the undeserving, the refugee and the economic migrant. The second is the tactic of adopting the position of bare life in order to politicize it. This latter move is exemplified by 'the non-violent protester who uses their own body to obstruct and draw attention to the violence of the state'. It finds one of its most iconic expressions in the image of the lone demonstrator, shopping bag in hand, standing in front of the tank in Tiananmen Square (2004, p. 16).

It seems to me quite valid to emphasize that the social and political struggles of migrants and their allies do not necessarily challenge the space of the camp but can in many circumstances merely reshape the lines which define it. At the same time, however, such a position risks a repeat of the mistake made by all those who, at the height of Western socialism, posed the relationship between reform and revolution in rather stark either/or terms. That is, it threatens to ignore, or worse, dismiss a whole range of practices and acts on the grounds that they do not qualify as sufficiently radical. What is needed, I want to insist, is a greater openness and sensitivity to the diverse, but often relatively minor ways in which migrants are constituted, and constitute themselves not just as subjects capable of acting, but as political subjects. With this in mind, I turn to the theme of acts of citizenship.

Acts of Citizenship, Acts of Demonstration, Politics

A particularly nuanced reading of the significance of the phenomenon of un-documented migration for citizenship studies is suggested by recent work that develops the theme of acts of citizenship. One important accomplishment of this idea, as I see it, is that it theorizes the politics of citizenship beyond the realm of formal entitlements, rights and laws. This is an accomplishment it shares with research into '*de facto*' or 'informal citizenship' (Sassen 2004). But what is especially important and truly novel about the idea of acts of citizenship is the insistence on a radical shift in focus. Instead of already-existing citizens or, for that matter, non-citizens – indeed, instead of actors *per se* – the objects of our closest attention are those constitutive moments, performances, enactments and events when a new identity, substance or relationship of citizenship is brought into existence. This move allows us a better understanding of situations through which subjects lacking formal rights or recognition constitute themselves – with or without the help of others – as capable of acting *like* citizens, and meriting treatment *as* citizens. Moreover, the emphasis on acts serves to draw our attention to moments of interruption: instances when something, however small and seemingly marginal, is changed, possibly for the first time. As Isin (Chapter 1, this volume) has emphasized, to speak of acts rather than, say, practices or habits, is to emphasize not that which is repeated or ingrained but those singular moments when action manages to accomplish a 'rupture in the given'.

Building on the work of Rancière and Honig, Nyers (2003) has shown how the political movements of people without status can be illuminated by this perspective on citizenship. Taking the example of the Comité d'Action des Sans-Statuts in Montreal, he shows how their political actions intrude upon the political order and challenge some of its most deeply held assumptions. Through inventive acts such as unannounced 'delegation visits' to the offices of Immigration Canada, this movement unsettles the dominant idea that refugees are passive objects who should have no political say in their own fate. A similar tactic of interruption is described by Chatterjee (2004) when he identifies a 'politics of the governed' by which squatters, migrants and homeless persons have managed to interrupt the official space and conventions of politics in Calcutta. Yet, as I hinted above, acts of citizenship are not confined to explicitly political under-takings. Seemingly minor and mundane things might also be considered in this way. For instance, the decision made by immigrants to set up soccer leagues in big US cities might also be considered an act of citizenship, not least because it has the potential to 'socially appropriate and culturally recompose public space' (Rodriguez 1995, p. 27).

There is much to recommend this line of analysis. While it shares with Agamben an appreciation that there are lines and manoeuvres that capture subjects outside political and legal space, it moves on from this observation in ways that are politically constructive. For its focus is not so much on the various mechanisms of capture (such as the camp) but rather on the multiple ways in which such sovereign spacings are unsettled. By investigating those moments when subjects constitute themselves as meriting recognition *as* citizens, a focus on acts of citizenship has the potential to reveal that the sovereign lines associated with the camp are considerably more mutable than otherwise might be assumed.

But it seems to me that at least one important oversight could follow from this focus on acts of citizenship. While it is certainly not inherent in the thematic focus, there is a risk that in placing acts of citizenship at the centre of our analytical strategies one specific kind of politics will be overlooked. I have in mind here a politics in which subjects refuse the identity of citizen, perhaps because they explicitly reject the rights, responsibilities and commitments that are associated with the citizen, or out of preference for other identities. My thinking on this point has been shaped by Hindess's (2004) recent criticisms of what we might call the rather 'enchanted' view which still prevails within much scholarly writing about citizenship.[5] Without dismissing the very real benefits which citizenship does bestow on many of its bearers, he urges that we bear in mind cases where citizenship is not sought, and sometimes explicitly or tactically refused. Judgments about the merits of being a citizen are, he insists, always 'circumstantial'. Very often in the past marginalized groups and peoples have viewed the status of citizenship as something desirable. But this depends on the particular historical and political context: 'there may well be circumstances in which the decision could go the other way. It is not difficult to find cases in which people appear to have preferred a way of life that did not involve citizenship, or involved it only in a weaker form' (Hindess 2004, p. 307). Hindess offers a wealth of cases to illustrate this point – including whole communities of citizens who had lived within or on the fringes of the Roman Empire, but seemed to prefer a life outside its institutions; Europeans who deserted their own civilizing missions in favour of a life amongst or alongside native people; and certain communities of indigenous people today who either reject the 'supposed benefits of citizenship' in modern states in favour of their own way of life, or seek some combination of the two.

Theoretical development of the idea of acts of citizenship would benefit from taking on board these cautions about the merits of citizenship. Seeking a better understanding of events where subjects do not act in the name of citizenship, and political commitment to a certain kind of citizenship is either ambiguous or explicitly refused, I want to suggest a conceptual supplement to 'acts of citizenship'. This is the idea of *acts of demonstration*. By foregrounding this theme I want to develop a concept that will be useful in making sense of certain political situations. These occur when an injustice is revealed, a relationship of power is contested, or a particular wrong is protested, but when the identity of the subjects at the heart of the protest is left relatively open.

Quite often we will find that the fields of acts of citizenship and acts of demonstration overlap considerably. To take one example from the world of migration politics, consider the unprecedented 2006 immigrant protests in the United States. Mobilizing as many as three million 'illegal aliens' and their allies in most of the major cities of the US, these rallies practised what Lomnitz calls a 'politics of visibility'. For the rallies demonstrated to the American public not only that undocumented people are living and working in their midst but that henceforth they will refuse to remain fugitive, underground, and hyper-exploited. Yet these acts of demonstration can also be regarded as acts of citizenship since they typically call for greater recognition – including the recognition of cultural difference – and, through mechanisms like regularization, inclusion within the polity. This combination of demonstration and insurgent citizenship was framed succinctly by marchers' signs which read: 'Today We March: Tomorrow We Vote' (Lomnitz 2007, p. 439).

However, it is not always the case that acts of demonstration are simultaneously or logically acts of citizenship. Not always does contestation find expression in the move which says: 'See/hear us, recognize us, respect us, empower us!' In certain circumstances it is important to identify that act of demonstration which refuses the identity of citizen, and does so in a way that opens space for other political possibilities. To illustrate and develop this point, the remainder of this chapter considers one particular act of demonstration, an act which returns us to the scene of Sangatte with which we began. The act that interests me is the project of mapping the refugee centre at Sangatte, a project undertaken by the group An Architektur.

Mapping the Territory of (Non-)Citizenship

An Architektur is a collective actor and the name of a journal associated with a group of critical architects based in Berlin. Founded in 2002 by certain members of the architects' collective Freies Fach (Willemsen 2006), *An Architektur* has to date published seventeen issues dealing with 'particular political and social aspects of architecture and the city under current capitalist conditions' (An Architektur n.d.). These range from the investigation of strategic sites at the very centre of contemporary geo-politics – for instance, issue 04 investigates the 'extraterritorial' space of the infamous US Naval base at Guantanamo – to the management of everyday space in the city. The latter is exemplified by issue 02, entitled 'Anti-Vandal'. This issue examines the activities of private companies whose product is the securing of unoccupied urban buildings. Besides publishing a magazine, members of An Architektur have also been active as the initiators and organizers of the first Camp for Oppositional Architecture, which took place in 2004 in Berlin's Wedding District. Staged in a vacant factory and office complex, this event sought to explore possibilities for resistance in the fields of architecture and planning.

It is quite significant that the first issue of the journal was dedicated to the work of the French sociologist and philosopher, Henri Lefebvre. For Lefebvre's pathbreaking observations on the place of different forms of space and spatialization within the reproduction of capitalism provide a point of departure for the kinds of projects An Architektur undertakes (Willemsen 2006). In particular, they take seriously Lefebvre's insistence that a critical analysis of spatial relations offers crucial insights about the proper character of a particular form of political order (An Architektur 2003).

But a second point of reference, and source of practical orientation for this collective is the work of the British historical geographer, John Harley (Willemsen 2006). Writing mostly in the 1980s, Harley made a series of important interventions in the field of geography when he brought certain insights from post-structuralist theory to bear upon the dominant con-ception of cartography. Harley argued that far from being an objective and purely communicative medium, cartography was a representational practice embedded within power relations (Crampton 2001). His call for a decon-struction of map making resonates with the work of a growing number of artists, activists, situationists and theorists, such as Bureau d'Etudes and Hackitectura. These groups experiment with the basic forms of maps, organigrams and flow-charts to devise representational practices adequate to the critique of contemporary forms of politics and power. In as much as An Architektur uses map-making to 'make visible the social relations inscribed in space that are invisible in normal maps', its map-making could be situated within this project of 'writing counter-geography' (Biemann 2003).

How has An Architektur engaged with questions of space and migration? Published in 2002, Issue 03 of *An Architektur* is entitled 'Grenzgeografie Sangatte' (An Architektur 2002). It utilizes on-site observations which

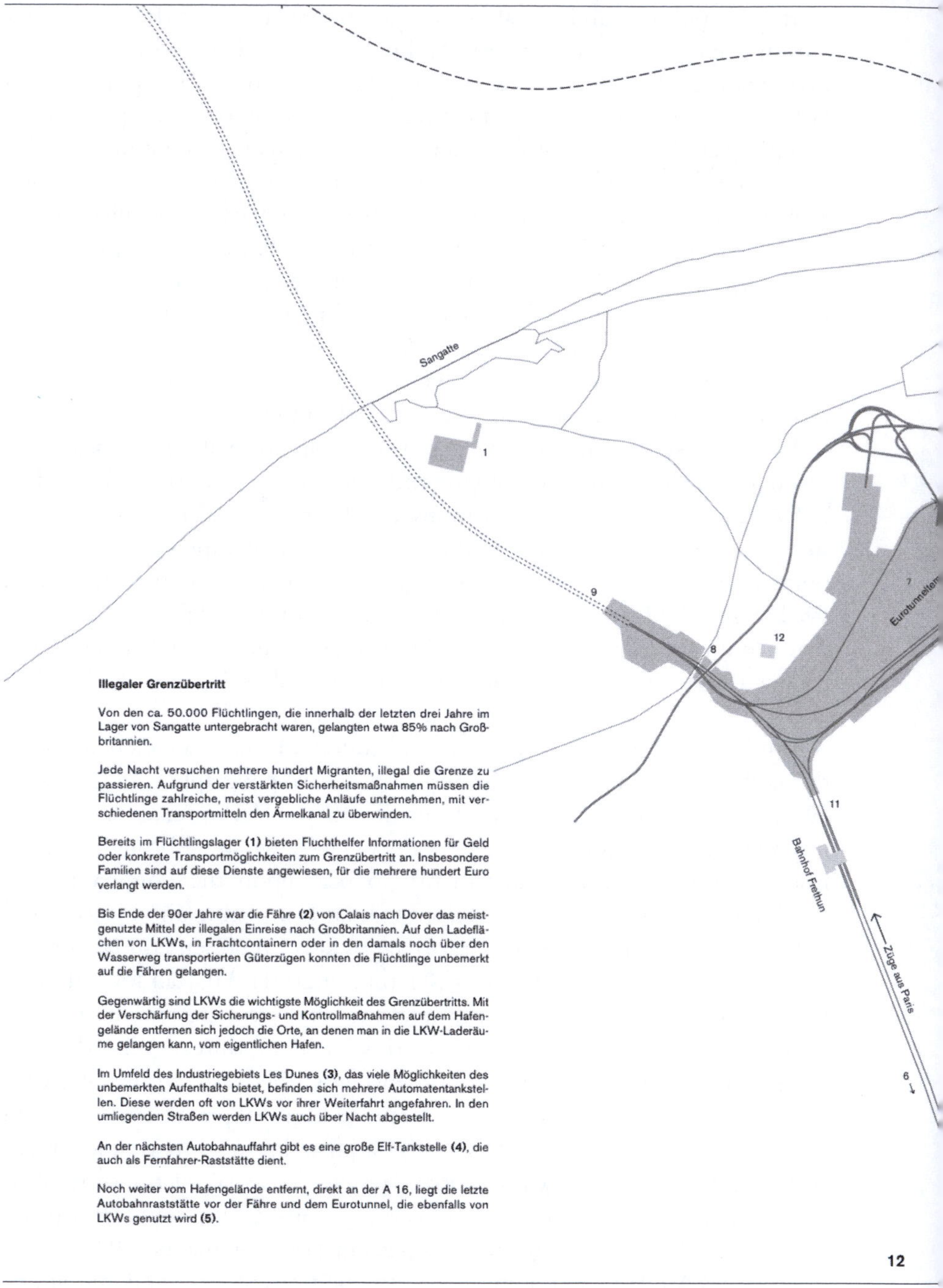

Sangatte

1

9

7 Eurotunnelterm

12

8

Illegaler Grenzübertritt

Von den ca. 50.000 Flüchtlingen, die innerhalb der letzten drei Jahre im Lager von Sangatte untergebracht waren, gelangten etwa 85% nach Großbritannien.

Jede Nacht versuchen mehrere hundert Migranten, illegal die Grenze zu passieren. Aufgrund der verstärkten Sicherheitsmaßnahmen müssen die Flüchtlinge zahlreiche, meist vergebliche Anläufe unternehmen, mit verschiedenen Transportmitteln den Ärmelkanal zu überwinden.

Bereits im Flüchtlingslager (1) bieten Fluchthelfer Informationen für Geld oder konkrete Transportmöglichkeiten zum Grenzübertritt an. Insbesondere Familien sind auf diese Dienste angewiesen, für die mehrere hundert Euro verlangt werden.

Bis Ende der 90er Jahre war die Fähre (2) von Calais nach Dover das meistgenutzte Mittel der illegalen Einreise nach Großbritannien. Auf den Ladeflächen von LKWs, in Frachtcontainern oder in den damals noch über den Wasserweg transportierten Güterzügen konnten die Flüchtlinge unbemerkt auf die Fähren gelangen.

Gegenwärtig sind LKWs die wichtigste Möglichkeit des Grenzübertritts. Mit der Verschärfung der Sicherungs- und Kontrollmaßnahmen auf dem Hafengelände entfernen sich jedoch die Orte, an denen man in die LKW-Laderäume gelangen kann, vom eigentlichen Hafen.

Im Umfeld des Industriegebiets Les Dunes (3), das viele Möglichkeiten des unbemerkten Aufenthalts bietet, befinden sich mehrere Automatentankstellen. Diese werden oft von LKWs vor ihrer Weiterfahrt angefahren. In den umliegenden Straßen werden LKWs auch über Nacht abgestellt.

An der nächsten Autobahnauffahrt gibt es eine große Elf-Tankstelle (4), die auch als Fernfahrer-Raststätte dient.

Noch weiter vom Hafengelände entfernt, direkt an der A 16, liegt die letzte Autobahnraststätte vor der Fähre und dem Eurotunnel, die ebenfalls von LKWs genutzt wird (5).

11

Bahnhof Fréthun

Züge aus Paris

6

12

Figure 8.1 Illegal border crossing (© An Architektur)

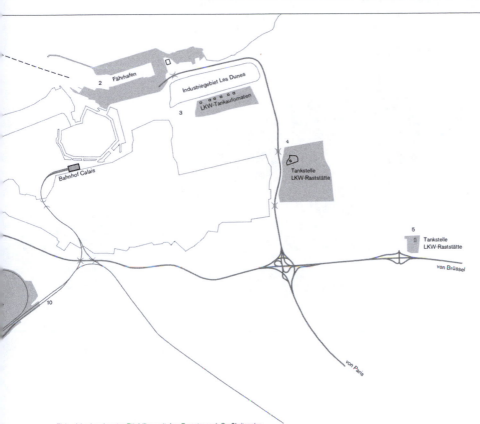

Einige Jahre lang konnten Flüchtlinge mit dem Eurostar nach Großbritannien fahren, wenn sie zwei Fahrkarten kauften, eine von Frethun (6) nach Paris und eine weitere von Paris nach London. In Paris konnten sie dann innerhalb des Zollbereichs bleiben und ohne Kontrolle weiterfahren. Seit Juli 1999, als darüber in Zeitungen berichtet wurde, gibt es diese Möglichkeit nicht mehr.

Mit der Verschärfung der Sicherheitsmaßnahmen im Fährbetrieb verlagerten sich die Versuche des Grenzübertritts auch auf den ebenfalls immer stärker gesicherten Eurotunnel. Um auf das Terminalgelände (7) zu gelangen, müssen mehrere bis zu vier Meter hohe und zum Teil elektrisch geladene Zäune überwunden werden. Dabei sollen mitgebrachte Decken vor dem elektrischen Schock schützen.

Das Aufspringen auf anfahrende Züge ist aufgrund der mangelnden Möglichkeiten, sich fest zu halten und wegen der hohen Geschwindigkeit insbesondere der Eurostar-Schnellzüge äußerst gefährlich. Dennoch versuchen einige Flüchtlinge, auf diese Weise in den Unterbau der Personenzüge oder auf die offenen Frachtzüge und in die darauf transportierten Lkws zu gelangen.

Es gab auch Versuche, von Brücken (8) auf anfahrende Züge zu springen, obwohl dies besonders wegen der elektrischen Oberleitungen im Tunnel lebensgefährlich ist. Mittlerweile befinden sich an den Brücken vor dem Eurotunneleingang zu beiden Seiten Gittervorrichtungen.

Den Tunnel zu Fuß zu durchqueren ist nicht möglich (9), da die Züge bei hoher Geschwindigkeit von einem starken Winddruck begleitet werden. Trotzdem ist es schon vorgekommen, dass der Zugverkehr wegen solcher Versuche angehalten werden musste. Weihnachten 2001 konnte eine Gruppe von 550 Flüchtlingen in zwei Gruppen zunächst das Wachpersonal und

die Absperrungen überwinden und anschließend einige Kilometer weit in den Tunnel hineinlaufen. Ein Großaufgebot der Polizei hielt die Flüchtlinge schließlich gewaltsam auf.

Die Güterzuggleise außerhalb des eigentlichen Terminalbereichs (10) sind weniger stark gesichert. Diese werden von Frachtzügen benutzt, die bereits in Lille oder Paris beladen wurden. Bis vor einiger Zeit warteten die Züge hier, doch mittlerweile fahren sie mit höherer Geschwindigkeit auf das Terminalgelände zu.

Kurz hinter dem Eurostar-Bahnhof Frethun ist ein Streckenabschnitt (11), auf dem versucht wurde, auf die anfahrenden Personenzüge zu gelangen.

In Folge der Einreiseversuche kam es zu zahlreichen, teilweise schweren Unfällen. Insgesamt kamen im Zusammenhang mit der illegalisierten Migration zwölf Flüchtlinge in den letzten zwei Jahren ums Leben. Auf dem Friedhof von Vieux Coquelles (12), ein Kilometer vom Tunneleingang entfernt, befinden sich die Gräber von fünf zum Teil unbekannten Flüchtlingen.

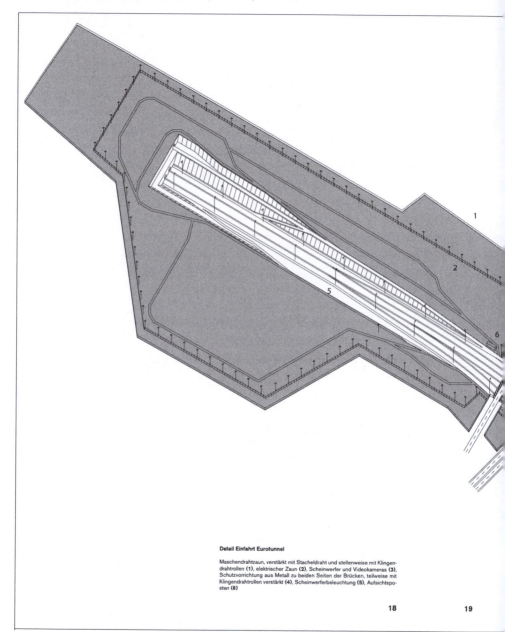

Detail Einfahrt Eurotunnel

Maschendrahtzaun, verstärkt mit Stacheldraht und stellenweise mit Klingendrahtrollen (1), elektrischer Zaun (2), Scheinwerfer und Videokameras (3), Schutzvorrichtung aus Metall zu beiden Seiten der Brücken, teilweise mit Klingendrahtrollen verstärkt (4), Scheinwerferbeleuchtung (5), Aufsichtsposten (6)

18   19

Figure 8.2 Detail: Eurotunnel entrance (© An Architektur)

members of the group made at Calais and Sangatte, as well as information drawn from news reports, the Red Cross and other refugee organizations. I noted at the outset that at the start of the twenty-first century, Sangatte had come to stand as a signifier for Europe's 'crisis' of 'immigration and asylum'. In the period from 1999 to 2002 it had featured prominently in a torrent of newspaper and TV coverage. An Architektur's coverage of this event is markedly different from the dominant representations of Sangatte. In what respects does this particular intervention into the mass-mediated 'border spectacle' (De Genova 2002) of Sangatte constitute an act of demonstration? In what ways is this act simultaneously expressive of a certain solidarity with the migrants and refugees at Sangatte, but reluctant to confer on its subjects any fixed or unambiguous identity? What political significance might we accord to the critical space that this act opens up?

An Architektur's border geography of Sangatte consists of nine maps and diagrams with titles like 'History of the refugee camp', 'Ground plan of the camp', and 'Detail, tunnel entrance'. In one it is the improvised living quarters of the refugees within the vast warehouse that is represented. Numbered annotations draw the reader's eye to mundane but telling little details: police buses permanently parked opposite a large rubbish bin; an open space at the back of the warehouse serving as a play area and a temporary mosque. Another map (Figure 8.1) locates the camp in relation to key elements in the transportation infrastructure of the area such as the ferry terminal, truck stops and petrol stations, and the railway lines which pass in and out of the Eurotunnel near Sangatte. Suggestive of a topography of escape attempts, this map charts the different routes which the migrants took from the camp, showing how some sought to break into the railway terminal and climb onto trains while others targeted nearby service stations in a bid to infiltrate trucks heading for Britain. Still another map (Figure 8.2) shows in meticulous detail the kinds of security provisions that the authorities have deployed around the entrance to the Eurotunnel, including barbed wire, electric fences, spotlights and video surveillance.

What are we to make of these representations? Certainly it would be possible to relate these to Agamben's theme of *homo sacer*. After all, isn't the converted warehouse an exemplary instance of a camp – an abandoned structure that is hurriedly and expeditiously pressed into service for the purpose of containing a population for which the social and legal order seems to have no place? Re-presenting the Eurotunnel – itself a potent symbol of a technologically interconnected Europe – An Architektur reveals a zone where certain classes of person become captured outside the European space of free movement. But the maps could also be read as evidence for the hypotheses of autonomous migration. For they speak to the determination of the migrants to find a way, somehow, by whatever means, to elude the system of border control, and pursue their chosen destination, in this case the shores of England. The great majority will fail, but not all.

But I think such a reading would tend still to understate the status of the maps and diagrams as interventions in their own right. It would miss the way in which this issue of *An Architektur* might be considered as an act which intervenes in, and re-presents the space opened up by the migrants in the course of their confrontation with national and European authorities and commercial actors like the railway companies. Here I think it is important to reflect on the aesthetic style and sensibility which An Architektur cultivates.

Perhaps the first thing that strikes the viewer is the abstract, technical and apparently neutral character of the plans and diagrams. They are intended to be 'somewhat abstract yet comprehensible' (An Architektur 2003). Yet there is more going on here. At first glance they could be the product of officialdom, almost: a set of diagrams used in the planning of the Eurotunnel and its environs; a series of maps designed to chart a space of transportation, organize its elements, diagram its flows, and secure its processes. Yet the maps are not neutral. As An Architektur explains in an interview (2003), all maps are necessarily selective and partial, diagramming some features, suppressing others. Even if their immediate appearance belies such selectivity, maps encode particular points of view, and assume particular ends and objectives on the part of their users. A tourist map is quite different from a map used for property acquisition or security. But in the diagram called 'illegal border crossing' (Figure 8.1) it is not the space of tourism or business that is charted but the shifting pathways of the migrants as they move back and forth from the improvised camp to the railway tracks, the ferry station, and other sites relevant to their quest for mobility. It seems that at least some of An Architektur's maps imagine the migrants themselves as their users. Given that these migrants have no sanctioned place in the political order, and only appear in social space as scandalous, quasi-criminal figures, the production of a such a map must count as a political act. For it insists that migrants are present at the scene of Sangatte not just as objects, but also, like any other user of maps, as purposeful subjects.

Continuing with the theme of the style of representation, I want to note how we might read An Architektur as practitioners of a certain form of simulation. It is not uncommon for political groups to protest the securitization of borders and the marginalization of migrants by utilizing shocking images of the conditions in which they are forced to live, perhaps portraying a humanitarian disaster. An Architektur avoids this idiom. As though mindful of the way in which scandalous images of desperate migrants can all too easily be re-inscribed within discourses of law and order, and used to underpin the call for still tougher immigration controls, An Architektur eschews the conventional grammar of outrage or denunciation. Instead, theirs is a potentially more subversive form of protest because of how it appropriates the iconography of technical design and technocratic administration in order to make its point.

These acts of appropriation are not just a matter of developing a new idiom of protest, one that is less vulnerable to immediate recuperation by mainstream discourses. It is also a matter of how one fashions a way to represent what are in many ways novel forms and experiences of migration. Here I want to note that the representational strategy of An Architektur appears to parallel the migration strategies of its subjects. In both cases it is a matter of infiltrating a given medium and making it work for different ends. Lacking the requisite identity papers, or simply the 'right' nationality, the migrants who pass through Sangatte have difficulty practising the kind of mobility available to most citizens of the EU and other wealthy regions. Like countless itinerants worldwide, 'freedom of movement' cannot be taken for granted but has to be seized. It has to be bought at inflated prices from 'smugglers'. It has to be taken by the tactics of the stowaway, the forger and the bribe. Quite often it takes the form of 'contained mobility' (Biemann 2004) – the cramped and often lethal movement that belongs to the individual smuggled into the shipping container; the mobility which requires its living subject to mimic the lifeless form of the commodity. Hence there is a kind of equivalence between the subversive and mimetic representational style of An Architektur, and the fact that our political culture has forced the very act of movement to become a subversive activity.

If my first point has concerned the representational style of the maps, a second point concerns their empirical character. An Architektur does not make the claim that its maps are 'objective'. For instance, they insist that that they do not attempt to achieve a direct representation of spaces (An Architektur 2003). But in as much as the generation of the maps entails certain activities of careful investigation, observation and measurement conducted at a particular locale, it can be said that they certainly are empirical. The viewer cannot but be impressed by the meticulous detail with which the interior of the camp, or the entrance to the Eurotunnel, has been recorded. For instance, in the case of the latter (Figure 8.2), each spotlight and video camera is carefully represented.

But why do these little details matter? What is the point of this seemingly painstaking labour of investigation? What is achieved by documenting the movements of the migrants and the counter-tactics on the part of the authorities in such abstract, diagrammatic terms? I want to suggest that in adopting this particular mode of representation An Architektur is actually constituting Sangatte as a relatively unknown – but not unknowable – space. Sangatte may be situated geographically near the old sea frontier between England and France but through their own practice An Architektur relocate it at a different frontier-space: the frontier of knowledge about new forms of migration. This is an act which disturbs established narratives about unauthorized migration. A great deal of commentary on Sangatte inscribed it within narratives that are already known and all too familiar. Migrants are either expressions of lawlessness and crime, or heroic, nomadic subjects. But An Architektur seems to be saying: we are confronted here with a relatively new and unfamiliar situation, for which we presently possess at best only heuristic concepts. Their graphic and empirical mode of representation serves to constitute Sangatte as a sort of experimental site. It becomes the scene of an encounter whose terms, forms and identities are not to be determined in advance. Rendering this encounter in the form of a mapping at once marks its present status as a kind of *terra incognito*, while gesturing towards the possibility of a better understanding of this phenomenon.

My final point concerns the identities of the different actors here. With this point we can elaborate the theme of acts of demonstration. As Andrew Barry has argued, new light is cast on the act of political demonstration once it is examined alongside the kind of demonstration that is more often associated with the world of science and technology, where particular truths are demonstrated by scientific experts in the context of the laboratory or the anatomy lecture theatre. The point is that, whether in politics or scientific life, the act of demonstration requires particular ethical and technical practices. In both cases it is a matter of 'making visible a phenomenon to be witnessed by others' (Barry 1999, p. 77). If the production of these maps and diagrams can be understood as an act of demonstration, this is because demonstration is not straightforward but an event that always has to be conducted under particular conditions and in the presence of particular witnesses.

But who are the witnesses, and what are they witnessing? Let us deal with the What before returning to the Who. One of the most interesting and significant features of An Architektur's demonstration of Sangatte, I want to suggest, is its refusal to ascribe a strong sense of identity to the migrants. From the text appended to the maps it is clear that An Architektur acts in solidarity with these migrants. This much is clear from the overall political tone of their writing, and the use of specific phrases like 'Fortress Europe' and 'the absurd socio-spatial geography of control'. At the same time, however, the project refrains from making strong assertions about the political and social identity of the migrants. There are no claims that they are quasi-citizens, victims, foreigners or nomads. Of course. this might be regarded as a somewhat irresponsible act of abstention on the part of An Architektur, a refusal to take an intellectual and political position. But it might also be regarded as an act of political modesty that purposefully leaves open the question of the identity of the actors. If so, this could actually be considered a timely and genuinely political move. For it resists the political urge to impose identity upon a fluid and ambiguous scene. It refuses the tendency in public as well as much academic debate to proceed as though we already know who and what we are dealing with.

And so to the who, and the question of the witness. For the question remains: who are these maps and diagrams – this *Grenzgeografie* – intended for? The point is that as a practice, every demonstration requires a witness who is qualified to confirm its evidence. Can we say then that an *act* of demonstration is that particular kind of event when the presence and the identity of the witness is uncertain, and when the prior existence of the witness, and the status of the event *as* a demonstration, cannot be taken for granted? If so, then acts of demonstration are those acts which appeal to an audience which is not already there. Here I want to speculate that with its avowedly empirical style, and its technical aesthetic, An Architektur is appealing to the possibility of a different kind of public than the one which presently observes the spectacle of migration – a public that is 'yet to come'.[6] It is both protesting the inadequacy of the current forms of publicity which dominate the politics of migration, and gesturing towards the need for a public space in which the genuine and intractable questions of migration might be discussed in a relatively open-ended and perhaps even experimental manner. This is perhaps why this political intervention is somewhat ambiguous about the identity or the purpose of the migrants themselves. This ambiguity may frustrate those looking for a firm statement of political allegiance, and an unequivocal appeal for migrants' rights. But the point is not to add one more voice seeking to stabilize their identity as this or that, and so to reproduce the existing dichotomies (citizens/aliens, legal/illegal, villains/heroes and so on). Instead, it is to make more explicit the limitations of existing modes of knowledge and dialogue; limitations that are all the more urgent in the face of new forms of migration for which there is not only an absence of simple or immediate answers, but also of adequate concepts.

If it is indeed the case that the particular act of demonstration we have examined puts at stake the limitations of our concepts of political community, then the territory of (non-)citizenship to which my subtitle refers should not be mistaken for a settled identity. It should not be taken to refer to a specific status or a group of people called non-citizens, the 'other' of 'the' citizen. Instead, it can be interpreted as a reference to the space of possibility which at any given moment surrounds our political identities. In his excellent essay on Foucault's method, Paul Veyne (1997, p. 158, his emphasis) writes: 'It is unquestionably an odd thing, well worth the attention of a philosopher, this capacity of human beings to remain unaware of their limits, their *exceptionality*, not to see that there is emptiness around them, to believe that at any given moment they are ensconced in the plenitude of reason.' The act of demonstration carries with it the hope and the possibility of a public that can register the conditions of its own exceptionality more fully.

Notes

1 I am grateful to the editors for helpful comments on earlier drafts of this chapter. I also wish to thank An Architektur for allowing me to reproduce their maps here, and for providing English translations of the map legends. I am grateful to Arne Rückert for his translation of their interviews and statements.

2 According to Faist (2002) issues become meta-issues when they operate as master signifiers within symbolic politics. He argues that 'migration' is today a meta-issue because of the way politicians and others invoke it as an explanation for countless different concrete problems, ranging from housing shortages to failing schools. Something similar can be said of 'terrorism'.

3 Amongst the best academic discussions of this idea are Mezzadra (2004), Mezzadra and Neilson (2003) and Rodriguez (1996).

4 On the apparent 'failure' of border control in the United States, see Cornelius (2005).

5 Answering the question of what a Foucauldian account of the French Revolution might look like, Keith Michael Baker (1994, p. 190) has suggested it 'would surely be a disenchanted one, seeking to reveal the mechanisms of power within the discourse of emancipation'. Conversely, an enchanted view of citizenship is one that readily accepts the progressivist assumptions embedded in this concept. It is a view that fails to interrogate the power relations and effects associated with what we might call governance through citizenship.

6 Deleuze and Guattari (1987, p. 345) speak of a 'people yet to come' in relation to creative interventions which act to destratify dominant forms of peoplehood. If 'the public' is already an effect of processes which territorialize and control a people – think of the technologies of 'public opinion' or 'public relations' – then my notion of a public yet to come.

References

Agamben, G. (1998) *Homo Sacer: Sovereign Power and Bare Life*, Stanford University Press, Stanford, CA.

—— (2000) *Means without End: Notes on Politics* (trans. V. Binetti and C. Casarino), University of Minnesota Press, Minneapolis, MN.

An Architektur (2002) 'The Geography of a Border: Sangatte, 2002', *An Architektur*, 3 <http://www.anarchitektur.com/aa03-sangatte/aa03-sangatte.html>.

—— (2003) 'Produktion und Gebrauch gebauter Umwelt' (an interview with An Architektur), June 1, <http://www.anarchitektur.com/presse/zone7.html>.

—— (n.d.) Introduction to the Website (English version), <http://www.anarchitektur.com/english.html>.

Andrijasevic, R. (2003) 'The Difference Borders Make: (Il)legality, Migration and Trafficking in Italy among Eastern European Women in Prostitution' in S. Ahmed, S., C. Castañeda, A.-M. Fortier and M. Sheller (eds), *Uprootings/Regroundings: Questions of Home and Migration*, Berg, Oxford.

Baker, K. M. (1994) 'A Foucauldian French Revolution?' in J. Goldstein (ed.), *Foucault and the Writing of History*, Blackwell, Oxford.

Barry, A. (1999) 'Demonstrations: Sites and Sights of Direct Action', *Economy and Society*, 28 (1), 75–94.

Biemann, U. (2003) 'Writing Counter-Geography', <http://www.geobodies.org/resources/_dl/Europlex_engl_red?dl>.

—— (2004) 'Contained Mobility', DVD.

Bull, M. (2004) 'Smooth Politics' in P. Passavant and J. Dean (eds), *Empire's New Clothes: Reading Hardt and Negri*, Routledge, New York.

Chatterjee, P. (2004) *The Politics of the Governed: Reflections on Popular Politics in Most of the World*, Columbia University Press, New York.

Cornelius, W. (2005) 'Controlling "Unwanted" Immigration: Lessons from the United States, 1993–2004', *Journal of Ethnic and Migration Studies*, 31 (4).

Coureau, H. (2003) '"Tomorrow Inch Allah, Chance!" People Smuggler Networks in Sangatte', *Immigrants and Minorities*, 22 (2/3), 374–87.

Coutin, S. B. (2003) 'Illegality, Borderlands, and the Space of Nonexistence' in R. W. Perry and B. Maurer (eds), *Globalization under Construction: Governmentality, Law, and Identity*, University of Minnesota Press, Minneapolis, MN.

Crampton, J. W. (2001) 'Maps as Social Constructions: Power, Communication and Visualization', *Progress in Human Geography*, 25 (2).

Daily Telegraph (2001) 'Eurotunnel Asks Court to Shut Calais Refugee HQ', 30 August.

De Genova, N. (2002) 'Migrant "Illegality" and Deportability in Everyday Life', *Annual Review of Anthropology*, 31, 419–47.

Deleuze, G. (1988) *Foucault*, University of Minnesota, Minneapolis, MN.

Deleuze, G. and F. Guattari (1987) *A Thousand Plateaus,* Athlone Press, London.

Diken, B. (2004) 'From Refugee Camps to Gated Communities: Biopolitics and the End of the City', *Citizenship Studies*, 8 (1), 83–106.

Diken, B. and C. B. Lautsen (2002) 'Zones of Indistinction – Security, Terror and Bare Life', *Space and Culture*, 5 (3), 290–307.

Edkins, J. (2000) 'Sovereign Power, Zones of Indistinction, and the Camp', *Alternatives*, 25 (1), 3–26.

Edkins, J. and V. Pin-Fat (2004) 'Introduction: Life, Power, Resistance' in J. Edkins, V. Pin-Fat and M. Shapiro (eds), *Sovereign Lives: Power in Global Politics*, Routledge, London.

Engbersen, G. (2001) 'The Unanticipated Consequences of Panopticon Europe: Residence Strategies of Illegal Immigrants' in V. Guiraudon and C. Joppke (eds), *Controlling a New Migration World*, Routledge, New York.

Faist, T. (2002) 'Extension du domaine de la lutte: International Migration and Security before and after 11 September 2001', *International Migration Review*, 36 (1), 7–14.

Guardian (2001) 'Why Refugees Prefer Britain to France', 6 September 2001.

Hardt, M. and A. Negri (2000) *Empire*, Harvard University Press, Cambridge, MA.

Hindess, B. (2004) 'Citizenship for All', *Citizenship Studies*, 8 (3), 305–15.

Isin, E. and K. Rygiel (2007) 'Abject Spaces: Frontiers, Zones, Camps' in E. Dauphinee and C. Masters (eds), *The Logics of Biopower and the War on Terror*, Palgrave Macmillan, Houndmills.

Kanak Attak (n.d.) 'Speaking of Autonomy of Migration… Racism and Struggles of Migration', <http://www.kanak-attak.de/ka/text/esf04.html>; accessed 28 April 2007.

Laacher, S. (2002) *Après Sangatte…: nouvelles immigrations, nouveaux enjeux*, La Dispute, Paris.

Lomnitz, C. (2007) '2006 Immigrant Mobilizations in the United States', in M. Feher, G. Krikorian and Y. McKee (eds), *Nongovernmental Politics*, Zone Books, New York.

Mezzadra, S. (2004). 'The Right to Escape', *Ephemera* 4 (3), 267–75.

Mezzadra, S. and B. Neilson (2003) 'Né qui, né altrove – Migration, Detention, Desertion: A Dialogue', *borderlands e-journal*, 2 (1).

Nyers, P. (2003) 'Abject Cosmopolitanism: The Politics of Protection in the Anti-Deportation Movement', *Third World Quarterly*, 24 (6), 1069–93.

Perera, S. (2002) 'What Is a Camp…?' *Borderlands*, 1 (1).

Prem Kumar, R. and C. Grundy-Warr (2004) 'The Irregular Migrant as *Homo Sacer*: Migration and Detention in Australia, Malaysia, and Thailand', *International Migration*, 42 (1), 33–64.

Rodriguez, N. (1996) 'The Battle for the Border: Notes on Autonomous Migration, Transnational Communities, and the State', *Social Justice*, 23 (3), 21–37.

Sassen, S. (2004) 'The Repositioning of Citizenship: Emergent Subjects and Spaces for Politics' in P. Passavant and J. Dean (eds), *Empire's New Clothes: Reading Hardt and Negri*, Routledge, New York.

Schwenken, H. (2003) '"Sangatte" – A Case Study about the Political Self-Organisation of Refugees and Migrants in the European Union', paper presented at ECPR Conference, Marburg, 18–21 September 2003.

Veyne, P. (1997) 'Foucault Revolutionizes History' in A. Davidson (ed.), *Foucault and His Interlocutors*, University of Chicago Press, Chicago.

Willemsen, M. (2006) 'An Architektur: Intervention Inevitable', <http://www2.cascoprojects.org/>.

ACTS II

❖

Exclusions
Without Names

Act 6

❖

Promising to Become European

ERKAN ERCEL

Drawing the universal out of difference rather than the other way around is a distinctly modern aspect of acts of citizenship. It is an open and unfinished narrative that continues to frame what might be called the contradiction of Other citizens. For example, on 3 November 2005 Turkish state authorities and the executive of the European Union Council signed a treaty – an act of promise. According to this agreement, Turkey promised to adopt EU regulations concerning human and minority rights and the supremacy of law, as well as to undertake a wide range of reforms in the economic, political and legal fields. In return, the EU promised that eventually it would make Turkey the first country identified as 'predominantly Muslim' to be granted full membership in what has to this point been seen as an 'exclusively Christian club'. This agreement marks an unprecedented moment of large-scale metamorphosis in the European perception of citizenship and identity. This distinguishes its occidental heritage from oriental (non-) citizenship forms and cultures. With this act of double promise, it is no longer possible to entertain the clear-cut distinction between the occidental and oriental forms of citizenship and identity.

Reform-oriented negotiations between Turkey and European states have a long history, preceding even the foundation of the Turkish Republic. As early as the mid-nineteenth century, the Ottoman state authorities, besieged by various problems, initiated a series of measures known as the Tanzimat Reforms (1839–76). These reforms aimed to modernize and centralize the state. During this process, European states not only served as a model for the Ottoman state authorities but also proactively intervened in Ottoman affairs, particularly with regard to reforms concerning non-Muslim subjects in the Empire. It is against this historical background that the significance of the recent turn of events should be appreciated. Through the promises exchanged in Brussels – the mutual act of promise – something new enters the world, a new possibility opens up.

For European subjects, historically the image of the Turk has conjured up notions of tyranny, despotism and the 'terror of the world'. In the eighteenth century, as the Empire was crumbling under military defeats and fiscal hardships, the image of the Ottoman Empire as the 'terror of the world' came to be replaced with that of the 'the sick man' of Europe. Despite this shift, the Empire for a long period continued to signify the intransitive/ radical other of both Europe and the Western conception of citizenship. In many senses this image of otherness continues to the present day.

In November 2005, however, with the exchange of promises in Brussels, the possibility of a cardinal shift in this representational relation emerged. In officially launching the accession negotiations and recognizing Turkey as a prospective fellow member, the EU has ushered in a new era of transitive relations between Europe and Turkey. Thus, the treaty in question not only extends a welcoming hand to Turkey, but in so doing also challenges long-held prejudices and animosities towards Turks. The very condition of possibility of this act of promise and profound change in the perception of the other (from a radical/transitive to an immanent/transitive other) resulted from the fear-mongering discourse of the clash of civilizations. Many European leaders saw recognition and negotiation with the Turkish other as the best means to prevent a confrontation between civilizations.

Within Europe, the legitimacy and the desirability of Turkey's membership in the EU remain controversial. For many Europeans, the accession agreement was brokered behind closed doors by elites and without the consent of the majority. Others are sceptical with regard to Turkey's ability to fulfil its obligations. What concerns us most here is the 'historic' shift in European identity and citizenship formations made possible by the act of promise. As contingent and contested as it might be, this act marks a fundamental metamorphosis in long-held Western perceptions of citizenship. It is no longer possible for European citizens to entertain the same relationship to their identity now that that identity has been broadened, however tentatively, to include a culture as 'alien' as the Turkish one. An act of promise has generated new subjects of citizenship.

Act 7

❖

Checkpoint Gazes

IRUS BRAVERMAN

The checkpoint in the occupied Palestinian territories (OPT) provides a unique space for examining how technologies of gazing are utilized by military and civil actors alike. It also exposes the power of these gazes both as acts of security and as subversive acts of citizenship. Originally, the checkpoints in the OPT were constituted as binary places where military officials observed the occupied Palestinian population. Through introducing a counter-gaze, the women of the organization Machsom Watch (MW) have attempted to disrupt this binary constellation of 'powerful versus powerless'. Herein, I consider this counter-gaze as an act of citizenship, especially in that it transforms the political, social, and ethical consciousness of its actors, and perhaps also that of the other actors who operate in the space of the checkpoint. While the gaze of security and calculability looks to empty its object of agency, what happens when MW women gaze back at security, exposing an otherwise clandestine aspect of its existence as such? For example, when MW mothers and sisters counteract the panoptic gaze of the soldiers by seeing them as sons and brothers, does this counter-gaze rupture the habitus of security enacted in this place, or is it further absorbed into the contagion of power that these women seek to disrupt? One way or the other, the women of MW constitute a third party in the checkpoint scene, rather than the usual two parties – soldiers and Palestinians – that confront each other in this space. But what happens when other actors intervene, this time with a different gaze and agenda? How does the dynamic between these various actors create and subvert the meaning of the gaze as an act of citizenship? The following paragraphs briefly explore these questions. Ultimately, I suggest that the interactions between the various gazes produced in and by the checkpoints are not only important indicators but are also constitutive of the changing relationships between the

211

actors that operate in this place, producing an increasingly complex set of hybrid gazes that constantly shift the power dynamics enacted in the checkpoint.

Machsom Watch (in English: Checkpoint Watch) is an organization of Jewish-Israeli women founded in February 2001 by three women as a concerned response to Israel's intensified closure policies in the OPT during and after the second Intifada. Approximately 500 Jewish-Israeli women are currently active in MW, which makes it one of the larger direct action organizations in Israel, if not the largest. Twice daily (usually during rush hours), groups of two to four women organize in shifts and set out to visit over forty checkpoints scattered throughout the OPT (with the exception of Gaza Strip). These checkpoints are either internal (regulating Palestinian movement within the OPT) or located along the borders of Israel (as defined by Israel). In the course of the shifts the women observe, document, and inquire into what they see. Then they follow up these inquiries by contacting commanders and reporters, while at the same time also posting the reports and responses on the organization's website. These forms of documentation are yet another important aspect of the technology of gazing. Potentially, they add a series of gazes to the scene of the checkpoint, sometimes even those of actors not physically present there. The act of inscription and documentation thus serves to further enhance the power of the gaze.

Primarily, the checkpoint is configured as a dichotomized space, a place of fixed binaries and of constant contestation between the 'powerful' and the 'powerless'. Indeed, already through its basic physical setting the checkpoint enables various forms of surveillance over the Palestinian residents of the OPT, in turn moulding them into docile, calculable, and governable bodies. Put differently, the checkpoint is a pivotal spatio-temporal site that serves to govern the movement and, even further, mould the identity of the Palestinian population. A major technology of surveillance, the practice of everyday gazing, is routinely performed at the checkpoints by Israeli soldiers and border police. Initially, such checkpoint gazes are unidirectional: they originate in the eyes of security and are directed outwards, towards the Palestinian other. By introducing their own gaze into this scene, the women of MW attempt to break the fixed binary dynamics routinely performed at the checkpoints.

Importantly, MW activists seem completely out of place at the checkpoint: they are women, some even elderly grandmothers, and most are of Ashkenazi (Western European) origin, highly educated, and from above-average socio-economic backgrounds. By routinely visiting the checkpoints, MW women resist their privileged spatial confinement within certain physical and mental boundaries, venturing to attain firsthand knowledge of the checkpoint space. This venturing is in itself a political, social and ethical statement, a questioning of the hegemonic scheme that attempts to monopolize access to and knowledge of checkpoint space through framing it as a dangerous military zone and an insecure place,

MW member gazes through camera lens at Israeli soldier gazing down at Palestinians.
El Hader checkpoint, June 2004 (© Irus Braverman)

especially for unarmed Jewish mothers of soldiers. Specifically, it is the gaze of
MW women that ruptures the habitus of the checkpoint, thereby constituting an act
of citizenship. Consequently, the checkpoint encompasses a triangular dynamic
between Israeli soldiers, Palestinian residents, and Jewish women. This makes for
a multitude of gazing encounters: the meaning of the soldiers' gaze is transformed
when they themselves are subjected to the gaze, thereby destabilizing the socio-
spatial power relations that existed prior to this (counter-)panoptic intervention by
MW women.

Or does it?

The security gaze of the IDF (Israel Defence Forces) and, by extension, of the
State of Israel also translates the gaze of MW women into a legitimizing scheme
in its ongoing checkpoint apparatus. Specifically, the IDF utilizes the presence of
MW women at the checkpoints as an indication of the humanistic and enlightened
nature of its occupation of the Palestinian territories. Despite its often stated
security concerns, the IDF 'grants' permission to MW women to observe the
checkpoints as an ongoing routine. In addition, Israeli military officials are
becoming increasingly open to meeting with MW women to address their

concerns. Moreover, soldiers of various military ranks routinely read the reports published electronically by MW, at times officially referring to them as an indication of the progressive approach that Israel has introduced in administering the checkpoints. This discourse of 'improvement' in turn increases the spatial stability and permanence of the checkpoints. At the same time, it also advances the positioning of the checkpoints as an inevitable and moral necessity, which goes against the most basic principles of MW. In other words, the counter-gaze of MW women cannot be interpreted as merely a simple disruption of the hegemonic gaze. In fact, their counter-gaze might even reinforce the hegemonic apparatus by lending it credibility, transparency, and stability.

To complicate the picture even more, it is interesting to note a third gaze that has been introduced to the checkpoint space recently. Women in Green, a right-wing women's group that consists mostly of settlers, has started visiting the checkpoints in order to counteract what they see as the interfering gaze of MW women in this space. They do so mainly by subjecting MW women to an act of gazing. (In one instance this gaze turned into a physical assault that led to the hospitalization of an MW member.) Further, there is also the gaze of the Palestinian National Authority. Although implicit, this gaze is also present at checkpoints, along with multiple gazes by various Palestinian and international non-profit organizations.

Indeed, a multitude of gazes are produced in and by the checkpoint, configuring less binary and more nuanced relationships between the various actors that operate in this space. This multitude of gazes does not necessarily organize neatly under the binary juxtaposition of hegemonic versus counterhegemonic gazing technologies. Instead, as in Giotto's thirteenth-century paintings, the gazes interact with one another, each affecting the configurations of others so as to produce an increasingly complex set of hybrid gazes that constantly shift the power dynamics enacted at the checkpoint.

Act 8

The Romani

EBRU ÜSTÜNDAG

In July 2000, the Romani World Congress declared itself a 'non-territorial nation' with a flag, constitution and anthem. This act of citizenship challenges the conceptualizations of citizenship employed by both the nation-state (citizens of a particular country) and the supranational state (citizens of the European Union).

The origins of the people who are known as Gypsies or Roma can be traced back to North-west India. As a result of invasions from the Ghaznavid Empire, they were forced to flee this area in the eleventh century. Although sharing common roots in ancient Punjabi and Hindi, the Romani language has many dialects. Based on these linguistic differences, Roma are divided into three populations: the Domari of the Middle East and Eastern Europe (the Dom), the Lomavern of Central Europe (the Lom), and the Romani of Western Europe (the Rom). Common to each dialect of the Romani language is an absence of words meaning 'duty', 'possession' and 'truth'. Perhaps related to this, historically the Roma have been stereotyped as thieves and cannibals.

Their history has been one of the most difficult of any community. Throughout the ages, the Roma have faced hardships including being outlawed, enslaved, tortured and killed. In 1510, for example, the Grand Council of France prohibited the Roma from residing in that country. The initial punishment for transgressing this law was banishment, with a second offence resulting in hanging. In 1773, the Empress of Hungary ordered all Romani children over the age of five to be taken from their parents, transported to distant villages and assigned to peasants. In early nineteenth-century Germany, *Heidenjachten* (Gypsy Hunts) were a popular 'sporting' activity. In 1885, the Roma were excluded by United States immigration policy. In 1921, the newly formed Czechoslovak Republic recognized Roma as a

'During the Cold' (© Arjen Zwart)

separate 'nationality'. In 1936, the German government stripped them of their voting rights.

Today it is estimated that there are more than 12 million Roma world-wide. As they are not generally considered citizens, however, their actual numbers are not recorded in official censuses. The Roma's struggles for civil, political and social rights, as well as for recognition from states and international organizations, are longstanding. The first World Romani Congress was held in London in 1971, drawing delegates from 14 countries. An international Romani flag and anthem were formally approved. A year later, the International Romani Union became a member of The Council of Europe, and in 1986 of the United Nations Children's Fund. In 1994 the British Criminal Justice and Public Order Act abolished the Caravan Sites Act, leaving about 5,000 families homeless. Although the Romani community has gained a certain degree of recognition, their struggle for rights continues.

When eventually the Romani World Congress declared itself a nation, it was the culmination of this specific history of and against oppression, marginalization and discrimination. While this act of citizenship may have drawn attention to this history of oppression, it is doubtful whether it will be heard by any nation-state as a claim for recognition, let alone rights.

Act 9

Return to Guatemala

KARINE CÔTÉ-BOUCHER

If there is such a thing as a pure act of citizenship it would have to be able to arise from abject conditions in which the most disenfranchised, least audible, and worst brutalized could retain or recover enough agency – through solidarity, international cooperation and political courage – to claim the right to have rights. Ironically, if such a pure act of citizenship were to exist it would also mean recognition that others have come from even more impossible conditions. On 20 January 1993, a group of Guatemalan refugees returned home after more than a decade of exile in Mexico. The community of refugees named this day of return Victoria 20 de Enero (Victory, 20 January). This name has come to symbolize a unique act of citizenship in which Guatemalan refugees negotiated an agreement with the government of their home country providing for their return. The accord permitting this return constitutes a historical precedent for the international refugee regime, which often depoliticizes refugees by casting them as ahistorical victims in need of international protection. In challenging the meaning of 'refugeeness', the refugees also opposed the violent segregation of indigenous Mayan Guatemalans. By constituting themselves as active members of the polity from which they had been expelled, the refugees blurred the borders within which acts of citizenships are thought possible, and reaffirmed their right to articulate their identities autonomously.

In the early 1980s, indigenous civilian peasants living in guerrilla-occupied areas fled an extremely violent counter-insurgency policy undertaken by the Guatemalan government. As a result of this experience, the refugees came to reject the legitimacy of both state and international authorities, instead autonomously organizing themselves in the refugee camps they inhabited in Southern Mexico. In 1987, the refugees created the Commissiones Permanentes (Permanent Commissions) that began negotiating the conditions of their return with the Guatemalan authorities, pressuring the government to recognize the importance of their return, and establishing alliances with social movements and organizations in Guatemala.

In 1992, the refugees and the Guatemalan government reached a six-point agreement that included recognition of the right to return on a voluntary individual basis, but in a collective fashion; the right to free association; the right to international accompaniment and monitoring during the return period; freedom of movement within Guatemala; the right to life and security; and access to land. While some of the elements of the accord were already inscribed within the Guatemalan constitution, this agreement bound the Guatemalan government to the refugees through the international monitoring of its implementation. International observers were able to oversee both the return process and the first years of the reinstallation of the refugees in Guatemala. Furthermore, the agreement guaranteed access to land, which is crucial in a country where 2 per cent of the population owns 65 per cent of the farmland, and an even greater majority of productive farmland. Land redistribution, however, was not simply an economic gain. Native Guatemalans see their attachment to *Madre Tierra*, or the motherland, as a fundamental aspect of their identity.

The Guatemalan refugees' act of citizenship challenges traditional notions of the refugee and of citizenship. The refugees organized politically and represented themselves as separate from both the receiving and home states, as well as the United Nations High Commissioner on Refugees, all of whom tend to promote individually based, often externally imposed repatriations. Through their promotion of the collective and voluntary aspects of what they forcefully designated as return, rather than repatriation, the Commission not only demonstrated the refugees' agency, but also questioned the very individualization and depoliticization of the refugee question. Furthermore, as their motto *'Luchar para Retornar! Retornar para Luchar!'* (Struggle to Return! Return to Struggle!) suggests, Guatemalan refugees asserted the right to their country and its land. They based their claim upon the guarantee that they would have what Arendt has called 'the right to have rights' upon their return. Claiming rights to the polity from which they fled, the Commission enacted citizenship on the margins of the territorial state. They demonstrated that the rights of refugees should not be confined to the framework of individual protection in a foreign country provided by international refugee law. Rather, those rights must also encompass the possibility to reclaim the right to return, as well as actively redefine to politics in their home country. The Commission achieved that possibility by securing alliances with Guatemalan popular organizations, allowing them to establish themselves as legitimate political actors in their homeland. Hence, the very status of Guatemalan refugees as rights claimants located outside the national polity to which they claim rights redefines the conditions of possibility under which refugees may act.

Collectively reclaiming the rights to which they were entitled, organized

Return to Sajolem Buena Vista, 1997 (© Karine Côte-Boucher)

refugees within the Commission obviously made a claim for justice. They reclaimed the lands they had lost when they escaped the massacres in the jungle; they reclaimed their right to free movement within their country and to a secure life, free from threats and violent deaths. Yet they believed they would not receive such justice without witnesses that could render their existence visible, audible and sayable, allowing their claim for dignity to be acknowledged and recognized. Having learned the lesson of the complete international silence during the massacres of the 1980s – when the Guatemalan government had closed the borders to international observers – the refugees demanded accompaniment through their return process. The accompaniment, upon which the refugees based their security, involved UN agencies and national human rights organiza-tions, as well as international NGOs and willing individuals. Accompaniers were not mere observers, as accompaniment meant support for a just return and for the refugees' endeavour to transform their society, which had been torn apart by three decades of civil war. By their non-interventionist yet bodily presence, the accompaniers bore witness to both living conditions and rights violations in the communities to which the refugees returned. This in turn altered the accompaniers' networks back home, resulting in increased pressure being applied to their own as well as the Guatemalan governments.

The condition of exile was also an occasion for Guatemalan refugees to redefine their identity, as well as to reclaim authorship over the definition of Mayahood. When organizing under the Commissions, Guatemalan refugees articulated their claims with a strong symbolic representation of themselves as Maya, a group sharing a common attachment to the land and shared experiences of repression since the Spanish Conquest. As a consequence of their interaction with various indigenous groups during their exile, the refugees' sense of identity was transformed, leading to a representation of a pan-Mayan community capable of organized communal action. As a dynamic and transformative condition, the exile of Guatemalan refugees suggests some consideration of the cultural aspects involved in acting as citizens. As rights claimants, refugees posited themselves as agents. Furthermore, they dynamically redefined their identity through their endeavour to build an autonomous political community.

Nevertheless, identity formation involves shifting processes. Women refugees problematized homogeneous definitions of Mayan identity within their own communities. By organizing within but also separately from the Permanent Commissions, women shed light upon the power relations within refugee communities that entitled some to define such identity for political purposes. Contesting their silencing, women called for closer attention to be given to their specific experiences as indigenous women (for example, rape and torture of indigenous women were widespread during the period known as *la violencia*). The struggles of women refugees for justice emphasized that refugees' rights claims were inseparable from a reorganization of power relations within communities.

If the organization of Guatemalan women in exile was generally well received, the ways in which their struggles for their rights brought about violent reprisal when refugees had returned to Guatemala indicates the ambivalence of political organizing and the downside of rights claims. In Ixcán, the Guatemalan region where the civil war had been waged most severely, active women were specifically targeted amidst spreading internal conflicts. Accused of having been part of the guerrilla movement, residences of refugee women's groups were burned, and many women threatened. Such internal conflicts challenge representations of Guatemalan refugee organizing as a cohesive endeavour undertaken by homogeneous communities. In this case, the extremely unequal gender relations within return communities point to the necessity of examining the role of power relations within groups that reclaim their rights. How do these relations contribute to the shaping of the claim, as well as the differential possibilities and constraints attached to acting as unequal members of such a polity? In short, the analysis of acts of citizenship should take into account the ambivalences involved in acting for justice.

Act 10

❖

Unintentional Acts
of Citizenship
(*The Joke*)

IAN MORRISON

When an act of citizenship occurs that is not intentionally directed towards issues of citizenship is it still an act of citizenship? Do accidental ruptures from official political ideology create unexpected spaces and rejoinders for potential acts of citizenship? In Milan Kundera's 1967 novel *The Joke*, a joke made by the protagonist and the state's response to this joke raise important questions concerning the relationship between the intention of the actor and the interpretation of his act as an act of citizenship.

The novel's protagonist, Ludvik, is a university student in Prague in the 1950s. Both Ludvik and his girlfriend are loyal members of a Communist party cell. To tease his more orthodox girlfriend, Ludvik sends her a postcard that reads: 'Optimism is the opium of the people! A healthy atmosphere stinks of stupidity! Long Live Trotsky!'

This joke has severe ramifications for Ludvik. Brought up on charges of anti-revolutionary activity, and condemned by his friend Pavel, Ludvik is expelled from the university and the Communist Party, and sentenced to work as a penal labourer in the mines, for the purpose of ideological retraining.

Thinking about this seemingly uncomplicated act of joking in terms of an act of citizenship necessitates the consideration of several questions. First, is Ludvik's act an act of citizenship? While the Czechoslovakian state's response to Ludvik's act is clearly an act of citizenship, as it delimits the permissible actions and rights of its citizens, and promotes a particular vision of the proper citizen, the nature of Ludvik's act is more ambiguous. Kundera is clear that Ludvik is attempting to make an innocent joke, not a political statement.

This leads to a second question: must one be consciously attempting to disrupt or affirm notions or practices of citizenship in order for one's act to be considered

221

an act of citizenship? Or is the response to an act (its interpretation as an act of citizenship) sufficient for it to be considered an act of citizenship? In other words, does the designation of an act as an act of citizenship depend on the intent of the actor, or the reception of the act?

Finally, can the act, its reception, and the response to its reception be separated? Can an act be separated from the manner in which others interpret it, and the response that this interpretation provokes? Is it possible or desirable to separate Ludvik's act of joking from its interpretation as an anti-revolutionary act, and his subsequent punishment by the state?

By addressing the temporal aspect of Ludvik's act in its singularity, as a once-occurrent historical act, it is possible to engage with these questions. A moment, an event or an act, while singular and once-occurrent, should not be conceived of as occurring in isolation. First, acts cannot be temporally divorced from, yet must not be folded into, the past and the future. An act is always implicated in the present, and therefore, both the past and the future. Second, and consequently, as the act is not in isolation from the future, its interpretation is also one of its constitutive elements. In other words, once an interpretation of an act is made, it becomes part of the act itself. An interpretation of an act allows for it to arrive in a particular form. Therefore, the interpretation of Ludvik's act as an act of citizenship enacts it as an act of citizenship, becoming thus implicated in what the act itself becomes. Approaching acts from this perspective enables us to de-centre the motivations (both conscious and unconscious) of the actor within the analysis of the act, while still locating the act in its historical specificity. By approaching Ludvik's act in this manner, we are able to avoid debates as to his conscious or unconscious motivation concerning the Communist regime, their significance to the accuracy of an interpretation of his act, and its designation as an act of citizenship.

While Ludvik's act may seem to exist only in the realm of fiction, it is vital to theorize the connection between the virtual and the actual in this act. In other words, a holistic analysis of Ludvik's joke must include an analysis of the relation between the fictional act and the act of the actual creation/production of this fictional act. In doing so, however, it is again vital to avoid examining the intentions (whether conscious or unconscious) behind Kundera's writing of Ludvik's act.

An analysis of Kundera's act that does not go beyond the realm of an analysis of his stated intentions fails to theorize how this act arrived in a particular context. *The Joke* was first published in the midst of the growing opposition to Antonin Novotny's hardline regime, and for the establishment of 'socialism with a human face'. Not only was *The Joke* published in this context, but its author was an important figure in the reformist movement. Moreover, in 1968, near the eve of the Soviet invasion, Jaromil Jires released a film adaptation of *The Joke* that was widely interpreted as a critique of Communist rule. In this context, Kundera's act

'Liberté', Jiri Sliva. Bronze Medal winner, International Satrykon Exhibition 2006, Legnica, Poland (© Satrykon)

arrived as an act of citizenship through its interpretation by, and the response of the post-invasion Czechoslovakian regime to it. Although repeatedly denying that the novel was anything but a love story, Kundera, rather like his fictional protagonist, was stripped of his membership in the Communist Party and his teaching post at the Prague Film Institute. Moreover, his writings, including *The Joke* (as well as the film adaptation) were banned. In 1975 Kundera went into self-imposed exile in France.

In the case of both Kundera's actual act and the virtual act of Ludvik, analysis of the act cannot rely on an interpretation of the motivations of the actor. The occurrence of an act cannot be separated from its arrival. An act does not exist as a now within a series of nows. Rather, acts are continually becoming and arriving in various forms.

PART III

❖

Sites and Scales
of Answerability

Chapter 9

❖

Citizenship,
Art and the Voices of the City:
Wodiczko's *The Homeless*
Projection

FRED EVANS

'The Voice of the City'

In one of his famous short stories, O. Henry tries to discover the 'voice' of New York City. He goes from citizen to citizen, looking for a 'homogeneous identity' that 'finds its oral expression through a common channel' (O. Henry 1953, p. 1254). But he concludes that the city has no univocal voice. Moreover, he seems satisfied with this result – as if the city contains a secret, as if it says 'I am neither a single voice nor a mere collection of voices, but something else again.' O. Henry's conclusion is especially important today. In our age we go beyond recognizing virtue as a fact; we value it as well. But we also fall too easily into ethnic cleansing and other forms of social and political exclusion. This problem is exacerbated by the difficulty we have in imagining any alternative for social-political unity beyond a homogeneous identity or a plurality held together by mere expediency. But O. Henry's exploration of the city and his satisfaction at the end of it suggest a third alternative: a unity composed of differences, or what I will call a 'multi-voiced body'.

   This alternative conception of the type of unity appropriate to and embodied in the city carries implications for acts of citizenship. After providing an initial characterization of a unity composed of differences, that is, the city as a multi-voiced body, I will show how a particular piece of art, *The Homeless Projection* by the Polish-Canadian artist Krzysztof Wodiczko, both helps to clarify this idea of unity and illustrates the acts of citizenship appropriate to it.

Plato and Jacobs on the City

We can begin clarifying this new notion of social unity by contrasting Plato's classical and Jane Jacobs's contemporary view of the city. Plato looks outside the city in order to find its key. From his transcendental perch, he sees the pure, eternal forms of the four virtues that he thinks are necessary for fulfilling the 'good' or 'health' of the city: wisdom, courage, moderation, and justice. In particular, Plato proclaims that justice prevails only when the soldiers and the producers of goods agree to let the guardians rule on the basis of their knowledge of the Forms – only when, that is, the inhabitants 'mind their own business' and vow not to usurp the role of the ruling elite and their sublime wisdom (Plato 1992, pp. 433a–435a).[1] For Plato, then, justice is derived from on high and dictates that a hierarchical form of order is proper for the city and ultimately for all societies.

In contrast to Plato, Jacobs is mesmerized by the sights of the city. Her immersion within the confines of urban spaces – her desire to stay in Plato's famous allegorical 'cave' rather than to join him in attempting to go outside it – constitutes a rejection of the Greek philosopher's lofty perspective and the hierarchical muzzle he places on the city's voices. Instead of hierarchical order and harmony, Jacobs sees heterogeneity and creativity as definitive of the city. More specifically, she says that cities are 'natural generators of diversity and prolific incubators of new enterprises and ideas of all kinds' (Jacobs 1961, pp. 143, 145).[2] In the light of her vision of the city, one can say that Plato achieves a hierarchical form of social solidarity by sacrificing diversity and fecundity. But Jacobs' emphasis on heterogeneity and fecundity presents us with the opposite problem: it seems to omit, and perhaps even to undermine, any basis for social solidarity.[3] Moreover, social solidarity – some fundamental internal bond between people – seems required if the notions of justice and citizenship are to have any hold on society. In short, Plato and Jacobs provide two extremes for understanding the city and leave us with this question: should we let the age-old fear of chaos drive us towards Plato's desire for order, or should we follow our penchant for what is new and different, and possibly deprive ourselves of the solidarity necessary for justice and a meaningful form of citizenship?

A City of Voices

In order to answer the question that I have just raised – in order to escape the two horns of the dilemma just encountered, fearful chaos or stifling order – we can follow O. Henry's lead and continue to speak of the city in terms of voices. In particular, we can identify Jacobs's 'generator of diversity' and 'incubator ... of new ideas' with the creative interplay among the heterogeneous voices of the city and the proliferation of new discourses and other practices that this interplay produces. Similarly, we can identity Plato's notion of order and O. Henry's initial quest for a 'homogeneous identity' with what I will call 'oracles.' An oracle is 'the one true God', 'the pure race', 'patriarchy', 'Capital' or any other voice whose social discourse is taken as absolute and seeks to be the inviolable basis for governance of the city. When the city is threatened by war, disease, or some other exogenous force, the ever-present but low-level fear of being overwhelmed by the production of new discourses and styles of existence is exacerbated. This heightened fear, in turn, gives rise to oracles and the rigid identities associated with them. At an extreme, this fear produces the mutilation of living and dead bodies, systematic rape and other atrocities that economic or national interests cannot by themselves explain.[4]

Society, then, is a contest between the creativity of interacting, heterogeneous voices and the aspirations of oracles to limit and channel this fecundity into a hierarchical form of order. We can specify the nature of this contest more precisely by first enlarging upon the notion of voices and justifying our reference to them as the primary dimension of the social body.[5] To begin this task, we can note three important aspects of voices. First, voices point in two directions at once – to social discourses and to the bodies that articulate these semiotic formations. In other words, each voice encapsulates the anonymous and personal dimensions of our existence, each joins 'heaven and earth', language and our bodies, within itself. But voices are much more than discourses and their bodily enunciators. They exist, from the very beginning, as responses to one another. In other words, the social body is neither a substance nor a mere collection of individuals; rather, it is the dialogic interplay among these voices, an interplay that simultaneously separates and keeps these social forces together.

This second aspect of voices also includes our discovery of ourselves as already uttering the discourse of the voice we are enunciating. We are these voices, but they are more than us, always throwing us ahead of ourselves into the ceaseless interplay that they perform with one another. We are both their vehicle and their agent, 'elliptically identical' with them, and therefore our existence has an anonymous as well as a personal dimension at once.[6] Before presenting the third aspect of these voices, some phenomenological reflection can help reinforce my claims about the first two aspects of these voices. Specifically, we can note that we never encounter ourselves apart from a dialogue with ourselves or with others. When we wake, we are already involved in an exchange that will continue throughout the day, switching interlocutors and topics, but always pulling us along in its train. To break from all dialogue would literally mean our disappearance as self-aware beings, as existences 'for ourselves' and 'for others'. Dialogue, or the interplay among voices, is therefore an omni-present and defining feature of our lives, not something incidental to us. We are dialogical creatures.[7]

Of course, the city involves more than linguistic discourse. It includes different kinds of music, fashion, architecture, food, institutions, and other ostensibly non-linguistic activities. But each of these activities is inter-twined with the words we use to speak about them or to further their modes of existence. It is not too much of a stretch, therefore, to claim that these non-linguistic activities and structures are, from the very beginning, already incorporated into the social discourses associated with voices.[8] In other words, all the activities or structures of the city can be incorporated into the voices that make up and contest with one another in the social body.

But these considerations concerning voices have not yet brought us to the heart of the endeavour to valorize heterogeneity and fecundity without effacing social solidarity. To accomplish this, we will have to go beyond Jacobs's view of the city as a 'generator of diversity' and an 'incubator ... of new ideas.' We will have to introduce the third aspect of voices, 'dialogic hybridity', and thereby characterize more fully the notion of a unity composed of differences, or a multi-voiced body.

Voices and Dialogic Hybridity

The notion of dialogic hybridity is manifested by all the voices of the city. But it can be made particularly clear by examining the emergence of a new language or idiom. Spanglish, for example, is pervasive on the streets of New York City and even theatrical productions have begun to be written and performed in this idiom.[9] As its name suggests, Spanglish is formed from English and Spanish. But this new language is not a mere synthesis of the other two. In each hybrid sentence, in each utterance of Spanglish, the original two languages remain alive within their progeny and challenge it and each other for audibility in the domain of the street or the theatre.[10]

These aspects of Spanglish, especially its hybrid character, can be clarified further by borrowing some ideas from the Russian linguist and culturologist, Mikhail Bakhtin. For Bakhtin, language is not a unitary system (1981, p. 288); rather, it is a plethora of intersecting social languages or languages of 'heteroglossia (1981, p. 292).[11] Each of these social languages is a 'form' for conceptualizing its surroundings in words and is 'characterized by its own objects, meaning and values.'[12] Each, moreover, is reflexive and evaluative, 'a particular point of view on the world and on oneself, the position enabling a person to interpret and evaluate his own self and his surrounding reality' (Bakhtin 1984, p. 47). Because these social languages are inherently evaluative, they are close in spirit to Nietzsche's 'value-creating powers' and to the 'agonism' that many contemporary political thinkers adopt as their primary understanding of the political dimension of societies (1981, p. 358, 304). They are, in other words, voices, and Bakhtin often refers to them as such.

Bakhtin uses the term 'hybridization' in order to speak of the inter-section among these social languages. More precisely, hybridization is 'a mixture of two social languages within the limits of a single utterance, an encounter, within the arena of an utterance, between two different linguistic consciousnesses, separated from one another by an epoch, by social differentiation or by some other factor' (1984, p. 193). This encounter can be explicit or implicit. In parody, for example, the repre-senting voice *overtly* introduces its 'semantic intention' or meaning into another person's discourse (the represented voice) and forces the latter to serve its (the representing voice's) opposing view of the common subject matter (p. 193). Sometimes, however, the voice we cite forces us to subordinate our own discourse to it. Thus W. E. B. Du Bois speaks of 'double-consciousness', the 'sense of always looking at one's self through the eyes of others, of measuring one's soul by the tape of a world that looks on in amused contempt and pity'. But even in this example, domination by the oracle of North American thought and values is still contested. Du Bois therefore goes on to say that the whiteness and the consciousness of Blacks are two rival voices in the 'American Negro', 'two souls, two thoughts, two unreconciled strivings; two warring ideals in one dark body, whose dogged strength alone keeps it from being torn asunder' (Du Bois 1904, p. 3).[13]

Not all examples of hybridization involve two or more *overt* voices. But even when a contesting voice is not mentioned explicitly, it is present implicitly. For example, we may speak about Plato's hierarchical view of the city without overtly mentioning democracy; nonetheless, that notion is tacitly present as a constituent and rival of the meaning of hierarchical order. In short, there are no monological or 'pure' utterances; every utterance, every voice, makes tacit reference to its friends and adversaries, each shaped by the others from the very beginning, and undergoing further changes as the interaction with them continues. This notion is of key importance because it provides a concrete and precise portrayal of how voices can be 'inside' or 'part of' one another, of how each voice is a dynamic or, as I can now say, a 'dialogic' hybrid.

In order for Bakhtin's notion of hybridization to apply fully to the example of Spanglish I gave earlier as well as to other hybrids, I must emphasize the ability of new voices to emerge out of the interplay among other ones. Thus Spanglish, as we saw, emerged from and contains within itself two other voices, English and Spanish. Moreover, the intersection now of these three languages, Spanglish, English, and Spanish, is a form of social solidarity, that is, the current identity of each of them depends upon that of the others. Yet each of these social languages or voices is still distinct from the others and contests with them for audibility on the streets of New York. With these qualifications in mind, the relation among the voices of society – their dialogic hybridity – can be summarized by saying that *each voice is part of the identity and, at the same time, the 'other' of the rest.* When this aspect of hybridization is taken into account, we see that dialogic hybridity both provides the social solidarity that Jacobs under-emphasized and preserves the heterogeneity and fecundity that Plato sacrificed for social order.

If we consult literature, there is ample proto-phenomenological evidence for the claim that the voices of society resound within one another – that each is a dialogic hybrid. For example, Salman Rushdie captures this hybridity in his novel *Midnight's Children*. He has his main character, Saleem, say there, and particularly in the context of the mega-city, Bombay, that each 'I,' each mind, 'contains a ... multitude,' that is, all the other voices of India, and that understanding any of these 'I's therefore requires 'swallow[ing] a world' (Rushdie 1980, p. 458).[14] In the context of Dublin, James Joyce illuminates the cacophony of voices that contend for audibility within the soul of his character, Stephen Dedalus: those of Stephen's father and schoolmasters urge him to be a 'gentleman', those of the gymnasium to be 'manly and healthy', of the national revival to be 'true to his country', of worldliness to 'raise up his father's fallen estate by his labours', of schoolmates 'to be a decent fellow ... and do his best to get free days for the school', and, finally and most satisfying to Stephen, the welcome words of 'phantasmal comrades' who provide escape from the 'hollow sounding voices' of the others (Joyce 1946, pp. 332–3).

This idea of hybridization can be construed more fully as the very schema of communication: each voice is directed towards three destinations at once – a referential object or subject matter, immediate or explicit interlocutors (for example, face-to-face exchanges) *and* the other voices that are implicitly at play in its social arena.[15] Communication, then, *is* the interplay among voices, each one of them articulating the world in the light of and often as a rival to the contesting viewpoints that surround and help constitute it. Put otherwise, communication signifies that society is the multi-voiced body of which I have been speaking and in which each voice is perpetually responding to the others. Because this interplay produces new voices, and because these changes bring about nuances in the identity of the rest, the very being of society is its creativity and consequent meta-morphosis, as well as the heterogeneity and social solidarity of its voices.[16]

Citizenship and Art in the Multi-voiced City: Wodiczko's *The Homeless Projection*

Now that the idea of society as a multi-voiced body has been clarified, its political significance can be developed. It should already be clear that justice in the city cannot follow Plato's dictum of 'minding one's own business'; justice must instead support and promote the very opposite, that is, the creative interplay among the voices of the social body and the interweaving of social solidarity, difference and fecundity that this interplay involves. For this creative form of communication to take place, inter-locutors must hear each other in a manner that leaves open the possibility of changes taking place in their social discourses. Without this openness, without this hearing that is willing to put the stability of the interlocutors' social discourses at risk, we forfeit the type of social solidarity that promotes heterogeneity and the production of new voices. Indeed, the nihilistic oracles of which I have spoken are voices whose social discourse prohibits its enunciators from accepting any significant changes in their discourse. These enunciators hear only in the sense of recording informa-tion and using it to manipulate others as a means of advancing the agenda stipulated by their oracular social discourses.

We can appeal to the extreme case of a neo-Nazi in order to clarify the nature of the hearing without hearing that is typical of oracles:

> [Neo-Nazi] groups like the one I was part of watch their enemies from a distance. They are afraid getting near might defuse their hate, or at least corrupt it with first-hand knowledge and second thoughts. This is what distinguishes a true ideological hate: the way members of the group carry it so carefully, keeping it sealed against all corruption. And this is also why bombs are a perfect weapon for terrorist groups: they allow them to maintain a cleansing distance from the target, and the violence is sudden; there is no time for arguments or counter blows. (Hasselbach and Reiss 1996, p. 55)[17]

Justice stands in opposition to oracles of this sort. We can capture its positive meaning by formulating it as 'the interplay among equally audible voices.' Because of its emphasis upon interplay and equal audibility, this principle of justice tacitly invokes the three main characteristics or hallmarks of the city as a multi-voiced body – its social solidarity, heterogeneity and fecundity. Despite the impossibility of completely fulfilling this principle,[18] it serves as an ideal that can be approximated in political life. In particular, its achievement requires acts of citizenship on the part of the city's inhabitants. Positively, these acts must involve and promote the open sort of hearing that maintains the solidarity, heterogeneity and fecundity of the city; negatively, they must resist oracles. They must, that is, create a rupture in the prevailing oracle and thereby increase the citizen standing or audibility of whatever groups and ideas have been silenced by the dominant forces in the city. This act helps perpetuate the solidarity or interplay among the voices of the city and at the same time ensures the city's heterogeneity, and that new voices will emerge within the social body. Acts of citizenship, then, simultaneously break up oracles and create the conditions for the city to be itself – an unimpeded multi-voiced body – and for its populace to be citizens in the substantive rather than merely legalistic sense of the term.

In order to make this idea of citizenship and its service to justice clearer and more concrete, I will show how a particular work of art, Krzysztof Wodiczko's *The Homeless Projection*,[19] functions as just the sort of act I have been describing. The use of Wodiczko's work is ironic in that it defies Plato's well-known dictum to exclude unregulated art from the city. His *Projection* will also serve to clarify further the major aspects of dialogic hybridity and the notion of a multi-voiced body.

Wodiczko's *The Homeless Projection* is similar to a number of other installations that he constructed in New York City during the 1980s. These installations consisted of images projected onto architecture and monuments of all sorts. In the case of *The Homeless Projection*, the images were cast onto various statues in Union Square Park and tacitly referred to the huge Zeckendorf Towers luxury apartment building situated adjacent to it. Wodiczko's aim with this particular work was to produce a counter-architecture and show through it that '[w]hat has been defined as architecture is really ... a merciless real estate system, embodied in a continuous and frightening mass-scale EVENT, the most disturbingly public and central operations of which are economic terror, physical eviction, and the exodus of the poorest groups of city inhabitants from the buildings' interiors to the outdoors' (Wodiczko 1986, p. 12).

Before elaborating on Wodiczko's projection at Union Square Park, it will be helpful to clarify further the 'frightening mass-scale event' or oracle in which his work intervened. Rosalyn Deutsche's essay on Wodiczko's projection and the history she provides of Union Square Park are revealing in regard to this task. When Union Square opened to the public in 1839, one of its stated purposes was to commemorate 'the theme and images of liberty secured by the War of Independence' (Deutsche 1996, p. 23). In subsequent years, a number of modifications were added to the park's original six pathways. These included statues of George Washington (1856), Lafayette (1873), and Abraham Lincoln (1868), as well as a bronze mother and children ensemble and an immense flagpole base with patriotic inscriptions, including the full text of the Declaration of Independence (1926) (Deutsche 1996, p. 35).

Whatever the intended meaning of these sculptures and the park, Deutsche shows that by the 1980s their allusion to liberty had become concentrated in the right to private property. More specifically, technological and financial enterprises replaced New York City's manufacturing base; members of the managerial and professional class increasingly displaced blue-collar workers and pushed service workers and others into marginalized housing or onto the streets. In order to meet the housing and office space requirements of the managers and professionals, and to exploit new avenues for the investment of capital, city officials and real estate developers sponsored the gentrification of large tracts of New York's buildings. Many of these edifices had already been abandoned or had fallen into disrepair, and many others provided cheap housing for New York City's poor (Deutsche 1996, pp. 4–5, 14–18, 44–8).

The changes taking place in New York affected the immediate Union Square Park area as well. Besides the construction of the luxury Zeckendorf Towers adjacent to it, the Park itself was 'revitalized'. This so-called revitalization included much more than preserving and refurbishing its four bronze monuments. For example, real estate advertisements rewrote the Union Square's history in order to emphasize the patriotic celebrations that took place there rather than the labour and other protests that were equally part of its past and present (Deutsche 1996, pp. 19–21, 25–6). Moreover, the officials in charge of the park agreed to change its entire spatial layout in order to ensure the type of Haussmanian or Panopticon surveillance that would discourage 'derelicts', 'thugs' and other 'undesirables' from loitering there.[20] Thus the original six radial paths were replaced by two sidewalks crossing the park and many trees were cut down. The beneficiaries of redevelopment, such as the corporate managers and residents of Zeckendorf Towers, would now have complete control over the park's public space (Deutsche 1996, pp. 28–9). They need not be too troubled by homeless or poor people, let alone the occasional pimp, drug dealer or thief that also used to haunt the Park's premises.

In response to these developments, Wodiczko performs an effective, indeed magical, intervention in the Park. Specifically, he transforms the statues on Union Square into homeless people by projecting slide-images seamlessly onto them. For example, a head bandage and a leg cast convert Lafayette's slim form into an unfortunate person asking for a handout (Figure 9.1); a crutch and beggar's cup change Lincoln into a vacant-eyed panhandler soliciting at a street corner (Figure 9.2); Washington's horse becomes a wheel-chair, his right hand now grasping a can of Windex and a cloth, and his imperial left arm motioning drivers to stop and get their windshields cleaned (Figure 9.3); similarly, an extended hand as well as a grocery cart transform the sculpture of the woman and her two children into a vagrant family (Figure 9.4) (Deutsche 1996, pp. 42–3).

Three aspects of Wodiczko's *The Homeless Projection* are particularly relevant to what I have been saying about the city. The first of these aspects concerns Wodiczko's undermining of homogeneity, hierarchical order and permanence. In her commentary on Wodiczko's projection, Deutsche says that it 'reinserts architectural objects into the surrounding city understood as a site of economic, social, and political processes'. His project therefore 'contests the belief that monumental buildings are stable, transcendent, permanent structures containing essential and universal meanings', and 'proclaims, on the contrary, the mutability of their languages and calls attention to the changing uses to which they are put as they are continually recast in new historical circumstances and social frameworks' (Deutsche 1996, pp. 6–7).[21] Indeed, the very form of *The Homeless Projection,* the ephemerality of the images it cast upon the statues, is the antithesis of permanence, including that of Plato's realm of Forms. In other words, Wodiczko's *The Homeless Projection* undermines not just this or that oracle, but oracularity itself. Like Michel Foucault's well-known genealogies, its aim is 'not the erecting of foundations' but to disturb 'what was previously considered immobile', to fragment 'what was thought unified', to show 'the heterogeneity of what was imagined consistent with itself' (Foucault 1998, pp. 374–5).

The second aspect of Wodiczko's counter-architecture is the particularization of the first aspect: it undermines a specific oracle, the real estate agencies' attempt to present their discourse of 'revitalization' as the most important story of the city. Thus Wodiczko proclaims that one of the aims of *The Homeless Projection* is 'to juxtapose the fake architectural real estate theatre with the real survival theatre of the homeless!' (Wosiczko 1986, p. 16)[22] This aim involves making the actual homeless (in small letters) into a new type of city monument or symbolic architectural form, THE HOMELESS (in capital letters):

THE HOMELESS appear more dramatic than even the most colossal and

Figure 9.1 Lafayette Monument, Union Square Park

Figure 9.2 Abraham Lincoln Monument, Union Square Park

Figure 9.3 George Washington Monument, Union Square Park

Figure 9.4 Mother and Child Fountain, Union Square Park

Krzysztof Wodiczko's *The Homeless Projection: A Proposal for the City of New York*, 1986 (photos © Krzysztof Wodiczko; courtesy Galerie Lelong, New York)

expressive urban sculptures, memorials, or public buildings . . . for there is nothing more disruptive and astonishing in a monument than a sign of life. To the observer the slightest sign of life in THE HOMELESS is a living sign of the possibility of the death of the homeless from homelessness. (1986, p. 12)

The first two aspects of Wodiczko's *The Homeless Projection*, therefore, are the undermining of oracularity and the insertion of a 'sign of life' that disrupts the real estate officials' own 'projection' of the meaning of Union Square Park. Put in positive rather than the negative terms just used, these first two aspects taken together champion diversity and the tendency of the city's heterogeneous forces to undermine or at least resist any oracle that would limit their audibility. More specifically, the 'sign of life' of which Wodiczko speaks is not simply the negation of the death sentence foisted upon the homeless by the real estate industry. It also affirms this life as one of a particular sort, a culture of the street poor, captured by the activities and postures of the homeless people depicted in the projection; furthermore, the amalgamation of these particular city dwellers with Washington, Lincoln and the other revered figures that make up the ensemble also conspires to prevent the viewer from reducing the homeless to examples of mere impoverishment: they gain just enough from their association with these revered figures to make us see them as embodying a way of life that, like all others, can develop in many directions if they are not oppressed, in this case by the real estate industry, and if healthcare and other resources are made available to them.[23] They gain just enough from this association for us to be reminded that they are citizens of the city like ourselves and thus even more worthy than usual of our allegiance and support.

The third aspect of Wodiczko's *The Homeless Projection* is related to the first two, that is, to the undermining of oracularity and the real estate industry's particular revitalization oracle, and to the positive side of their meaning, the affirmation of the city's heterogeneity. This third aspect concerns *The Homeless Projection*'s embodiment of the city's dialogic hybridity or solidarity – that is, of the role that voices play in constituting and contesting each other's identity and place in the city, and in producing new voices through this interplay. Wodiczko's own voice, as articulated in his counter-architecture, affirms the city's resistance to oracles and, hence, the city's heterogeneity. But his counter-architecture also establishes itself in part through the other voices it cites. In the case of the real estate developers, Wodiczko's projected images insert an alien, parodic meaning into their 'revitalization' discourse. This parody undermines the oracle status of the developers' discourse and shows it to be a death sentence for homeless people rather than a harbinger of new life for the city. But it also establishes Wodiczko's voice as the opposite of that of the real estate developers. *The Homeless Projection's* contest with the real estate industry's discourse makes the latter a dimension of the counter-architecture's meaning and hence of Wodiczko's voice: what we negate contributes to who we are just as much as what we endorse.

Another voice is also at play in Wodiczko's conversion of Union Park through his slide-projections. This voice is liberty, for which the statues in the Park were originally supposed to provide the testimony. Wodiczko's *The Homeless Projection* both appropriates this voice of liberty as its own (the increased audibility of the homeless) and, at the same time, reveals the hypocritical character of its original meaning within the context of the city's rampant capitalism and, more specifically, New York City's real estate industry. Within Wodiczko's counter-architecture, therefore, two other voices, Liberty and Capital, help constitute it and simultaneously contest with it and each other for audibility.[24] When we realize that capitalism, liberty, the homeless and art are all themselves composed of many voices or sub-dialects, the voices at play in Wodiczko's *Homeless Projection* seem innumerable, even if certain ones are more salient, more audible, in this particular historical moment than they might be in other such moments.

Moreover, the emergence of Wodiczko's counter-architecture produces a metamorphosis of the other voices. Just as the addition of a new colour or of a new sex would change the meaning of their traditional counterparts, so *The Homeless Projection* transforms the significance of the 'liberty' and 'revitalization' articulations of Union Square Park: both now take on the cast of a lie and must revise themselves if they are to counter the interloper's, indeed, their progeny's, parody of them. These forced revisions, too, can be put in more positive terms: they, like the voice of Wodiczko's *Homeless Projection*, are new voices, produced by the interplay among the voices of the city. As I said earlier, the very being of the social body is its continuous metamorphosis as well as its solidarity and its heterogeneity.

Wodiczko's *The Homeless Projection*, then, embodies the dialogic hybridity of voices. But it is also a superlative act of citizenship. Because of Wodiczko's ability to hear other people, his projection increases the audibility of voices that had been marginalized – especially those of the homeless and radical art – and contributes to the social solidarity, heterogeneity and ongoing metamorphosis of the city. In other words, his artful intervention helps the city to achieve the justice (an interplay among equally audible voices) demanded by the city's status as a multi-voiced body.

Beyond Communitarianism and Political Liberalism

Despite the support of Wodiczko's project, we cannot yet congratulate ourselves on discovering the core meaning of justice and citizenship within the city's hybrid body. We must, just as Plato tried to do, also say why anyone should feel compelled to be just and to take citizenship seriously.[25]

The major reason for being just and a good citizen on the multi-voiced body view concerns social solidarity, that is, the sense in which each voice is at once part of the identity and the other of the rest. This intersection of heterogeneous voices implies that the automatic affirmation we make of our own voice is simultaneously the valorization of the multitude resounding within that voice. In other words, we have two primary identities related to citizenship: our identity as the legal member of a nation-state and our identity as a substantive member of the multi-voiced body itself. Whatever our legal citizenship might be, we are also citizens of the multi-voiced body and thus citizens in a substantive as well as a legal sense. Once we recognize this dual citizenship, we will be motivated to be just because justice amounts to us being ourselves, to fulfilling our dual identity and the affirmation it carries for the other voices resounding within our own – most immediately, in this case, the voices of the city.

This dual identity and citizenship provide an advantage over political liberalism and over traditional forms of communitarianism. The abstract and universal principles or rights of political liberalism have great difficulty in outweighing the power of identity as a motivating factor: we all too easily engage in unnecessary wars and even the torture of those whom we see as outside 'our own kind'. On the other hand, the identity provided by religion, race or tradition to which many communitarians appeal is too narrow, too socially and politically exclusionary, to bring us together across the many issues that divide us: what traditional communitarianism gains in motivating justice and acts of citizenship, it loses by the narrowness of the allegiance it inspires.[26] In contrast, the multi-voiced body view of the city and society provides the motivation for justice usually attributed to communitarianism *and* the universality claimed by political liberalism. Indeed, these two traits, motivation and universality, are built into each other on the multi-voiced body view of society. We desire to fulfil our identity, but that identity also includes the other voices of society; thus the motivation to hear ourselves is equally the basis for hearing others, for universality.

One can see, then, that the notion of dialogic hybridity or social solidarity peculiar to the multi-voiced body view of the city allows the twin issues of motivation and universality to be addressed effectively. But the very idea of this form of social solidarity also raises a problem that would seem to undermine any value that the multi-voiced body view might have. For doesn't the affirmation of the other voices of society include racist, sexist and other nihilistic discourses – that is, voices whose enunciators, in the name of an impossible 'purity', deny their dialogic hybridity and their origin in the multi-voiced body? But if I am right in claiming that society is a multi-voiced body and that each voice is a dialogic hybrid, then the very denial by these social discourses of their origin legitimates us in doing what would have seemed to be a paradox: to exclude the excluders. We may have to hear the enunciators of these nihilistic voices for both structural and pragmatic reasons,[27] but we cannot justifiably give them a policy-making role in a body that they repudiate in principle. Oracles of this nihilistic sort, then, are aberrations in relation to the city, albeit ones made all too prevalent historically and geo-graphically by our too easily exacerbated fear of diversity and novelty. These aberrant voices must join the ranks of Plato's hierarchical regime and the real estate industry's revitalization discourse as unjust in relation to the city and as a proper target for acts of citizenship such as Wodiczko's *The Homeless Projection*.

Unfortunately, this attempt to exclude the excluders opens the multi-voiced body view to a second and final objection. This objection points out that the view of the city as a multi-voiced body, including its principle of justice and its idea of citizenship, itself appears to be an oracle. My response to this objection is to agree that the multi-voiced body view is an oracle, but to show that it is simultaneously an anti-oracle. The multi-voiced body view is an oracle because it provides a utopian vision of the city as well as a direction for critical thought and political activism. As we have seen, this utopian vision is the solidarity, heterogeneity, and fecundity of the city's multi-voiced body; and the political direction it prescribes and motivates is the fulfilment of the city's principle of justice through mediating acts of citizenship. But the multi-voiced body view is also an anti-oracle because the very idea of it is in principle unfinalizable. Our affirmation of the city's multi-voiced body commits us to hear other voices and thus to remain open to possible revisions of our idea of this body.[28] A commitment to the idea of the city as a multi-voiced body, in other words, valorizes the very conditions that maintain this idea as a lure for new articulations of itself and thus for the unending contestation over which version of it will represent society at any given time. Stated more succinctly, the status of the multi-voiced body as the continual production of new versions of itself intrinsically undermines any finalized idea of the nature of that body.

This reason for the anti-utopian character of the multi-voiced body is stronger than it may at first appear. The multi-voiced body not only acts as a lure for articulations of itself; it invites divergent rather than convergent versions of itself, new voices rather than closer approximations to old truths. And yet these divergences, as divergences *of* the idea of the multi-voiced body and not, say, of fascism or any other idea of society, fall within the range permitted by this generative and essentially incomplete or inexhaustible idea. The idea differs, then, from the convergence-orientation implicit in Kantian regulative ideals and phenomenological horizons. In operational terms, this anti-utopian aspect of the multi-voiced body acts as a disrupter of any pretender to the throne, of any oracle that would attempt to give that body a final destination or claim to be intrinsically closer to the right path than other articulations of this vision of society.

To summarize these claims and this chapter, the idea of the city as a multi-voiced body is oracular in that it provides a utopian vision of society; but it is equally anti-oracular in that it intrinsically undermines any attempt to present an articulation of itself as final or even as closer to it than are other articulations. For practical or political reasons one articulation will usually win out over another, but never because it is closer to some absolute standard, some Platonic form, of what this body would be. Because these articulations of the idea of the multi-voiced body are not final, and in so far as they affirm the heterogeneity, solidarity and creativity of the city, they, like Wodiczko's *The Homeless Projection*, will always accord with the spirit of the city, will always be preferable to the oracles that declare themselves to be the unchangeable truth and are for that very reason the antithesis of the city and the dialogic hybridity of its voices. O. Henry's 'voice of the city,' then, has turned out to be many voices. In particular, it has turned out to be the interplay among them, a social solidarity that thrives on their heterogeneity, produces new social discourses, and continually metamorphoses itself.

Notes

1   Wisdom resides in the guardians who rule the city, bravery in the soldiers who command obedience to the municipal laws generated by the wisdom of the rulers, and justice and harmony throughout the three parts, that is, as their two principles of interrelationship. The producers or entrepreneurs' desire for money, when controlled by the city's laws, helps to maximize the production necessary for meeting the city's material needs. Plato's emphasis on order as the chief virtue or need of the city has been reiterated in many of the utopian dreams that historically succeeded his work and in the notions of cosmos over chaos that both preceded and succeeded it. For the utopian dreams concerning cities, see David Pinder's *Visions of the City* (2005) as well

as Jane Jacobs's critical review of these dreams (1961, pp. 16–25); for the more enduring issue of the struggle between cosmos and chaos, see Norman Cohn (1993).

2   See also her comments about the city as a 'natural' setting for human beings (1961, pp. 444–5). Jacobs, of course, is not alone in lauding these aspects of the city. In particular, see Pinder's treatment of the 'situationists' in his *Visions of the City* (2005).

3   Jacobs does directly address the issue of order in the city. But she treats it as a mechanical problem of the interrelationship of multiple variables – 'organized complexity' (1961, p. 434) – and not in terms of the type of social solidarity or political/social 'unity composed of differences' towards which I am headed in this paper.

4   In a book I have just completed (see note 5 for the reference), I develop a notion, the 'social unconscious,' in order to enlarge upon this explanation of the tendency to produce oracles (Evans, forthcoming).

5   For a full treatment of the idea of voices and the accompanying notion of society as a multi-voiced body, see Evans (forthcoming). I have also published a number of articles involving these notions. See, for example, Evans 2004, 2001, 2000.

6   In *The Multi-Voiced Body*, I argue that we have a special relation to these voices, that we are 'elliptically identical' with them, that we are them, but that they are also, in their ongoing dialogue or contestation with one another, more than us (and thus that we are always more than ourselves). In other words, as I say above, our existence has both an anonymous and a personal dimension; we are both vehicle and agent of the forces that comprise us.

7   Moreover, each voice in these exchanges has the ability, because of the complex syntax of discourse, to make an object of itself or of another social discourse and imagine them as different than they are at present. In this sense, voices and their dialogic relation to one another, including our so-called soliloquies, are the basis of human freedom and thus deserve the prominence I am giving them here. This notion of freedom is treated at length in *The Multi-Voiced Body*.

8   In *The Multi-Voiced Body*, the relation of voices to bodies, perception and social structures is fully treated. This treatment relies on the notion of 'reciprocal pre-supposition' as developed in Gilles Deleuze and Felix Guattari, *A Thousand Plateaus* (1987, p. 145; see also pp. 91, 108, 140–1,146). It also addresses the traditional problem of the relation between 'base and superstructure' that is associated with Marxism.

9   In the plays that use Spanglish as their linguistic medium, the dynamic hybridity of this idiom, its fecundity and dialogic intersection with its constituent languages, becomes crystal clear. It is no longer a language that people speak only on the street; it becomes, in this literary context, what the Russian linguist and culturologist Mikhail Bakhtin calls 'the image of a language' – a language that is now formally presented to us as existing through its constant interplay with other social-linguistic viewpoints. Specifically, in *The Dialogic Imagination* Bakhtin says that the presence of a language in a novel transforms the idiom into 'the image of a language', that is, a language as it appears to the other 'linguistic consciousnesses' that make up the novel and, vice versa, how they appear to it (1981, p. 359).

10   Moreover, the identities of these two languages take on a new nuance once Spanglish arises from them; in particular, their perceived 'purity' gains in salience relative to the perceived 'impurity' of their progeny. The tendency is then to condemn Spanglish for its hybridity and praise the other two for their 'unsullied' character.

11   Bakhtin 1981, p. 291; see also pp. 170, 365.

12   See also pp. 382, 356. Bakhtin also refers to these social languages as 'voices'. He often speaks of voice as including 'personality' and defines it explicitly in his notes as including 'height, range, timbre, aesthetic category (lyric, dramatic, etc.) ... [and] a person's worldview and fate' – see Bakhtin 1984, p. 293. Moreover, Bakhtin sometimes refers to social languages as 'form-shaping ideologies' (1984, p. 97).

13   For a systematic treatment of 'whiteness' and resistance to it by the 'black body' in the North American context, see Yancy, forthcoming.

14   On this page, Rushdie is speaking of all of India; but it's clear in his novel that the exemplar of India is a city, Bombay.

15   This implicit interplay is similar to what Dallmayr (1996, p. 291) calls 'lateral universalism', 'an ingathering hospitable to all other beings', at least when oracles are not ordering it up for their own homogenizing purposes.

16   The full meaning of this idea of communication is discussed in *The Multi-Voiced Body*.

17   We should bear in mind that bombs dropped from the air maintain this 'cleansing distance' as well, and perhaps constitute a form of 'dispassionate terrorism' in comparison with the neo-Nazi's emotionally invested form.

18   The principle is impossible to fulfil because if all voices were equally audible at once, none could be heard for the din they would produce. The role of law, then, is to ensure that the institutions and inhabitants of the city always approximate the fulfilment of this ideal to the highest degree possible without the self-cancellation just mentioned.

19   My exposition of Wodiczko's *Homeless Projection* is also based on Deutsche 1996. *Homeless Projection* was originally displayed as an installation in New York at the 49th Parallel, Centre for Contemporary Canadian Art, in 1986. The brochure distributed there is the material reprinted in *October* (Wodiczko 1986) and cited above.

20   These references are, respectively, to Georges Haussmann, Napoleon III's architect and transformer of Paris, and to Jeremy Bentham's famous tower proposed for use in prison control.

21   See also Deutsche 1996, p. 38.

22   Cf. Deutsche 1996, pp. 12, 37, 38, 39, 42, 43, 46.

23   In support of this idea as homelessness as a way of life (not necessarily a chosen one), there is a newspaper for the homeless in Cambridge, Massachusetts, *Spare Change News*.

24   For example, the voice of homeless people is actually many voices, some of which might contest Wodiczko's rendition of them.

25   As is well known, Plato claims that nothing is more fulfilling or pleasurable than knowing the perfect forms. But they can't be known unless the soul is 'just' and in harmony with itself. Thus Plato takes this sublime pleasure as the motivation for being just. See Plato 1992, pp. 583b–588a.

26   For a discussion of this issue see my *The Multi-Voiced Body*, Chapter 10; Kymlicka 2002, pp. 209–10 and *passim*; Greg M. Nielsen's (2002) extended treatment of *ethnos* and *demos*; as well as Thompson 1998, pp. 188–90, and *passim*.

27   These reasons are worked out in *The Multi-Voiced Body*.

28   If my version of the idea of the multi-voiced body should be the governing voice of society, then this same commitment means that I must be open to its replacement by a rival version of the idea of the multi-voiced body.

References

Bakhtin, M. (1981) *The Dialogic Imagination* (trans. C. Emerson and M. Holguist), University of Texas Press, Austin, TX.

—— (1984) *Problems of Dostoyevsky's Poetics* (trans. C. Emerson and M. Holguist), University of Texas Press, Austin, TX.

Cohn, N. (1993) *Cosmos, Chaos and the World to Come: The Ancient Roots of Apocalyptic Faith*, Yale University Press, New Haven, CT.

Dallmayr, F. (1996) 'Democracy and Multiculturalism' in S. Benhabib (ed.), *Democracy and Difference: Contesting the Boundaries of the Political*, Princeton University Press, Princeton, NJ.

Deleuze, G. and F. Guattari (1987) *A Thousand Plateaus: Capitalism and Schizophrenia*, (trans. B. Massumi), University of Minnesota Press, Minneapolis, MN.

Deutsche, R. (1996) 'Krzysztof Wodiczko's *Homeless Projection* and the Site of Urban "Revitalization"' in *Evictions: Art and Spatial Politics*, MIT Press, Cambridge, MA.

Du Bois, W. E. B. (1904), *The Souls of Black Folk: Essays and Sketches,* fifth edition, A. C. McClurg and Co., Chicago, IL.

Evans, F. (2000) 'Voices of Chiapas: The Zapatistas, Bakhtin, and Human Rights', *Philosophy Today*, 42, 196–210.

—— (2001) 'Genealogy and the Problem of Affirmation in Nietzsche, Foucault, and Bakhtin', *Philosophy and Social Criticism*, 27 (3).

—— (2004) 'Multi-Voiced Society: Philosophical Nuances on Salman Rushdie's *Midnight's Children*', *Florida Journal of International Law*, 16 (3).

—— (forthcoming), *The Multi-Voiced Body: A Philosophy of Society and Communication in the Age of Diversity*, Columbia University Press, New York.

Foucault, M. (1998) 'Nietzsche, Genealogy, History', in Faubion, J. D. (ed.) *Michel Foucault: Aesthetics, Method, and Epistemology*, The New Press, New York.

Hasselbach, I. with T. Reiss (1996), 'How Nazis are Made', *The New Yorker*. 8 January.

Henry, O. (1953) 'The Voice of the City' in *The Complete Works of O. Henry*, Vol. 2, Doubleday and Company, Garden City, NY.

Honig, B. (1996) 'Difference, Dilemmas, and the Politics of Home' in S. Benhabib (ed.), *Democracy and Difference: Contesting the Boundaries of the Political*, Princeton University Press, Princeton, NJ.

Jacobs, J. (1961) *The Death and Life of Great American Cities*, Vintage Books, New York.

Joyce, J. (1946) *A Portrait of the Artist as a Young Man*, in H. Levin (ed.), *The Portable James Joyce*, Penguin Press, New York.

Kymlicka, W. (2002) *Contemporary Political Philosophy*, second edition, Oxford University Press, Oxford.

Laclau, E. and C. Mouffe (1985) *Hegemony and Socialist Strategy: Towards a Radical Democratic Politics*, Verso, New York.

Nielsen, G. M. (2002) *The Norms of Answerability: Social Theory between Bakhtin and Habermas*, State University of New York Press, Albany, NY.

Nietzsche, F. (1967) *On the Genealogy of Morals* (trans. W. Kaufmann and R. J. Hollingdale), Vintage Books, New York.

Pinder, D. (2005) *Visions of the City: Utopianism, Power and Politics in Twentieth-Century Urbanism*, Edinburgh University Press, Edinburgh.

Plato (1992). *Republic* (trans. G. M. A. Grube), Hackett: Indianapolis, IN.

Rushdie, S. (1980) *Midnight's Children*, Penguin Books, New York.

Thompson, J. (1998) 'Community Identity and World Citizenship' in D. Archibugi, D. Held and M. Köhler (eds), *Re-imagining Political Community: Studies in Cosmopolitan Democracy*, Stanford University Press, Stanford, CA.

Wodiczko, K. (1986) '*The Homeless Projection*: A Proposal for the City of New York', *October* 38 (Autumn), 3–22.

Yancy, G. (forthcoming) *Black Bodies, White Gazes*, Rowman and Littlefield, New York.

Chapter 10

❖❖

Acts of Chinese Citizenship:
The Tank Man and
Democracy-to-Come

YON HSU

On 4 June 1989 a young Chinese man attempted to stop tanks that were en route to Tiananmen Square to participate in a crackdown on the student movement. The name 'Tank Man' has been given to this actor whose true identity remains unknown to this day. What is known is that he used his body as a roadblock, making the column of tanks move to avoid him five times. The only way for the tanks to advance would have been to roll over him. When they stopped just short of him he climbed onto the leading vehicle in order to attempt to persuade the commander to turn around. After jumping off the tank, he furiously swung his grocery bags to the ground and, shouting out, expressed his anger at the military brutality. This unique event ended when the Tank Man was pulled aside by some onlookers (or secret agents) and then disappeared into the crowd. This moment of defiance was captured and disseminated by Western journalists in a nearby hotel. The global audience experienced feelings of awe related to the man's courage, as well as fear for his safety. The image had also created a sense of hope concerning the possibility that the column of tanks would back down at the Tank Man's request.

It is difficult to explain this act of bodily struggle through the rational language of formal entitlement and legal status usually associated with the concept of citizenship in the West. It also seems inappropriate to subject the Tank Man's act to schematic divisions of political membership, programmatic categories of individual autonomy or other procedural articulations of democratic practices. Furthermore, the case of the Tank Man is fraught with risks, charged with strong emotions, and accented by a type of martyrdom that contains few references to rights and obligations otherwise recognizable in contemporary citizenship practices. If *Time* magazine could select the Tank Man as one of the most influential figures of liberty and democracy in the past century, how do we make sense of his act without leaping to the hasty conclusion of the triumph of Western democracy over Chinese authoritarianism? Another question remains: if principles of liberal democracy cannot be applied to Tank Man's acts of defiance, how does this case shed light on citizenship studies in general?

The absence of a language of rights in Chinese political culture at the time and the inadequacy of explanation of the Chinese case from the liberal model turns out to be advantageous: an examination of this act requires recourse to alternative theoretical considerations that otherwise might not occur. The Tank Man acted both irrationally and with an emotional and volitional anger. The following argument makes use of a series of concepts drawn from three disparate thinkers that together help me to make sense of acts of citizenship outside the Western context. I contrast and integrate elements from Jacques Derrida's philosophy of justice and concept of democracy-to-come; Mikhail Bakhtin's concept of double-sided answerability and philosophy of the act; and Judith Butler's critique of norms and philosophy of the subject. First, drawing on concepts developed by Bakhtin, I focus on the importance of emotional-volitional acts in citizenship studies. Without acts from lived experiences, citizenship is petrified in a theoretical world of abstraction, political ideology or regime dogma. In these worlds citizenship takes place through the pretender's ritual acts in the service of glorifying or maintaining a regime. While questioning rationalism and its privileging of reason over emotion, I further argue for the significance of emotional-volitional engagement in acts as an axiological position for quality and value as well as a key nuance of citizenship.

I then turn to Jacques Derrida's discussion of justice and democracy-to-come in order to help unravel just how acts of citizenship, such as that performed by the Tank Man, create moments of political rupture. These are the moments when citizens refuse to perform what Bakhtin calls the pretender's ritual acts; instead they reveal and confront the violence of state authority. The confrontation itself is what Derrida calls an act of faith in justice or in democracy-to-come. 'To-come' has less to do with the messianic waiting for something to happen in the future than with the imperceptivity of justice and democracy that in turn demands us to act to their potentiality. When acts of citizenship are performed as defiance against the violence of the regime, they put faith in what must be addressed as the urgent demand of the here and now. They are also open to the demands of other future possibilities beyond what is claimed by authority to be legal, just or democratic. At the same time, acts of citizenship create political rupture as an injunction to the aporia of citizenship backed by what Derrida calls the 'mystical violence' of law and authority.

Acts of citizenship not only concern the juridical and the political, but also the ethical. These three realms of concern cannot be separated easily. To advance this point, I turn first to Butler's work on norms and subject formation. Acts of citizenship bring about ruptures not only in the legal sense of citizenship defined by the regime, but also to political subjectivity. However, as Derrida also argues, acts cannot be total ruptures. The significance of acts lies in the actor's determination to work out the aporia, albeit maintaining an evaluative yet transformative relation to the given political structure and the preceding sense of the self. Almost twenty years after the event, the Tank Man remains enigmatic. Who is the Tank Man? What is his name? Where is he from? Was he a student or a worker? Perhaps his identity will never be known. In any case the Tank Man's background and identity are less significant than the way he defined himself through his act. This defining process entails what Bakhtin calls double-sided answerability towards the universal and the particular. First, it is the universal obligation of acts of citizenship to address the urgent demand of the here and now and the potential of other possibilities in the name of justice or democracy-to-come. Second, the act addresses the particular 'ought' that political subjects should give an account of their own irreplaceable uniqueness. Therefore, acts of citizenship not only address the other, as Derrida would suggest, but also the self, as both Bakhtin and Butler would insist. Before developing the main points of this chapter, the context of the Tiananmen protest in 1989 is outlined briefly.

The Tiananmen Protest

Ten years after Deng Xiaoping announced a programme of economic reform and opened China to capitalism in 1979, the Chinese regime had already become saturated with various problems in 1989. These included corruption, official profiteering, the stagnation of political leadership, and manipulation of and by the press. Chinese intellectuals have long been central in the (re)making of Chinese history, but they were no longer certain of their roles and positions in the process of transformation. They shared the same grievances as ordinary Chinese. Moreover, they felt cast out from participation in the process of reformation. Capitalist development tended to invert the traditional social hierarchy by elevating the mercantile class, while the activities of intellectuals remained tightly controlled and limited by the regime.

As a result, the discussion of social and political issues became popular within Beijing universities. Nevertheless, it was not until the spring of 1989 that students seized opportunities to express their grievances and act against the regime. Initially crowds gathered in Tiananmen Square on 15 April to mourn the death of the former Communist Party general secretary, Hu Yaobang, 'the only' uncorrupted leader. This political space was frequently used to stage people's support for the Chinese regime. Students constructed another window of opportunity by reincarnating the spirit of democracy through their commemoration of the student movement of 4 May 1919, which had marked a genealogical starting point for Chinese democracy. Students in 1989 believed that they could act like the previous generation in contributing to China's modernization and shaping the direction of national development. In this sense the protest was not simply a demand for liberty and democracy. Students also saw themselves as patriotic citizens who sought to offer solutions to social and political problems in China.

Small gatherings with posters and speeches first took place in the Haidian District that hosts most of the 76 universities in Beijing. On 18 April, thousands of students marched to Tiananmen Square to mourn Hu, and to express their dissatisfaction with the *status quo*. On 27 April, one million people joined in a march in response to the harsh criticism of student protests by government officials. This march was especially pivotal in amplifying the need to act and in opening the concern from student self-interest to the good of all the Chinese people. The protest became heated when students started to organize camps in the square. Political engagement went deeper when students gained support from workers and ordinary citizens from Beijing and elsewhere. The 1989 pro-democracy protest then became more complex, involving political acts ranging from a demand for dialogue with Chinese officials, to the establishment of a statue of liberty, to hunger strikes (Calhoun 1997).

The Chinese government could not ignore the extent to which the protest evolved. After hardliners within the regime had won the battle against reformists, the protest came to be regarded as a threat to social security, and martial law was declared on 19 May. Protest tactics included barricades, emotional persuasion, physical roadblocks, bodily assemblies and the destruction of public objects (buses) in order to impede the march of the PLA (People's Liberation Army) towards the square from different sectors of the city. It was not until midnight on 4 June that the Chinese government determined the need to end the protest in bloodshed. This was also the context in which the Tank Man acted against the PLA.

While the existing literature concerning the 1989 Tiananmen protests focuses on the socio-political background and the aftermath of the events, it also tends to contextualize the event from the perspective of social movements (Fewsmith 2001; Calhoun 1997; Lin 1992; Cheng 1990). The political acts of defiance described above are understood as tactics, or are treated as a means to an end. In other words, acts are seen either as the making of Chinese democracy or as the building blocks of a movement towards democracy. As a result, these existing approaches overlook the acts of defiance themselves. How can an understanding of these acts themselves make a contribution to citizenship studies in general?

Moments of Political Rupture for Justice and Democracy-to-Come

The Tank Man's defiance of the PLA reflects the limit of subjecting citizenship to objective, legal and political categories. First, it is difficult to analyse the Tank Man through the language of rights. This central theme of theorizing citizenship in the West was foreign to China at the time. We often discuss Western citizenship *vis-à-vis* membership and belonging. This implies challenges brought by the other, the third party, the alien or the foreigner. However, this is less the case for the Tank Man, as he confronted an army that is 'supposed' to protect and liberate its own people. Second, it is rather awkward to subject the case of the Tank Man to the question of legitimacy or legality because he is regarded as a political rogue from the perspective of the Chinese government. Third, it is ironic that military violence preserves law. This implies that there is a limit in our conceptual explanation of citizenship based on a systematic, statutory and programmable apparatus with which we are familiar in the West. In this part of the discussion, I argue that emotional-volitional acts are significant for citizenship as they rupture the violence of law and the taut regime authority that prevails in the Chinese context. I argue further that acts of citizenship must be acts of faith in justice and in democracy-to-come.

Bakhtin provides us with conceptual tools for resolving some of the difficulty of analysing the example of the Tank Man. We tend to treat citizenship as an abstract ideology or a system of legal relations that transcends the acts of citizens. In Bakhtin's terms, acts are translated into 'a theoretical world, [but] not the world in which an act or deed is actually performed' (Bakhtin 1995, p. 27). Citizenship can only become alive when acts take place as lived experiences. Otherwise, citizenship is subject to theoreticism and can only ever determine what acts should be for the sake of abstract thought, political ideology or regime dogma. In other words, citizenship as such renders acts into ritual and habitual acts that require citizens' repeated performances in order to maintain the legitimacy and legality of the political system. Consequently, when citizenship is fixated on regulated or codified prescriptions, it is exercised with the pretension that the maintenance of the regime in the name of the citizens' well-being or social security is ontologically more fundamental than anything else. Thus, any threat to the superiority of the regime is considered to be an act of 'turmoil'. Anyone who renounces the performance of ritual acts is in turn regarded as a rogue or a criminal.

To break away from ritual and habitual acts of citizenship in this context, we need first to take up critical and evaluative positions. In other words, acts of citizenship have to be emotionally and volitionally engaged as they mark out value-governed axiological positions at the moments of political rupture. They cannot be based solely on reason or reasonable knowledge. Following Kierkegaard, Derrida suggests that 'the instant of decision is madness' (Derrida 2002, p. 255). This sense of madness conjoins with Bakhtin's emphasis on the importance of emotions in acts: '[e]verything that is actually experienced as something given and as something-yet-to-be-determined, is intonated, has an emotional-volitional tone, and enters into an effective relationship to me within the unity of the ongoing event encompassing us. An emotional-volitional tone is an inalienable moment of the actually performed act' (Bakhtin 1995, p. 65). Acts of citizenship have to be emotional-volitional intonations precisely because they give force to where and how the act is originated and situated. These tones further facilitate the expression of citizens' unique evaluation of the referential object. This helps to clarify that citizenship not only entails *meanings* to fight and risk for, but also specific *values* to be attached and addressed. Citizenship becomes meaningless without concrete acts. Acts of citizenship without emotions can only constitute political subjects with the legality of rights and responsibility by leaving motives, characters, values and tonality behind.

Some might argue in response that emotions can be a danger to social stability when they are deemed to be manipulated by the few. For instance, the Tank Man is regarded as a rogue in the eyes of the Chinese regime because he acted as if he was angry at the approaching PLA and as if he himself was mad (insane). It is possible that emotions can be instrumentally manipulated through propaganda and that they inscribe deceit in the general sentiment of public culture, as was seen during the Cultural Revolution.[1] However, this should not be a reason to undermine the indispensability of emotions in acts of citizenship. If emotional-volitional acts are subject to manipulation, so is rational argumentative discourse. As Bakhtin points out, rationalism is 'elemental and blind outside the bounds of an answerable consciousness, just as any being-in-itself is'. Rationality cannot be free from manipulation 'precisely because of the law inherent in the logical – the law of immanent necessity' (Bakhtin 1995, p. 29). To further theorize acts of citizenship, I turn now to Derrida and examine how he defines 'the law of immanent necessity' as grounded on a violence that creates injustice and yet remains legal.

Acts of citizenship take place because the legal sense of citizenship itself is problematic. It is derived from the mystical foundation of a regime where citizenship can be deprived from justice. To develop this argument, Derrida first distinguishes 'mystical violence' from 'divine violence'. The former makes law and the latter challenges law. Derrida argues that state authority or political sovereignty names itself, and it possesses absolute privilege and infinite prerogative. That is, the origin and the maintenance of authority in and through the making of law 'cannot by definition rest on anything but themselves, they are themselves a violence without ground' (Derrida 2002, p. 242). Derrida emphasizes that it is *always* in and for its own interests that state sovereignty relies on and monopolizes violence. 'This monopoly does not strive to protect any given just and legal ends but law [that protects state authority] itself' (Derrida 2002, p. 267). This is the case for *all* sovereign states, regardless of scale, history or democratic/authoritarian type.

The *raison d'être* of the military and the police is to found, support and maintain the social order and thus the interests of authority. Even though their existence and presence are always in the name of the well-being of all citizens, they in fact are the force of law. Whenever they are present, they are always effective. The tanks approaching Tiananmen Square indicate the presence of law-preserving violence enforced by the PLA. When martial law has to be enforced for the sake of national security it can quickly become brutally violent, especially when authority is threatened by what Derrida calls 'divine violence'. Simply put, the military operation by the PLA was legal, but was not just.

As law is enforced to exclude other forms of violence perceived as a threat to the order of the regime, Derrida argues that it is an attempt 'to exclude the other witness, to destroy the witness of the other order, of a divine violence whose justice is irreducible to law, of a violence hetero-geneous to the order both of law and right' (Derrida 2002, pp. 295–6). This best explains the split between justice and law. On the one hand, mystical violence presents itself as the violence of injustice when citizens bring rupture to authority. On the other hand, divine violence is enforced as an injunction to what is given as law. It questions whether law is just. It also demands what must be addressed immediately beyond law. Finally, it refuses the mystical violence of authority. As Derrida argues, 'one must reject all mystical violence, the violence that founds law, which one may call governing violence. One must also reject the violence that preserves law, the governed violence in the service of the governing' (Derrida 2002, p. 292).

Rejection as such is a decision to act beyond applied rules, program-mable routines or calculable results. Acts of defiance as injunction to injustice or as demands for opening up to possibilities other than law must go through 'the test and ordeal of the undecidable' (Derrida 2002, p. 253). To act is a decision to risk without a foreseeable, guaranteed result. This echoes Butler's remark that 'we must recognize that ethics requires us to risk ourselves precisely at moments of unknowingness, when what forms us diverges from what lies before us' (Butler 2005, p. 136). The undecid-able and unknowingness create moments of suspension like the one faced by the Tank Man. When the Tank Man violated martial law by stopping the approaching tanks, it could not be done with decidable knowledge or knowledge of whether the tanks would stop or whether it would be a triumph of justice at those particular moments. Nevertheless, if one is compelled to act, or if one takes a chance beyond the predictable, it has to be for something worthy of its name. Overall, it is not habitual for citizens to challenge the mystical violence of law by overcoming fear or risking life. The Tank Man stunned the global audience precisely because he acted as if his life was no longer more important than his demands for what must be done. As Derrida argues, '[i]f there are responsibilities to be taken and decisions to be made, responsibilities and decisions worthy of these names, they belong to the time of a risk and of an act of faith' (Derrida 2003, p. 118).

In his earlier work, Derrida singles out justice as something worthy to act for, to take a chance on, and therefore to risk for. Citizens must act for justice in order to deconstruct and exceed law, to push boundaries of injustice set by sovereignty, to challenge the delineation of political membership, and to open up to alterity. Nevertheless, we cannot deter-mine the exact content or categorical imperative for justice since justice does not entail specific promises, nor a universal model applicable to all situations. Rather, it is an occasion when one addresses and works out the possibility of differences or otherness. If, keeping this understanding of justice in mind, we seek to address the existing problems of citizenship, we need to address other possibilities beyond the given limits of legality. Otherwise, we lose the capacity to interrogate the violence of injustice inherited in the nature of citizenship that sustains state authority. When we do not take the risk to act beyond the sovereign boundaries of injustice, we also lose opportunities to invigorate citizenship by broadening its legal scope of inclusion. Finally, we lose openness towards the future if we do not consider the coming of other possibilities of citizenship.

For Derrida, what is worthy of the name for which we act and risk is also democracy. Throughout his work, there is a conjunction between justice and democracy, since there is a need to inscribe democracy into the distinction between law and justice. In his own words, 'democracy would be a degeneration of law, of the violence, the authority, and the power of law. There is not yet any democracy worthy of this name. Democracy *remains* to come: to engender or to regenerate' (Derrida 2002, p. 281). While justice is not tantamount to law, democracy is 'neither the name of the regime nor the name of a constitution' (Derrida 2005, p. 26). In addition, if justice exceeds law, a democracy worthy of its name must go beyond current democratic regimes and constitutions. Therefore, 'the perfect democracy, a full and living democracy does not exist' (Derrida 2005, p. 73). Democracies are always to come in the sense that we cannot be satisfied with what claims to be just or democratic. 'To come' especially indicates infinite imperfectability or even impossibility. Justice and democracy have to be questioned, deconstructed and criticized in an open-ended process with a promise that there is potential for less mystical violence.

As mentioned above, risking something worthy of its name has to entail faith. Derrida emphasizes that '[t]his act of faith belongs – it *must* belong – to what is incalculable in assurance of certainty – in truth, with knowledge – is ordained by the very structure of confidence or of credence as faith' (Derrida 1997, p. 16). Faith here does not mean passive anticipation or an excuse for deferral. Nor does it subject justice or democracy to a utopia. Rather, a promise, a duty or a responsibility is inscribed in the act of faith. This is important because 'to come' implies that justice or democracy is 'not something that is certain to happen tomorrow, not the democracy (national or international, state or trans-state) of the future, but a democracy that must have the structure of a promise – and the memory of that which carries the future, the to-come, here and now' (Derrida 2002, p. 78). This also indicates that there is a gap between actual conditions and potentialities with regards to justice and democracy. This gap can only be bridged by acts of faith in three senses: first, there is an urgency and precipitation to act so as to address actual problems of law and legality immediately. Second, to act is to have faith in the values and potentiality of justice and democracy. Third, to stress the urgency and the problems of the here and now is to 'inscribe a performative and attempt to win conviction by suggesting support or adherence, an "and yet it is necessary to believe it", "I believe in it, I promise, I am in on the promise and in messianic waiting, I am taking action or am at least enduring, now you do the same...'" (Derrida 2005, p. 91).

We do not wait for justice and democracy to come, nor do we wait for them to be given or imposed by someone else. Otherwise, it would not be 'the ought' for everyone to act. Nor would it be a duty or a responsibility for everyone to shoulder. We must act, risk and venture into the terrain of the unknown without an alibi, detour or proceedings. Otherwise, justice and democracy remain something empty, and their potentialities remain to be limited. To juxtapose with Bakhtin, only through the correlation with acts does 'the eternity of meanings [like justice and democracy-to-come] become something actually valued – something actually valid or operative' (Bakhtin 1995, p. 29). That is, the promise of justice and democracy remain to be universal in an empty sense until they are realized by actual acts in addressing concrete, specific problems of citizenship.

Acts of citizenship thus ought to be acts of faith in justice and democracy-to-come. This is also the only way to reveal the aporia of state authority and citizenship. For Derrida (1997), it is a legal fiction in political discourses to resort to birth or nature in relation to nations, since state sovereignty is always established and maintained by mystical violence. For instance, the force of the People's Liberation Army only liberated the people in name. It killed them in reality. It is equally questionable to associate citizenship with the idea of universal brotherhood, since the mystical violence of state sovereignty already sets the boundaries of political membership in the processes of inclusion and exclusion. For instance, the Chinese government classified those against its authority as rogue citizens. But the Tank Man acted with the faith that the PLA could bridge the gap between its name and deeds. He also acted with the faith that 'the sovereign's identity, that is, the identity of "the people" – is not fixed, and in principle (at least) cannot be determined other than by the interpretations and continuous re-definitions of the people themselves' (Fritsch 2002, p. 580). The process of contesting the sovereign's identity is characterized by instability, internal differentiation and indefinite becoming. In short, it is the process of democracy through which we discuss and contest who belongs and whose goods count in the political community. Therefore, democracy is always to-come because it has to be constantly open to criticism and transformation.

When a regime refuses to be democratic, it violently fixes the political sense of belonging, unjustly demarcates obedient from rogue citizens, and stubbornly prioritizes the maintenance of *status quo* over transformation. In other words, it refuses the coming of democracy, and rejects the possibility of re-examining citizenship. Acts of citizenship like the Tank

Man's, therefore, become indispensable when the legal sense of citizenship itself relies on mystical violence to stagnate itself. Acts of citizenship involve more than merely following the particular rules of a legal order: they must defy the legal sense of citizenship, which is framed in favour of the interests of the regime. Acts of citizenship therefore are also acts of transgression that create and invigorate democracy beyond law and authority.

(Un)Making Political Identity

Derrida does not shy away from the normative language of must, obligation and responsibility when it concerns acts against law and authority. That is, acts of citizenship are not only juridical-political battles, but also ethical struggles. Nevertheless, is it sufficient to act in the name of justice and democracy-to-come while addressing the demands of others or other possibilities? Can acts of citizenship address the political subject at the same time? What significance does it give to the Tank Man himself? When the Tank Man decided to act and to cast his life away, what was the must of the here and now for himself? To answer this set of questions, I turn to the ethical dimension of acts of citizenship. I argue that political subjects are unmade and made at the same time through challenging the given political order in order to invent new law and sovereignty. In addition, they involve double-sided answerability that orients towards the realization of universal values worthy to fight for in name, and towards the particular confirmation of irreplaceable uniqueness in political identity.

For Derrida, to decide to act is to decide to invent. It cannot be a repetition or extension of identity. Judith Butler makes a similar point in arguing that '[o]ne is dependent on this "outside" to lay claim to what is one's own. The self must, in this way, be disposed in sociality in order to take possession of itself' (Butler 2004, p. 7). This is another way of saying that acting outside of the habitual implies the demand of justice or democracy-to-come because what is challenged is law and authority. At the same time, what is interrupted is the fixed sense of the political subject. To follow this logic, there is no determined subject that precedes acts. However, this does not suggest that acts of citizenship can bring a total break from the past or a complete overthrow of sovereignty. New law and sovereignty can only be worked out or negotiated on the basis of the given order. It is rather unrealistic or romantic to argue for a completely different political order, as none can escape mystical violence that founds and maintains sovereignty. In addition, the sovereignty of the political being cannot be totally made anew through acts. We cannot naïvely expect that acts can produce a completely different quality and disposition of citizenship. In fact, acts occur in the midst of working out the aporia between conformation to the pre-existing condition and the invention of political subjectivity.

Political subjects are unmade and made at the same time through the aporia. This argument resonates well with Judith Butler's work on gender where she develops the argument that the doubled truth of norms constrains or transforms subjects through gender work. 'If I am someone who cannot be without *doing*, then the conditions of my doing are, in part, the conditions of my existence. If my doing is dependent on what is done to me or, rather, the ways in which I am done by norms, then the possibility of my persistence as an "I" depends upon my being able to do something with what is done with me.' We need norms, rules, law, legality and so on to live and to thrive. However, we can also be constrained by them if they do violence to us or if they violate justice. Like Derrida, Butler makes an ethical demand that we must act and oppose such violence for the sake of justice, although it cannot be a total denial of the conditions in which we are situated. 'My agency does not consist in denying this condition of my constitution. If I have any agency, it is opened up by the fact that I am constituted by a social world I never chose. That my agency is ridden with paradox does not mean it is impossible. It means only that paradox is the condition of its possibility' (Butler 2004, p. 3).

Butler's remarks on acts and norms are equally insightful when it comes to comprehending acts of citizenship. Political subjects can only be constructed in acts that (re)affirm, claim, deny, transform and create new standards of political normality. In other words, acts are only partially conditioned by what is present in the given order and what lies outside of the making of political identity. 'This does not mean that I can remake the world so that I become its maker. That fantasy of godlike power only refuses the ways we are constituted, invariably and from the start, by what is before us and outside of us' (Butler 2004, p. 3). Thus, it would be naïve to assume that acts of citizenship can bring total rupture from either the given political order or subjectivity. While such assumptions endow acts with a power of constructing a brand-new sense of citizenship, they risk leading analysis away from the specific conditions of the ways through which political subjects are made. Acts of citizenship therefore have to be understood in the moments when political beings find themselves at once constituted by and dependent on the foregone citizenship. Nonetheless, they strive to maintain a critical yet transformative relation to the way citizenship is defined by law and authority.

To use the Tank Man as an example, it would be hard to imagine that he acted outside of the given socio-political framework or values at the time.[2] As patriotism is central to the way political subjects of the Chinese regime acted, it cannot be disposed of easily. Students were upset by the Chinese government and demanded the correct naming of their protest; rejecting the accusation of an 'unpatriotic turmoil' against the 'People', they claimed the status of a patriotic democratic student movement. It is true that the Tank Man's acts were out of concern for the illegitimacy of the crackdown, but they were also out of his love for his country. These emotions of aporia allowed the Tank Man to work out the difference between support of the regime's authority as the habitual pattern of patriotism and the revolt against martial law as the invigoration of patriotism.

If it is impossible to uproot acts of citizenship from the pre-existing political order and normality, acts claiming independence of the other citizens are also questionable. For Derrida, anything that claims to be pure and free from the influence or 'contamination' of the other is a fiction. He takes one more step to prioritize the concern for the other over the autonomy of the self in the ethical relation of acts. Since it is impossible to keep the other away from self-identity, it is a must to act in order to address the other or even to address 'myself *as* the other' (Derrida 2002, p. 245). Simply put, the subject is authorized by consideration of the other, and is consequently going through a process of becoming by opening up to the other. Acts of citizenship therefore must consider the demands of aliens, the non-citizens, rebels or revolutionaries. Even when one tries to apply a universal prescription, implement programmable rules, or confirm the core values of justice, the uniqueness or the singularity of the other must be reconciled. In Derrida's own words, the act of justice 'must always concern singularity, individuals, groups, irreplaceable existences, the other or myself *as* other, in a unique situation, with rule, norm, value, or the imperative of justice that necessarily have a general form' (Derrida 2002, p. 245). This also provides the opportunity to work out the aporia of the universal and the particular. Acts thus define self-identity in the consideration of how the uniqueness of the other can or cannot be well treated by universal imperatives like justice or democracy-to-come.

However, questions remain: can acts also concern addressing the particularity of the political subject? Can acts of citizenship address the unique situation and determination of a political being? The Tank Man's acts help to deepen rejoinders to these questions. The Tank Man acted as if there was no expectation that he would continue the process of self-transformation since he was ready to sacrifice himself. Furthermore, he acted as if it was the final moment of his life. Some might argue that the sense of martyrdom embodied in the Tank Man's acts was not special and it already had a universal appeal during the student protest. For instance, students went through hunger strikes or formed human roadblocks to stop the approaching PLA prior to the night of the crackdown. Indeed, all these acts, whether planned or improvised, were oriented towards another possibility for China in the universal call for justice and democracy-to-come. However, if we overemphasize the sense of martyrdom as something common among acts of citizenship during the Tiananmen protest, we might gloss over the uniqueness of each act. Furthermore, if we simply focus on how acts of citizenship orient towards the universal call, we might neglect how they also gravitate towards the particular sense of political subjectivity meaningful enough for self-sacrifice. This is the reason why Bakhtin's formulation of two-sided answerability can be interpreted to mean that no political representative or representation can satisfy the actual experience of every citizen, although the universal side gives the impression of covering every political member's demands. Political representation frequently de-roots citizens' personal participation in the once-occurrent context through political acts. Consequently, when citizens are detached from the once-occurrent political context, they also lose the chance to mark out their unique axiological participation.

As discussed previously, an act worth putting faith into can only be confirmed by taking up an axiological position. Otherwise the universal imperative remains abstract, theoretical or ideological, without any empirical consideration or actual significance. In addition, universality in the theoretical realm can hijack acts and transform them into ritual acts, as they are detached from faith and sincerity. The act is also stripped from the urgent injunction of the ought, or rigorous anticipation. In other words, ritual acts can only be performed by someone with an alibi. In Bakhtin's words, 'an alibi in being', a pretender or an impostor cannot be answerable to the universal ought. At the same time, a pretender lacks 'an acknowledgement of [one's] obligative (ought-to-be) uniqueness', and so performs only ritual acts (Bakhtin 1995, p. 42). If this is the case, even addressing the demands of the other in the universal name of justice or democracy-to-come is an alibi. That is, to act as a response to the other can be an excuse to escape from the recognition of one's unique place at a particular moment.

This emphasis on being answerable to both universal and particular demands is what Bakhtin calls the double-sided answerability in acts. 'An act must acquire a single unitary plane to be able to reflect itself in both directions: in its sense or meaning and in its being, it must acquire the unity of two-sided answerability – both for its content (special answerability) and for its Being (moral answerability)' (Bakhtin 1995, pp. 2–3). In addition, to be answerable to the universal appeal in which people put faith means to challenge the habitual violence against justice or disrespect for life and this has to be generated from one's special position. This special position is once-occurrent and never repeatable. Nobody else can perform the same act. Even when one is not situated in the same time and space, it does not guarantee the same act. Thus, Bakhtin remarks that 'the concrete and once-occurrent ought of the answerably performed act, is not something I come to know of and to cognize but is something I acknowledge and affirm in a unique or once-occurrent manner' (Bakhtin 1995, p. 40). It is as if one is thrown into a unique situation, or as if one enters into a given structure of time and space. However, once the decision is made to act with the acknowledgement of one's uniqueness, one escapes the whirlpool of alibi and pretension.

To bring out special answerability in acts 'involves the performance of an existential dialogue' through which one authorizes oneself (Bakhtin 1995, p. 80n9). One is no longer simply authorized by the other, as Derrida suggests. One stops being an unfinished first draft or an unsigned document that is obliged to act in an answerable way. For Bakhtin, to decide to act, thus, is an engagement to unmake and make self-identity through which one 'transforms an empty possibility into an actual answerable act or deed' (Bakhtin 1995, p. 42). To juxtapose this with Derrida, the demands of the here and now arise from a once-occurrent event that requires the engagement of acts as the immediate injunction to the given order and to the fixed identity. As a result, this is not simply about transforming the empty possibility of the universal imperative in the theoretical world. It is also about producing weight and 'compellentness' in acts that help one to anchor orientation in life. 'To live from within oneself does not mean to live for oneself, but means to be an answerable participant from within oneself, to affirm one's compellent, actual non-alibi in Being' (Bakhtin 1995, p. 49). Special answerability thus does not suggest cutting off the other in the ethical relation of acts. It rather sheds light on the chances created by acts that stop one from drifting through life, to be decided and possessed by others, or to have the other as an excuse for acts. For Bakhtin, the ought is a category of the individual act, or even a category of individuality, for which nothing else can substitute.

Bakhtin's double-sided answerability helps us to get closer to the Tank Man's act of sacrifice. It was the Tank Man's dialogic engagement with his own unique existence that paradoxically sought life, not death. This paradox exists because the demand to be faithful to his unique, once-occurrent situation in life can only be made in the guise of martyrdom. It was a guise not because he pretended to be a hero, but because only through the determination of martyrdom could the Tank Man bring himself to life. Thus, his act revived himself from the sense of being 'determined, predetermined, bygone or finished, essentially not living' (Bakhtin 1995, p. 9). Simply put, to challenge the PLA and to choose to sacrifice, the Tank Man already gave an account of himself.

The Tank Man could not be indifferent to the bloodshed that occurred on 4 June. As one of the participants in the 1989 protest, Chiu, puts it: The Tank Man's martyrdom 'was a "rite of passage" through which one secured one's "personhood" by joining the coming-into-being of a "Greater Self" (*da wo* in Chinese)' (Chiu 1991, p. 343). To achieve one's special sense of identity in the unity of the collective aspiration was something universal during the 1989 Tiananmen protest. Fearless martyrdom also enacted a sense of historical responsibility while linking itself to the previous generations of Chinese students who strove for democracy. This included the May Fourth movement in 1919, and the first and second Tiananmen movements in 1976 and 1986 respectively. It thus entailed a historical sense of responsibility towards the Chinese nation rooted in a genealogical demand reaching back to the early twentieth century.

We are certainly curious about the Tank Man's fixed identity: his name, occupation, background and aftermath. However, it becomes clear that he had already authorized himself and told us who he was/is through acts of defiance against the approaching tanks. Finally, it is unquestionable that by addressing the immediate demands of the here and now, that is, the desired retreat of military forces against citizens' justice and democracy-to-come, the Tank Man gave signature to a life in which obligation and responsibility in both universal and particular senses became concrete.

Conclusion

Illuminated by the Tank Man's strong emotional-volitional act, this chapter has laid out the significance of acts of citizenship across a series of steps. Citizenship studies have a tendency to subject citizenship to a theoretical world where concrete actual experiences are emptied out, where acts are rendered into ritual acts whose rational language can stifle entitlement or rights, and where citizens become pretenders who act out the demands of the regime. I have argued instead for the importance of emotional-volitional acts in invigorating citizenship studies. I have demonstrated that acts of citizenship take place at moments of political rupture that challenge the mystical foundation of authority and question the legitimacy of violence in establishing and maintaining law and regime. More importantly, they address the immediate demands of the here and now in the name of justice and democracy-to-come. Acts of citizenship occur especially when the legal sense of citizenship becomes problematic and requires citizens to issue an injunction to inherent injustice. This is a universal ought enforced by citizens in acts of faith. That is, it requires every citizen to promise to participate, to act and to risk for something worthy of its name, albeit justice and democracy-to-come. 'To-come' implies the impossibility and imperfection in justice and democracy. Nevertheless, it is the must or the ought to act them, because that is the only way in which we can open up to the demands of the other political possibility where the mythical violence of state authority is questioned.

Acts of citizenship cannot be satisfied with the universal orientation towards justice and democracy-to-come. In considering the Tank Man's acts of martyrdom, it has helped to stress the processes of unmaking and making political subjects through acts of citizenship. Through rethinking Butler's work on the double truth of norms and identities, I have argued that acts of citizenship take place between the given and created structures of political order and subjectivity. On the one hand, acts of citizenship cannot simply be derived from the outside. If this were the case, acts could be imposed that might lack the answerable engagement through which political subjects make sense of themselves in comprehensive political languages and values. On the other hand, acts of citizenship cannot simply occur without transforming the given and the known. Otherwise, they also would lack answerable engagement because they could be performed as the habitual or the ritual. Thus, acts of citizenship are unique precisely because they have to work out the paradox of the given and creative senses of political structure and subjectivity. Consequently, the uniqueness of acts of citizenship also lies in their answerability towards both universal demands of the juridical-political situation and the particular demands of political subjects. I have thus argued both away from and with Derrida, who prioritizes the demands of the other over those of the self, and I have relied on Bakhtin's double-sided answerability. Acts of citizenship have to be answerable to the ethical demands of citizens in order to assure the sense of self-identities.

To combine juridical, political and ethical dimensions in acts of citizenship, we can reach the following concluding remark: when acts of defiance erupt, there is a chance for citizenship to be detached from the service of regime authority. With emotional-volitional engagement, acts of citizenship can mark out the values, quality and heaviness of citizenship. Addressing the demands of the other and of the here and now in justice and democracy-to-come, acts of citizenship entail the universal ought. Finally, when acts of citizenship simultaneously address the demands of authorizing the sense of the subject in the aporia of the given order and invention, they are answerable to the particular ought of the political being in facing the unique, irreplaceable event.

Acknowledgement

I would like to thank Greg Nielsen for his insightful comments on a previous draft.

Notes

1 Acts in the Tiananmen protest have to be distinguished from those of the Cultural Revolution, although both were marked by acts of strong emotional velocity and volitional intensity. They were different because the former was a bottom-up movement for justice and democracy, while the latter was initiated from the top. In addition, the former did not involve mutual class hatred, an emotion that was central to the latter.

2 Another good example to illustrate the demands to work out the aporia between the given and the created subjectivity is the case of hunger strikers during the 1989 protest. The hunger strikers radicalized the student protest because of the explicit violence against the self. Theirs were extreme acts in a society that inscribes familial, paternal values in body politics. As bodies are given by parents, it is important to keep them intact. Moreover, since Chinese history has been ridden by famine, the traditional culture values food as scarce and sacred to the vitality of life. Fasting thus became an act that potently indicated the students' self-sacrifice for the nation. However, their bodily struggles were also ridden by paradoxes. On the one hand, hunger strikers demanded respect, equal dialogue and proper naming. On the other hand, the hunger strikers were self-positioned as children struggling against elders – fathers, uncles and aunts. For instance, Chai Ling, a student leader, initiated the hunger strike on the night of 12 May with the following words: '[W]e, the children, are ready to die. We, the children, are ready to use our lives to pursue the truth. We, the children, are willing to sacrifice ourselves' (Shen 1990, p. 237, quoted in Calhoun 1997). Altlization in China where students radicalized their acts without alienating the ordinary Chinese people from recognizing them. Through working out this aporia between children and citizens, students were able to take advantage of the ideals of innocence and purity we associate with the image of the children. It sharpened the contrast with corrupted 'uncles and aunties' by amplifying the urgent demands of saving the 'mother'(land).

References

Bakhtin, M. (1995) *Toward a Philosophy of the Act*, University of Texas Press, Austin, TX.

Borradori, G. (2003) *Philosophy in a Time of Terror: Dialogues with Jürgen Habermas and Jacques Derrida*, University of Chicago Press, Chicago, IL.

Butler, J. (2004) *Undoing Gender*, Routledge, New York.

—— (2005) *Giving an Account of Oneself*, Fordham University Press, New York.

Calhoun, C. (1997) *Neither Gods nor Emperors: Students and the Struggle for Democracy in China*, California University Press, Berkeley, CA.

Cheng, C.-Y. (1990) *Behind the Tiananmen Massacre: Social, Political, and Economic Ferment in China*, Westview, Boulder, CO.

Chiu, Y.-L. (1991) 'The Specificity of the Political on Tiananmen Square, or a Poetics of the Popular Resistance in Beijing', *Dialectical Anthropology*, 16, 333–47.

Derrida, J. (1997) *Politics of Friendship* (trans. G. Collins), Verso, London.

—— (2002) 'Force of Law – The "Mystical Foundation of Authority"' in J. Anidjar (ed.), *Acts of Religion*, Routledge, New York.

—— (2005) *Rogues*, Stanford University Press, Stanford, CA.

Fewsmith, J. (2001) *China since Tiananmen: The Politics of Transition*, Cambridge University Press, New York, Cambridge.

Fritsch, M. (2002) 'Derrida's Democracy to Come', *Constellations*, 9 (4).

Lin, B.-J. (1992) *The Aftermath of the 1989 Tiananmen Crisis in Mainland China*, Westview, Boulder, CO.

Chapter 11

❖

Answerability with Cosmopolitan Intent: An Ethics-Based Politics for Acts of Urban Citizenship

GREG M. NIELSEN

In this chapter I look to explain how acts of citizenship with cosmopolitan intent are situated within the paradox of a necessary indifference towards otherness in urban culture. Acts of citizenship are understood as events that contain several overlapping and interdependent components: they claim rights and impose obligations in emotionally charged tones; pose their claims in enduring and convincing arguments; and look to shift established practices, status and order. My concern is not with either social movements or the immediate juridical, economic or transnational languages used in any of their specific components, but rather with sketching an ethics-based politics that can account for acts of citizenship. At the outset I recall the observation, first remarked by Georg Simmel in his 1903 article on 'The Metropolis and Mental Life', that a measure of the 'blasé attitude' is an important background dimension of urban life (Simmel 1971). I argue accordingly that a certain measure of indifference and non-participation is a key precondition for citizenship enactment with cosmopolitan intent; this in turn has consequences for the parallel distinction between politics as the administration of power and the political as a form of antagonism between various states of co-being.

Theorizing answerability with cosmopolitan intent and an ethics-based politics for acts of citizenship requires reference to a specific combination of theorists not usually discussed together. Through immanent critical readings and concrete illustrative examples I both distinguish and draw together Mikhail Bakhtin's philosophy of dialogue and critique of the limits of pluralism; Georg Simmel's urban sociology and neo-Kantian ethics; and Jacques Derrida's deconstructions of politics, law and justice. Acts of citizenship are interpreted from these approaches in four separate sections – Bakhtin: The Bus Uncle and the Limits of Dialogic Pluralism; Simmel on Sources of Cosmopolitan Co-being; Derrida: Political Citizens and Citizen Politics after 9-11; and Derrida and Simmel: Catching Acts Between Law and Justice. Before reaching these sections I briefly contrast the thinkers' similarities and differences; define acts of citizenship in more detail; and clarify the chapter's core argument that the paradox of a necessary indifference towards others is a basic precondition for answerability with cosmopolitan intent.

Similarities and Differences

It is striking how each of these thinkers takes such different approaches to theorizing acts and their relation to otherness. For Derrida, following Levinas, the other is the one who authors me and so I owe a debt of responsibility through acts across my life. In different ways for Simmel and Bakhtin the other is a limited co-participant in my life history and the focus is on the consummation between the more active 'I' in the act and the other in the creation and aesthetics of co-being. In short, each thinker contributes to an ethics of alterity in ways that allow me to draw their contributions together into a mutually reinforcing approach. While Derrida's conceptual genealogies recall that absolute definitions encounter contradictory and doubled meanings, Simmel, and especially Bakhtin, help clarify how acts have a two-sided answerability to both general ideals and unique performances. Drawing on concepts of otherness from all three thinkers, I look to explain how acts of citizenship should be interpreted beyond substantive practices or formal legal status, while maintaining reference to how they might move both these poles.

Simmel (1968) argues that an act cannot be preceded by a universal law that is void of subjective content. For him, only those acts that conform to unique gestures are universal, whereas universal laws can never be individual. For Simmel there is no finite number of experiences a subject can take towards representations or what he calls objective culture. The question arises then of how experiences might be understood inside acts of citizenship. Both Bakhtin and Derrida, in different ways and to different degrees, explore the role of language in centering a finite number of forces that combine to shape emotional-volitional orientations in objective culture. Inspired and influenced in part by Simmel, Bakhtin develops the concepts of answerability and dialogism, or the pluralist mixture of emotional-volitional tones between utterances and points of view, as a means of capturing the subjective exchange that occurs in acts. Like Simmel and Bakhtin, Derrida develops Kant's philosophy of representation without being Kantian, but also reverses the traditional Western relation that privileges speech over writing in acts. Bakhtin argues that the answerability of the act suggests a two-sided process in which a speaker anticipates a general or objective response as well as a unique subjective rejoinder. An act is answerable in the sense that its actor is responsible for it, but the answerability of the act also lies beyond conventional responsibility. It lies in its capacity to evoke a response. Like answerability, Derrida's concepts of the 'traversal' and of the 'trace' also assume a cross-over or travelling between the objectively real and the possible subjective rejoinder. In a similar way Bakhtin's dialogism kicks in 'when equally weighted, simple or complex utterances' address the same theme or set of themes so that they cannot help but gravitate towards one another subjectively 'whether they confirm, mutually supplement, or (conversely) contradict one another' (1984, p. 189). As in all dualisms, one side cannot help but refer to the other for its own definition. Bakhtin's concept of dialogism and Derrida's concept of writing help recall how this opposition needs to give way to a multiplicity of identifications that find unity out of difference.

Defining Acts of Citizenship

Emotionally charged acts of citizenship often challenge the objective moral order and the rule of law and may also resort to non-legitimate means of violence to achieve their goal. However, acts beyond civil disobedience are already no longer acts of citizenship in the ethics-based politics that is my topic. Revolutionary, terrorist, or state-sponsored terrorist violence are pre-politically instituted when the rule of law and the politics of persuasion and shame fail. They are thus enacted under one authority, or simply through the spectacle of violence, whether to put forward a subaltern response or to maintain imperial order. I understand acts of citizenship in the broadest non-violent sense to include the multiple ways in which actors come out of the non-participatory blasé urban attitude to engage in disputes over a wide variety of common goods. These disputes have to do with how common goods and various orientations towards them should be shared, cared for, encouraged, protected, or transformed, disciplined, outlawed, abandoned – all in the language of rights and obligations.

As events acts of citizenship are unique moments where local and/or transnational actors 'claim the right to claim rights' or impose obligations against injustices and already instituted practices. Such acts also need to improvise creative but also enduring and convincing arguments for justice against unjust laws as well as their intended or unintended exclusionary consequences. Acts of citizenship have the capacity to subvert already instituted forms of citizenship and challenge legal norms and moral codes. Acts of citizenship should be understood in themselves as unique and distinct from forms of rational, emotional, traditional or habitual action (Weber 1978) because they are also actively answerable events. Acts that step into the participatory out of the non-participatory are answerable to both general ideals and unique performances. Other forms of social actions are not bound by the same two-sided answerability that is both particular and universal. Acts of citizenship are thus politically participatory in so far as they help organize public presentations of often-contradictory statements from actors who claim rights or impose social responsibilities. But, at another level, such statements are potentially transcultural as they are named in and across the languages of domestic and international flows. Acts of citizenship need each of these overlapping and interconnecting components to sustain themselves; otherwise they dissolve, collapse, fragment or otherwise break down into uncivil acts.

Necessary Indifference and Answerability with Cosmopolitan Intent

A key paradox for acts of citizenship is that the more blasé the attitude becomes in the city towards difference, the less likely the need to act. And yet indifference is clearly needed to accommodate a variety of levels of answerability with cosmopolitan intent. A point to keep in mind is that indifference towards strangeness is already so much a part of cosmopolitanism in the city that it is easy to miss the important place it should have in theorizing citizenship and by extension acts of citizenship. I am aware of, and in full agreement with those who put emphasis on improving citizenship participation or on easing constraints that would impede individual or group actors from exercising rights. Increasing participation is a means of resolving the fragmentation in social solidarity and the sense of inequality and exclusion that are the marks of injustice in modern societies. I begin, however, from this other vantage point of the non-participatory politics of citizenship and its already established moral and legal order in order to define acts of citizenship as events of the participatory political citizen.

Bakhtin: The Bus Uncle and the Limits of Dialogic Pluralism

The transition from the non-participative into the participatory act is explained in this section with reference to Bakhtin's concept of dialogism and his argument about the limits of pluralism. His concepts are explicated through analysis of an example of a failed act of citizenship in everyday urban culture as presented through an intense verbal conflict between two individuals recorded live on a Hong Kong bus and broadcast with English language subtitles on the Internet to a massive global audience. The example provides a demonstration of how partial acts of citizenship can emerge and break with assumed civic norms and habits. An alternative approach to citizenship – one that shifts its focus to acts – reminds us that we live together not only across difference but also with necessary indifference. The point is made that acts of citizenship are not legitimated by the participatory stand alone but that they also need to defend creative and enduring arguments through two-sided answerability.

Bakhtin's approach to the act and to dialogue permit us to ask not only how we enact citizenship when drawn out of mutual indifference but also to think about how unique individuals might do this across divisions within civil society. 'My entire life as a whole, he writes, can be considered as a single complex act or deed that I perform: I act, i.e. perform acts, with my whole life, and every particular act and lived-experience is a constituent moment of my life – of the continuous performing of acts' (Bakhtin 1993, p. 3). He goes on to say that in dialogue 'what underlies the unity of an answerable act is not a principle as a starting point, but the fact of the actual acknowledgement of one's own participation' (1993, p. 40). Participation in dialogue is not limited to a conventional exchange of utterances as in a conversation between two interlocutors that can be decoded according to linguistic conventions. The act of dialogue is understood as a much broader framing that takes place in the imagination of speakers and their image, however distant or intimate, of the potential listener. It has an attitude of answerability that is opposite to the blasé because it takes up the performative stand. It crosses from the non-participatory by learning some aspect of the emotional and volitional inner life of the listener. 'Only a dialogic and participatory orientation takes another person's discourse seriously and is capable of approaching it both as a semantic position and as another point of view' (Bakhtin 1984, p. 64). Once we've been brought out of the blasé into dialogue, a cross-pollination or 'transgredience' between points of view happens. Through two-sided answerability participants draw on broader cultural resources and background lifeworld convictions for ways to respond to the questions of how to act when faced with someone who can answer back, and possibly how to answer someone who might not share the same habitus, moral doctrine or ideology.

But what happens when the dialogue is distorted or breaks down and when there is no retreat to the blasé? What are the limits of dialogic pluralism? The popular Cantonese video 'The Bus Uncle' (titled and subtitled by an internet forum) helps illustrate the danger of a failed act of citizenship as it circulates in an everyday event of transition between the non-participatory and the participatory. The video taken by a passenger using a cell phone captures a live and intense verbal conflict between a middle-aged man ('The Bus Uncle') and a twenty-something younger male on a Hong Kong city bus travelling down a busy boulevard late on an April evening in 2006. Although the two citizens come from the same culture they also belong to different generations and are attached to different social strata. The local culture becomes an artefact of global culture in that the film was uploaded to *Google Video* and *You Tube* and was one of the most frequently viewed Internet videos around the world in April and May of 2006. Although Internet videos appear monologic in terms of their relation to audiences, the fact that they anticipate a response from them suggests a dialogic relationship in the broadest sense. The video received global press coverage and became something of a cult hit among Hong Kong youth, entering their vernacular speech and appearing in a variety of popular cultural products including spin-off music videos, chat forums and other media. Naming the phenomenon and measuring its meaning, as in the case of 9/11 discussed below, has the appearance of an outward ripple effect that expands in a series of concentric circles from the most indigenous participatory experience to the broadest objective representation at a global level.

The video begins with a middle-aged man complaining angrily that the younger man sitting directly behind him should not have touched him on the shoulder and interrupted his telephone conversation to ask him to speak more softly. He points out early in the exchange that the young man was talking on the phone earlier and he did not impose any requests to soften his tone. The middle-aged man makes a claim about civility in the form of a right: 'I have the right to use my cell phone without being interrupted because you are also talking on your cell phone.' This is a very crude example of a citizen claiming the right to have rights and trying to impose an obligation on his fellow citizen. On the other hand, it becomes apparent very quickly that the claims are not situated in any enduring argument and that they are not made in a convincing manner, so the act of citizenship quickly breaks down into a one-sided act of incivility. Leaving aside reception for those on the bus who might be unfamiliar with the given culture and language, or for those who are most vulnerable to this form of harassment, the lower threshold of 'bus' sociability presented in the initial stages of the Bus Uncles's utterance would be accepted without much reflection in most places in the world.

Such habitual courtesies are among innumerable banalities that are easily taken in stride as we encounter one another in urban public space. At the upper threshold we are intuitively and intensely aware of how to turn our gaze away or towards one another to best accommodate the boundaries of culture, politics and political citizenship in street life. No citizen who carries the blasé attitude gives much of a second thought about travelling on a bus filled with strangers and we mostly ignore each other even when we bump up against one another. This is a clear example of the precondition of indifference needed for cosmopolitan intent in the city. For Simmel, the blasé attitude adopted as a reaction to the mixture of everyday and every-night rhythm allows citizens to traverse spaces normally, safely, creatively and ethically, even as it multiplies individual contingency and corporal exchanges.

But the Bus Uncle forces his interlocutor out of the blasé by gradually escalating his tones of anger across the six minutes of the exchange. The young man seems to withhold his rejoinder, though he does break silence by referring to his interlocutor on at least three occasions in passively aggressive tones as 'boss', by laughing briefly at the absurdity of the requests and demands being made, and by 'warning' his interlocutor at the end of the conflict (possibly) to stop mentioning his mother. At each point where it appears the reproach should be arrested, the middle-aged man repeats even more angrily the phrases 'This is not yet resolved! Not yet resolved! Not yet resolved!' and 'I have pressure. You have pressure'. In the latter part of the video the Bus Uncle persuades the young man to shake hands but then again escalates the anger and continues to utter numerous profanities, threats, and sexual statements about the young man's mother. The video ends with the Bus Uncle returning to his seat to take another telephone call.

Bakhtin's concept of dialogic pluralism is not relativist. Failed acts of citizenship like this demonstrate the limits of pluralism when they do not recognize the active role of the listener and so do not value 'the interplay of equally audible voices'. In defining the limits of pluralism from the dialogical point of view, Fred Evans argues, we should legitimately withhold recognition '(though not audibility) from racist, sexist, and other politically exclusionary doctrines. These doctrines deny their hybridity and we cannot therefore justifiably cede power to or affirm them, even though hearing them is inescapable, at least as voices that we reject' (Evans 2004, p. 739). In other words, to make an enduring and convincing argument work in an act of citizenship the speaker and the listener first have to take each other's discourse seriously and give each other access to an ultimate word about themselves.

A key point in the video is about having the final word on one's self. This civil dimension is important to acts of citizenship because so much of citizenship politics is about orientating in the world of others' words, whereas an act of citizenship means making the word your own or at least injecting it with a capacity for answerability in the double sense. The group or the individual, in enacting citizenship, is implicated in the unique moment of subjective culture but has no foundational principle other than the self-acknowledgement of involvement in the act itself. Answerable words are populated by the evaluations and emotional-volitional tones of others. The word is only my own when I have enacted it. 'When there is no access to one's own ultimate word, then every thought, feeling, experience must be refracted through the medium of someone else's discourse' (Bakhtin 1984, p. 202). When voices of the alien 'other' are deprived of their own ultimate word, 'the direct, unconditional word appears barbaric, raw, and wild' (p. 203).

Thus, only when we can act on our own word and when we can take the other's word seriously, are we out of the blasé, deep into two-sided answerable acts of citizenship. The young man in the video, who seems at points to simply accept or go along with the rudeness of the Bus Uncle, also refuses the two-sided form of answerability. This leads to two potentially conflicting questions about an act of citizenship. The first is: what should I do when I'm pulled out of the blasé attitude and faced with an adversary – say an irrational one like the Bus Uncle – who refuses to respect my choice to ignore his ultimately unanswerable claim? The second is: how can I reach understanding creatively with another who may or may not share my values, and in fact insults me violently in my own language and traditions? The answers to these questions take two different theoretical directions. The first has no choice but to lead back to the metanorms of justice, or the most ideal agreements about justice that are practically necessary and entered into voluntarily. Acts of citizenship, though, are more than the exercise of rational procedures or legal practices. They are also answerable performances. This means that law alone cannot tame political citizenship, nor can it only be about controlling a clash over power differentials or antagonisms over common goods and identities. The second question posed above requires a loosening of the grip of proceduralism in order to address the question of transgenerational or transcultural understandings of the just and the right. These understandings are needed to accommodate the creative dimension that occurs when different lifeworlds intersect. Here the goal of answerability is for each to gain as much access to the other's background convictions as possible without harming the least well off or most excluded.

All the way through, *The Bus Uncle* draws its audience into witnessing a recognizable tension between civic habit or etiquette and what we are calling acts of citizenship. For the young man the blasé attitude is as close as he can get to an ethics-based politics in the sense that it seems that being as non-responsive as possible is the right approach to the situation. To put it another way, by not responding to the Bus Uncle he struggles to bring the scene back towards the non-participatory so as to avoid escalating the conflict. But this only increases the conflict to the point where the Bus Uncle breaks Hong Kong law by using obscene and threatening language in public against the young man. In addition to the audience on the bus, a world audience is there to witness he is in the wrong. He is named and shamed in popular culture as somebody so 'other' as to be an outcast and at the same time so popular as to be at once both imitated and degraded. Could this cosmopolitan witnessing and decrowning be inherent to acts of citizenship? Could this explain how listeners recognize the young man's right to the non-participatory blasé attitude over the middle-aged man's claim to freedom (to use his cell phone)? In the next section I leave the example of the Bus Uncle to review the concept of unconditional hospitality as a defining characteristic of cosmopolitan culture and continue to trace the sources of a conditional cosmopolitan co-being through Simmel's urban sociology.

Simmel: Cosmopolitan States of Co-being?

A new blasé cosmopolitan vision has emerged since Simmel first described the blasé attitude and the stranger as generic types for the city. For some the new cosmopolitan vision has been declared a triumph of the contemporary global city while others caution against its monologic effects. The everyday cosmopolitan vision, to quote Ulrich Beck, is one in which 'differentiation between us and them is becoming confused both at the national and international levels'. Everywhere the local is becoming 'the playground of universal experience' (Beck 2006). On the other hand, for Craig Calhoun (2003), an unrepentant critical realist, the cosmopolitan vision takes its genesis from empires and retains a democratic deficit, whereas the nation-state both created modern democracy and remains rooted in it. For philosophers as diverse and separated by time and outlook as Immanuel Kant, Kwame Anthony Appiah and Jacques Derrida, there is agreement that the cosmopolitan vision has important blindspots, internal constraints and hidden forms of domination. Kant (1992) argued that hospitality for all foreigners is never unconditional, but that it is an obligation and contingent on domestic law. For Appiah (2006) this hospitality cannot be offered by just any 'us' to just any 'them'; rather, it is limited to those who would enter dialogue between 'different ways of life'. Derrida (2002) goes further and concludes that the subject of hospitality also contains an opposite element of hostility. He coins the term hostipality to capture the conflict between radical unconditional hospitality and the control over the guest that is implied in the exchange from the host. He argues nonetheless that only an 'audacious call for a genuine innovation in the history of the duty to hospitality', can evoke a possible solution to injustices in our time (2000, p. 3).

To avoid a conceptual overload and in order to move with and beyond cosmopolitan citizenship studies, it is helpful to draw a distinction from the outset between a cosmopolitan intent with unconditional hospitality towards the other and one that seeks to be inclusive of multiple states of co-being. The latter is a more constrained form of cosmopolitan intent in as much as it is built from a two-sided answerability that recognizes universal duty towards the guest-other and the guest's particular reciprocal responsibilities towards the host culture. It is at best utopian to defend one-sided unconditional hospitality as a politics towards the other, because politics and law would need to be erased or relativized. In a cosmo-politanism of co-being, acts of citizenship retain the dialogic capacity for answerability, antagonism and adversarial opposition that allow actors to shift in and out of the blasé and the participatory and to maintain the final word on themselves, as seen above.

This doesn't explain, however, how cosmopolitan intent through co-being evolves from Simmel's urban sociology. His proposition is that the seemingly disassociative 'blasé attitude' has an unexpected consequence that allows much more complex acts of citizenship within equally complex forms of association, individual contingency and bodily demarcations. In 'The Metropolis and Mental Life' Simmel presents us with classic socio-logical concepts that explain human association in terms of the paradox between the individual and society, the difference between urban and rural formations, the tragic triumph of objective forms of economic exchange over subjective cultures of feeling and the intellectual response to extreme bodily stimulus. The street mentality, he argues, includes a multiplicity of individual possibilities of intellectual reaction: out of these the subject creates 'a protective organ for itself against the profound disruption with which the fluctuations and discontinuities of the external milieu threaten it'. The blasé attitude we take towards other persons is an important predisposition in that it numbs our sensibility towards the multi-sided associations with emotional experiences of the real-life contents of other individual lives. As Simmel puts it, the 'incapacity to react to new stimulations with the required amount of energy constitutes in fact that blasé attitude which every child of a large city evinces when compared with the products of the more peaceful and more stable milieu' (1971, p. 329).

It is important to note that the blasé attitude is uncommitted to any political project of citizenship or ethical stand whatsoever, even when the citizen is surrounded – as in almost any street – by political and ethical messages. It is the attitude, writes Simmel, that 'results first from the rapidly changing and closely compressed contrasting stimulations of the nerves'. It allows for a range of strategies and emotions that include reserve (or 'holding back from fully responding to others'), alienation (where 'one nowhere feels as lonely and lost as in the metropolitan crowd') and even nihilism ('money, with all its colourlessness and indifference ... becomes the common denominator of all values') (Simmel 1971). For example, walking or standing in a crowd among others in the street is most often a multi-sided way of associating that has its own habits, distinct rhythms, distance and degrees of sociability among participants – depending on the given occasion, ritual, frame, or objective form that is in play. It is not political at all – but each kind of association in the city depends on the blasé attitude of others for a calming of nervous energy between participants. Otherwise navigating the association would not be possible.

On the other hand, as was seen in *The Bus Uncle* video, everyday contexts can be transformed instantly out of the blasé into pre-political misunderstandings and dangerous breakdowns in civic habits. Symbolic and real violence, crime, civil disobedience and protest are other flashpoints that break open the imaginary barriers of street culture. When these boundaries are transgressed through the political or pre-political, the meaning of walking or standing in the street is in turn transformed into a subjective state such as confrontation, fear, anxiety, collective solidarity or euphoria. The point here is that by examining the paradox observable at street level whereby our way of being together requires us to be indifferent towards each other in a way that enhances our capacity for difference, we quickly come up against the dividing line between subjective and objective cultures. This doubled background condition is parallel to the manifest division between acts of citizenship at the emotionally engaged moment when rights or obligations are publicly claimed, on the one hand, and, on the other, situations in which administrative or juridical actions define citizenship in the neutral disengaged language of right, membership, policy or law, as defined after the fact.

Simmel's definition of the transition between subjective and objective cultures differentiates between the emotional and volitional orientation towards a 'common good', on the one hand, and the good as a 'thing' on the other. Objective culture is made up of all the languages, signs, images, constitutions, religious doctrines, literatures and technologies produced by generations over time. Objective cultures of citizenship, we could say, are public in the sense that they are there for anyone to use as much as they like or are able to. Although for Simmel the 'tragedy of culture' is about the loss of subjective culture to the objective culture of all kinds of industry, the paradox is that the one cannot completely exhaust the other (Simmel 1997).

On close scrutiny then, for Simmel, the cognitive response to over-determined bodily and social stimulus encountered in the street needs to be understood as a capacity to simultaneously withdraw from emotions and corporality into a more complex and subtle form of individuation. The blasé attitude 'appears to be the most profound cause', Simmel says, 'of the fact that the metropolis places emphasis on striving for the most individual forms of personal existence – regardless of whether it is always correct or always successful' (1971, p. 337). Bakhtin's dialogic pluralism is opposite to the blasé attitude because when the performative attitude is taken up it crosses the threshold of the blasé attitude and suspends it in favour of positing a new level of answerability through knowing some of the emotional and volitional life of the other with whom we are in dialogue. The effect Simmel has theorized remains the key predisposition that permits an expansion of public capacity for ever greater degrees of difference. The turn from emotion and volition in the blasé mentality is synonymous with the shift from objective (non-participatory) to subjective (participatory) culture that allows for greater degrees of differentiation in everyday practices. The distinction further parallels the one between citizenship politics and political citizenship in that both sides take from each other. This needs further explanation before we can return to the question of an ethics-based politics for acts of citizenship in the next section.

Derrida: Citizen Politics and the Political after 9/11

Simmel was both a patriot and a nationalist during the First World War. Even though he lived in a context that would soon give new meaning to Clausewitz's infamous doctrine 'war is politics by other means', it is very hard to imagine how he could have pictured anything like the attack on the twin towers of the World Trade building on 11 September 2001 and the events that led to the current so-called 'war on terrorism'. Like the *Bus Uncle* video, representations of global media events like 9/11 begin from the moment of occurrence in the street and ripple outward across the minutes and hours that follow and continue to unfold over months and years. Tales of heroic acts of citizenship emerge as quickly as the mediated political call for retribution and ultimately for retaliation against known or unknown enemies. Over time it remains a divisive event in debates within the global politics of war and peace. To many in the Islamic world and elsewhere, 9/11 is understandable and forgivable, if not condoned, as an act of war. How can an objective cosmopolitan world culture respond to this 'other' emotional-volitional orientation and what act of citizenship can we hope for? The two sides of citizenship that come out of such events, in the forms of practice and legal status, seem to grind against each other in a contradiction between cosmopolitan intent and domestic identification.

Derrida recalls that the proprietor of a Shanghai café informed him and his friends that a plane had crashed into one of the towers. They knew within an hour via CNN news that there was something like a major event happening not just in the city but in the world. But how could such an event be named? How could the enemy be identified when anyone could be the enemy? Later, while in New York, Derrida comments on the unspoken sense in which in any public or private conversation the name of the event could only be 9/11. He couches the analysis of the trauma and the wound of the event in the metaphor of autoimmunization, 'where a living being immunizes itself against its own immunity in quasi-suicidal fashion' (2003, p. 93). Suicide bombers obtain American weapons in American cities, and pass through American airports to 'commit two suicides: their own and those who welcomed them'. The blasé has been broken. We cannot remain indifferent in the city, not because of the event but because we are terrorized by the future of a possible incomprehensible aggression.

Absolute definitions of the concept of politics as administrative or of the political as a sphere of pure antagonism between friend and enemy encounter contradictory and doubled meanings. In his critique of Carl Schmitt's definition of the political, for example, Derrida questions whether the opposite of friend is not enemy but rather hostility or the threat of hostility. For Schmitt, according to Derrida, 'even if in all conceptual purity, it is not known what war, politics, friendship, enmity, hate or love, hostility or peace are, one can and must know – first of all practically, politically, polemically – who is the friend and who is the enemy' (Derrida 2005, p. 116). Derrida takes issue with this idea that the political can be isolated to a friend–enemy distinction 'in the first instance', or that if the enemy were to be removed the result would be depoliticization. If the political is a point of hostility then it is not only the enemy but also anyone who is hostile that creates the condition of the political. I conclude from this that citizens cannot move out of the blasé into fear and hostility without distinguishing between a private and public enemy. The moment rights are claimed for self-defence against the enemy–non–citizen (though suicide and other bombers can also be citizens), and the moment the obligation is imposed to launch into a world war against terrorists, the shift from the blasé to hostility turns away from the juridical towards the penal system on a massive scale.

The blasé attitude is not the type of concept to be measured in terms of the conceptual purity called for by the friend–enemy distinction. Although it is situated on one side of the dividing line that distinguishes it from active citizenship in the city, it is not appropriate to speak of a pure apathy as a precondition of the political. One is either indifferent towards difference or one is not. There may be a possible range of indifference in a given situation – as in being more or less indifferent towards poverty, suffering or crime, or more or less open to a greater degree of strangerness in terms of lifestyles or cultures – but complete numbness or utter indifference would seem to indicate a comatose state in which nothing could shift the agent out of non–participation into the realm of the participative where acts of citizenship occur. If the capacity to be indifferent created by the blasé expands our ability to accept difference, then how might acts of citizenship emerge from this, and how do justice and law and the tension between politics and the political limit such acts? Unconditional cosmopolitan intent would seek an ideal or objective world culture that would transform indifference into an emotional–volitional right to refuge, a duty towards hospitality, and acceptance of strangers. But any sense of global justice needs to accommodate domestic rules of residence and rights to security. And so the impossibility of complete tolerance towards difference (which always in some way sees 'the strong give up something to the weak', as in amnesty for so-called illegal immigrants), comes up against the symbolic and real constraints of domestic law and criminal violence.

How do politics, law and justice impact on acts of citizenship in such a context, and how does the shift from the blasé cosmopolitan attitude towards antagonism affect the ethical-political-juridical regime? Defining politics as the overall impersonal organization and administration of antipathy between people means that almost everything, including the smallest details of street culture, is affected at some point by background regulatory regimes of administration and law (Rose 1989, 1999). Yet acts of citizenship are not reducible to legal status or political practice. On the one hand, they break from the regime of politics and even law, while on the other they add a new regime. If political citizenship, as distinct from citizenship politics, is first about charged emotional-volitional antagonism between imaginary but not fictional adversaries, and about their overt and intense disputes over what constitutes the common good and the limits of antagonism, then the spectacles, rituals and habits of everyday street life presumably cannot be sustained without the mediation of citizenship politics. If, however, political citizenship is about active, intense emotional-volitional points of agency, it also relies on citizenship politics as a means of measuring thresholds and channels of public communication. Disputes over common goods and limits of pluralism need to be resolved through citizenship politics, but sometimes enduring and convincing arguments inside acts of citizenship are about direct challenges to the regulatory regimes that citizenship politics has built over time. The paradox is that the one cannot exercise itself without the other, and so the question needs to be asked regarding what are the limits of an act of citizenship that seeks to negate a regulatory regime. If in the extreme example the subjective perception prevailed that the street has too great a potential to be implicated in the political – in other words, if the street is too intensely antagonistic as in 9/11 – all citizens would hesitate a lot more before leaving the house in the morning.

Obviously in places in the world where there are wars, checkpoints, contested border crossings and open violence between gangs or national minorities and nation-states, people do hesitate a lot more before they go out into the street. The growing number of homeless people in liberal democracies and the growing number of refugee camps emerging within and especially at the borders of liberal democracies around the world are extreme examples of how public disputes over common goods and identities are playing themselves out on the street (Arnold 2004; Davis 2006; Neuwirth 2006). Both the homeless and the refugee camps are made up of communities of unique individuals and both are subjected to hostile citizen politics (either domestic or global) not of their choosing. When, for example, local and national public housing budgets in liberal democracies like the United States are slashed significantly over long periods of time, and when citizen politics are subsequently reduced to a politics of zero tolerance and police administration of city streets, then whole communities of unique individuals are put into a position where organizing acts of citizenship can only mean changing the regulatory regimes of political citizenship so that it becomes responsive to those who have seen their citizenship stripped away (Bratt et al. 2006).

Although at first glance the need for acts of citizenship that appeal to justice and not the law appears to lead to an immediate reduction or overthrowing of citizenship politics, Simmel might argue that such acts of citizenship remain deeply associative rather than disassociative in that they lead to a new politics – or, as Derrida would say, 'a politics in the future'. On the other hand, if an act of citizenship calls for a violent overthrow of existing political citizenship, then the territory is neither politics nor the political, but rather the pre-political: for such an act collapses multi-sided association under a single authority (Arendt 1958).

Derrida and Simmel: Catching Acts between Law and Justice

Whereas Simmel's work in philosophy attempts to provide an ethics for the modern individualism that accompanies the multiple metropolitan sociological type, Derrida's concepts of hospitality and hostility help recall that other concepts like politics and the political, and law and justice, are doubled and contradictory. Simmel's reflections on the city, and especially on the metropolitan mentality, need to be interpreted through his ethics. In a strikingly similar vein, Derrida, following Pascal and Montaigne, argues that law is not justice and that acting out of duty or law does not make the act just. Simmel reverses Kant's position by arguing that if the general law means the agent can give a universal value to an act, and yet the act can only be carried out by the agent's own definition, or judged on the merits of the individual case, then law is no longer general but only particular to that agent's situation. Thus each specific case has to include the formulation of a new universal law. Derrida says almost exactly this when talking about the role of the judge in courts: 'Each case is other, each decision is different and requires an absolutely unique interpretation, which no existing, coded rule can or ought to guarantee absolutely' (1992, p. 23). For Simmel the objectivity of individual law is possible, because the connection between the subjective and the individual is broken: the decisive point, as Simmel puts it, is that 'individual life is nothing subjective but – without somehow losing its restriction to this individual – it is as an ethical ought (*sollen*) that is absolutely objective' (1968, p. 217).[1]

For Derrida, justice and law are not equivalent terms. Law is not reducible to a universal category but, as Derrida says, 'lucky for politics, it is deconstructable' (1992, p. 15). Derrida defines 'justice as being infinite, incalculable, rebellious to rule, and foreign to symmetry, heterogeneous and heterotropic'. The definition is opposed to 'the exercise of justice as law or right, legitimacy or legality, stabilizeable and statutory, calculable, a system of regulated and coded prescriptions' (1992, p. 22). For Simmel only individual law is just. For Derrida 'law is not justice'. Law is the element of calculation, 'and it is just that there be law' (1992, p.17). Taking a position between Simmel and Derrida, I propose that the first condition for an act of citizenship to be just would be that it be unique and non-repeatable and yet able to make an enduring and convincing argument (as in Simmel's individual law). The second condition for justice is that the act be divisive (as in Derrida's concept of justice as law 'that cuts, that divides'). Let me try and separate these two parts out before bringing them back together for acts of citizenship.

In the essay on individual law Simmel argues against Kant's categorical imperative (that you should only ever act in a way whereby you can at the same time will that everyone else should act in the same way). He argues for the opposite of duty or deontological ethics – for an ethics of individual law that would itself be immanently emotional and transcendentally objective, or what he calls the 'immanence of transcendence' (Joas 2000). The Kantian formula, Simmel says, is seen to 'determine the morality of an action and even to establish a possible generalization. However, if our act is understood as it really stands in life – with its seamless, interwoven wholeness – then it cannot be generalized, because this would mean nothing else than to think the whole life of this individual as a general law' (1968, pp. 189–90). At the same time, he insists on the importance of distinguishing between 'moral subjectivism' and 'individual law'. We can think of the former as a collective emotion that defines the universality of enacting a culture of citizenship, while the individual law is the unique expression of the person who acts out of a life history. As Simmel puts it, 'the individual is not necessarily subjective, and objectivity is not necessarily supra-individual' (Simmel 1968, p. 241).

Like Simmel, Derrida insists on the individuality of general law and the emphasis of his critique opposes the notion that a norm or regulative ideal should guide an act. Acting out of duty is like being 'deployed with the automatism attributable to machines' (p. 134). 'There is no longer any place for justice or responsibility whether juridical, political or ethical' (p. 135). The question becomes how to reconcile an act of citizenship that 'must always concern singularity, individuality, irreplaceable groups and lives in a unique situation, with rule, norm, value, or the imperative of justice which has a general form, even if this generality prescribes a singular application in each case' (1992, p. 17).

Let's think about this against the thesis on the blasé for a moment. If it is true that the blasé attitude permits ethical subjectivity but is not itself an ethical stand, then what is the ethical status of this condition? For Simmel, the question of how the individual ought to act in the street is linked to a given context, but at the same time his or her ethics also transcends context in that the ethical act by the individual is a law and therefore is also objective. Here there is little distinction between an ordinary act and an act of citizenship, except that the latter is not a calculated intention but rather an individual law. There is confusion, though, about the meaning of the individual law that needs to be clarified before it can be applied to acts of citizenship. Does the individual law mean that every time I engage in multi-sided association I should ask myself how this act is going to determine the rest of my life? The point for Simmel is that every performance counts in the life history of the agent, and yet the agent is never determined by a single act other than an act that is an entire life history. In other words, my act defines me as I perform my act. For an act of citizenship to have this same quality it must acknowledge a similar ethical responsibility. According to Simmel the responsibility for one's life history lies in 'the ought of every single doing' (1968, p. 238). For the actor in the act of citizenship, the ethical question of how I ought to act in this individual answerability is based 'on all I have ever done, been and ought to have done or been' (1968, p. 238).

The blasé attitude falls somewhere between an ethical and political stand and belongs to neither. It provides a psychological distance needed for subjective culture to thrive in highly individuated ethical form. Alienation and nihilism is one end on a continuum of extreme outcomes. At another end, however, the blasé attitude creates room for the individual to manoeuvre without ending up in an infinite regression that would hold anyone back from taking up any kind of act for fear it might not measure up to some absolute categorical imperative or will to power. As we have seen, objective and subjective cultures take from one another, as do political citizenship and citizenship politics. Even though the former dominates the latter in each case, the paradox is that the one cannot completely exhaust the other. We can all engage in as many acts of citizenship as we like or are able to, but no single individual is able to exhaust all of citizenship politics in the form of One Big Act of political citizenship. The subjective culture of the political citizen (the impulse for making rights claims) and objective citizen politics (the administrative or juridical subject), both struggle – sometimes together and sometimes against one another – to discipline and unify subjective culture as much as is seen to be necessary or is possible. But objective cultures cannot completely eliminate the capacity of subjective culture to respond or resolve centripetal forces. This is because there is always the citizen's loophole of ethical subjectivity where she or he refuses to see herself or himself as simply equivalent to other objects of the political process.

Conclusion

Following Simmel's lead and the insights of Derrida and Bakhtin, the argument in this chapter has been that citizenship politics, understood as the administration of a common good and a conditional variety of difference within it, also requires a built-in degree of indifference to be able to act anew beyond its limits. Citizenship politics is objective and administrative but at the same time is not divorced from subjective culture and a sense of justice. My main counter-intuitive conclusion is that a certain measure of indifference is a precondition for acts of citizenship that test the limits of cosmopolitan intent and of political citizenship (the thresholds for rights claims and capacity for hospitality). The blasé attitude Simmel theorized is neither ethical, political nor discursive in itself, and as such it is not the context for citizenship enactment but rather part of its groundwork. I have tried to make this point on the assumption that expanding the cultural capacity of citizenship enactment to bridge between greater degrees of strangerness is an important ethical component of dialogic pluralism and acts of citizenship to come. Our capacity to take a blasé attitude towards the other's differences or specificities creates a condition where various degrees of strangerness can operate in the city, and where we do not cease becoming ourselves in unique ways as we encounter each other. In other words, I have tried to show that the blasé attitude provides a distance needed for subjective culture to thrive in highly individuated form, so that the most incommensurable moral subjectivities might be able to occupy the same space.

Grounding citizenship enactment in urban answerability with a conditional cosmopolitanism of co-being does not mean basing it simply on an objective or reasonable form of cooperation or communicative action. Nor is it a state of permanent antagonism. Dialogic pluralism includes elements from each of these approaches in that it provides an explanation of the limits of pluralism in terms of how opposite sides come to understanding together out of a tension issued from struggles about the ultimate word on oneself and on one's others. Bakhtin's principle of two-sided answerability assumes an anticipation of justice and the right response at the same time as values are exchanged, on the one hand, and potentially creative transcultural hybridization, on the other. Theorizing an ethics-based politics means accounting for structure and agency, order and disorder, subjectivity and objectivity, self and other, inclusion and exclusion. Defining the limits of pluralism within the dialogic approach means that no matter how closed off an ideology or a comprehensive doctrine – as long as the agents are alive – they are answerable to those they might exclude or do violence if they should choose, or be able to choose, to put themselves into acts of citizenship. An answerable act of citizenship with cosmopolitan intent needs to provide rejoinders that overcome barriers of exclusion through unique performances that display rigorous defence of an enduring and convincing ideal of justice. The concept of acts of citizenship thus provides a powerful conceptual tool for citizenship studies because it focuses on the act as an event that reveals the moment of exclusion of 'others' for reasons of legal entitlement, but also reveals the moment of inclusion of 'others'. Acts of citizenship are distinct in that they need both an aesthetic way of shaping the political and a convincing deliberative politics for transforming administrative, moral and legal imperatives – whether or not an act seeks to recover, preserve or transform the common good.

Acknowledgements

Thanks to Fred Evans, Yon Hsu and Engin Isin for suggestions on earlier drafts, and to Dominique Legros for detailed comments and criticism on the most recent version.

Note

1   I draw freely here from the translated English version of Simmel's text that Tapani Laine and I developed in our research for a paper on Simmel and Bakhtin (1999). See also Nielsen (2002).

References

Appiah, K. A. (2006) *Cosmopolitanism: Ethics in a World of Strangers*, Norton, New York.

Arnold, K. (2004) *Homelessness, Citizenship and Identity: The Uncanniness of Late Modernity*, State University of New York Press, Albany, NY.

Bakhtin, M. (1984) *Problems of Dostoevsky's Poetics* (trans. C. Emerson and W. Booth), University of Minnesota Press, Minneapolis, MN.

— (1993) *Toward a Philosophy of the Act* (ed. M. Holquist, trans. V. Liapunov), University of Texas Press, Austin, TX.

Beck, U. (2006) *The Cosmopolitan Vision* (trans. C. Cronin), Polity, London.

Bratt, R., M. E. Stone and C. Hartman (eds) (2006) *A Right to Social Housing: Foundation for a New Social Agenda*, Temple University Press, Philadelphia, PN.

Calhoun, C. (2003) 'The Class Consciousness of Frequent Travelers: Toward a Critique of Actually Existing Cosmopolitanism', *South Atlantic Quarterly*, 101 (4), 869–97.

Davis, M. (2006) *Planet of Slums*, Verso, London.

Derrida, J. (1992) 'Force of Law: The "Mystical Foundation of Authority"' in *Deconstruction and the Possibility of Justice*, Routledge, London.

— (2001) *On Cosmopolitanism and Forgiveness*, Routledge, London.

— (2002) *Acts of Religion* (ed. G. Anidjar), Routledge, New York.

— (2003) 'Autoimmunity: Real and Symbolic Suicides' in G. Borradori, *Philosophy in a Time of Terror: Dialogues with Jurgen Habermas and Jacques Derrida,* University of Chicago Press, Chicago, IL.

— (2005) *The Politics of Friendship* (trans. G. Collins), London, Verso.

Evans, F. (2004) 'Multi-Voiced Society: Philosophical Nuances on Salmon Rushdie's *Midnight's Children*', *Florida Journal of International Law*, 16 (3), 727–41.

Joas, H. (2000) *The Genesis of Values* (trans. G. Moore), University of Chicago Press, Chicago, IL.

Kant, I. (1983) *Perpetual Peace and Other Essays* (trans. T. Humphrey), Hackett, Cambridge.

Leger, F. (1989) *La pensée de Georg Simmel: Contribution à l'histoire des idées au début du XXe siècle*, Éditions Kimé, Paris.

Neuwirth, R. (2006) *Shadow Cities: A Billion Squatters, A New World*, Routledge, London.

Nielsen, G. (2002) *The Norms of Answerability: Social Theory Between Bakhtin and Habermas*, State University of New York Press, Albany, NY.

Nielsen, G. and T. Lane (1999) 'Simmel's Shadow'. Ninth International Bakhtin Meetings, Frei Universitat, Berlin, July.

Rose, N. (1989) *Governing the Soul: The Shaping of the Private Self*, Routledge, London.

— (1999) *Powers of Freedom: Reframing Political Thought*, Cambridge University Press, Cambridge.

Simmel, G. (1968) *Das Individuelle Gesetz* (ed. M. von Landmann), Suhrkamp, Frankfurt am Main (first published 1913 in *Logos*, 4 (2), Musaget, Moscow).

— (1971) *Georg Simmel: On Individuality and Social Forms* (ed. D. Levine), University of Chicago Press, Chicago, IL.

— (1997) *Simmel on Culture: Selected Writings* (eds D. Frisby and M. Featherstone), Sage, London.

The Bus Uncle video (2006) <http://www.youtube.com/watch?v=RSHziqJWYcM>.

Weber, M. (1978) *Economy and Society: An Outline of Interpretive Sociology* (eds G. Roth and C. Wittich, trans. E. Fischoff *et al.*), University of California Press, Berkeley, CA.

ACTS III

❖

Rituals
and Performance

1916 Memorial, Dublin City Hall (© irishwarmemorials.ie)

Act 11

❖

Acts of
Commemoration

IAN MORRISON

Acts of citizenship break from everyday habits as well as broader institutional practices in both official and non-official ways. Whether they are acts of remembering or acts of forgetting, rituals of commemoration are among the most important instances of the enactment of citizenship. In what follows I examine an official act of state commemoration of the 1916 Easter Uprising evoked in September 2005 by the Irish Taoiseach Bertie Ahern. An analysis of this kind of official act demonstrates the lively and complex struggles over the claiming and interpretation of that which is to be commemorated.

Citizenship is not only a legal status; it is also enacted through practices and rituals. Consequently, acts of citizenship comprise not only the establishment or challenging of rights and obligations, but also the construction, interpretation and reinterpretation of those practices and rituals that act to sustain the myths underlying particular conceptions of citizenship.

Rituals of commemoration occupy a central position among the practices that sustain particular myths of belonging. Whether revolutions, wars, heroes, heroic deeds or the founding of a state is commemorated and memorialized, analyses of the struggles involved in the claiming and reclaiming of the events to be commemorated, and the interpretation and reinterpretation of that which is to be commemorated, are vital acts of citizenship, crucially implicated in the manner in which citizenship is enacted and re-enacted.

In precisely such an act of citizenship, the Irish Taoiseach Bertie Ahern decreed in September 2005, during a speech at his party's annual conference, that the Irish government would immediately undertake the planning of two commemorative projects. First, the Irish state would recommence the commemoration of the anniversary of the 1916 Easter Uprising with an annual military parade through the streets of Dublin. Second, a 1916 committee would be struck in order to immediately begin preparations for the centennial commemorations of the events of Easter 1916.

Ahern's acts of citizenship, which in positioning the event of Easter 1916 as an event worthy of national commemoration reinvoked it as the founding moment of the Irish Republic, was itself irrevocably dependent on and linked with the act that was enacted on Easter, 1916. On Easter 1916, the Irish Republican Brotherhood, a small group of revolutionary Irish nationalists, revolted against British rule in Ireland. After occupying several buildings in the centre of Dublin, the group declared the formation of an Irish Republic, and named itself the provisional government. The widely circulated Proclamation of the Republic asserted 'the right of the people of Ireland to the ownership of Ireland, and to the unfettered control of Irish destinies', and declared Ireland to be 'sovereign and indefeasible'. Perhaps most interestingly, the group implicated the remainder of the Irish population in their act, affirming that, 'The Irish Republic is entitled to, and hereby claims, the allegiance of every Irishman and Irishwoman.'

While the revolutionaries were initially scorned by the general public, the brutal response of the British armed forces, including the execution of all of the signatories to the Proclamation (the image of a seriously wounded James Connolly, tied to a chair in order to be executed by a firing squad, is burned particularly deeply into the republican memory) and an assault on the civilian population turned public sentiment towards the revolutionary cause. In 1921, after a campaign of guerrilla warfare by the Irish Republican Army, a treaty creating the Irish Free State was signed. Thus, five years after the first act of founding, a second act of founding was enacted. This act, however, proved divisive, leading to a civil war between those who supported the treaty and recognized the newly formed state, and those who opposed the treaty and did not recognize the legitimacy of the new state.

Until 1966, under the leadership of Eamon De Valera (himself a participant in the 1916 Uprising), the Irish military played a prominent role in official government commemorations of the Easter Uprising. While the events of Easter 1916 have always retained a central place within Irish nationalist imagery, there has also been, since 1916, and especially since the renewal of the 'Troubles' in Northern Ireland in the late 1960s, opposition to their glorification. Opponents argued that commemoration equalled glorification, and sought to reinterpret the events of 1916 and their legacy. The act's appropriation as a sentimental heroic nationalist myth leaves unexamined the act's other face, the glorification of martyrdom, the deed and blood sacrifice.

As previously mentioned, while the 1916 Uprising was a courageous act of anti-colonial revolt, and a radical act of founding, it was also an undemocratic and exclusionary act, in which a small faction violently instituted the republic 'on behalf of' all others, and demanded from them – in fact, saw itself as entitled to – their unconditional allegiance. Any commemoration of the 1916 Uprising that wishes to dissociate itself from violent republicanism does not do justice to the multifaceted legacy of this event.

By re-involving the state, and particularly the military, in the commemoration of the Easter Uprising, Ahern stated that he hoped to associate it more closely with the events of 1916, and thereby reclaim images of heroism from militant republicanism.

Thus, Ahern's attempt to divorce the actions of 1916 from the armed republican movement and Sinn Féin, and to associate them more closely with the modern Irish state, fails to engage critically with the event. Rather than acknowledging the problematic and complex legacy of 1916, the military commemoration of the Easter Uprising serves to glorify the armed republican tradition. Although the 1916 Uprising has been interpreted as an act of heroic sacrifice, it must also be rendered as an act of a small revolutionary vanguard, which lacked broad popular support, yet attempted to pronounce and determine the nature of Irish citizenship and 'Irishness'. The 1916 Uprising, therefore, must be reinterpreted as the attempt by an armed group to claim/demand the allegiance of every 'Irishman and Irishwoman' (an identity, which, despite the pluralism of the Declaration, was largely based on essentialist notions of Irish identity) to their vision of an Irish Republic. In this transcendental vision of republicanism, a being emerges that pretends to enact all members of the republic. The emergence of this being defines and redefines the republic and the citizen of the republic at every moment, continually marginalizing all other identities, individuals or groups.

Act 12

Non-Citizens'
Politics

JOHN SAUNDERS

Although the genesis of acts of citizenship is situated in being political, they also have the capacity to be generated through the administrative or formal dimension of politics. In their two-sided answerability they can be seen to be both about politics and the political, about claiming the right to have rights and about expanding the inclusion of those who are excluded. This paradox is considered below through a discussion of an example of how an administrative innovation in the definition of voting rights can be seen to join a deeper sense of the political engaged as an act of citizenship.

Formal citizenship remains securely tied to administrative nation-state institutions and their legal and political practices. However, cities in North America and Europe have seen various forms of voting rights – mainly at the municipal government and school board levels – conferred on non-citizens.

By conferring voting rights on non-citizens, municipalities challenge the dominance of the nation-state as arbiter of rights and obligations, and create an opening for the renegotiation of the boundaries between citizens and strangers. The 2003 decision of Cambridge, Massachusetts to extend voting rights to all residents, regardless of their citizenship status, is exemplary of such acts of citizenship. This decision expanded 1999 legislation that would have allowed documented non-citizens to vote in school board elections, in effect granting full municipal voting rights to undocumented or 'illegal' immigrants. By 2007 the legislation was still awaiting approval by the Massachusetts state government (as is a similar law passed by Amherst).

Other towns in the state have also engaged in public discussions concerning the expansion of local franchise, raising interesting tensions regarding both formal and substantive understandings of citizenship. In these cases, questions arise

Members and supporters of the Cambridge Campaign for Immigrant Voting participate in the Rights Immigrant Workers Freedom Ride in New York City, 4 October 2003 (© Kathleen Coll)

concerning the authority of nation-state institutions to confer or delimit citizenship, as well as the means by which rights are claimed and groups recognized.

The move to extend the municipal vote confronts conventional understandings of citizenship, which position the nation-state as the ultimate arbiter of status and rights. The challenge, however, is a limited one. State legislatures must also endorse such municipal legislation for it to become law, while national citizenship status remains under the purview of the US federal government.

Proponents of the legislation argue that the extension of franchise would strengthen civic participation and local democracy, and help support a sense of belonging for all residents. Some emphasize the economic contributions of immigrants to their municipalities, while others draw direct parallels with other efforts to grant rights to excluded groups. According to Kathy Coll, a representative of the Cambridge Campaign for Immigrant Voting Rights, 'Cambridge has a strong tradition of sharing the vote. For example, in 1879, 40 years before the federal government enfranchised women, women in Cambridge were enfranchised in school board, tax and bond elections' (Immigrant Voting Project). Others draw attention to earlier contexts, dating from independence to the 1920s, in which municipal voting rights were granted to non-status immigrants. Recent years have seen growing efforts to extend the franchise in various American cities, including New York and San Francisco, as well as in Europe.

These attempts can also be seen as a way of opening up substantive notions of citizenship, drawing connections between the places where immigrants live and work and the broader geographic context of their lives. Local efforts that seek to include the excluded recognize identities that are unsettled, despite their categorization according to legal or bureaucratic status (citizen, landed immigrant/resident alien, undocumented, illegal).

Moreover, these attempts are also the product of immigrants themselves organizing for rights and recognition. In Cambridge, expanded voting rights are linked with previous years of work to claim services such as housing for immigrants. Thus basic economic needs have been tied to legal, political struggles for recognition. For example, in 1993 the Campaign for Immigrant Voting Rights launched an initiative led by the pro-affordable housing non-profit organization Eviction Free Zone that was endorsed by immigrant and civic groups. Through such coalitions, boundaries among citizens and strangers, outsiders and aliens are opened up for renegotiation.

Legally, efforts to expand the franchise may seem in some respects to be only symbolic, but this is the case only if they are considered separately from the struggles in which they emerge. Substantively, they can be seen as a desire to dissolve categories of citizenship, and to place it within the realm of the material, the everyday spaces in which included and excluded live.

Act 13

Flash Mobs

JOHN SAUNDERS

The rupture from habitus belongs with the first moment of an act of citizenship. It renders the place where the right to claim rights is made accessible. In the following illustration the focus is not on the act of citizenship in itself or for itself, but on its performance as an event.

By participating in a small, almost unnoticed piece of street theatre (known as a 'flash mob') in downtown Montreal, city dwellers opened up a range of possibilities for examining what it means to act as a citizen. Residents coming together as a group, claiming space and interrupting the everyday order of things in the city can be seen as a form of resistance and a challenge to existing patterns and practices.

On 9 August 2003, dozens of people gathered at Montreal's Place des Arts to participate in what some observers already considered a fading fad – a flash mob. Following a pre-arranged signal (four people opening umbrellas simultaneously at 1 p.m.), the crowd made quacking noises for several minutes, tossed rubber ducks into a public fountain, and then left.

As part of a series of flash mobs that have taken place in recent years, the incident garnered press attention as an inexplicable curiosity, largely attributed to young people with access to new technologies. Cell phones, web sites, chat rooms and text messaging are seen as facilitating what are deemed to be spontaneous actions in public spaces.

Despite the appearance of spontaneity, for the Place des Arts mob, plans were coordinated in the preceding days, with rubber ducks handed out at the event itself. 'By 1.25 p.m. the mobbers had dispersed, leaving 200 plastic ducks bobbing in the water, with many a confused onlooker wondering what had just happened' (King 2003).

As an act of citizenship, it is possible to read the flash mob as a means of

Participants 'released' rubber ducks into a Montreal fountain during an
August 2003 flash mob (© Julien Smith and David Leaman)

creating spaces in which claims to rights and recognition occur. It can be seen as
a pleasurable implication of the body within the city, in which categories of citizen,
stranger and outsider may become blurred through shared performance that
interrupts conventional spaces and practices.

The interruption of the everyday also interrogates the meaning of the mob
itself, reflecting back on the condoned and the usual, and the everyday uses of
the spaces of the city by its residents. With only rubber ducks remaining as
material traces of the event, the flash mob can be seen as a tactic, a temporary
appropriation of public space in unintended, open-ended ways.

However, the flash mob contains tensions and contradictions, which unsettle
attempts to claim it as a spontaneous, irrational/non-rational act. It requires
organization and planning (even if sporadic, vague and cursory), not visible within
the immediate event itself. It is potentially deeply calculated, following intentions
set out by participants or organizers, who may clash on the logistics as well as the
interpretation of the event. (Following the Montreal event, one observer suggested
the rubber ducks could have detracted from the success, as they required
cleaning up afterwards.)

Some argue that the absurdist nature of flash mobs deprive them of political
meaning, since overt, specific claims are rarely articulated. The risk here is to
reproduce conventional (and oppositional) understandings of the political,
conflating it solely with acts of resistance (to power, to domination). Through its
temporality and jarring presence, the flash mob confronts efforts to name it or
define it, and allows for reconsidering how subjects embody the city.

Act 14

❖

Spike Lee's
25th Hour

ERKAN ERCEL

An act of citizenship mediated through art disrupts the taken-for-granted – as any other act of citizenship might. Yet such mediated acts aren't required to defend an enduring profane argument. An act of citizenship through the mediation of art has the liberty to explore special ethical meanings that move against the habitus of general culture. At the same time such acts do not have the burden of being ethical themselves or responsible towards policy or laws that are required in direct political acts. Mediating acts through art thus allows us access to speech and images about the habitus that are otherwise unshowable or unspeakable.

A scene from Spike Lee's film *25th Hour* merits investigation from the perspective of acts of citizenship as an artistic intervention that calls for a different ethics of relating to our fellow citizens, strangers, outsiders or aliens – an ethics that warns of the perils of seeing the other as a thief of our enjoyment. The film follows Montgomery Brogan's final 24 hours as a free man. Sentenced to eight years in prison for drug dealing, Brogan has only one day left before turning himself in to the state penitentiary. During his last round of visits to friends and family, Brogan stops at a local pub run by his father. While in the restroom, he notices a piece of graffiti – 'fuck you' – scrawled across the bottom edge of the mirror. The flurry of rage that follows has the dubious honour of being probably the most scandalously politically incorrect racist tirade ever caught on camera. Hardly any city dweller escapes the wrath of Brogan: the squeegee, Sikhs and Pakistanis, the Chelsea boys, the Korean grocers, the Russians in Brighton Beach, the Wall Street brokers, the black-hatted Hasidim, the Puerto Ricans, the Dominicans, the Upper East Side wives, the Uptown brothers, the corrupt cops. The familiar faces of vibrant, cosmopolitan city life suddenly turn into a motley crew of 'others' and into objects of hatred. This is not only because, unlike Brogan, they will continue to enjoy the city while he is incarcerated, but also and more importantly because 'they' have always deprived Brogan of full enjoyment by enjoying themselves in ways that are so alien and inaccessible to him. Whether they are 'the Puerto Ricans, twenty to a car, swelling up the welfare rolls' or 'Sikhs and Pakistanis bombing down the avenues in decrepit cabs, curry steaming out their pores stinking up my day, terrorists in fucking training' or 'the Korean grocers with their pyramids of overpriced fruits and their tulips and roses wrapped up in plastic' or 'the Chelsea boys with their waxed chests and their pumped-up biceps', the 'other' always enjoys at our expense, always steals our enjoyment. Hence, 'Fuck the whole city and everyone in it … Let an earthquake crumble it. Let the fires rage. Let it burn to fucking ash and then let the waters rise and submerge this whole rat-infested place.'

In an earlier scene shot through the window of Brogan's brother's office, the viewer is confronted by the giant emptiness where the World Trade Towers used to stand. Consequently, we are made aware that Brogan's rant is not only meant as a reflection of his inner turmoil. It is, first and foremost, a social commentary on life in the aftermath of 9/11. And a very sad commentary it would have been, had Brogan ended his monologue by summoning all the disastrous forces of nature to wipe out the city; the quintessential fascist utopia whereby the old and the degenerate are to be completely purged to make way for the new and the pure. But Brogan knows better than that. 'No. No, fuck you, Montgomery Brogan. You had it all and you threw it away. You dumb fuck.' Through this cathartic experience, our protagonist finally comes to the realization that he has not the other but himself to blame for his misfortune. And it is this last gesture that not only gives Brogan's otherwise hateful outburst its redeeming quality, but also renders it an act.

Of course, it is only in the diegetic reality of the film that Brogan is the agent of this act. Since it is through the mediation of the camera's eye that we are privy to this solitary act, it is therefore Spike Lee who really deserves the credit for the staging of this act and, by that token, for the act itself. Lee's artistic act – or better put, his act through art – is noteworthy in two respects. First, through the disarming bluntness of Brogan, Lee confronts the audience with the dark underside of liberal multiculturalism and its politically correct discourse. Such ridicule of the pretentiousness and hypocrisy of political correctness, however, is all too common today – ranging from books (*Politically Incorrect Bedtime Stories*) to sitcoms (*Curb Your Enthusiasm, The Office, Extras*), and comedy shows (*Mr Show*) – to the point where it hardly commands any subversive edge. Mere exposés of the disingenuousness of political correctness are of no use in figuring out what to do with the critique of multiculturalism. Actually, to the extent that they breed cynicism, they might very well feed into the hardening of essentialist identity claims. And therein lies the significance of Brogan's concluding line. It is only when Brogan finally turns his scorn on himself that the stream of flashback images of the stereotypes reflected in the restroom mirror is replaced by his own self-image. He displaces his anger from one group to the other only, in the end, to discover that he himself is the cause of his own deadlock. This is the ethical lesson that most criticisms of multiculturalism stop short of. As Žižek has pointed out on many occasions, the real issue at stake here is not whether Indians smell of curry or Korean markets are overpriced or Chelsea boys work out all the time. The point is, even if these stereotypes are empirically verifiable, why do we feel so strongly about them? Why do the other and the other's way of living fascinate us so much? How does it trigger so much fury in us? And Spike Lee's forceful scene demonstrates that this very moment of self-questioning is possible only when Brogan manages to snap out of his obsession with the other and is once again able to discern his face in the mirror. In that sense, Spike Lee's act may be better characterized as an ethic of citizenship that can inform a myriad acts of citizenship – an ethic by way of an admonition: beware that your fascination with the other might have to do less with them than yourself.

INDEX

❖